Data Analysis for Social Science

Fundamental Methods

You can access the exercise materials
and updated content
by scanning the QR code.

도서출판 윤성사 220

Data Analysis for Social Science
Fundamental Methods

제1판 제1쇄   2024년 3월 4일

지 은 이   Haeil Jung (정해일)
펴 낸 이   정재훈
꾸 민 이   안미숙

펴 낸 곳   도서출판 윤성사
주   소   서울특별시 용산구 효창원로 64길 10 백오빌딩 지하 1층
전   화   대표번호_02)313-3814 / 영업부_02)313-3813 / 팩스_02)313-3812
전자우편   yspublish@daum.net
등   록   2017. 1. 23

ISBN 979-11-93058-23-7 (93350)
값 25,000원

ⓒ Haeil Jung, 2024

지은이와의 협의에 따라 인지를 생략합니다.

이 책의 전부 또는 일부 내용을 재사용하려면 반드시 사전에 저작권자와
도서출판 윤성사의 동의를 받아야 합니다.
All Rights Reserved. Please do not use or cite without permission.

잘못 만들어진 책은 구입하신 서점에서 교환 가능합니다.

Data Analysis for Social Science

Fundamental Methods

Haeil Jung

Data Analysis for Social Science

Fundamental Methods

Preface

Statistics or data analysis has been a challenging subject for many students since it is based on mathematics, and there are difficult concepts related to probability. I experienced similar frustration when I was in college and graduate school. Ironically, despite such difficulties, my interest in data analysis grew and led me to my current research and teaching. Since I was a graduate student, I have taught data analysis courses for more than 15 years, and I have been trying to find a better way to teach this subject. From my teaching, I have learned a new path to teaching data analysis. This textbook is the outcome of my experience as a student and a teacher in the data analysis courses.

This book is an introductory data analysis textbook for college and graduate students who have not studied this subject before. Different from other textbooks in data analysis, it focuses on the methods that are commonly used in quantitative reports and research papers in social science. Particularly, it covers how the sample mean and the regression model can be widely applicable to the cross-sectional data for various purposes. On the other hand, this book does not cover some of the conventional empirical methods that could be well replaced by the OLS regression analysis, such as the Chi-square test, ANOVA, and ANCOVA. Also, to help students understand, this book includes practical examples and exercises.

This textbook is designed for a one-semester course. Most of the instructors would cover all chapters over 15 weeks by teaching one chapter within one to two weeks. After the course with this book, students would be able to empirically analyze various topics in social science using the sample mean and regression model.

February, 2024
Haeil Jung

Contents

Preface / 7

Chapter 1
How do we examine our interests with data?: Distribution and mean / 13

- Understanding our world with data / 13
- Mapping what we want to study into numbers / 14
- Less likely or more likely? Think about the probabilities of events / 20
- Which group of subjects do we want to study?: The population of interest and the random sample / 23
- Random sample assumption and sampling methods / 24
- What useful information can we have from a sample?: sample mean and sample variance / 26
- Normal distribution and its application: One of the most popular and useful distributions / 32
- Alternative measures to mean: median and mode / 40
- Chapter Summary / 42
- Exercises / 43

Chapter 2
Do more with the sample mean: Inference / 49

- Sampling distribution of the sample mean and the Central Limit Theorem / 49
- The confidence interval (CI) for the population mean μ / 56
- Hypothesis test for the population mean μ / 68
- How to choose an appropriate sample size in the survey for inference / 79
- Chapter Summary / 85
- Exercises / 87

Chapter 3
Examining the relationship between the two quantitative variables I: Correlation coefficient and introduction to the OLS regression analysis / 92

- Covarience and correlation coefficent / 92
- Introduction to the OLS regression analysis / 100
- Chapter Summary / 118
- Exercises / 120

Chapter 4
Examining the relationship between the two continuous variables II: Inference in the OLS regression analysis / 125

- The normally of the error term and the sampling distribution of the OLS estimator / 125
- The linear regression model when the sample size becomes larger / 128
- The Confidence Interval (CI) for the regression parameter $ß_1$ / 133
- Hypothesis test for the regression parameter $ß_1$ / 137
- Chapter Summary / 149
- Exercises / 151

Chapter 5
Handling two or more explanatory variables in OLS regression analysis I: Multivariate Regression Analysis / 155

- Partialling out and multicollinearity in multivariate regression analysis / 155
- Omitted variable bias in the linear regression model / 164
- Adding an explanatory variable and the efficiency of OLS estimators / 168
- Chapter Summary / 173
- Exercises / 174

Chapter 6
Handling two or more explanatory variables in OLS regression analysis II: Hypothesis tests and more in Multivariate Regression Analysis / 179

- Hypothesis tests in multivariable regression analysis / 179
- Adjusted R-squared / 192
- Chapter Summary / 194
- Exercises / 195

Chapter 7
The OLS regression analysis when comparing the outcomes of the two or more groups: Use of binary explanatory variables / 201

- Estimating group differences in an outcome variable / 202
- Estimating group differences in an outcome variable without the constant / 209
- Estimating group differences using an interval variable / 211
- Estimating group differences in a slope coefficient / 213
- Estimating group differences in all explanatory variables / 217
- Estimating the nonlinear relationship between an explanatory variable and an outcome variable / 219
- Subsample analysis based on exogenous explanatory variables / 222
- Chapter Summary / 224
- Exercises / 225

Chapter 8
Developing and completing the OLS regression analysis by using rescaling and functional specifications / 231

- Rescaling of the outcome and explanatory variables / 231
- Linearity in the OLS analysis / 238
- Linear and nonlinear specifications in the OLS analysis / 238
- Choosing specifications by considering three different types of causal paths / 246

- General rules for including additional variables and making specifications in multivariate regression analysis / 253
- Chapter Summary / 254
- Exercises / 255

Chapter 9
The OLS regression analysis when the variance of the error term depends on the explanatory variables: Heteroscedasticity / 264

- Chapter Summary / 273
- Exercises / 274

Chapter 10
The regression analysis when the outcome variable is binary: LPM, Logit, and Probit / 277

- Linear Probability Model (LPM): Using OLS when the outcome variable is binary / 277
- The estimation of logit and probit models / 281
- Statistical inference and goodness of it for probit and logit models / 296
- Chapter Summary / 304
- Exercises / 305

Appendix
A. Software programs for data analysis: SPSS, SAS, Stata, R / 313
B. How to do a reliable empirical study / 313
C. z distribution table: standard normal curve tail probabilities / 314
D. t distribution table: critical values of the t distribution / 315
E. Chi-square distribution table: critical values of the Chi-square distribution / 316
F. F distribution table: critical values of the F distribution / 318

References / 325
Index / 326

Data Analysis for Social Science

Fundamental Methods

Chapter 1
Data Analysis for Social Science: Fundamental Methods

How do we examine our interests with data?: Distribution and mean

Understanding our world with data

We would like to learn about our world: astronomical phenomena like the sun, moon, and stars; wild lives like plants and animals; human behaviors like child-rearing, education attainment, work choices, and death. Some of them are out of pure curiosity, and others are done for usefulness in private management or public governance in a different scale of organizations, from a family to a village to a nation to a multinational organization. There are many ways to study our world. The easiest way has been observing and guessing. Historically, observing, guessing, and correcting our guessing has made progress in many fields. Initially, we thought that Earth was the center of the universe even till the middle age. Then, people came up with new ways of observing and guessing by inventing telescopes and developing math and astronomy to better understand the sun is at least the center of our solar system. Our knowledge about the universe has grown even further with more powerful cameras, spacecraft, and more. Statistics has been a way of observing and guessing by collecting and studying reliable data. For a long time, people called it statistics, and recently, people like to call it data science from a larger perspective. It is an objective and scientific way of observing and guessing. It starts with an acknowledgment of the scientific revolution during the Renaissance that we don't know the truth or that unknowns are out there. Collecting and analyzing reliable data does not give us complete certainty about the truth but guides us to make a sound prediction about the truth. The knowledge accumulated through this process has been used to persuade ourselves and our fellow humans to make many advances, such as exploring space, better medicines, and better public policies.

For the purpose of this book on data analysis for social science, let's narrow down our interests to our society. Specifically, first, we would like to study the average of our interests, such as which candidate would win the presidential election in 2020 in the U.S., the average obesity rate in Canada in 2020, the high school dropout rates in Indiana, the U.S. in 2021, and so on. Second, the relations between our interests could be whether voters' ideology is related to how they voted in the presidential election in 2020 in the U.S., whether the obesity rate was related to the sedentary hours per day in Canada in 2020, whether the regional unemployment rates are related to the high school dropout rates in the U.S. in 2022, and so on. We start with the first topic and then move to the second topic later on.

Mapping what we want to study into numbers

To study our world with empirical tools, we need to transfer the events and characteristics into meaningful numbers we can analyze. Without doing so, it is too burdensome and tedious. Some of the events and characteristics are already in numbers, such as height, weight, salary, wage, age, weekly work hours, and so on. But some of them are not in numbers, such as men and women, liberal and conservative, pro-choice and pro-life, white and nonwhite, and so on. Thus, more care is needed to transfer those events and characteristics into appropriate numbers attached to them. There are some definitions and rules when we may assign numbers to events and characteristics.

First, assigning a number to represent our topic of interest is called a variable. Typically, one-to-one matching is common between what we know in reality and matched numbers that a variable can be. For example, as shown in Figure 1.1, we can make a variable to study height, weight, and BMI. And each value of height is one-to-one matched to numbers. In other words, the different numbers cannot indicate the same thing; for instance, 5.6 feet and 6 feet are not the same things. They represent the different heights of people. However, it is possible that several things in reality at the same time can be assigned to one number. The short (less than 5 feet), medium (5 to less than 7 feet), and tall individuals (7 feet or more), respectively, can be assigned to 1, 2, and 3, respectively. Then, in this case, 1 can represent any height less than 5 feet.

Next, as shown in Figure 1.2, it is possible to assign 1 and 0 to two qualitative events: currently employed and otherwise, respectively. This is called a binary variable or a

Figure 1.1 Quantitative random variable: mapping of events in our world to real numbers

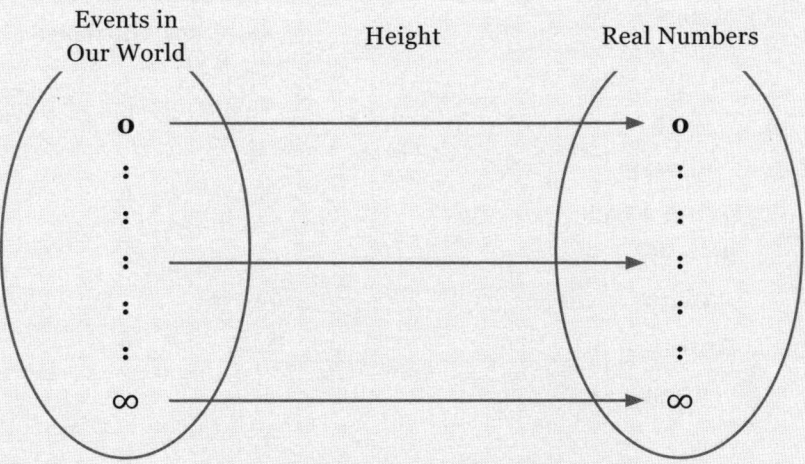

Notes: Many events in our world are directly mapped into real numbers.

Figure 1.2 Binary random variable: mapping of events in our world to real numbers

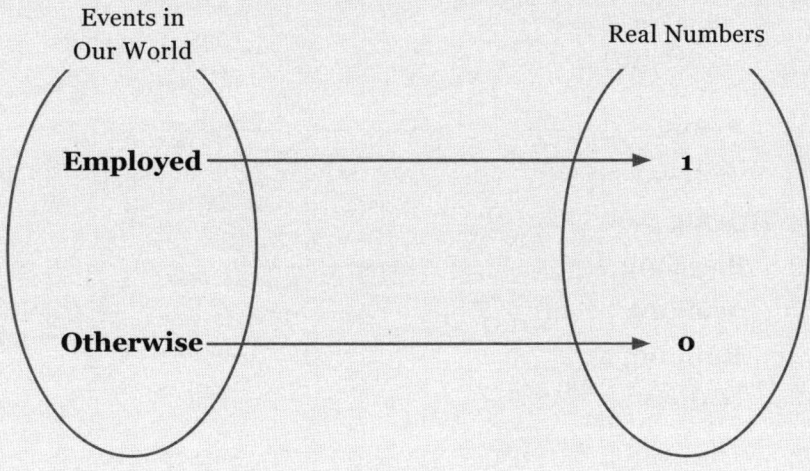

Notes: Binary events are typically mapped into 0 and 1. The reference event is usually 0.

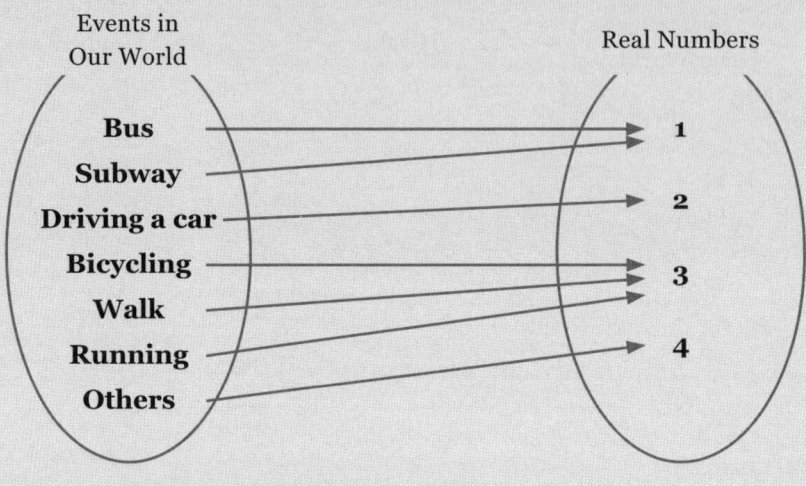

Figure 1.3 Multinomial random variable: mapping of events in our world to real numbers

Notes: Two or more events can be mapped into one number.

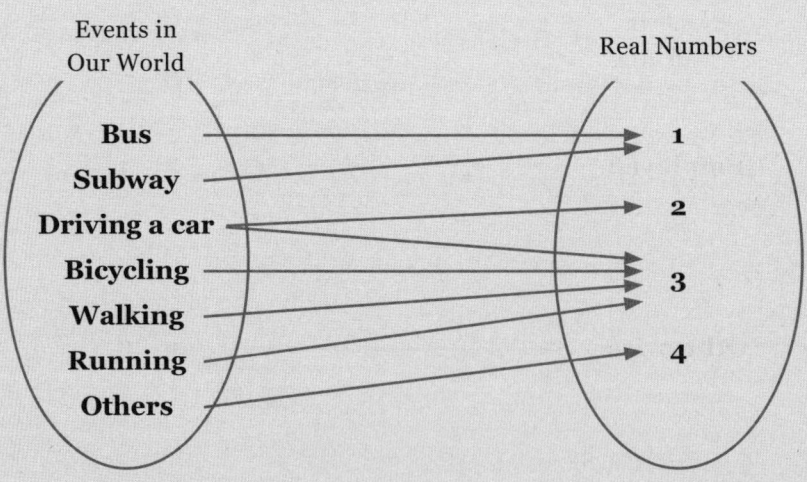

Figure 1.4 Multinomial random variable: mapping of events in our world to real numbers

Notes: One event (Driving a car) cannot be mapped into two numbers. It is a wrong practice to create random variables.

dummy variable. Instead of using other pairs of numbers, such as 1 and 2, 2 and 3, or 1 and 100, opting for 1 or 0 is mathematically advantageous as 1 represents 100% and 0 represents 0%. When the outcome variable is binary, with 1 indicating employment and 0 indicating otherwise, the sample mean indicates the percentage of employed individuals.

Furthermore, additional qualitative events are depicted in Figure 1.3. When studying the commuting choices of individuals, it is possible to assign values of 1, 2, 3, and 4 to commuting by bus or subway, driving a car, commuting by walking, running, or bicycling, and other modes, respectively. In this example, 1 can represent commuting by public transportation, such as a bus or subway. It is termed a multinomial variable or a categorical variable. In this example, 1, 2, 3, and 4 are used instead of 10, 20, 30, and 40 or -1, -2, -3, and -4 because 1, 2, 3, and 4 are more easily understood and practical for use.

Table 1.1 Types of variables and related examples

Quantitative variables		Qualitative variables	
Continuous variables	Counting variables	Nominal variables	Ordinal variables
Height	Number of customers in a coffee shop for each hour	men (0), women (1)	No college education (0), some college or more (1)
Weight	Number of children per family	otherwise (0), currently married (1)	bad (1), good (2), excellent (3)
Income	Number of doctor's visits per adult	otherwise (0), currently working (1)	do not like (1), neutral (2), like (3)
Wage	Number of hospitalizations per adult	Take a bus (1), drive a car (2), ride a bicycle (3), walk (4), others (5)	highly liberal (1), liberal (2), moderate (3), conservative (4), highly conservative (5)
GPA	Number of homicides per year	Christian (1), Muslim (2), Hinduism (3), Buddhism (4), Judaism (5), others (6)	~$10,000 (1), $10,000~$20,000 (2), $20,000~$50,000 (3), $50,000~$100,000 (4), $100,000~ (5)

Thus, a variable can be a function that transfers things of interest to numbers. As mentioned earlier, it is possible that multiple things or events can be assigned to one number. However, it is not allowed to assign one thing or event to multiple numbers since it creates confusion in our data analysis. For example, as shown in Figure 1.4, if 2 and 3 indicate the same event, driving a car, we cannot identify an event by a specific number in the data.

In summary, there are four types of variables: two for quantitative variables and the other two for qualitative variables. Please see the details in above Table 1.1.

Some quantitative variables are continuous, and others are counting. Continuous variables are those that have values with no gaps, such as height, weight, wage, income, and academic scores. Continuous variables are already in numbers and are easy to be found around us. Also, they can be rescaled to other numbers, for example, miles to meters. On the other hand, counting variables are integer numbers, such as the number of doctor's visits per year, the number of hospitalizations per year, and the number of customers per hour.

Some qualitative variables are nominal, and the others are ordinal. Nominal variables are those without any orders or ranking, such as gender, ethnicity, and marital status. For binary nominal variables (binary or dummy variables), it is common to assign 0 or 1 to the two possible events. Nominal variables that are multinomial can have multiple numbers, such as 1 to 6, in an example of religion in Table 1.1. However, these numbers have no meaning. Ordinal variables are those with order or ranking. The numbers that are assumed to represent different values depend on the context and the purpose of the research. For a binary event of some college education or not, we can assign 1 to some college education or more and 0 to otherwise. In this case, 1 is higher than 0. For a multinomial event of political ideology, we can assign higher numbers to more conservative people, such as 1 for highly liberal, 2 for liberal, 3 for moderate, 4 for conservative, and 5 for highly conservative. In this case, there is ranking, depending on how conservative a person is. Also, we can make an interval variable from a continuous variable, and it can have orders as a result. As shown in an example of Table 4.1, the yearly earnings can have five values of 1 to 5: ~$10,000 (1), $10,000~$20,000 (2), $20,000~$50,000 (3), $50,000~$100,000 (4), and $100,000~ (5). Higher numbers indicate higher yearly earnings.

Example 1.1

The table below is the list of random variables in the year 1990 of the NLSY79

(National Longitudinal Survey of Youth - 1979 Cohort) data set.

rhw1984: real hourly wage in 1984 U.S. dollars
edu: number of education in years
lcexpy: job experience in years
afqt: AFQT score (cognitive test scores from 1 to 100)
female: 1 for female and 0 for male

In this list of variables, rhw1984 and afqt are continuous while edu and lcexpy are counting. On the other hand, female is nominal and binomial since 1 is not higher than 0. We can create another binary variable using edu. For example, a new variable indicating some college education or more (called collmore) can be 1 for 13 years or more years of education and 0 for 12 years or fewer years of education. This can be ordinal and binomial since 1 is higher than 0.

collmore: 1 for some college or more and 0 for high school or less

Also, we can create a new variable indicating the level of cognitive skills using afqt. The new variable called cogskills can be 1 for 0 to 25 in afqt, 2 for 26 to 50 in afqt, 3 for 51 to 75 in afqt, and 4 for 76 to 100 in afqt. Therefore, cogskills is ordinal and multinomial.

cogskils: 1 for 0 to 25, 2 for 26 to 50, 3 for 51 to 75, and 4 for 76 to 100 in afqt.

Notes:
the NLSY79 (National Longitudinal Survey of Youth - 1979 Cohort) data set
https://www.nlsinfo.org/content/cohorts/nlsy79

AFQT score: In NLSY79, a composite score derived from select sections of the battery can be used to construct an approximate and unofficial Armed Forces Qualifications Test score (AFQT) for each youth. The AFQT, developed by the U.S. Department of Defense (DOD), is a general measure of trainability and a primary criterion of enlistment eligibility for the Armed Forces.

https://www.nlsinfo.org/content/cohorts/nlsy79/topical-guide/education/aptitude-achievement-intelligence-scores

Less likely or more likely? Think about the probabilities of events

There is no certainty in life. Our every move and decision may lead to various consequences with different chances. For example, after a college education, there is a high chance you will get a job you want, but there is also a chance you will end up with no job. If a person is single, there is a different chance to be married next year, depending on age, ethnicity, job status, etc. If a boy is from a particular neighborhood and specific family background, there is a high or low chance that this person would be an MLB player. If someone is obese, what is the chance that this person has diabetes in 10 years? If someone starts smoking at age 20, what is the chance this person would get cancer at age 60? Such chances and probabilities can be studied scientifically and rigorously. This is a part of our study in this textbook.

Let's see how to formalize the chances and probabilities we hope to study.

Suppose that the random variable X represents the number from rolling a die. Thus, the value of X could be 1 to 6. The random variable Y is assumed to represent whether a head or a tail shows up when flipping a coin. Let the value of Y be 1 for the head and 0 for the tail.

Then, assuming that the dice and the coin are fair.

We can express the probabilities as follows.

$P(X = 1) = \frac{1}{6}, P(X = 2) = \frac{1}{6}, ..., $ and $P(X = 6) = \frac{1}{6}$ are saying that the probability of each event of rolling a fair die is 1/6.

$P(Y = 1) = \frac{1}{2}$ and $P(Y = 0) = \frac{1}{2}$ are saying that the probability of each event of flipping a fair coin is 1/2.

$P(X = 2, Y = 1) = P(X = 2) \cdot P(Y = 1) = \frac{1}{6} \times \frac{1}{2} = \frac{1}{12}$, the chance of having 2 in rolling die and a head in flipping a coin at the same time is 1/12. We can get this number by multiplying the probabilities of two events since the two events are independent (not related to each other whatsoever).

Table 1.2 Political orientation and its probability

Political Orientation	Probability
$Y = 1$: Liberal	0.490
$Y = 2$: Neutral	0.133
$Y = 3$: Conservative	0.377
Total	1

Let's look at another example of survey results.

Consider the political orientation of people in South Korea. Suppose that Table 1.2 from the survey represents the political orientation of people in South Korea.

Thus, $P(Y = 1) = 0.490$, $P(Y = 2) = 0.133$, and $P(Y = 3) = 0.377$. The total probability of adding three events is 1, which implies the total probability required for studying any events in probability. In other words, in South Korea, the chances of being liberal and conservative are about 49 and 38 percent, respectively, while the chance of being neutral is about 13 percent. It does not mean that we know what political orientation a certain person has in South Korea. It says that we have a scientific and reliable guess about the political orientation of the average person in South Korea. This information is valuable enough when we try to understand the political landscape of South Korea. That is the beauty of data analysis.

Now, let's go further. In Table 1.3, consider the joint distribution of the random variables X and Y, where X indicates whether people in South Korea support the increasing military spending. Here, $X = 1$ for support and 0 for no support. Suppose that $P(X = 1) = 0.547$ and $P(X = 0) = 0.453$, which says that about 54.7 percent of South Korean adults support the expansion of military spending, and about 45.3 percent of South Korean adults do not support it.

Table 1.3 The Joint Distribution of X and Y

	$X = 0$: Do not support an increase in military spending	$X = 1$: Support an increase in military spending	Total
$Y = 1$: Liberal	0.274	0.216	0.490
$Y = 2$: Neutral	0.056	0.077	0.133
$Y = 3$: Conservative	0.123	0.254	0.377
Total	0.453	0.547	1.000

It is important to note that the total probability adds to 1 for the two random variables, X and Y, which makes this joint distribution valid. This table says that $P(X = 1, Y = 1) = 0.216$ and $P(X = 0, Y = 1) = 0.274$, which are called joint probabilities between two variables. Thus, it is found that about 21.6 percent of adults are liberal and support an increase in military spending, while about 27.4 percent of adults are liberal and do not support military spending expansion.

Since these two events are not independent, $P(X = 1, Y = 1) = 0.216$ is not $P(X = 1) \cdot P(Y = 1) = 0.547 \times 0.490 = 0.268$.

Then how do we calculate $P(X = 1, Y = 1)$?

We usually update our knowledge when we learn something new. For example, as we have more chances to meet someone, we keep updating our knowledge about who this person is in terms of personal chaterstistics based on our experiences. This idea leads to Bayes' theorem in probability and statistics, which updates the probability of some event conditional on other given events.

Suppose that X and Y are dependent on each other like in the example above.
Then, by Bayes' Rule, $P(Y = y | X = x) = \frac{P(X=x, Y=y)}{P(X=x)}$.

Bayes' Rule or Bayes' Theorem:

$$P(Y = y | X = x) = \frac{P(X = x, Y = y)}{P(X = x)}$$

Bayes' Rule, also known as Bayes' Theorem, is a mathematical formula that provides a way to update the probability of an event of our interest, $Y = y$, based on a new event, $X = x$. It states that the posterior probability, $P(Y = y | X = x)$, is the joint probability of the two events, $P(X = x, Y = y)$, divided by the probability of the new event, $P(X = x)$. Bayes' Rule is commonly used in statistics, machine learning, and other fields to make predictions and update beliefs based on new information.

As a result, $P(X = x, Y = y) = P(Y = y | X = x) P(X = x)$ from $P(Y = y | X = x) = \frac{P(X=x, Y=y)}{P(X=x)}$.

Therefore, if we know $P(Y = y | X = x)$ and $P(X = x)$, we can calculate $P(X = x, Y = y)$.

If X and Y are independent,
$P(X = x, Y = y) = P(Y = y) P(X = x)$ since $P(Y = y | X = x) = P(Y = y)$ in $P(X = x, Y = y) = P(Y = y | X = x) P(X = x)$.

Then, what is the conditional probability that an adult supported a military expansion, given that she/he is conservative?

$$P(X = 1 | Y = 3) = \frac{P(X = 1, Y = 3)}{P(Y = 3)} = \frac{0.254}{0.377} = 0.674$$

Also, $P(X = 1, Y = 3) = P(X = 1|Y = 3)P(Y = 3) = 0.674 \times 0.377 = 0.254$.

We can think about the probability of a continuous variable, too.

IQ scores are known as one of the most popular measurements of a person's cognitive ability. IQ scores can be considered to be a continuous variable in the data analysis. It is constructed to have the following probabilities for the general population.

About 50% of the population has IQ scores greater than 100, which can be presented as $P(100 < X) = 0.5$. It is equivalent to $P(100 \leq X) = 0.5$; < and ≤ are interchangeable because a value, such as 100 in this example, has no probability in the distribution of a continuous variable.

About 95% of the population has IQ scores between 70 and 130, which can be presented as $P(70 < X < 130) = P(70 \leq X \leq 130) = 0.95$.

About 2.5% of the population has IQ scores greater than 130, and about 0.15% of the population has IQ scores greater than 145, which can be shown below.

$P(130 < X) = P(130 \leq X) = 0.025$

$P(145 < X) = P(145 \leq X) = 0.0015$

Thus, it is quite rare to see some persons' IQ scores greater than 130 or even 145.

Suppose that we would like to know the probability of IQ scores greater than 130, given that the individuals are all college graduates. X is a continuous random variable for IQ scores while Y is a binary random variable for a college degree, 1 for a college degree, and 0 for otherwise.

Then, we can calculate $P(X > 130 | Y = 1) = \frac{P(X > 130, Y = 1)}{P(Y = 1)}$ if we know $P(X > 130, Y = 1)$ and $P(Y = 1)$.

Which group of subjects do we want to study?: The population of interest and the random sample

If we would like to study height, weight, and BMI, then we need to choose which group of people we are interested in. Children under age 10, adolescents aged 13 to 18, or adults aged 30 to 50? Or women aged 65 or older? We should identify our group of interest whatever we would like to study. This group of interest is called the population of interest.

If we would like to study the third-grade students in a particular elementary school, we may survey all the students in that school. However, in general, we cannot survey every individual in our population of interest since it is usually large and ambiguous. For example, if we would like to study all children aged 6 to 10 in the U.S., the total number of children this year in the U.S. is very large and unknown. Depending on the survey period, the total number of children may change due to international migration and other reasons. Also, it takes a lot of time and money to survey all the subjects in the population of interest. Therefore, we use a sample (the limited number of individuals that we can handle in a survey) that represents the population of interest.

Random sample assumption and sampling methods

Then, how can we have a sample representing the population of interest? For example, suppose that we are interested in the BMI level of children aged 6 to 10 in the U.S. In an ideal case, we may have a list of all the children in the U.S. To get a representative sample consisting of 1,000 children, we may randomly choose 1,000 children from the list and ask a question about height and weight to get the BMI. This is simple random sampling. Therefore, each child in the population has an equal chance of being chosen. A sample obtained by simple random sampling is called a random sample. Children in the random sample are not related to one another (they are independent of one another), and they are expected to have possible values from the same distribution (they are identically distributed). Through this book, a random sample is assumed for the usual data analysis. By this assumption, the representativeness of the sample for the population of interest is secured.

However, in reality, we do not have a list of children in that group in the U.S. because it is difficult to find a public system that records all the children in the U.S. Even with such a system, we may miss some of the children who migrate in and out of the U.S. every day. Therefore, as we mentioned earlier, the population of interest is usually large and sometimes not completely known. To get around this difficulty, statisticians came up with an idea of sampling methods: one method is to survey the children in each randomly chosen regional area, such as the areas indicated by zip codes. Of course, it is not perfect for obtaining the sample representing the population of interest, but it is close to an ideal random sampling. This is called cluster random sampling. Another popular sampling method is sampling based on strata, groups with some particular characteristics, such as gender, age, education, and so on. This is called stratified random sampling. Most of the surveys are based on a mix of these two sampling methods in some way.

Cluster random sample

A cluster random sample divides the population into numerous clusters, like city blocks or regional boundaries. Then, it randomly chooses a simple sample of these clusters and includes all individuals within those selected clusters as the sample.

Stratified random sample

A stratified random sample involves dividing the population into distinct groups known as strata and then selecting a simple random sample from each stratum. For example, race, gender, or political preference can be strata. When the sampled strata proportions align with those of the entire population, it is referred to as proportional stratified random sampling. On the other hand, if the sampled strata proportions differ from the population proportions, it is known as disproportional stratified random sampling.

In a stratified sample, every stratum (meaningful group) is utilized for sampling. The strata are carefully chosen groups that we want to compare and study in the population. On the other hand, a cluster sample involves selecting only a sample of the clusters, where clusters are not necessarily meaningful groups but just a convenient way to divide the population. Therefore, in contrast to stratified sampling, which involves including all strata, cluster sampling selects only a portion of the clusters, resulting in a less precise approach for studying specific population groups.

Example 1.2

Example of cluster random sampling
Burnham, G., Lafta, R., Doocy, S., & Roberts, L. (2006). Mortality after the 2003 invasion of Iraq: a cross-sectional cluster sample survey. *The Lancet*, 368(9545), 1421-1428.

"Methods: Between May and July 2006, we did a national cross-sectional cluster sample survey of mortality in Iraq. 50 clusters were randomly selected from 16 Governorates, with every cluster consisting of 40 households. Information on deaths from these households was gathered.

> Findings: Three misattributed clusters were excluded from the final analysis; data from 1849 households that contained 12,801 individuals in 47 clusters was gathered. 1,474 births and 629 deaths were reported during the observation period. Pre-invasion mortality rates were 5·5 per 1,000 people per year (95% CI 4.3–7.1), compared with 13.3 per 1,000 people per year (10.9–16.1) in the 40 months post-invasion. We estimate that as of July 2006, there have been 654,965 excess Iraqi deaths as a consequence of the war, which corresponds to 2.5% of the population in the study area. Of post-invasion deaths, 601,027 were due to violence, the most common cause being gunfire."
>
> Example of multistage random sampling
> The American Community Survey (ACS) uses a combination of stratified and cluster random sampling methods by treating counties (or census tracts) as clusters. It selects a random sample of a certain number of them. It also incorporates strata based on age groups, income levels, education levels, and other demographic variables to ensure representation from various segments of the population.
>
> "The American Community Survey (ACS) is the cornerstone of the U.S. Census Bureau's effort to keep pace with the nation's ever-increasing demands for timely and relevant data about population and housing characteristics. The ACS is conducted throughout the United States and Puerto Rico, where it is called the Puerto Rico Community Survey (PRCS). For ease of discussion, the term ACS is used here to represent both surveys. The ACS is an ongoing monthly survey that collects detailed housing and socioeconomic data. The ACS includes people living in both housing units (HUs) and group quarters (GQs)."
> https://www.census.gov/programs-surveys/acs/methodology/design-and-methodology.html

What useful information can we have from a sample?: sample mean and sample variance

Assume that we have a random sample of the population of interest. Then, the next question is what useful information we can obtain about our topic of interest from the sample and what we can learn from that information. Our analytical strategy will depend on what we would like to know about the population of interest. Generally, one of the most popular and useful information is the sample average or the sample mean, such as the voting rate, the employment rate, the average academic score, the average height, the average weight, the average BMI, etc. The next is the sample variance to examine how far an individual point of information is from the sample average or how diverse the individual characteristics are. For example, a higher variance in the student's academic score may indicate the widening academic inequality among students.

Usually, we assume that a random sample represents the population and gives us the ability to know information about the population. Using the sample, we can calculate the sample mean for the population mean and the sample variance for the population variance.

For a random variable X, the population mean is defined as
$E(X) = \mu$, which is unknown and to be estimated using the random sample.
The population variance is defined as
$Var(X) = \sigma^2$, which is unknown and to be estimated using the random sample.

Greek letters are popular to denote the population parameters, such as the population mean and the population variance. We typically put a hat on Greek letters to indicate the estimators for the population parameters. For example, the sample mean is $\hat{\mu}$ for the population mean, μ, while the sample variance is $\hat{\sigma}^2$ for the population variance, σ^2. We also use $\bar{X}$ for the sample mean and S^2 for the sample variance.

The sample mean, $\hat{\mu}$ or $\bar{X}$, for the population mean, μ, is obtained as follows:

$$\hat{\mu} = \bar{X} = \frac{X_1 + X_2 + \cdots + X_n}{n} = \sum_{i=1}^{n} \frac{X_i}{n}$$

The sample variance, $\hat{\sigma}^2$ or S^2, for the population variance, σ^2, is obtained as follows:

$$\hat{\sigma}^2 = S^2 = \frac{(X_1 - \bar{X})^2 + (X_2 - \bar{X})^2 + \ldots + (X_n - \bar{X})^2}{n-1} = \sum_{i=1}^{n} \frac{(X_i - \bar{X})^2}{n-1}$$

The sample standard deviation is the square root of the sample variance as shown below.

$$\hat{\sigma} = S = \sqrt{\frac{(X_1 - \bar{X})^2 + (X_2 - \bar{X})^2 + \ldots + (X_n - \bar{X})^2}{n-1}} = \sqrt{\sum_{i=1}^{n} \frac{(X_i - \bar{X})^2}{n-1}}$$

The sample mean indicates the center value of our sample, and the sample variance (or the sample standard deviation) suggests how spread or diverse our sample is in the value of interest, such as BMI. The sample mean and variance are the estimators for the population mean and variance that inform us about the random sample we collect.

Example 1.3

The table below is the list of AFQT scores (cognitive test scores from 1 to 100) of black women aged 30 with 14 years of education in the year 1990 of the NLSY79 (National Longitudinal Survey of Youth - 1979 Cohort) data set.

AFQT Score	Frequency
3	2
10	1
12	1
15	1
19	1
20	1
27	2
37	1
41	1
43	2
46	1
52	1
69	1
81	1
82	1
n	18

Then, we can obtain the sample mean and the sample standard deviation as below.

$$\hat{\mu} = \bar{X} = \frac{X_1 + X_2 + \cdots + X_n}{n} = \sum_{i=1}^{n} \frac{X_i}{n} = 35$$

$$\hat{\sigma} = S = \sqrt{\frac{(X_1 - \bar{X})^2 + (X_2 - \bar{X})^2 + \cdots + (X_n - \bar{X})^2}{n-1}} = \sqrt{\sum_{i=1}^{n} \frac{(X_i - \bar{X})^2}{n-1}} = 25.58$$

For the same sample, the following table is about hourly wage in 1984 U.S. dollars.

Hourly wage in 1984 U.S. dollars	Frequency
2.59	1
3.38	1

3.47	1
3.58	1
3.78	1
4.79	1
4.81	1
4.98	1
5.03	1
5.35	1
5.73	1
6.41	1
6.46	1
6.57	1
7.08	1
10.33	1
15.10	1
16.05	1
n	18

Again, we can obtain the sample mean and the sample standard deviation as below.

$$\hat{\mu} = \bar{X} = \frac{X_1+X_2+\cdots+X_n}{n} = \sum_{i=1}^{n}\frac{X_i}{n} = 6.42$$

$$\hat{\sigma} = S = \sqrt{\frac{(X_1-\bar{X})^2+(X_2-\bar{X})^2+\cdots+(X_n-\bar{X})^2}{n-1}} = \sqrt{\sum_{i=1}^{n}\frac{(X_i-\bar{X})^2}{n-1}} = 3.78$$

Notes:
the NLSY79 (National Longitudinal Survey of Youth - 1979 Cohort) data set
https://www.nlsinfo.org/content/cohorts/nlsy79

Before going further, it is time to make a clear distinction between the population of interest and the sample. As mentioned earlier, the population of interest can be defined by us but cannot be directly obtained or analyzed. Of course, we can think about the possible shapes of the population distribution with possible values and their range, although it is all in our imagination. For example, it is commonly accepted that the population distribution of individuals' heights and weights is bell-shaped and symmetric based on our experience and many sample studies. Then, we also can think about the population mean, the average value of the population, and the population variance, the diversity of the population. Although we do not know them, we know they are there. It is intuitive to see that the sample mean is an estimate for the population mean, and the sample variance is an estimate for the population variance. But, again, the sample mean is not the population mean, and the sample variance is not the population variance.

Estimating the sample mean is widely used to examine and understand our world. Example 1.4 below shows the trend in U.S. birth rates using the yearly mean of births per 1,000 women aged 15 to 44 in the U.S.

Example 1.4

The Trend in U.S. Birth Rates

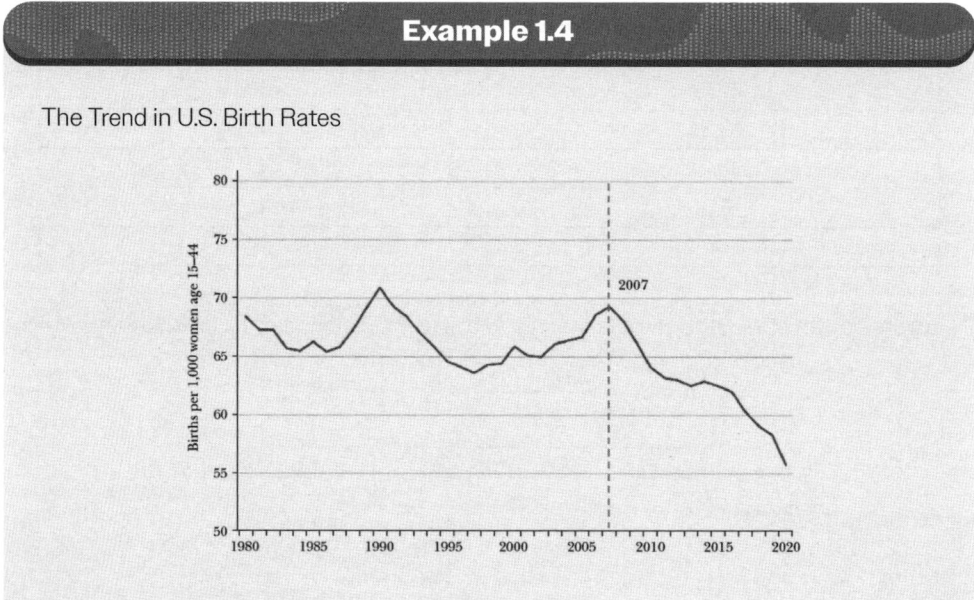

Kearney, Levine, & Pardue. (2022). p.152.
Kearney, M. S., Levine, P. B., & Pardue, L. (2022). The Puzzle of Falling U.S. Birth Rates since the Great Recession. *Journal of Economic Perspectives*, 36(1), 151-76.

This graph displays the patterns in birth rates for women aged 15 to 44 in the United States. From 1980 to 2007, the fertility rate in the U.S. remained relatively stable, with only slight fluctuations. However, after the onset of the Great Recession in 2007, there was a decline, and it took around seven years, starting from 2014, for the rate to recover. Since then, there has been a significant drop in the U.S. fertility rate, reaching

55.8 births per 1,000 women in 2020, which is almost 20 percent lower than thirteen years ago. Unfortunately, there are no indications of a recovery from this downward trend.

Another figure in Example 1.5 shows the employment-to-population ratio by age groups between 1965 and 2018 to examine the labor market participation of U.S. adults.

Example 1.5

Employment-to-Population Ratio by Age, 1965-2018

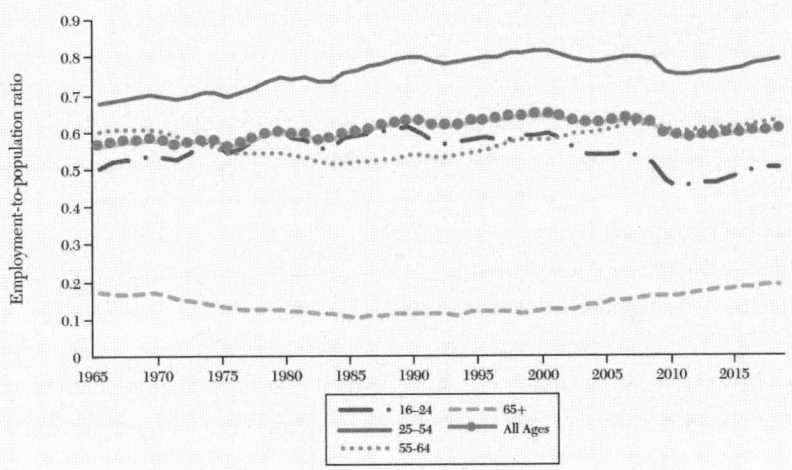

Abraham & Kearney. (2020). p.591.
Abraham, K. G. & Kearney, M. S. (2020). Explaining the decline in the U.S. employment-to-population ratio: A review of the evidence. *Journal of Economic Literature*, 58(3), 585-643.

This graph indicates a sharp drop in the overall employment-to-population ratio during the 2007-2009 recession, followed by a partial recovery, but the ratio still remains lower than pre-recession levels. The significant decrease in the employment rate of workers in their prime working-age has become a topic of increasing discussions and concerns. The employment rate for the age group of 16-24 has decreased by more than 5 percentage points from 1999 to 2018.

As shown in Example 1.6, it is important to understand the difference between percent (percentage) and percentage point when you interpret descriptive statistics.

Example 1.6

Case A:
Change from 80% to 90% in high school graduation rate
Increase by ten percentage points
Increase by 10/80=12.5 percent or percentage

In case A, a percentage-point increase is similar to a percent increase in magnitude.

Case B:
Change from 5% to 7% in cancer survival rate
Increase by two percentage points
Increase by 2/5=40 percent or percentage

In case B, it seems like a small increase in percentage point change, but it is actually a big increase in terms of percent change.

Normal distribution and its application: One of the most popular and useful distributions

The sample mean and variance do not provide a complete understanding of the random sample. For example, the random sample of girls aged 10 to 13 may have the same mean and variance in BMI as the random sample of boys aged 10 to 13. However, it does not mean that the distribution of girls' BMI is the same as that of boys' BMI. This is why sometimes researchers would like to show the distribution of the sample in frequency tables, bar graphs, and histograms. The description of the sample is one main area of data analysis.

Particularly, histograms are popular to show the shape of the sample distribution of the quantitative variables as below.

Example 1.7

This example presents a histogram of real hourly wage in the year 1990 of the NLSY79 (National Longitudinal Survey of Youth - 1979 Cohort) data set.

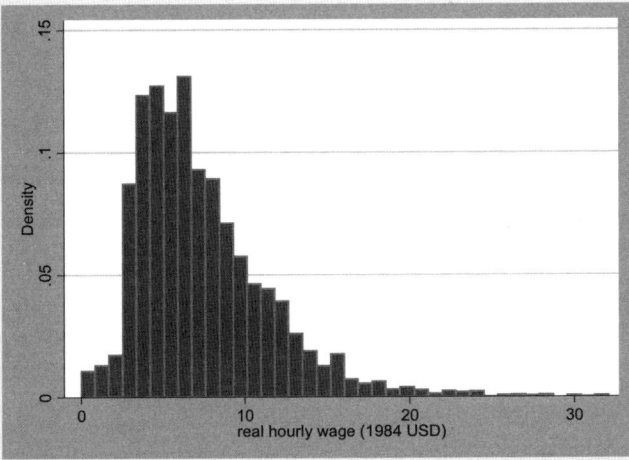

A histogram is a type of graph that plays a crucial role in statistics. Its primary purpose is to represent the distribution of a data set. In this case, we are interested in hourly wage. Each bar in a histogram corresponds to a range of values, often referred to as a 'bin'. The bins collectively cover the range of the entire data set, providing a segmented view of the data distribution. We can choose different ranges of values depending on our research interests and purposes.

A key feature of the histogram is the way it conveys information through the height of each bar. The height is indicative of the number of values from the data set that fall within the range of that particular bin. This aspect of the histogram makes it exceptionally useful for visualizing and understanding the spread and concentration of data points within a data set. In this example, the distribution of real hourly wage is not symmetric. A larger number of people are concentrated in the lower wage range (less than $10) on the left side of the distribution, whereas only a few earn higher

> wages (more than $20) on the far right.
>
> Notes:
> the NLSY79 (National Longitudinal Survey of Youth - 1979 Cohort) data set
> https://www.nlsinfo.org/content/cohorts/nlsy79

Then, how can we study the shape of the sample distribution? One of the most popular benchmarks is the normal distribution, which is bell-shaped and symmetric.

The bell-shaped and symmetric distribution has been with us throughout history and in nature. Statisticians developed the mathematical equations and frameworks of the normal distribution to mimic such bell-shaped and symmetric distributions closely and to explain many events and natural phenomena we experience. If any sample distribution in our study is similar to the normal distribution, we can study it using the normal distribution. Further, statisticians came up with an idea to transform all the normal distributions with different means and variances into the standard normal distribution with the same mean, 0, and the same variance, 1, which becomes a yardstick to compute the probability of any events or characteristics that follows a normal distribution. Specifically, the probabilities under the standard normal distribution are calculated and presented in the z table. For example, if the students' math score follows a normal distribution, it is easy to figure out the chance that a student can have a math score less than 70 by finding a transformed value of 70 in the z table of the standard normal distribution.

Let's look at the z table below, one of the z tables that are popularly used. In this z table, rows and columns indicate the z-score on the standard normal distribution. Right tail probabilities of the z-score, $P(Z > z)$, are found inside the table. For example, $P(Z > 0.43)$ is found by looking up the probability where the row of 0.4 and the column of 0.03 meet. It is 0.3336. In other words, the probability of z-score greater than 0.43 is 0.3336 or 33.36%. Since there is no probability at a real number, $P(Z > 0.43) = P(Z \geq 0.43) = 0.3336$. Using the fact that the total probability is 1, $P(Z < 0.43) = 1 - P(Z > 0.43) = 1 - 0.3336 = 0.6664$. Also, since the standard normal distribution is symmetry, $P(Z > 0.43) = P(Z < -0.43) = 0.3336$. Thus, probabilities of negative z-scores can be drawn from this table, too.

Then, how do we convert the normal distribution to the standard normal distribution?

Let Y be a random variable with a normal distribution with mean $E(Y) = \mu$ and

Appendix C of the text book: Standard normal probability in right-hand tail (for negative values of z, probabilities are found by symmetry).

z table

z	0.00	0.01	0.02	0.03	0.04	0.05	0.06	0.07	0.08	0.09
0.0	0.5000	0.4960	0.4920	0.4880	0.4840	0.4801	0.4761	0.4721	0.4681	0.4641
0.1	0.4602	0.4562	0.4522	0.4483	0.4443	0.4404	0.4364	0.4325	0.4286	0.4247
0.2	0.4207	0.4168	0.4129	0.4090	0.4052	0.4013	0.3974	0.3936	0.3897	0.3859
0.3	0.3821	0.3783	0.3745	0.3707	0.3669	0.3632	0.3594	0.3557	0.3520	0.3483
0.4	0.3446	0.3409	0.3372	0.3336	0.3300	0.3264	0.3228	0.3192	0.3156	0.3121
0.5	0.3085	0.3050	0.3015	0.2981	0.2945	0.2912	0.2877	0.2843	0.2810	0.2776
0.6	0.2743	0.2709	0.2676	0.2643	0.2611	0.2578	0.2546	0.2514	0.2483	0.2451
0.7	0.2420	0.2389	0.2358	0.2327	0.2296	0.2266	0.2236	0.2206	0.2177	0.2148
0.8	0.2119	0.2090	0.2061	0.2033	0.2005	0.1977	0.1949	0.1922	0.1894	0.1867
0.9	0.1841	0.1814	0.1788	0.1762	0.1736	0.1711	0.1685	0.1660	0.1635	0.1611
1.0	0.1587	0.1562	0.1539	0.1515	0.1492	0.1469	0.1446	0.1423	0.1401	0.1379
1.1	0.1357	0.1335	0.1314	0.1292	0.1271	0.1251	0.1230	0.1210	0.1190	0.1170
1.2	0.1151	0.1131	0.1112	0.1093	0.1075	0.1056	0.1038	0.1020	0.1003	0.0985
1.3	0.0968	0.0951	0.0934	0.0918	0.0901	0.0885	0.0869	0.0853	0.0838	0.0823
1.4	0.0808	0.0793	0.0778	0.0764	0.0749	0.0735	0.0721	0.0708	0.0694	0.0681
1.5	0.0668	0.0655	0.0643	0.0630	0.0618	0.0606	0.0594	0.0582	0.0671	0.0559
1.6	0.0548	0.0537	0.0526	0.0516	0.0505	0.0495	0.0485	0.0475	0.0465	0.0455
1.7	0.0446	0.0436	0.0427	0.0418	0.0409	0.0401	0.0392	0.0384	0.0375	0.0367
1.8	0.0359	0.0351	0.0344	0.0336	0.0329	0.0322	0.0314	0.0307	0.0301	0.0294
1.9	0.0287	0.0281	0.0274	0.0268	0.0262	0.0256	0.0250	0.0244	0.0239	0.0233
2.0	0.0228	0.0222	0.0217	0.0212	0.0207	0.0202	0.0197	0.0192	0.0188	0.0183
2.1	0.0179	0.0174	0.0170	0.0166	0.0162	0.0158	0.0154	0.0150	0.0146	0.0143
2.2	0.0139	0.0136	0.0132	0.0129	0.0125	0.0122	0.0119	0.0116	0.0113	0.0110
2.3	0.0107	0.0104	0.0102	0.0099	0.0095	0.0094	0.0091	0.0089	0.0087	0.0084
2.4	0.0082	0.0080	0.0078	0.0075	0.0073	0.0071	0.0069	0.0068	0.0066	0.0064
2.5	0.0062	0.0060	0.0059	0.0057	0.0055	0.0054	0.0052	0.0051	0.0049	0.0048
2.6	0.0047	0.0045	0.0044	0.0043	0.0041	0.0040	0.0039	0.0038	0.0037	0.0036
2.7	0.0035	0.0034	0.0033	0.0032	0.0031	0.0030	0.0029	0.0028	0.0027	0.0026
2.8	0.0026	0.0025	0.0024	0.0023	0.0023	0.0022	0.0021	0.0021	0.0020	0.0019
2.9	0.0019	0.0018	0.0018	0.0017	0.0016	0.0015	0.0015	0.0015	0.0014	0.0014
3.0	0.0013	0.0013	0.0013	0.0012	0.0012	0.0011	0.0011	0.0011	0.0010	0.0010
3.1	0.0010	0.0009	0.0009	0.0009	0.0008	0.0008	0.0008	0.0008	0.0007	0.0007
3.2	0.0007	0.0007	0.0005	0.0005	0.0005	0.0006	0.0006	0.0005	0.0005	0.0005
3.3	0.0005	0.0005	0.0005	0.0004	0.0004	0.0004	0.0004	0.0004	0.0004	0.0003
3.4	0.0003	0.0003	0.0003	0.0003	0.0003	0.0003	0.0003	0.0003	0.0003	0.0002

standard deviation $Sd(Y) = \sigma$.

We can construct $z = \frac{Y-\mu}{\sigma}$, a new random variable, by subtracting $E(Y) = \mu$ from Y and dividing it by $Sd(Y) = \sigma$. As a result, z follows the standard normal distribution with mean 0 and standard deviation 1. Figure 1.5 shows how we can compute the probability between a and b when Y follows the normal distribution. When we standardize the Y distribution, then a becomes $\frac{a-E(Y)}{Sd(Y)}$ and b becomes $\frac{b-E(Y)}{Sd(Y)}$. To compute the probabilities between a and b can be done by looking up the probability between $\frac{a-E(Y)}{Sd(Y)}$ and $\frac{b-E(Y)}{Sd(Y)}$ in the z table.

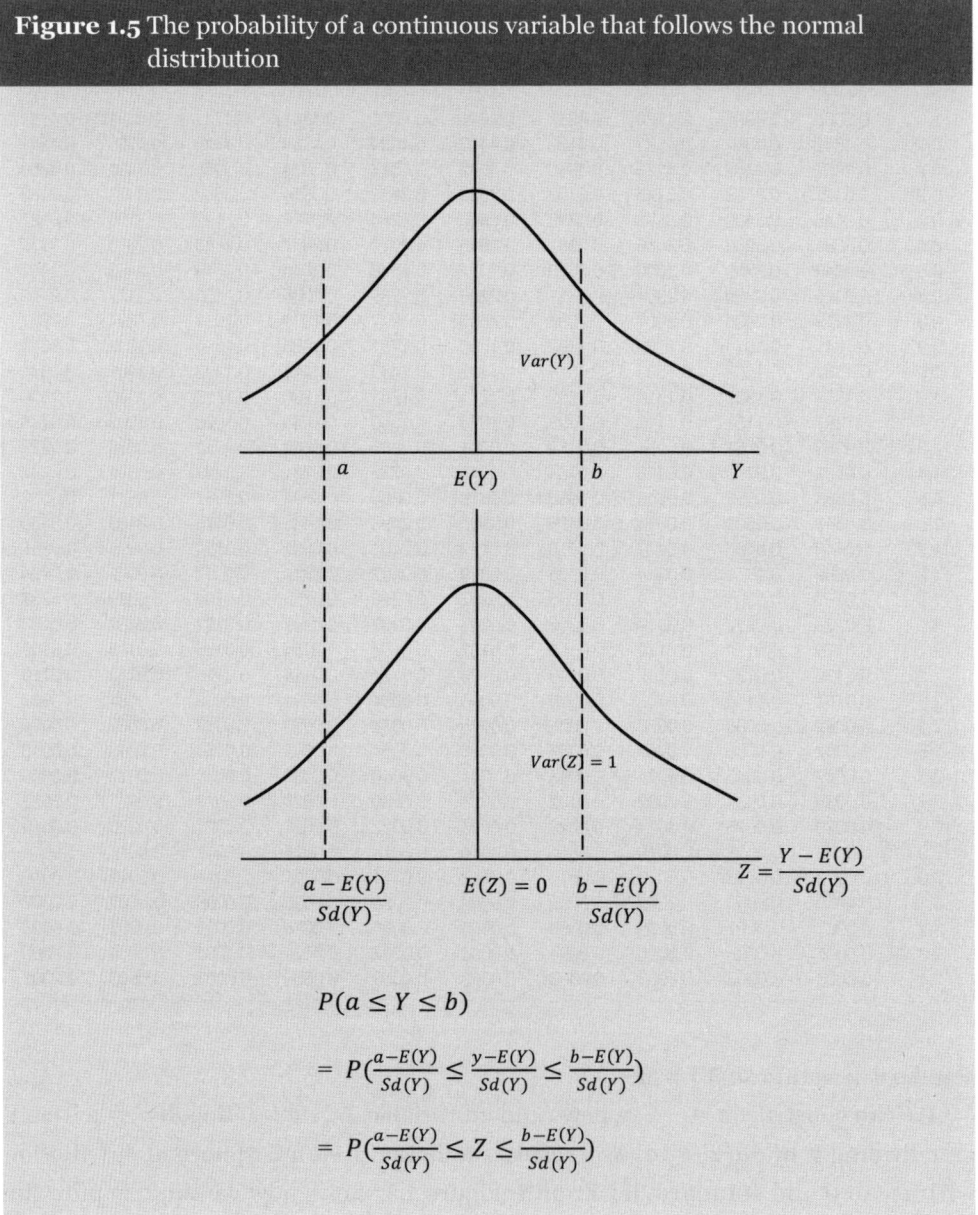

Figure 1.5 The probability of a continuous variable that follows the normal distribution

Example 1.8

For a random variable Y with a normal distribution with mean = 3 and standard deviation = 4, obtain $P(Y<3.5)$ and $P(3<Y<5)$.

$P(Y < 3.5)$

$= P(\frac{Y-3}{4} < 0.125)$

$= P(Z < 0.125)$

$= 1 - P(Z > 0.125)$ using the symmetry of the z distribution

$= 1 - 0.4522$

$= 0.5478$

$P(3 < Y < 5)$

$= P(\frac{3-3}{4} < \frac{Y-3}{4} < \frac{5-3}{4})$

$= P(0 < Z < 0.5)$

$= 1 - P(0 > Z) - P(Z > 0.5)$ using the symmetry of the z distribution

$= 1 - 0.5 - 0.3085$

$= 0.1915$

Example 1.9

For a random variable Y with a normal distribution with mean = 3 and standard deviation = 4,

Obtain a, a^*, b, and b^* such that $P(a<Y<a^*) = 0.90$ and $P(b<Y<b^*) = 0.95$
Make sure that two end values are equally distant from the mean of Y.

$P(a<Y<a^*) = P(\frac{a-E(Y)}{sd(Y)} < Z < \frac{a^*-E(Y)}{sd(Y)}) =$

$P(\frac{a-3}{4} < z < \frac{a^*-3}{4}) = 0.90$

$\frac{a-3}{4} = -1.645 \qquad \frac{a^*-3}{4} = 1.645$ from the z table

➔ $a = -3.58 \qquad a^* = 9.58$

$P(b < Y < b^*) = P(\frac{b-E(Y)}{sd(Y)} < z < \frac{b^*-E(Y)}{sd(Y)}) =$

$P(\frac{b-3}{4} < z < \frac{b^*-3}{4}) = 0.95$

$\frac{b-3}{4} = -1.96 \qquad \frac{b^*-3}{4} = 1.96$ from the z table

➔ $b = -4.84 \qquad b^* = 10.84$

There are some events that may not follow the normal distribution. Some of them may show more subjects on the right or left with long tails on the other side. When the distribution has a longer left tail and more information on the right tail, it is called skewed to the left. On the other hand, when the distribution has a longer right tail and more information on the left tail, it is called skewed to the right. Please see Figure 1.6.

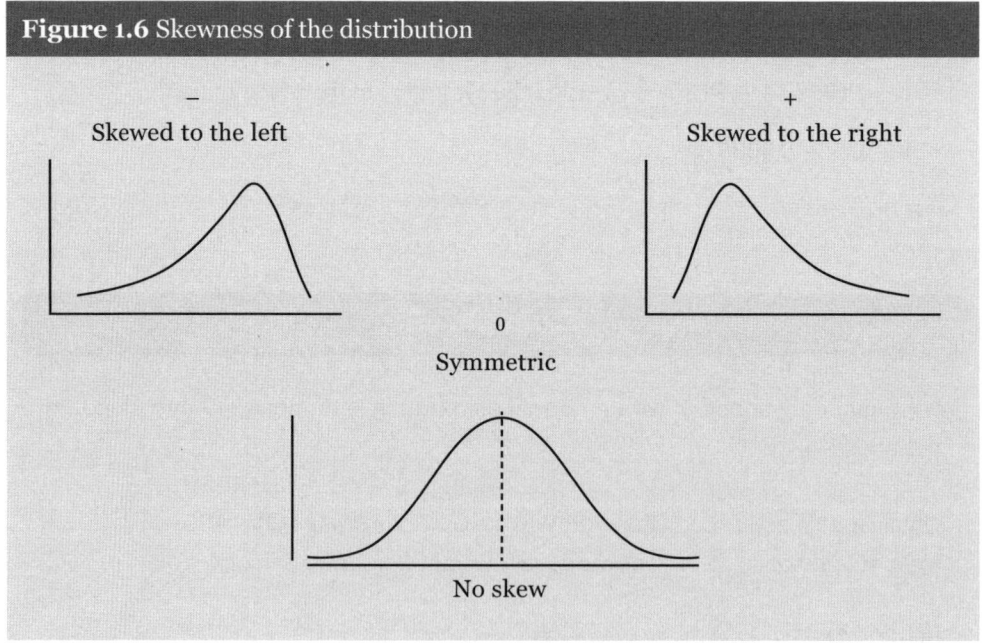

Figure 1.6 Skewness of the distribution

Example 1.10

The example below shows a histogram of real hourly wage and another histogram of the log of real hourly wage in the year 1990 of the NLSY79 (National Longitudinal Survey of Youth - 1979 Cohort) data set.

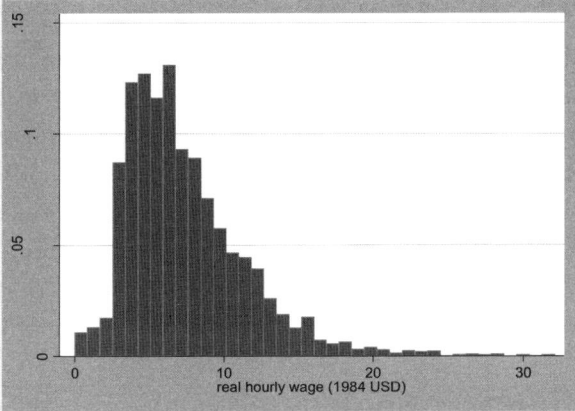

As shown here, the real hourly wage is skewed to the right. This kind of shape of distribution is typical for the hourly wage.

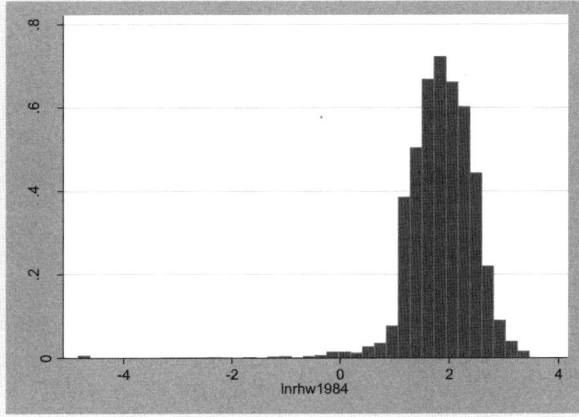

On the other hand, the histogram of the log of real hourly wage (lnrhw1984) is close to normal distribution. This implies that we can transform a right-skewed distribution into a normal (symmetric) distribution by applying a logarithmic function.

Notes:
the NLSY79 (National Longitudinal Survey of Youth - 1979 Cohort) data set
https://www.nlsinfo.org/content/cohorts/nlsy79

Alternative measures to mean: median and mode

There are two major alternative measures to mean. One is the median, the middle value, and the other is the mode, the most frequent value. Although mathematically inconvenient to obtain median and mode, they have their own advantages in some studies. Particularly, the median is popular to summarize the sample when the sample distribution is highly skewed to the left or right. In this situation, the sample mean may be highly affected by the extremely low or high values since the sample mean gives equal weight to all the values in the sample. For example, many studies of housing prices and household incomes use the median to minimize the influence of extreme values.

Specifically, in Figure 1.7, as shown in the middle, in a perfectly normal distribution, the mean, median, and mode are all located at the same point, at the center of the distribution. As we can see in the right, in a positively skewed distribution, the mean is greater than the median, which is greater than the mode. The tail of the distribution is longer on the right side. As presented in the left, in a negatively skewed distribution, the mean is less than the median, which is less than the mode. The tail of the distribution is longer on the left side.

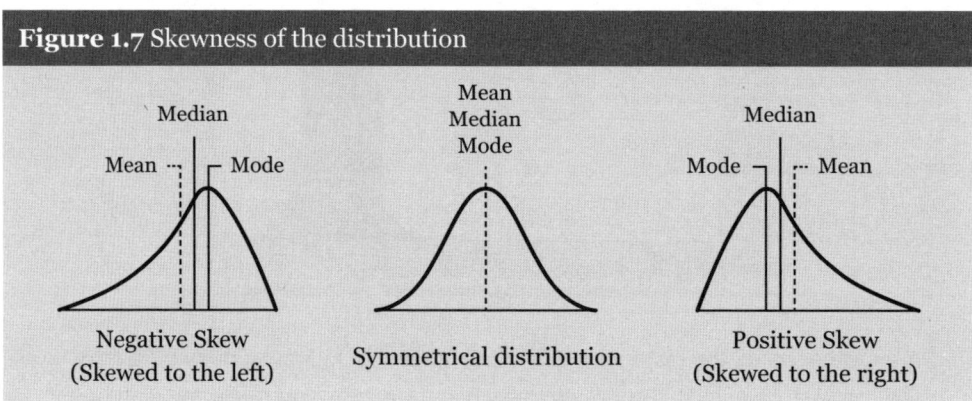

Figure 1.7 Skewness of the distribution

Particularly, it is important to note whether the mean is greater or smaller than the median. For household incomes and housing prices, the mean is typically greater than the median, which implies a positively skewed distribution.

Example 1.11

Suppose that you have a sample below. Please find the mean, median, and mode.

1, 2, 3, 4, 5, 5, 6, 6, 6, 7, 8, 9, 10

Mean: 5.538
Median: 6
Mode: 6

Example 1.12

Distribution of annual household income in the United States in 2011

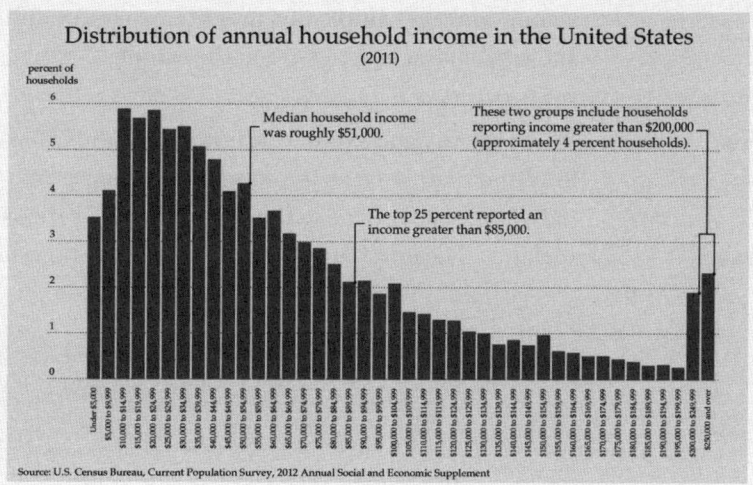

Since the distribution of annual household income is skewed to the right, and the considerable number of households are concentrated in extremely high income, it is common to report the median household income, $51,000, as shown here.

Chapter Summary

How to start the data analysis	Find your question to answer using the data analysis. Ex) I would like to know the proportion of adults who were working in the U.S. in 2022. Define the subjects of your study. Ex) Adults aged 20 to older in the U.S. in 2022 Find reliable data that include the representative sample of your interest and information you would like to examine. Ex) Current population survey in the U.S. in 2022 Find a relevant variable and code your interest of characteristics into appropriate numbers? Ex) Currently working = 1, otherwise = 0
What to estimate	Typically, the sample mean suggests an average value of the sample and the sample variance indicates how different subjects' characteristics are in the sample.
Addressing common misunderstandings and mistakes	When the variable of interest is nominal and categorical (multinomial), such as the commuting choices of individuals, do not make the sample mean or the sample variance. The numbers in that variable have no value.

Exercises

Chapter 1
How do we examine our interests with data?: Distribution and mean

1. Please identify and explain whether the following variables are quantitative (continuous or counting) or qualitative (nominal or ordinal).

(1) Number of children in a family

(2) Voting behavior: early voting, election day voting, or no voting

(3) Distance between home and nearest public transportation

(4) Smartphone user or not

(5) Years of education

(6) Yearly earnings

(7) Attitude toward same-sex marriage (highly unfavorable, unfavorable, neutral, favorable, highly favorable)

2. Suppose that a study calculates the yearly household earnings of families residing in public housing in New York in 2010. A random sample of 10 families reveals their annual incomes (in hundreds of U.S. dollars).

      122   83   90   77   100   83   64   78   92   73

(1) Find and interpret point estimates of the population mean and standard deviation.

3. As a researcher, you want to see if 90% of 32-year-old nonblack women have at least 12 years of education. Using the data from NLSY79, you have a sample proportion of 0.865 with a sample size of 378. NLSY79 is assumed to be a random sample.

(1) What is your research question?

(2) What is your population of interest?

(3) Define your random variable. Is it qualitative or quantitative? Explain your answer.

4.

	$X = 0$ did not vote for Obama in 2012	$X = 1$ voted for Obama in 2012	Total
$Y = 0$: did not support a military campaign against Syria or no opinion.	400	200	600
$Y = 1$: supported a military campaign against Syria.	50	350	400
Total	450	550	N= 1,000

Suppose that a poll of 1,000 US adults who voted in 2012 reported the figures in this table. Let X be a dummy variable indicating whether a person voted for President Obama in 2012 and Y be a dummy variable indicating whether a person supported a possible military action against Syria.

(1) What is the probability that a person voted for Obama in 2012?

(2) What is the probability that a person supported military action against Syria?

(3) What is the conditional probability that a person supported military action against Syria given that he/she voted for Obama in 2012?

5. Consider the joint distribution of X and Y described in the table below. Assume that the figures roughly correspond to election results for the 2008 Presidential Election and 2010 Midterm Election in Indiana. Let X be a dummy random variable indicating whether a voter voted for President Obama in 2008 and Y be a dummy random variable indicating whether the voter voted for a Democrat in 2010.

	$X = 0$ did not vote for Obama in 2008	$X = 1$ voted for Obama in 2008
$Y = 0$ did not vote for a Democrat in 2010	.274	.216
$Y = 1$ voted for a Democrat in 2010	.245	.265

(1) Is the joint distribution valid? Why?

(2) What is the probability that an Indiana voter voted for Obama in 2008?

(3) What is the probability that an Indiana voter did not vote for a Democrat in 2010?

(4) What is the conditional probability that a voter voted for a Democrat in 2010 given that he or she voted for Obama in 2008?

6. Suppose that the number of SPEA (School of Public and Environmental Affairs) master students who took V506 (introductory data analysis course) and V507 (intermediate data analysis course) after the first year is in the following diagram. For example, the number of SPEA master students who only took V506 is 100 and the number of students who took V506 and V507 is 120.

Enrollment in V506 and V507

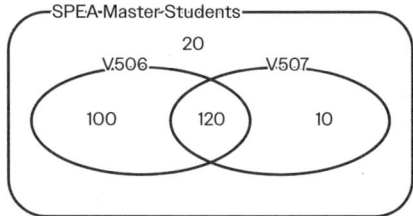

Please calculate the following probabilities and show your work with explanations.

(1) $P(V506) =$

(2) $P(\text{not } V506) =$

(3) $P(V506 \text{ and } V507) =$

(4) $P(V506 \text{ or } V507) =$

(5) $P(V506|V507) =$

(6) Please discuss the difference between $P(V506 \text{ and } V507)$ and $P(V506|V507)$.

7. Suppose that you want to study the BMI of new freshmen at Korea University. You randomly collected 15 students out of the population and recorded their Body Mass Indexes (BMI).

| 27 | 24 | 20 | 22 | 21 | 40 | 35 | 35 | 30 |
| 25 | 29 | 28 | 33 | 32 | 38 | | | |

(1) Calculate the sample estimates of the population mean and variance.

(2) Please explain the meaning of your sample mean and variance in (1).

8. Suppose that there is a high-tech company in the U.S. Suppose that 1,000 people (800 men and 200 women) were promoted to managerial positions last year from the pool of candidates (60% women and 40% men). It is known that women and men, on average, are equally capable of performing the managerial positions. Based on this result, female workers of the company sued the company for discrimination against women. Let our outcome variable $Y = 1$ for women and 0 for men.

(1) What should be the number and proportion of women promoted if there were no discrimination against women?

(2) What is the sample proportion of women promoted to managerial positions?

10. It is known that IQ scores follows a normal distribution with mean = 100 and standard deviation = 15.

(1) Suppose that your IQ score is 125. Please find the probability that someone has a higher IQ score than you.

(2) Please find what percentage of people in the population fall between 90 and 110 in terms of IQ scores.

(3) Please find an IQ score such that 25% of the population has a higher score. Show all steps.

Chapter 2
Data Analysis for Social Science: Fundamental Methods

Do more with the sample mean: Inference

In the last chapter, we were interested in the population of interest. We learned how to get the sample mean and variance using the sample to understand the population. Also, we learned how frequency tables and histograms from the sample are useful. Now, using the sample, let's go further to learn about the population. Specifically, although we know that the sample mean is not the population mean, we can scientifically guess the population mean using the sample mean. It is called inference in data analysis. This chapter is about how to rigorously develop the inference of the population mean, using the statistical properties of the sample mean.

Sampling distribution of the sample mean and the Central Limit Theorem

To get to the inference of the population mean, we first need to talk about the sample mean and its distribution. It sounds odd to say the distribution of the sample mean, $\bar{Y}$. But suppose that we calculate infinitely many sample means using infinitely many random samples with the same sample size n. Then, let's make a distribution of the sample means. This is the sampling distribution of the sample mean. Of course, it is not possible in reality, but such imagination turns out to be very useful and insightful for statistical inference.

Suppose that we have a random sample of $\{Y_1, Y_3, Y_3 \ldots \ldots Y_n\}$ with the population mean $E(Y) = \mu$ and the population variance $Var(Y) = \sigma^2$. Then, the population distribution of the sample mean, $\bar{Y}$, is called the sampling distribution of $\bar{Y}$. As shown in

Figure 2.1, the mean of this distribution is the population mean, μ, and the variance is $\frac{\sigma^2}{n}$, the population variance divided by the sample size, n. Therefore, by its nature, this distribution is getting narrower (the variance of $\bar{Y}$ gets smaller and close to 0) as the sample size, n, gets larger. As n goes to infinity ($n \to \infty$), Y converges to the population mean, μ. In other words, when we have more or more information by increasing the sample size, any $\bar{Y}$ is getting close to the population mean, μ. This is known as the law of large numbers (LLN). It makes sense and is a good thing for a larger sample study.

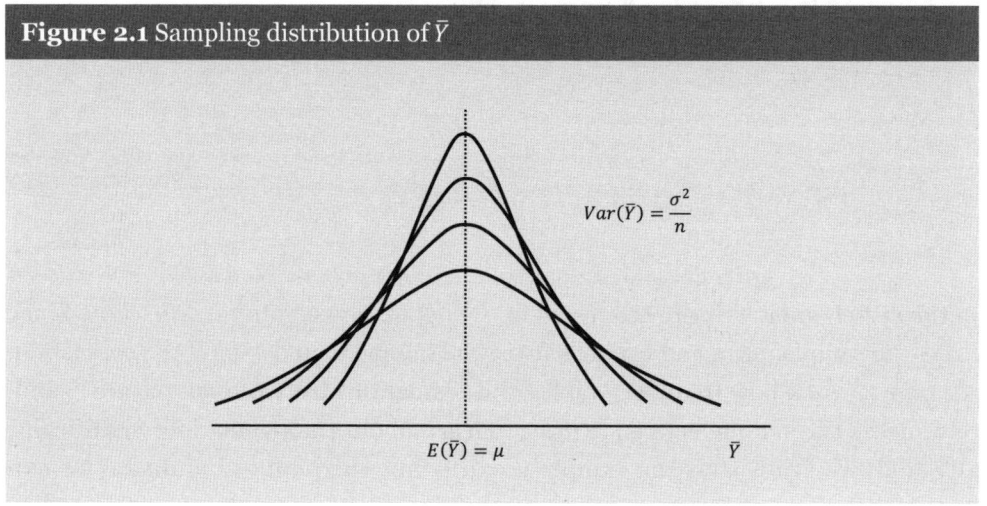

Figure 2.1 Sampling distribution of $\bar{Y}$

Law of Large Numbers (LLN)

Suppose that $Y_1, Y_2, ..., Y_n$ are independent and identically distributed random variables with mean μ and variance σ^2.

Then, the sample mean, $\bar{Y}$, converges to μ since the variance of $\bar{Y}$ converges to 0 as n gets larger and goes to infinity.

To minimize any confusion, I would like to explain the differences among the three types of distributions: the population distribution of Y, the sample distribution of Y, and the sampling distribution of $\bar{Y}$. They seem all similar, but they are absolutely different from one another.

Let's make two popular examples of a random variable. One is continuous, and the other is binary.

As shown in the figure below, there are three distributions we can think about when we study a continuous variable Y, reflecting what we want to study, such as BMI, IQ, wage, or academic scores. First, the population distribution of Y represents a plausible figure of data points over the possible values of Y, with height indicating possibilities of the range of values. The center of the distribution is the population mean, $E(Y_i) = \mu$, and the diversity of the distribution is the population variance, $Var(Y_i) = \sigma^2$. Thus, in this example, most of the data points are located in the middle of the distribution. As mentioned earlier, since we cannot collect all the information on Y to calculate the population distribution of Y, the population distribution of Y is in our imagination. However, it is useful theoretically. The sample distribution of Y is what we can make with our sample. It is tangible, and we can obtain the sample mean and sample variance by calculation. The sampling distribution of $\bar{Y}$ is the distribution of all possible values of the sample mean. Thus, we also cannot see or obtain this figure. This is only in our imagination for theoretical convenience. For the continuous variable Y, it is easy to see these three distributions and compare their similarities.

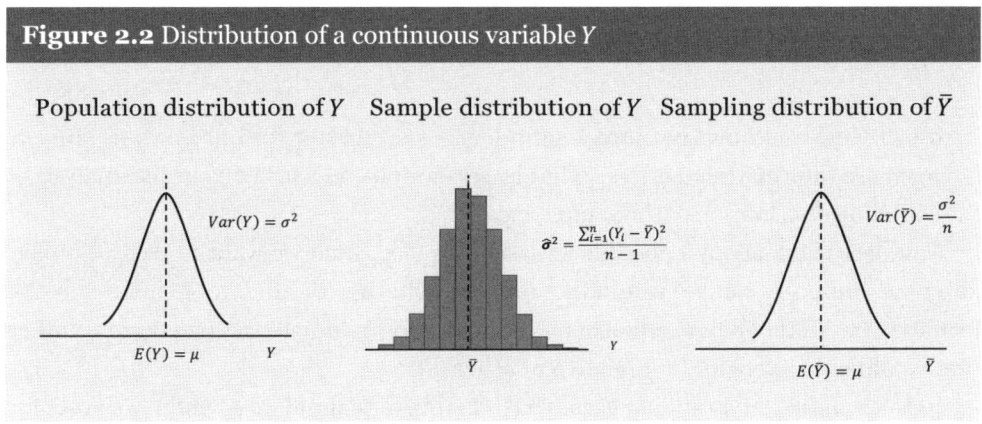

Figure 2.2 Distribution of a continuous variable Y

Let's suppose that Y is binary this time, such as men or women, having a college degree or not, currently married or not, currently having a child under age 18 or not, and so on. In this case, we can come up with the population distribution of Y, the sample distribution of Y, and the sampling distribution of $\bar{Y}$ below. It is easy to understand that the population distribution of Y is for the population we cannot obtain in reality, and the sample distributions of Y are drawn using the sample we have. These two distributions have two bars since they are only two valid values in this distribution, 0 and 1. Then, let's look at the sampling distribution of $\bar{Y}$. Some people may think it is odd to see that the sampling distribution of $\bar{Y}$ is different from the shape of the population and sample distributions of Y. However, when we realize that $\bar{Y}$ is the sample mean of the sample consisting of 0 and 1, its value is between 0 and 1. Thus, $\bar{Y}$ can be treated as a continuous variable and can have this smooth shape of the distribution shown below. Of course, since we cannot have infinitely many $\bar{Y}$s in reality, the sampling distribution of $\bar{Y}$ with a binary Y variable exists theoretically in our imagination.

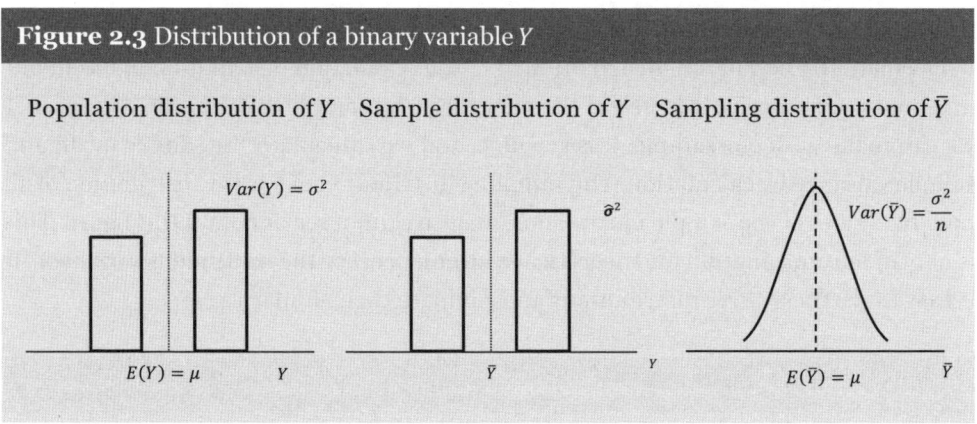

Figure 2.3 Distribution of a binary variable Y

Intuitively, we know that larger sample sizes are better for our analysis since it means more information. Let's see what larger sample sizes bring us in the analysis of the sampling distribution of the sample mean.

Now, let's think about a possible situation we face when we want to study a binary outcome. Suppose that we would like to know whether Candidate A would win the incoming election. We have a poll of n randomly chosen individuals by asking whether they would like to vote for Candidate A or others.

In this sample, let a random variable $Y = 1$ (vote for candidate A) and $Y = 0$ (vote for other candidates). Let's assume that we have 10,000 random samples with a sample size of n. In other words, there are 10,000 random samples drawn from the population, and each sample's size is the same as n. Of course, in reality, we often draw only one sample from the population.

The 10,000 sample means using 10,000 random samples.

Let's assume that each cell below indicates a sample, and we have 10,000 samples and calculate $\bar{Y}$ for each sample whose size is the same as n. Therefore, we have $\bar{Y}_1, \bar{Y}_2, ..., \bar{Y}_{10,000}$.

$\bar{Y}_1$ using the first sample of $\bar{Y}_1, \bar{Y}_2, ..., Y_n$	$\bar{Y}_2$ using the second sample of $\bar{Y}_1, \bar{Y}_2, ..., Y_n$	$\bar{Y}_3$ using the third sample of $\bar{Y}_1, \bar{Y}_2, ..., Y_n$	......		
		......			
		......			
					$\bar{Y}_{10,000}$ using the 10,000th sample of $\bar{Y}_1, \bar{Y}_2, ..., Y_n$

Then, we obtain a sample mean from each sample.

Thus, we have 10,000 sample means, such as 0.45, 0.5, 0.55, 0.56, 0.57, ...

Let's make a distribution using 10,000 sample means and see what the distribution looks like. According to the Central Limit Theorem (CLT), such a distribution of sample means is getting close to a normal distribution as n becomes larger. In other words, a distribution of our 10,000 sample means with a sample size of 100 is more similar to the normal distribution than a distribution of our 10,000 sample means with a sample size of 10.

Why is this property of the sampling distribution useful? First, regardless of whether a random variable Y is continuous, discrete, or binary, the sampling distribution of $\bar{Y}$ gets more likely to be the normal distribution as the sample size, n, gets larger. This property is powerful because it enables us to study the sample mean of any events or characteristics using the normal distribution when the sample size is large enough. Second, the normal distribution has many useful properties, such as symmetry, bell-shape, and standardization.

Central Limit Theorem

Suppose that $Y_1, Y_2, ..., Y_n$ are independent and identically distributed random variables with mean μ and variance σ^2. Then, for any random sample $Y_1, Y_2, ..., Y_n$ with a sample size n, **as n gets larger**, the sampling distribution of the sample mean $\bar{Y}$ approaches to a normal distribution (**regardless of the distribution of Y_i**). The approximate normality of the sampling distribution of **the sample mean $\bar{Y}$** applies no matter what the shape of the population distribution of Y_i.

- CLT: Distribution of $\bar{Y}$ approaches to **a normal distribution as sample size n gets larger**
- CLT: Standardized Distribution of $\bar{Y}$ approaches to a **standard normal distribution as n gets larger**

Suppose that Y_i does follow a normal distribution. Then, $z = \frac{\bar{Y}-\mu}{\left(\frac{\sigma}{\sqrt{n}}\right)}$ **exactly** follows a standard normal distribution.

Suppose that Y_i does not follow a normal distribution. Then, as n gets larger, $z = \frac{\bar{Y}-\mu}{\left(\frac{\sigma}{\sqrt{n}}\right)}$ **approximately** follows a standard normal distribution.

From time to time, there is some confusion between the central limit theorem (CLT) and the law of large numbers (LLM). The law of large numbers is not about the shape of the sampling distribution of $\bar{Y}$ but about the convergence of $\bar{Y}$ to the population mean, μ, as the sample size gets larger and larger. On the other hand, the central limit theorem is mainly about the shape of the sampling distribution of $\bar{Y}$ that converges to the normal distribution, as the sample size gets larger and larger. Both do not assume what distribution Y_i follows.

Let's apply the CLT to the following example.

Election poll of 100 individuals: Candidate A vs. Others
Random variable $Y = 1$ (vote for candidate A) and $Y = 0$ (vote for other candidates)
$P(\text{vote for Candidate A}) = P(Y=1) = \pi$
$P(\text{vote for Other Candidates}) = P(Y=0) = 1-\pi$

Mean of $Y = E(Y) = P(Y=1) = \pi$ is unknown.
Variance of $Y = Var(Y) = P(Y=1)*(1-P(Y=1)) = \pi(1-\pi)$ is unknown.

Notes: When employing a binary random variable, its population variance is calculated as the product of the probability of $Y=1$ and the probability of $Y=0$.

Then,
Mean of $\bar{Y} = E(\bar{Y}) = \pi$.
Variance of $\bar{Y} = Var(\bar{Y}) = \frac{\pi(1-\pi)}{n}$ and standard deviation (error) of $\bar{Y} = Se(\bar{Y}) = \sqrt{\frac{\pi(1-\pi)}{n}}$.

The standard deviation of the sampling distribution is called the standard error.
Suppose that conventional belief for an unknown parameter $\pi = 0.5$.
What is the probability that $\bar{Y} = \hat{\pi}$ falls greater than 0.6 when we have the sample with 100 voters?
We can find the probability, $P(0.6 < \bar{Y})$, in this question as follows using the CLT:

$P(0.6 < \bar{Y})$

$= P(\frac{0.6 - 0.5}{\sqrt{\frac{0.5(1-0.5)}{100}}} < \frac{\bar{Y} - 0.5}{\sqrt{\frac{0.5(1-0.5)}{100}}})$

$= P(2 < Z)$

$= 0.0228$

Let's see another example. Suppose that we want to examine the math score of 6th-grade students in the U.S. in 2019. Let the random variable Y = math score of a student that is assumed to follow the normal distribution.

Then, the population mean of $Y = \mu = E(Y)$ is unknown, and the population variance of $Y = \sigma^2 = Var(Y)$ is unknown.

Then, the population mean of $\bar{Y} = E(\bar{Y}) = \mu$ and the population variance of $\bar{Y} = Var(\bar{Y}) = \frac{\sigma^2}{n}$ and the standard deviation (error) of $\bar{Y} = Se(\bar{Y}) = \sqrt{\frac{\sigma^2}{n}} = \frac{\sigma}{\sqrt{n}}$.

Suppose that a previous study shows that $\mu = E(Y) = 60$ and $\sigma^2 = Var(Y) = 100$
What is the probability that $\bar{Y}$ falls less than 58.5 with a random sample of 100 students? We can easily answer this using the standard normal distribution.
We can find the probability, $P(\bar{Y} < 58.5)$, in this question as follows:

$P(\bar{Y} < 58.5)$

$= P(\frac{\bar{Y}-60}{\sqrt{\frac{100}{100}}} < \frac{58.5-60}{\sqrt{\frac{100}{100}}})$

$= P(Z < -1.5)$

$= 1 - P(Z > 1.5)$

$= 1 - 0.0668$
$= 0.9332$

What is the probability that $\bar{Y}$ falls between 59 and 60.5 with a random sample of 400 students?

Let's see below:

$P(59 < \bar{Y} < 60.5)$

$= P(\frac{59-60}{\sqrt{\frac{100}{400}}} < \frac{\bar{Y}-60}{\sqrt{\frac{100}{400}}} < \frac{60.5-60}{\sqrt{\frac{100}{400}}})$

$= P(-2 < Z < 1)$

$= 1 - P(Z > 2) - P(Z > 1)$

$= 1 - 0.0228 - 0.1587$
$= 0.8185$

In this example, if Y does not follow the normal distribution, we can use the CLT to obtain the probability above.

When we use the sampling distribution of the sample mean and the Central Limit Theorem (CLT), we can do more interesting things with the sample. The first thing is the Confidence Interval (CI) and the second thing is the hypothesis test. They are the process of using data from a sample to make a scientific guess about a population, which is called inference in data analysis. Using these two tools, we infer more information about the population from the sample.

The confidence interval (CI) for the population mean μ

The sampling distribution of $\bar{Y}$ consists of the infinitely many values of the sample mean, and we don't know where the population mean is. But if we use the CLT and the characteristics of the population, we can figure out the chance of where the population mean may be located. Of course, nothing is certain in empirical studies, but determining the likelihood of the potential location of the population mean is useful for making a good decision and drawing a sound conclusion. This is much better than random guessing or guessing with unreliable evidence.

Suppose that we are studying a continuous variable, such as the SAT scores of college applicants. It is reasonable to assume that Y_i follows a normal distribution. Then, $Z = \frac{\bar{Y} - \mu}{\sigma/\sqrt{n}}$ follows a standard normal distribution. Thus, we can have the following steps using the z table.

$$P\left(-1.96 < \frac{\bar{Y} - \mu}{\sigma/\sqrt{n}} < 1.96\right) = 0.95$$
$$\Rightarrow P\left(-1.96 * \left(\frac{\sigma}{\sqrt{n}}\right) < \bar{Y} - \mu < 1.96 * \left(\frac{\sigma}{\sqrt{n}}\right)\right) = 0.95$$
$$\Rightarrow P\left(-\bar{Y} - 1.96 * \left(\frac{\sigma}{\sqrt{n}}\right) < -\mu < -\bar{Y} + 1.96 * \left(\frac{\sigma}{\sqrt{n}}\right)\right) = 0.95$$
$$\Rightarrow P\left(\bar{Y} - 1.96 * \left(\frac{\sigma}{\sqrt{n}}\right) < \mu < \bar{Y} + 1.96 * \left(\frac{\sigma}{\sqrt{n}}\right)\right) = 0.95$$

The first equation indicates that the probability that the random variable Z, following the standard normal distribution, is bounded by -1.96 and 1.96 is 95%. Then, the second to fourth equations show how we can move around the terms using algebra by understanding that the inequality terms should be held by multiplying, adding, or subtracting the same terms on both sides.

According to the last equation, although we don't know the exact value of the population mean (μ), we can make a scientific guess about its true value. As a result, the estimated range between $\bar{Y} - 1.96 * \left(\frac{\sigma}{\sqrt{n}}\right)$ and $\bar{Y} + 1.96 * \left(\frac{\sigma}{\sqrt{n}}\right)$ is called the 95% confidence interval (CI) and it is presented as $[\bar{Y} - 1.96 * \left(\frac{\sigma}{\sqrt{n}}\right), \bar{Y} + 1.96 * \left(\frac{\sigma}{\sqrt{n}}\right)]$.

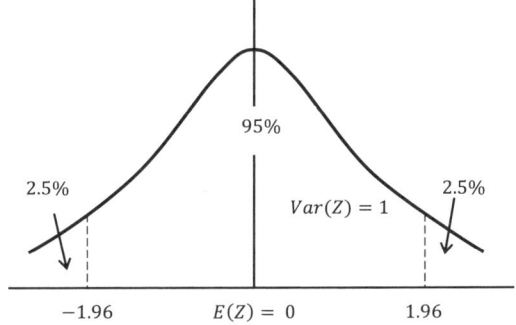

This time, let's assume that Y_i does not follow a normal distribution.

Then, $Z = \frac{\bar{Y} - \mu}{\sigma/\sqrt{n}}$ is more likely to follow a standard normal distribution as n gets larger by the Central Limit Theorem (CLT).

$$P\left(-1.96 < \frac{\bar{Y} - \mu}{\sigma/\sqrt{n}} < 1.96\right) \approx 0.95$$
$$\Rightarrow P\left(-1.96 * \left(\frac{\sigma}{\sqrt{n}}\right) < \bar{Y} - \mu < 1.96 * \left(\frac{\sigma}{\sqrt{n}}\right)\right) \approx 0.95$$
$$\Rightarrow P\left(-\bar{Y} - 1.96 * \left(\frac{\sigma}{\sqrt{n}}\right) < -\mu < -\bar{Y} + 1.96 * \left(\frac{\sigma}{\sqrt{n}}\right)\right) \approx 0.95$$
$$\Rightarrow P\left(\bar{Y} - 1.96 * \left(\frac{\sigma}{\sqrt{n}}\right) < \mu < \bar{Y} + 1.96 * \left(\frac{\sigma}{\sqrt{n}}\right)\right) \approx 0.95$$

In the same manner we showed earlier, the last equation implies that although we don't know the exact value of the population mean (μ), we can make a scientific guess about the true value of it. This time, the probability is approximately 95% since we are using the CLT. As before, the 95% confidence interval (CI) is presented as $[\bar{Y} - 1.96 * \left(\frac{\sigma}{\sqrt{n}}\right), \bar{Y} + 1.96 * \left(\frac{\sigma}{\sqrt{n}}\right)]$.

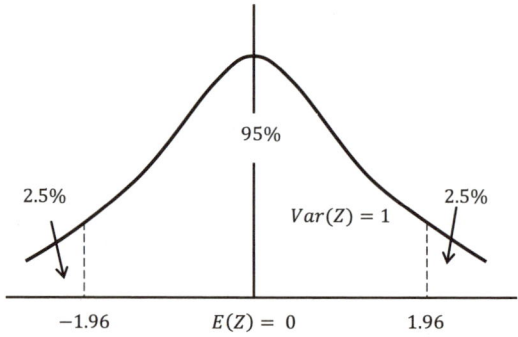

There has been some confusion and misunderstanding about the interpretation of the estimated CI. It is easy to make a mistake by saying that the 95% CI means "with a 95% probability, μ lies within the estimated interval, $\bar{Y} \pm 1.96 * \left(\frac{\sigma}{\sqrt{n}}\right)$." But this is not correct.

The 95% CI itself is an estimator with $\bar{Y}$. Thus, when we interpret the estimated 95% CI, it is important to be aware of this and use the correct interpretation. The correct interpretation is "If we repeatedly selected random samples of size n and each time estimated a 95% confidence interval, then in the long run about 95% of intervals would contain μ" or "For 95% of all potential random samples, the estimated interval $\bar{y} \pm 1.96 * \left(\frac{\sigma}{\sqrt{n}}\right)$ would contain the population mean μ." Since this interpretation is too long and tedious, the statisticians come up with a statement like "We are 95% confident that the estimated interval would contain the population mean μ" or "We are 95% confident that μ would lie within the estimated interval."

Interpretation of the C.I.

Incorrect Interpretation

With a 95% probability, μ lies within the estimated interval, $\bar{Y} \pm 1.96 * \left(\frac{\sigma}{\sqrt{n}}\right)$.

Correct Interpretation

1) We are 95% confident that μ would lie within the estimated interval, $\bar{Y} \pm 1.96 * \left(\frac{\sigma}{\sqrt{n}}\right)$.

2) For 95% of all potential random samples,

   the estimated interval $\bar{Y} \pm 1.96 * \left(\frac{\sigma}{\sqrt{n}}\right)$ would contain the population mean μ.

3) If we repeatedly selected random samples of size n and each time estimated a 95% confidence interval, then in the long run about 95% of estimated intervals would contain μ.

In summary, for any random sample of a continuous or discrete variable, $Y_1, Y_2, ..., Y_n$, with a sample size n, there are four cases we can think about the 95% CI.

	Y follows a normal distribution.	Y does not follow a normal distribution.
Small n	$[\bar{Y} - 1.96 * \left(\frac{\sigma}{\sqrt{n}}\right), \bar{Y} + 1.96 * \left(\frac{\sigma}{\sqrt{n}}\right)]$	CI cannot be constructed.
Large n	$[\bar{Y} - 1.96 * \left(\frac{\sigma}{\sqrt{n}}\right), \bar{Y} + 1.96 * \left(\frac{\sigma}{\sqrt{n}}\right)]$	Approximately, $[\bar{Y} - 1.96 * \left(\frac{\sigma}{\sqrt{n}}\right), \bar{Y} + 1.96 * \left(\frac{\sigma}{\sqrt{n}}\right)]$ by CLT

For the 99% CI, 1.96 can be replaced by the z-score for the 0.5% tail probability, 2.58.

Therefore, the 99% CI is summarized as follows.

	Y follows a normal distribution.	Y does not follow a normal distribution.
Small n	$[\bar{Y} - 2.58 * (\frac{\sigma}{\sqrt{n}}), \bar{Y} + 2.58 * (\frac{\sigma}{\sqrt{n}})]$	CI cannot be constructed.
Large n	$[\bar{Y} - 2.58 * (\frac{\sigma}{\sqrt{n}}), \bar{Y} + 2.58 * (\frac{\sigma}{\sqrt{n}})]$	Approximately, $[\bar{Y} - 2.58 * (\frac{\sigma}{\sqrt{n}}), \bar{Y} + 2.58 * (\frac{\sigma}{\sqrt{n}})]$ by CLT

Now, it is time to consider another twist in statistics that has confused a lot of students and researchers. Assume that Y follows the normal distribution. In the 95% CI, the sample mean, $\bar{Y}$, is estimated and the sample size, n, is known. Then, how about the population standard deviation, σ? This must be estimated, too. When we obtain the sample standard deviation, $s = \sqrt{\frac{\sum_{i=1}^{n}(Y_i - \bar{Y})^2}{n-1}}$, and replace σ with it, $\frac{\bar{Y} - \mu}{s/\sqrt{n}}$ follows the t distribution, not the z distribution. The t distribution is also bell-shaped and symmetric like the z distribution, but the shape changes depending on the sample size. When the sample size is small, the t distribution is more spread to the left and right sides and has thicker tails than the z distribution. However, when the sample size is larger than 100, the t distribution is almost the same as the z distribution. We live in an era of large samples. It is very rare to see a study with a sample size of less than 100. Therefore, it is most common to keep using the z distribution even after the sample standard deviation, s, replaces the population standard deviation, σ.

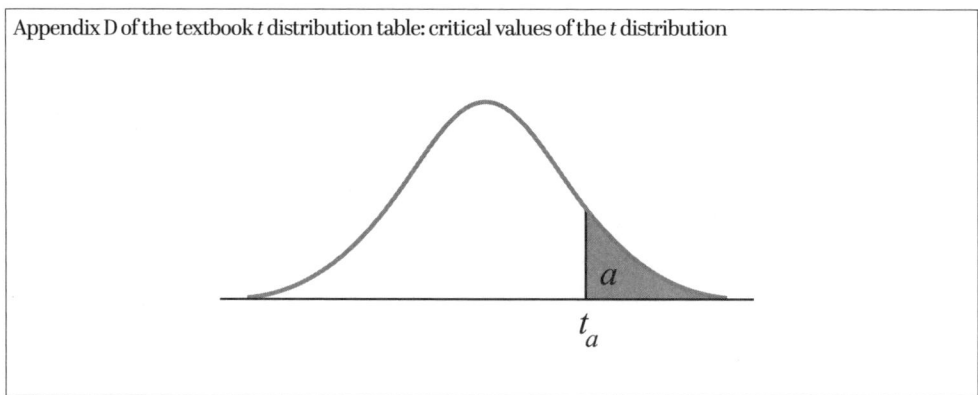

Appendix D of the textbook t distribution table: critical values of the t distribution

df	Right-Tail Probability					
	$t_{.100}$	$t_{.050}$	$t_{.025}$	$t_{.010}$	$t_{.005}$	$t_{.001}$
1	3.078	6.314	12.706	31.821	63.656	318.289
2	1.886	2.920	4.303	6.965	9.925	22.328
3	1.638	2.353	3.182	4.541	5.841	10.214
4	1.533	2.132	2.776	3.747	4.604	7.173
5	1.476	2.015	2.571	3.365	4.032	5.894
6	1.440	1.943	2.447	3.143	3.707	5.208
7	1.415	1.895	2.365	2.998	3.499	4.785
8	1.397	1.860	2.306	2.896	3.355	4.501
9	1.383	1.833	2.262	2.821	3.250	4.297
10	1.372	1.812	2.228	2.764	3.169	4.144
11	1.363	1.796	2.201	2.718	3.106	4.025
12	1.356	1.782	2.179	2.681	3.055	3.930
13	1.350	1.771	2.160	2.650	3.012	3.852
14	1.345	1.761	2.145	2.624	2.977	3.787
15	1.341	1.753	2.131	2.602	2.947	3.733
16	1.337	1.746	2.120	2.583	2.921	3.686
17	1.333	1.740	2.110	2.567	2.898	3.646
18	1.330	1.734	2.101	2.552	2.878	3.611
19	1.328	1.729	2.093	2.539	2.861	3.579
20	1.325	1.725	2.086	2.528	2.845	3.552
21	1.323	1.721	2.080	2.518	2.831	3.527
22	1.321	1.717	2.074	2.508	2.819	3.505
23	1.319	1.714	2.069	2.500	2.807	3.485
24	1.318	1.711	2.064	2.492	2.797	3.467
25	1.316	1.708	2.060	2.485	2.787	3.450
26	1.315	1.706	2.056	2.479	2.779	3.435
27	1.314	1.703	2.052	2.473	2.771	3.421
28	1.313	1.701	2.048	2.467	2.763	3.408
29	1.311	1.699	2.045	2.462	2.756	3.396
30	1.310	1.697	2.042	2.457	2.750	3.385
40	1.303	1.684	2.021	2.423	2.704	3.307
50	1.299	1.676	2.009	2.403	2.678	3.261
60	1.296	1.671	2.000	2.390	2.660	3.232
80	1.292	1.664	1.990	2.374	2.639	3.195
100	1.290	1.660	1.984	2.364	2.626	3.174
∞	1.282	1.645	1.960	2.326	2.576	3.091

As shown in the t table here, we can find the t-score based on the right-tail probabilities in the column and the degrees of freedom (n-1 in our sample mean analysis) in the row.

Thus, when the sample size is small, and Y follows a normal distribution, for the 95% CI, 1.96 is replaced by t-score, $t_{0.025, df=n-1}$, where 0.025 indicates the right-tail probability and the degree of freedom is n-1 for the t table. For example, $t_{0.025, df=20-1} = 2.093$, larger than 1.96. However, when n is larger than 100, $t_{0.025, df=n-1}$ approaches to 1.96, as found in the t table.

The 95% CI in this case can be constructed as shown below:

$$[\bar{Y} - t_{0.025, df=n-1} * \left(\frac{s}{\sqrt{n}}\right), \bar{Y} + t_{0.025, df=n-1} * \left(\frac{s}{\sqrt{n}}\right)] \text{ from}$$

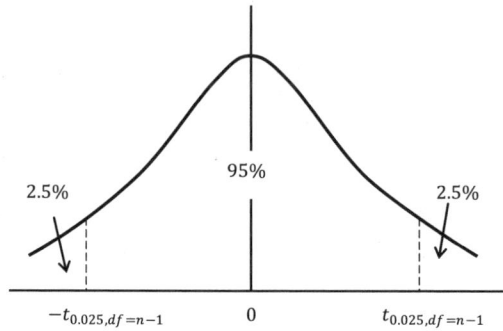

$$P\left(-t_{0.025, df=n-1} < \frac{\bar{Y}_n - \mu}{s/\sqrt{n}} < t_{0.025, df=n-1}\right) = 0.95$$

$$\Rightarrow P\left(\bar{Y}_n - t_{0.025, df=n-1} * \left(\frac{s}{\sqrt{n}}\right) < \mu < \bar{Y}_n + t_{0.025, df=n-1} * \left(\frac{s}{\sqrt{n}}\right)\right) = 0.95 \text{ where } \frac{s}{\sqrt{n}}$$

is called the standard error.

Also, for the 99% CI, the t-score ($t_{0.005, df=n-1}$) corresponds to the z-score (2.58) for the 0.5% tail probability. For example, $t_{0.005, df=25-1} = 2.797$, larger than 2.58. Again, as n is becoming larger (typically larger than 100), for the 99% CI, t-score is becoming close to 2.58.

The characteristics of t distribution can be stated below.
- The t distribution displays a symmetrical, bell-shaped curve centered at a mean of 0.
- The t distribution generally has fatter tails and is more dispersed compared to the standard normal distribution.
- The t distribution's standard deviation is slightly greater than 1, and its exact value is determined by the degrees of freedom (df), where df equals n-1, with n representing the sample size.
- For each specific value of degrees of freedom (df), the t distribution displays a slightly varying spread, and distinct t-scores apply for each df value.
- As the degrees of freedom (df) or sample size (n) increases, the t distribution increasingly resembles the standard normal distribution because the estimated standard error approaches the true standard error with larger sample sizes.

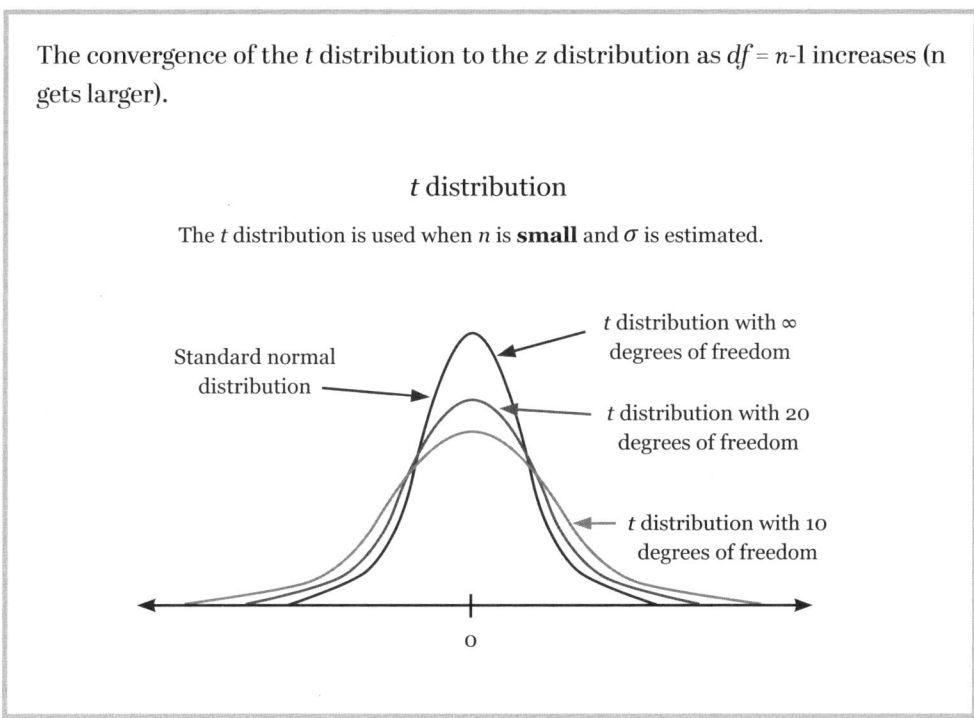

The convergence of the *t* distribution to the *z* distribution as *df* = n-1 increases (n gets larger).

In summary, for any random sample of a continuous or discrete variable, $Y_1, Y_2, ..., Y_n$, with a sample size of n and the estimated standard deviation, $s = \sqrt{\frac{\sum_{i=1}^{n}(Y_i - \bar{Y})^2}{n-1}}$, there are four cases we can think about the 95% and 99% CI.

95% CI

	Y follows a normal distribution.	Y does not follow a normal distribution.
Small n	$[\bar{Y} - t_{0.025, df=n-1} * \left(\frac{s}{\sqrt{n}}\right),$ $\bar{Y} + t_{0.025, df=n-1} * \left(\frac{s}{\sqrt{n}}\right)]$	CI cannot be constructed.
Large n	$[\bar{Y} - 1.96 * \left(\frac{s}{\sqrt{n}}\right), \bar{Y} + 1.96 * \left(\frac{s}{\sqrt{n}}\right)]$	Approximately, $[\bar{Y} - 1.96 * \frac{s}{\sqrt{n}}, \bar{Y} + 1.96 * \left(\frac{s}{\sqrt{n}}\right)]$ by CLT

99% CI

	Y follows a normal distribution.	Y does not follow a normal distribution.
Small n	$[\bar{Y} - t_{0.005, df=n-1} * \left(\frac{s}{\sqrt{n}}\right),$ $\bar{Y} + t_{0.005, df=n-1} * \left(\frac{s}{\sqrt{n}}\right)]$	CI cannot be constructed.
Large n	$[\bar{Y} - 2.58 * \left(\frac{s}{\sqrt{n}}\right), \bar{Y} + 2.58 * \left(\frac{s}{\sqrt{n}}\right)]$	Approximately, $[\bar{Y} - 2.58 * \frac{s}{\sqrt{n}}, \bar{Y} + 2.58 * \left(\frac{s}{\sqrt{n}}\right)]$ by CLT

Example 2.1

6th grade students' math scores out of 100 points in the U.S. in 2008
Random variable Y = math score of a student

Mean of $Y = \mu = E(Y)$ is unknown.
Variance of $Y = \sigma^2 = Var(Y)$ is unknown.

Then,
Mean of $\bar{Y} = E(\bar{Y}) = \mu$.
Variance of $\bar{Y} = Var(\bar{Y}) = \frac{\sigma^2}{n}$ and

Estimated standard Deviation (Error) of $\bar{Y} = \sqrt{\frac{s^2}{n}} = \frac{s}{\sqrt{n}}$.

Suppose that $n=100$, $s=10$, $\bar{Y}=45$.
95% CI for μ?

Please use $[\bar{Y} - t_{.025, df=n-1}\left(\frac{s}{\sqrt{n}}\right), \bar{Y} + t_{.025, df=n-1}\left(\frac{s}{\sqrt{n}}\right)]$.

We know that $\bar{Y} = 45$, $\frac{s}{\sqrt{n}} = \frac{10}{\sqrt{100}}$, the degree of freedom = 99, and $t_{.025, 99} = 1.984$
Plug those into $[\bar{Y} - t_{.025, df=n-1}\left(\frac{s}{\sqrt{n}}\right), \bar{Y} + t_{.025, df=n-1}\left(\frac{s}{\sqrt{n}}\right)]$

Then, we have $[45 - 1.984 * \frac{10}{\sqrt{100}}, 45 + 1.984 * \frac{10}{\sqrt{100}}] = [43.016, 46.984]$.

Then, we can say that we are 95% confident that the population mean lies between 43.016 and 46.984.

When Y is a binary variable, such as voting for candidate A or others, men or women, passing an exam or not, and the sample size n is large, $\hat{\pi}$ is the sample mean of a binary variable and replaces $\bar{Y}$ for notational convenience. Also, $s = \sqrt{\hat{\pi}(1-\hat{\pi})}$. The tables above can be re-summarized as below since binary Y does not follow a normal distribution.

95% CI

	Y follows a normal distribution.	Y does not follow a normal distribution.
Small n	Not Available (NA)	CI cannot be constructed.
Large n	NA	Approximately, $[\hat{\pi} - 1.96 * (\frac{s}{\sqrt{n}}), \hat{\pi} + 1.96 * (\frac{s}{\sqrt{n}})]$ by CLT

99% CI

	Y follows a normal distribution.	Y does not follow a normal distribution.
Small n	NA	CI cannot be constructed.
Large n	NA	Approximately, $[\hat{\pi} - 2.58 * (\frac{s}{\sqrt{n}}), \hat{\pi} + 2.58 * (\frac{s}{\sqrt{n}})]$ by CLT

Example 2.2

As a researcher, you want to study whether 80% of 32-year-old nonblack women had at least 12 years of education in 1990. In your random sample of nonblack women aged 32 in 1990, Y = 1 if women have at least 12 years of education and Y = 0 otherwise. You have a sample proportion of 0.865 with a sample size of 378. Let's construct a 95% confidence interval for the population proportion.

95% confidence interval for π

$$\hat{\pi} \pm z_{0.025} * \left(\sqrt{\frac{\hat{\pi}(1-\hat{\pi})}{n}}\right) = 0.865 \pm 1.96 * (0.018)$$

Thus, the 95% confidence interval for the population mean π is (0.83, 0.90).
We are 95% confident that the population proportion π is likely to fall between 0.83 and 0.90.

Assume that you have a sample size of 1,600 with the same sample proportion. Obtain a new 95% confidence interval and explain any differences between this confidence interval and the 95% confidence interval above.

95% confidence interval for π with n = 1,600

$$\hat{\pi} \pm z_{0.025} * \left(\sqrt{\frac{\hat{\pi}(1-\hat{\pi})}{n}}\right) = 0.865 \pm 1.96 * (0.009)$$

Thus, 95% confidence interval for the population mean π is (0.85, 0.89).
We are 95% confident that the population proportion π is likely to fall between 0.85 and 0.89.

Since sample size n increased from 378 to 1,600 with other things fixed, the margin of error, $z_{0.025} * \left(\sqrt{\frac{\hat{\pi}(1-\hat{\pi})}{n}}\right)$, decreases, and we have a narrower 95% confidence interval.

The confidence intervals are widely used in many studies. Example 2.3 shows the share of mammograms that are true positive and false positive and its confidence interval at each age of women in the U.S. from January 2008 through December 2012.

Example 2.3

Share of mammograms that are true positive and false positive

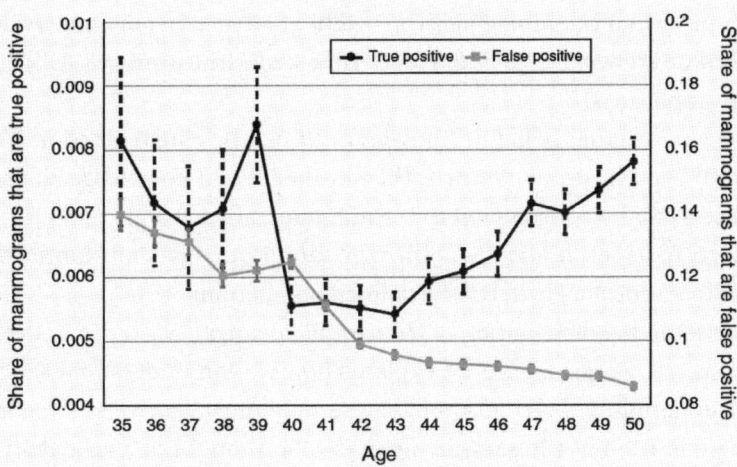

Einav, Finkelstein, Oostrom, Ostriker, & Williams. (2020). p. 3847.

Einav, L., Finkelstein, A., Oostrom, T., Ostriker, A., & Williams, H. (2020). Screening and selection: The case of mammograms. *American Economic Review*, 110(12), 3836-70.

This figure focuses on privately insured women who underwent mammograms, specifically those included in the analysis sample, which consisted of 7,373,302 woman-years from private insurance claims data from January 2008 through December 2012. The graph displays the percentage of mammograms that are true positive (on the left-hand axis) and false positive (on the right-hand axis) for each age group, based on their age at the start of the calendar year. The category of negative mammograms is not included in the graph. The graph also includes confidence intervals denoted by dotted vertical lines for each age group. When the confidence intervals of the true positive and false positive do not overlap, they are likely statistically different. The chance of a true positive increases while the chance of a false positive decreases as women age, resulting in a wider gap between the two.

Hypothesis test for the population mean μ

The second tool of inference is the hypothesis test. The main purpose of the hypothesis test is to do a scientific examination of whether our starting belief or knowledge is reliable or not. Then, it is important to set what our original belief or knowledge could be. For example, when we think about the height of all men in our country, what is our original belief or knowledge? Is it 5.8 feet? How about the average SAT scores of this year's college applicants?

If we have an original belief or knowledge, it can be constructed in a statement called the null hypothesis. In contrast, the new belief and knowledge challenging the null hypothesis can be constructed in a statement called the alternative hypothesis. Thus, the hypothesis test is about whether the sample provides substantial evidence to challenge the conventional belief of the defined population.

Using the sampling distribution of the sample mean, $\bar{Y}$, let's try to understand how the hypothesis test works. Figure 2.4 explains how we can understand the hypothesis test using the sampling distribution of the sample mean. As we studied earlier, the sampling distribution of the sample mean can be thought of as the distribution of infinitely many sample means from the infinitely many samples with sample size n.

The sampling distribution below follows a normal distribution since, by the CLT, the sampling distribution is approaching the normal distribution as n gets larger. Or, if the sample size is small, we assume that Y follows a normal distribution. Then, the sampling distribution follows the normal distribution.

Originally, as shown in Figure 2.4, the mean of the sampling distribution, μ, is unknown. If we assume that we set the population mean as a certain number, μ_0, the null hypothesis can be expressed like H_0: $\mu = \mu_0$ in this figure. In this null hypothesis, our original belief says that the population mean is known as μ_0. The alternative hypothesis, H_a: $\mu \neq \mu_0$, says that our original belief is not true. In other words, it says that the true population mean is smaller or greater than μ_0. When the alternative hypothesis indicates the two possible alternatives, it is called the two-sided hypothesis test.

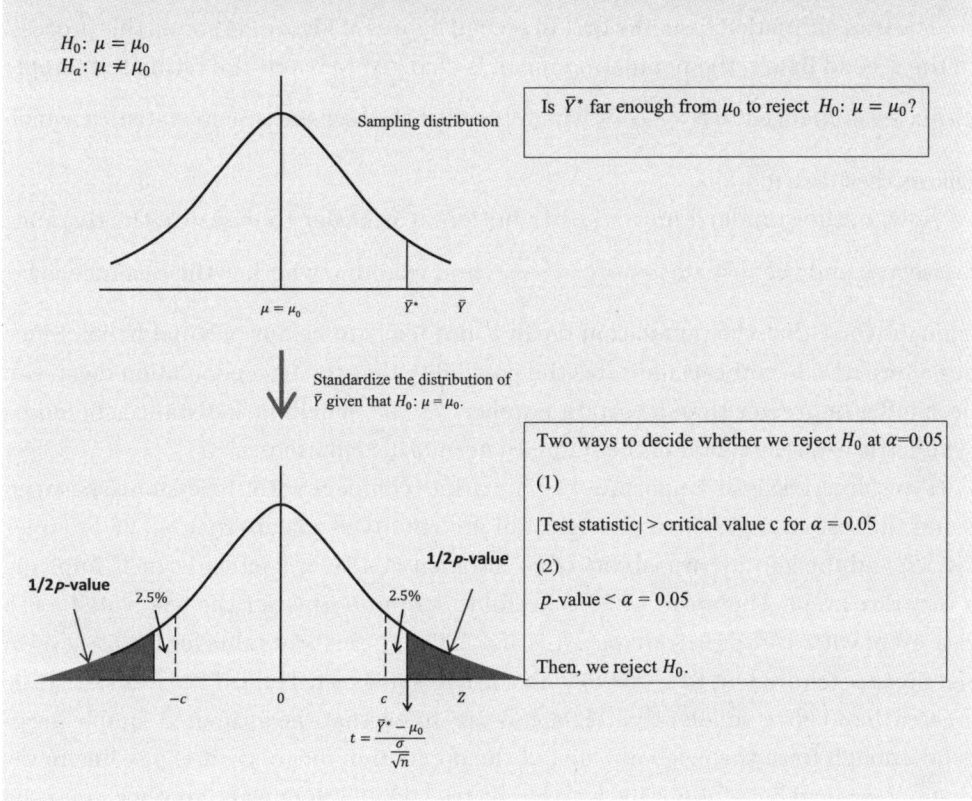

Figure 2.4 How to understand the two-sided hypothesis test using the sampling distribution of the sample mean $\bar{Y}$

Thus, under our original belief, our population mean in the sampling distribution is μ_0 in the first figure. Then, let our estimated sample mean be $\bar{Y}^*$ in this distribution. Assume that our estimated sample mean, $\bar{Y}^*$, is from a random sample representing the population of interest. Then, we may expect that our estimated sample mean is close to the population mean. If it is far from the population mean, there are two possible scenarios. First, under our assumption that our sample is randomly drawn and represents the population, the true population mean may not be equal to our original belief, μ_0. Second, our random sample may not represent the population, which questions the validity of the estimated sample mean. Of course, we assume the first scenario, and it gives the validity of our analysis. Then, how do we know that our estimated sample is far from the population mean? How far is far enough to say that the true population mean is not likely to be our original belief? Statisticians came up with a method to understand this. They say that it is better to measure the distance between the population mean under the null hypothesis and our estimated sample mean in the more formalized condition, called the standard normal distribution.

The transformation from the first to second figures of Figure 2.4 shows this process. In the second figure, the population mean is changed to 0 and the estimated sample mean, $\bar{Y}^*$, is changed to $t = \frac{\bar{Y}^* - \mu_0}{\frac{\sigma}{\sqrt{n}}}$, which is called the test statistic in statistics, which follows the z distribution.

Now, in the standard normal distribution, it is easier to measure the distance between 0 and the test statistic, $t = \frac{\bar{Y}^* - \mu_0}{\frac{\sigma}{\sqrt{n}}}$, and examine whether the distance is far enough to say that the population mean is not likely to be our original belief. Since our alternative hypothesis indicates the possibility that the true population mean can be smaller or greater than a certain number, μ_0, the benchmark distance should be symmetric from the center of the standard normal distribution, 0.

Typically, ±1.96 is an important benchmark to compare with the distance between 0 and the test statistic since the right tail probability of z-score that is 1.96 or larger is 2.5% and the left tail probability of z-score that is -1.96 or smaller is 2.5%, implying a very rare event. Therefore, ±1.96 is useful to examine whether the test statistic is a rare event with a 5% or less chance. It is also called the critical value for the 5% level of significance (equivalent to $\alpha = 0.05$) with the two-sided test. Then, if the test statistic is greater than 1.96 or smaller than -1.96, it is safe to say that the estimated sample mean is far enough from the original belief of the population mean. Or it is possible to say that our original belief is not likely to be the true population mean. Another well-used benchmark is ±2.58 since the right tail probability of a z-score that is 2.58 or larger is 0.5%, and the left tail probability of a z-score that is -2.58 or smaller is 0.5%. Thus, ±2.58 is another benchmark to examine whether the test statistic is a rare event with 1% or less chance. It is called the critical value for the 1% level of significance (equivalent to say $\alpha = 0.01$) with the two-sided test.

When we use the sample standard deviation, $s = \sqrt{\frac{\sum_{i=1}^{n}(Y_i - \bar{Y})^2}{n-1}}$, and replace σ with it, $\frac{\bar{Y} - \mu}{s/\sqrt{n}}$ follows the t distribution, not the z distribution. Then, we need to be careful to construct the test statistic considering the sample size and the normality of Y distribution.

First, let's see the hypothesis test for the population mean when the sample size is small. When the sample size is small and Y follows a normal distribution, the t table is used to get these benchmarks to examine the distance between 0 and the test statistic.

As a result, ±1.96 from the z table can be replaced by $\pm t_{0.025, df = n-1}$ and ±2.58 from the z table can be replaced by $\pm t_{0.005, df = n-1}$. Then, the test statistic follows the t distribution with $df = n-1$. However, it is important to note that when the sample size is small and Y does not follow a normal distribution, we cannot construct the test statistic for the population mean.

Second, when the sample size is large, we have more flexibility in constructing the hypothesis test for the population mean with the help of the Central Limit Theorem (CLT). Specifically, when the sample size is large, we can construct the test statistic for the population mean due to the CLT, regardless of whether Y follows the normal distribution. Also, the z-score can be used as critical values to do the hypothesis test since the t distribution converges to the z distribution when the degree of freedom, n-1, becomes larger. In conclusion, when the sample size gets larger, it is okay to use the z-score to do the hypothesis tests, regardless of whether the distribution of Y follows the normal distribution.

Let's assume a large sample. Also, assume the test statistic in our example, $t = \frac{\bar{Y}^* - \mu_0}{\frac{s}{\sqrt{n}}}$, is 2.1. Using the logic above, since 2.1 is greater than 1.96, it is possible to say that we have considerable evidence to challenge the original belief. Therefore, we say that we reject the null hypothesis with the 5% level of significance in the two-sided test.

There is another way to examine whether the distance between the original belief of the population mean and the sample mean is large enough. The main idea is to compare the tail probability of the critical value with the tail probability of the test statistic. Thus, if the tail probability of the test statistic is smaller than that of the critical value, it is equivalent to the situation that the test statistic is far enough from 0 to reject the null hypothesis. The tail probability of the test statistic is called the "p-value." In the case of the two-sided hypothesis test, the p-value (the tail probability of the test statistic) is two times the probability that the z-score is larger than a test statistic. Since $P(Z>2.1) = 0.0179$, the p-value for the test statistic of 2.1 is $0.0179 \times 2 = 0.0358$. Since it is less than 5%, it is possible to say that we reject the null hypothesis at the 5% level of significance.

Let's move to the following null hypothesis with the alternative hypothesis that has only one possibility.

$$H_0: \mu = \mu_0$$
$$H_a: \mu > \mu_0$$

Specifically, the null hypothesis is the same as the first example: the population mean is the same as a certain number, μ_0, the original belief about the true population mean. However, different from the previous example, the alternative hypothesis says that the true population mean is greater than the original belief.

The first figure in Figure 2.5 is the same as the first figure in Figure 2.4. As before, the sampling distribution follows a normal distribution since, by the CLT, the sampling distribution is approaching the normal distribution as n is getting larger. When the sample size is small, we assume that Y follows a normal distribution to have the normally distributed sampling distribution.

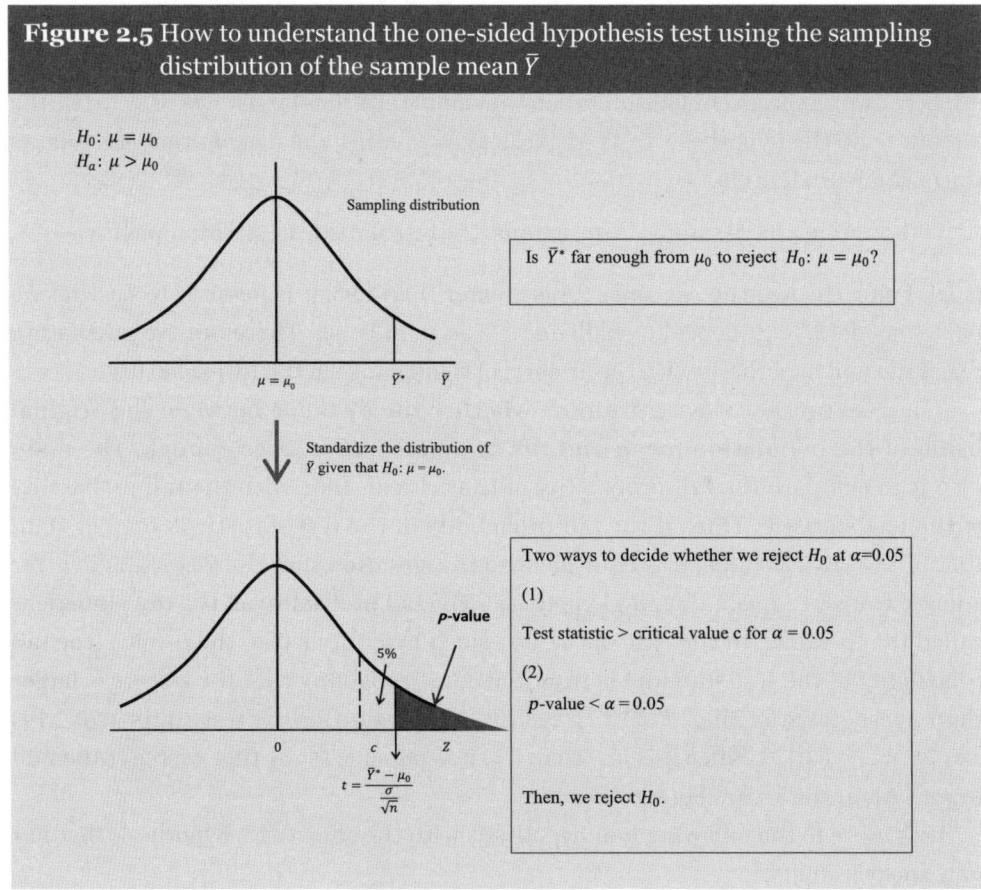

Figure 2.5 How to understand the one-sided hypothesis test using the sampling distribution of the sample mean $\bar{Y}$

Again, we are interested in whether the distance between the original belief of the population mean and the estimated sample mean is large enough to challenge our original belief. To do so, we can standardize the sampling distribution to create a new distribution that is compatible with the standard normal distribution. Since the alternative hypothesis in this example includes the one-tailed possibility when the original belief is not true, the benchmark in the standard normal distribution is only considered on one side. In this case, the right-hand side of the standard normal distribution. The guided probability of the typical rare event is 5% or 1%. Since the right side of the population mean is considered, the benchmark to measure the distance between the original belief of the population mean and the test statistic is marked on the right side of the standard normal distribution. For the 5% level of significance, 1.645 is the critical value since the right tail probability of the z-score that is 1.645 or larger is 5%. For the 1% level of significance, 2.326 is the critical value since the right tail probability of the z-score that is 2.326 or larger is 1%.

As before, assuming that the test statistic is 2.1 with a large sample, it is greater than 1.645 but smaller than 2.326. Therefore, it is possible to say that there is considerable evidence to challenge the original belief at the 5% level of significance, but it is not enough to challenge the original belief at the 1% level of significance. In other words, we say that we reject the null hypothesis with the one-sided hypothesis test at the 5% significance level, while we don't reject the null hypothesis with the one-sided hypothesis test at the 1% level of significance.

Again, we can compare the tail probabilities of the critical value and the test statistic to examine whether the distance between the original belief of the population mean and the test statistic is large enough. In the case of the one-sided hypothesis test, the p-value (the tail probability of the test statistic) is the probability that the z-score is larger than the test statistic. Since $P(Z>2.1) = 0.0179$, the p-value for the test statistic of 2.1 is 0.0179. Since it is less than 5%, it is possible to say that we reject the null hypothesis at the 5% level of significance. On the other hand, since it is greater than 1%, we don't reject the null hypothesis at the 1% level of significance. This is the same conclusion as earlier when we compare the critical value and the test statistic.

There are two major mistakes we can make in the hypothesis test. The first one is that the test statistic is far enough from 0 to reject the null hypothesis, but it turns out that the original belief is true. This is called Type I Error. The second one is that the test statistic is not far enough from 0 to reject the null hypothesis, but it turns out that the original belief is not true. This is called a Type II error. So, for a valid and effective hypothesis test, it is natural to minimize the probabilities of Type I and II errors. The typical hypothesis test using the standard normal distribution fairly minimizes the probability of Type II error. Thus, it is critical to set the probability of Type I error that we can tolerate, which is equivalent to setting the significance level or α. Therefore, finding the critical value for the significance level to examine whether the test statistic is far enough from 0 is the process of minimizing the probability of

Type I error. For example, if we set up the critical value for the 5% significance level in the standard normal distribution, it is equivalent to saying that the test statistic should be 5% or less chance in the distribution. It is a very rare chance. If everything is perfect, such as a random sample, the valid test process, and so on, the test statistic of 5% or less chance indicates that the original belief is not likely to be true. However, 5% indicates the probability that we reject the null hypothesis even if it is true, which is the probability of Type I error. It is also popular to set up the critical value for the 1% level of significance. Then, the probability of Type I error is reduced to 1%, but it is also more difficult to challenge the original belief with this more stringent benchmark.

	Two Types of Errors in Hypothesis Tests
Type I error	Reject the null hypothesis when the null hypothesis is true. The probability of Type I error is the significance level. Therefore, setting the smaller significance level is desirable, but it leads to a lower chance of rejecting the null hypothesis. Typically, setting the 5% and 1% significance levels are generally used.
Type II error	Don't reject the null hypothesis when the null hypothesis is false. The conventional hypothesis tests fairly minimize the probability of Type II error.

In summary, for any random sample of a continuous or counting variable, $Y_1, Y_2, ..., Y_n$, with a sample size of n and the estimated standard deviation, $s = \sqrt{\frac{\sum_{i=1}^{n}(Y_i - \bar{Y})^2}{n-1}}$, there are four cases we can think about the test statistic.

	Y follows a normal distribution.	Y does not follow a normal distribution.
Small n	Test statistic $t = \frac{\bar{Y} - \mu_0}{\frac{s}{\sqrt{n}}} \sim t_{df=n-1}$ where $s = \sqrt{\frac{\sum(Y_i - \bar{Y})^2}{n-1}}$	Test statistics cannot be constructed.
Large n	Test statistic $t = \frac{\bar{Y} - \mu_0}{\frac{s}{\sqrt{n}}} \sim N(0, 1)$ where $s = \sqrt{\frac{\sum(Y_i - \bar{Y})^2}{n-1}}$	Test statistic $t = \frac{\bar{Y} - \mu_0}{\frac{s}{\sqrt{n}}} \stackrel{a}{\sim} N(0, 1)$ where $s = \sqrt{\frac{\sum(Y_i - \bar{Y})^2}{n-1}}$ by CLT

df	Right-Tail Probability					
	$t_{.100}$	$t_{.050}$	$t_{.025}$	$t_{.010}$	$t_{.005}$	$t_{.001}$
1	3.078	6.314	12.706	31.821	63.656	318.289
2	1.886	2.920	4.303	6.965	9.925	22.328
3	1.638	2.353	3.182	4.541	5.841	10.214
4	1.533	2.132	2.776	3.747	4.604	7.173
5	1.476	2.015	2.571	3.365	4.032	5.894
6	1.440	1.943	2.447	3.143	3.707	5.208
7	1.415	1.895	2.365	2.998	3.499	4.785
8	1.397	1.860	2.306	2.896	3.355	4.501
9	1.383	1.833	2.262	2.821	3.250	4.297
10	1.372	1.812	2.228	2.764	3.169	4.144
11	1.363	1.796	2.201	2.718	3.106	4.025
12	1.356	1.782	2.179	2.681	3.055	3.930
13	1.350	1.771	2.160	2.650	3.012	3.852
14	1.345	1.761	2.145	2.624	2.977	3.787
15	1.341	1.753	2.131	2.602	2.947	3.733
16	1.337	1.746	2.120	2.583	2.921	3.686
17	1.333	1.740	2.110	2.567	2.898	3.646
18	1.330	1.734	2.101	2.552	2.878	3.611
19	1.328	1.729	2.093	2.539	2.861	3.579
20	1.325	1.725	2.086	2.528	2.845	3.552
21	1.323	1.721	2.080	2.518	2.831	3.527
22	1.321	1.717	2.074	2.508	2.819	3.505
23	1.319	1.714	2.069	2.500	2.807	3.485
24	1.318	1.711	2.064	2.492	2.797	3.467
25	1.316	1.708	2.060	2.485	2.787	3.450
26	1.315	1.706	2.056	2.479	2.779	3.435
27	1.314	1.703	2.052	2.473	2.771	3.421
28	1.313	1.701	2.048	2.467	2.763	3.408
29	1.311	1.699	2.045	2.462	2.756	3.396
30	1.310	1.697	2.042	2.457	2.750	3.385
40	1.303	1.684	2.021	2.423	2.704	3.307
50	1.299	1.676	2.009	2.403	2.678	3.261
60	1.296	1.671	2.000	2.390	2.660	3.232
80	1.292	1.664	1.990	2.374	2.639	3.195
100	1.290	1.660	1.984	2.364	2.626	3.174
∞	1.282	1.645	1.960	2.326	2.576	3.091

In this t table, when Y follows a normal distribution, and the sample size is small, we need to look up the critical value in the t table at the 5% or 1% significance level. $t = \frac{\bar{Y} - \mu_0}{\frac{s}{\sqrt{n}}} \sim t_{df = n-1}$ is the t-test statistic and indicates that the test statistic follows the t distribution with the degree of freedom = n-1. However, as the sample size gets larger, we can use the critical value in the z table. The test statistic follows the standard normal distribution when n is large, expressed as $\frac{\bar{Y} - \mu_0}{\frac{s}{\sqrt{n}}} \sim N(0, 1)$. When Y does not follow a normal distribution, the test static approximately follows the standard normal distribution by CLT, presented as $t = \frac{\bar{Y} - \mu_0}{\frac{s}{\sqrt{n}}} \overset{a}{\sim} N(0, 1)$.

Example 2.4

Suppose that our population of interest is women aged 25 to 33 in 1990 in the U.S., and we would like to investigate whether their hourly wage is enough to support their living cost.

Suppose that for women, their real hourly wage in 1984 dollars is $6.5. We can set the null hypothesis as below.

$$H_0: \mu = \$6.5$$

μ_0 is a particular value for the population mean μ that is accepted as a convention or is to be challenged. It is 6.5 here.

We can think about two types of alternative hypotheses.

Assuming that we don't know whether the real hourly wage of women is larger or smaller than $6.5, the alternative hypothesis for the two-sided hypothesis test is $H_a: \mu \neq \$6.5$ (two sided hypothesis).

Assuming that the real hourly wage of women could be larger than $6.5, the alternative hypothesis for the one-sided hypothesis test is $H_a: \mu > \$6.5$ (one sided hypothesis)

When Y is a binary variable, such as voting A candidate or others, men or women, passing an exam or not, and the sample size n is large, $\hat{\pi}$ is the sample mean of a binary variable and replaces $\bar{Y}$. Also, $s = \sqrt{\pi^0(1 - \pi^0)}$ where π^0 is the population proportion under the null hypothesis. The table above can be re-summarized as follows since Y does not follow a normal distribution.

	Y follows a normal distribution.	Y does not follow a normal distribution.
Small n	Not available (NA)	Test statistics cannot be constructed.
Large n	NA	Test statistic $t = \frac{\hat{\pi} - \pi^0}{\frac{s}{\sqrt{n}}} \overset{a}{\sim} N(0,1)$ where $s = \sqrt{\pi^0(1-\pi^0)}$ by CLT

Example 2.5

As a researcher, you want to study whether 80% of 32-year-old nonblack women had at least 12 years of education in 1990. In your random sample of nonblack women aged 32 in 1990, $Y = 1$ if women have at least 12 years of education and $Y = 0$ otherwise. You have a sample proportion of 0.865 with a sample size of 378.

Let's test whether 80% of 32-year-old nonblack women have at least 12 years of education. The sample size is 378. First, we construct the null hypothesis and two-sided alternative hypothesis. Then, we conduct the hypothesis test at α=0.01, using the critical value.

$$H_0: \pi = 0.8$$
$$H_a: \pi \neq 0.8 \ (two\ sided\ hypothesis)$$

Significance Test at $\alpha = 0.01$

$$test\ statistic\ t = \frac{\hat{\pi} - \mu_0}{se\ (\hat{\pi})\ under\ H_0} = \frac{0.865 - 0.8}{\sqrt{\frac{0.8(1-0.8)}{378}}} = 3.16$$

$$critical\ value = z_{0.005} = 2.58$$

Since $test\ statistic\ t > |z_{0.005}|$, we reject H_0 at $\alpha = 0.01$. It seems that the proportion of nonblack women at age 32 with a high school education or more is different from 80% at the 1% significance level.

In conclusion, the general steps of hypothesis tests of the population mean are summarized as follows.

> **<Hypothesis tests of the population mean or proportion>**
>
> (1) Think about a research question and check the characteristics of a random variable (continuous or binary) you would like to use
> (2) Develop H_0 & H_a based on a research question: Two-sided test or one-sided test?
> (3) Construct the relevant test statistic $\qquad t = ?$
> (4) Choose the significance level $\qquad \alpha = 0.05$ or 0.01 (Prob of type I error: Prob of rejecting H_0 when H_0 is true)
> (5) Find the critical value considering the chosen significance level based on whether you have a two-sided test or a one-sided test
> c such that
> $P(t > c \mid H_o) = \alpha$ $\quad$ One-sided test (e.g., $H_a: \mu > 0$)
> $P(t < c \mid H_o) = \alpha$ $\quad$ One-sided test (e.g., $H_a: \mu < 0$)
> $P(|t| > c \mid H_o) = \alpha$ $\quad$ Two-sided test (e.g., $H_a: \mu \neq 0$)
> (6) Compare the test statistic with the critical value
> Test statistic > critical value c ($H_a: \mu > 0$) ⎤
> Test statistic < critical value c ($H_a: \mu < 0$) ⎬ Reject H_0
> |Test statistic| > critical value c ($H_a: \mu \neq 0$) ⎦
>
> Or
>
> (6) Compare your p-value with the significance level, $\alpha = 0.05$ or 0.01.
> If p-value $< \alpha$, then reject H_0.
> In a two-sided test, the p-value corresponds to double the tail probability of the test statistic.
> In a one-sided test, the p-value corresponds to the tail probability of the test statistic.

In this chapter, we cover a significance test and the confidence interval as useful inference tools to investigate the population mean. However, it is important to remember that a significance test can be more deterministic while the CI, an interval estimate, can be more informative.

Also, we need to be aware of the difference between statistical significance and practical significance when we conduct the hypothesis tests. It is misleading to report results only if they are statistically significant. Among all the tests you try, some may be statistically significant just by chance. This is a type I error. Also, it is possible that some estimated mean are considerably different for the population mean in the null hypothesis in practice, but the hypothesis tests are not statistically significant. In this case, we need to examine plausible reasons why test statistics are not large enough to reject the null hypothesis, such as small sample sizes and large sample variance.

Let's see the following example.

For women, their real hourly wage in 1984 dollars is $6.5.

$$H_0: \mu = \$6.5$$
$$H_a: \mu \neq \$6.5$$

- Study 1: $\bar{Y} = 6.9$, $t = \frac{\bar{Y} - \mu_0}{se} = \frac{6.9 - 6.5}{0.4} = 1$
- Study 2: $\bar{Y} = 6.6$, $t = \frac{\bar{Y} - \mu_0}{se} = \frac{6.6 - 6.5}{0.025} = 4$

The estimated mean is much larger in Study 1 than in Study 2. However, the standard error is much smaller in Study 2 than in Study 1. As a result, the hypothesis test in Study 2 rejects the null hypothesis even at $p<0.01$ (the 1% significance level), but there is no statistically significant result in Study 1.

Therefore, the statistical significance does not always mean the sizable difference between the original belief of the population mean and the estimated sample mean. The hypothesis test may indicate the statistical significance to reject the null hypothesis, while the difference between the original belief of the population mean and the estimated sample mean is small. On the other hand, it is also possible that the difference between the original belief of the population mean and the estimated sample mean is large, although the test is statistically insignificant. Therefore, when we interpret the test results, we need to think the socio-economic significance beyond the statistical significance. The statistical significance could be easily achieved by simply using a large sample (increasing the sample size n) since the test statistic gets larger as the sample size gets larger.

How to choose an appropriate sample size in the survey for inference

Before a survey, it is critical to ask what sample size is most appropriate for inference. Of course, large samples are better than small samples. However, since time and money are limited, we cannot always increase the sample size to as large as we want. Then, what is the most appropriate sample size to reduce the CI's size or to get a more precise

CI? Also, what is the most appropriate sample size to get the statistically significant results in the hypothesis test?

Suppose that Y is a continuous or discrete variable.

First, let's find the smallest sample size, n, to make the CI most efficient given the budget, time constraints, and statistical circumstances.

Before the estimation, the CI is $[\bar{Y} - z\left(\frac{\sigma}{\sqrt{n}}\right), \bar{Y} + z\left(\frac{\sigma}{\sqrt{n}}\right)]$ where $z = 1.96$ for the 95% CI and $z = 2.58$ for the 99% CI. $z\left(\frac{\sigma}{\sqrt{n}}\right)$ is called the marginal of error, m, that determines how wide the CI is.

Then, we can have $n = \sigma^2 (\frac{z}{m})^2$ from $m = z\left(\frac{\sigma}{\sqrt{n}}\right)$ by algebra.

Depending on how wide the CI is, we can set m to be some number or less.

Depending on which confidence level we choose, $z = 1.96$ for the 95% CI and $z = 2.58$ for the 99% CI.

We can choose a value for σ^2 from the previous research or findings.

Then, we can calculate the smallest sample size n for the desirable margin of error.

Also, we have the following lesson from $n = \sigma^2 (\frac{z}{m})^2$.

- The required sample size increases as the confidence level increases from 95% to 99% since the increasing confidence level indicates the increasing reliability of the CI.
- The required sample size increases as m decreases since m indicates the precision of the CI.
- The required sample size increases as σ^2 increases since σ^2 indicates the variability of the population (the population is more heterogeneous).

Second, let's find the smallest sample size, n, to make the hypothesis test most efficient given the budget, time constraints, and statistical circumstances.

Before the estimation, the test statistic $t = \frac{\bar{Y} - \mu_0}{\frac{\sigma}{\sqrt{n}}}$. Assume that we plan to do the two-sided hypothesis test.

Then, we can have $n = \sigma^2 (\frac{t}{\bar{Y} - \mu_0})^2$ from $t = \frac{\bar{Y} - \mu_0}{\frac{\sigma}{\sqrt{n}}}$.

Depending on how significant the hypothesis test is, we can set $t = 1.96$ for 5% significance and $t = 2.58$ for 1% significance.

From the previous research and $H_0 : \mu = \mu_0$, we can set $\bar{Y} - \mu_0$ to be some number.

We can choose a value for σ^2 from the previous research or findings. Then, we can calculate the smallest sample size n for the significant hypothesis test. We have the following lessons from $n = \sigma^2(\frac{t}{\bar{Y}-\mu_0})^2$.

- The required sample size increases as the significance level of the hypothesis test becomes stricter from 5% to 1% since the stricter significance level indicates the increasing reliability of the hypothesis test.
- The required sample size increases as $\bar{Y} - \mu_0$ decreases since the decreasing difference in $\bar{Y} - \mu_0$ requires more precise tests to have a statistical distinction.
- The required sample size increases as σ^2 increases since σ^2 indicates the variability of the population (whether the population is more heterogeneous).

Example 2.6

Suppose that you would like to know the appropriate sample size to see the statistically significant test results in the analysis of students' math scores in school district A.

You want to know a sample size n such that, with $\alpha = 0.05$, the difference between the sample mean and the population mean ($\bar{Y} - \mu_0$) under the null hypothesis will not exceed 3. Let's impute the population standard deviation σ as 10 from a previous study.

$$n = \sigma^2\left(\frac{t}{\bar{Y} - \mu_0}\right)^2 = 10^2\left(\frac{1.96}{3}\right)^2 = 42.684$$

Thus, the sample size needs to be at least 43.

How about for $\alpha = 0.01$?

$$n = \sigma^2\left(\frac{t}{\bar{Y} - \mu_0}\right)^2 = 10^2\left(\frac{2.58}{3}\right)^2 = 73.96$$

Thus, the sample size needs to be at least 73.

How about for the difference between the sample mean, and the population mean under the null hypothesis will not exceed 1?

$$n = \sigma^2 \left(\frac{t}{\bar{Y} - \mu_0}\right)^2 = 10^2 \left(\frac{1.96}{1}\right)^2 = 384.16$$

Thus, the sample size needs to be at least 385.

How about for population standard deviation as 15?

$$n = \sigma^2 \left(\frac{t}{\bar{Y} - \mu_0}\right)^2 = 15^2 \left(\frac{1.96}{3}\right)^2 = 96.04$$

Thus, the sample size needs to be at least 97.

This time, suppose that Y is a binary variable.

First, we would like to find the smallest sample size, n, to make the CI most efficient given the budget, time constraints, and statistical circumstances.

Before the estimation, the CI is $[\hat{\pi} - z\left(\frac{\sigma}{\sqrt{n}}\right), \hat{\pi} + z\left(\frac{\sigma}{\sqrt{n}}\right)]$ where $z = 1.96$ for the 95% CI and $z = 2.58$ for the 99% CI. $z\left(\frac{\sigma}{\sqrt{n}}\right)$ is called the margin of error, m, that determines how wide the CI is. Also, $\sigma = \sqrt{\pi(1 - \pi)}$.

Then, we have $n = \pi(1 - \pi)\left(\frac{z}{m}\right)^2$ from $m = z\sqrt{\frac{\pi(1-\pi)}{n}}$.

Depending on how wide the CI is, we can set m to be some number or less.

Depending on which confidence level, we choose, $z = 1.96$ for the 95% CI and $z = 2.58$ for the 99% CI.

We can choose a value for π from the previous research or findings.

Then, we can calculate the smallest sample size n for the desirable margin of error.

Also, we have the following lesson from $n = \pi(1 - \pi)\left(\frac{z}{M}\right)^2$.

- The required sample size increases as the confidence level increases from 95% to 99% since the increasing confidence level indicates the increasing reliability of the CI.
- The required sample size increases as m decreases since m indicates the precision of the CI.

- The required sample size increases as $\pi(1-\pi)$ increases since $\pi(1-\pi)$ indicates the variability of the population (the population is more heterogeneous).

Second, we want to find the smallest sample size, n, to make the hypothesis test most efficient given the budget, time constraints, and statistical circumstances.

Before the estimation, the test statistic $t = \frac{\hat{\pi} - \pi^0}{\frac{s}{\sqrt{n}}}$ where $s = \sqrt{\pi^0(1-\pi^0)}$ under $H_0 : \pi = \pi^0$. Let's assume that we plan to do the two-sided hypothesis test.

Then, we can have $n = s^2 (\frac{t}{\hat{\pi} - \pi^0})^2$ from $t = \frac{\hat{\pi} - \pi^0}{\frac{s}{\sqrt{n}}}$.

Depending on how significant the hypothesis test is, we can set $t = 1.96$ for 5% significance and $z = 2.58$ for 1% significance.

From the previous research and $H_0 : \pi = \pi^0$, we can set $\hat{\pi} - \pi^0$ to be some number. We can choose a value for $s^2 = \pi^0(1 - \pi^0)$ from the null hypothesis.

Then, we can calculate the smallest sample size for the significant hypothesis test.

We have the following lessons from $n = s^2 (\frac{t}{\hat{\pi} - \pi^0})^2$.

- The required sample size increases as the significance level of the hypothesis test becomes stricter from 5% to 1% since the stricter significance level indicates the increasing reliability of the hypothesis test.
- The required sample size increases as $\hat{\pi} - \pi^0$ decreases since the decreasing difference in $\hat{\pi} - \pi^0$ requires more precise tests to have a statistical distinction.
- The required sample size increases as s^2 increases since s^2 indicates the variability of the population (whether the population is more heterogeneous).

Example 2.7

Suppose that you would like to know the appropriate sample size to see the statistically significant test results in the analysis of students' passing rate in math exams (pass for a score of 75 or over) in school district A.

You want to know a sample size n such that, with $\alpha = 0.05$, the difference between the sample proportion and the population proportion $\hat{\pi} - \pi^0$ under the null hypothesis will not exceed 0.03. Let's impute the population proportion π^0 as 0.4

under $H_0: \pi = 0.4$.

$$n = \pi^0(1-\pi^0)\left(\frac{t}{\hat{\pi}-\pi^0}\right)^2 = 0.4(1-0.4)\left(\frac{1.96}{0.03}\right)^2 = 1024.427$$

Thus, the sample size needs to be at least 1,025.

How about for $\alpha = 0.01$?

$$n = \pi^0(1-\pi^0)\left(\frac{t}{\hat{\pi}-\pi^0}\right)^2 = 0.4(1-0.4)\left(\frac{2.58}{0.03}\right)^2 = 1775.04$$

Thus, the sample size needs to be at least 1,776.

How about for the margin of error less than 0.05?

$$n = \pi^0(1-\pi^0)\left(\frac{t}{\hat{\pi}-\pi^0}\right)^2 = 0.4(1-0.4)\left(\frac{1.96}{0.05}\right)^2 = 368.79$$

Thus, the sample size needs to be at least 369.

Chapter Summary

Inference for the population mean	The sample mean formula ($\sum_{i=1}^{n} \frac{Y_i}{n}$) represents a random variable before the estimation, and it has its own distribution called the sampling distribution. According to the Central Limit Theorem (CLT), the sampling distribution of the sample mean gets close to the normal distribution as the sample size n becomes larger. This is critical for us to use the confidence intervals and hypothesis tests, regardless of whether our events follow the normal distribution.
How to precisely estimate the population mean	More information (larger sample size) and similar subjects in the sample (less sample variance) lead to a narrower sampling distribution of the sample mean, which helps the better estimation of the population mean. Specifically, we can have narrower and more precise confidence intervals for the population mean and the hypothesis tests that are more likely to reject the null hypothesis when the null hypothesis is false.
Addressing common misunderstandings and mistakes	When the sample size is small, we cannot use the confidence intervals and hypothesis tests of random variables that do not follow the normal distribution. The constructed 95% confidence interval for the population mean does not mean that the true population mean lies within the confidence interval with a 95% chance. The constructed 95% confidence interval itself is an estimator, which implies that the true population mean is included in 95% of all the constructed 95% confidence intervals from the infinitely many random samples with sample size n. Therefore, it is an accurate way to say that we are 95% confident that the true population mean lies within the confidence interval.

When we find the implications of the hypothesis tests, we need to consider not only the statistical significance but also the estimates are sizable in terms of the socio-economic significance.

Exercises

Chapter 2
Do more with the sample mean: Inference

1. Suppose that you are examining 6th grade students' math scores (X = 0 to 100 points) in the U.S. in 2008. Also, suppose that a previous study gave you that $\mu = E(X) = 60$ and $\sigma^2 = \text{Var}(X) = 100$ Assume that X follows the normal distribution.

(1) What is the probability that $\bar{X}$ falls between 59 and 60.5 with a random sample of 100 students?

(2) What is the probability that $\bar{X}$ falls between 59 and 60.5 with a random sample of 450 students?

(3) Discuss why the probabilities in (1) and (2) are different.

2. Suppose that a research calculates the yearly household earnings of families residing in public housing in New York in 2010. A random sample of 10 families reveals their annual incomes (in hundreds of U.S. dollars).

| 122 | 83 | 90 | 77 | 100 | 83 | 64 | 78 | 92 | 73 |

(1) Construct and interpret a 95% confidence interval for the population mean.

(2) What assumption do we need to construct a 95% confidence interval for the population mean for a small sample like this one?

(3) Previous research shows that the annual family income for those families living in public housing should be at least $7,500. Test whether the annual family income for those families in New York is statistically different from $7,500. Construct the null hypothesis and one-sided alternative hypothesis. Test at the 0.05 level and the 0.01 level, using the critical value and interpret the test result. Explain how the 95% confidence interval for the population mean in (1) is related to the significance test in this question.

3. Suppose that as a researcher, you want to see if 90% of 32-year-old nonblack women have at least 12 years of education in 1990. Using the data from NLSY79, you have sample proportion of 0.865 with sample size 378. NLSY79 is assumed to be a random sample.

(1) Identify the notation for the population proportion. Identify the variance and standard deviation of the random variable using the population proportion. Draw and describe the population distribution of the random variable you are studying.

(2) Identify the notation for the sample proportion for the population proportion and the sample standard deviation for the population deviation. Show the process for obtaining these sample estimates.

(3) Draw and describe the sampling distribution of the sample proportion (estimator for the population proportion). Remember that you have a large sample. Describe what happens to the sampling distribution of the sample proportion as the sample size increases, and explain why this property is useful in constructing confidence intervals and performing significance tests. What is the mean and standard error of the sample proportion? Estimate the standard error of the sample proportion.

(4) Show the process of obtaining a 95% confidence interval for the population proportion using the sample proportion and the estimated standard error obtained

in the previous question. Briefly interpret the confidence interval.

(5) Now assume that you have a sample size of 1,600 with the same sample proportion. Obtain a new 95% confidence interval and explain any differences between this confidence interval and the 95% confidence interval in the previous question.

(6) Now show the process of testing to see whether 90% of 32-year-old nonblack women have at least 12 years of education. Sample size is 378. Construct the null hypothesis and two-sided alternative hypothesis. Test at the 0.05 level and the 0.01 level, using the critical value. Interpret the test result.

(7) Let's do a different hypothesis test. Please test whether 85% of 32-year-old nonblack women have at least 12 years of education. Sample size is 378. Construct the null hypothesis and two-sided alternative hypothesis. Test at the 0.01 level, using the critical value. Interpret the test result.

4. Suppose that you are working for a government agency. You want to estimate the proportion of men aged 30 in country A who have ever been arrested. Your goal is to have a reasonably precise estimate. However, since you do not have enough funding for this research, you want to figure out a necessary sample size. You decide to use a sample size such that, with 95% confidence($a = 0.05$), the difference between the sample proportion and the population mean under the null hypothesis (marginal of error) would not exceed 0.02.

(1) Previous research suggests that the benchmark proportion of men aged 30 in country A who have ever been arrested is 0.2. Find the necessary sample size.

(2) The benchmark proportion is now 0.3. Find the necessary sample size. Discuss why your new sample size is larger or smaller than the one in question (1).

(3) Now you want the margin of error not to exceed 0.01. The benchmark proportion is still 0.3. Find the necessary sample size. Discuss why your new sample size is larger or smaller than the one in question (2).

(4) Suppose that there will be a funding cut in your agency. Please discuss the possible impacts of a funding cut on this type of research based on your findings in questions (1), (2), and (3).

5. Suppose that you want to know whether the BMI of new freshmen at Korea University is 30 (threshold of obesity). You randomly collected 15 students out of the population and recorded their Body Mass Indexes (BMI).

27	24	20	22	21	40	35	35	30
25	29	28	33	32	38			

(1) Construct and interpret a 95% confidence interval for the population mean.

(2) What assumption do we need to construct a 95% confidence interval for the population mean for a small sample like this one?

(3) Construct the null hypothesis and two-sided alternative hypothesis to test whether the BMI of new freshmen at Korea University is 30. Test at $\alpha = 0.05$, using the critical value and interpret the test result.

(4) Explain how the 95% confidence interval for the population mean in (1) is related to the significance test in (3).

6. Suppose that there is a high-tech company in the U.S. Suppose that 1,000 people (800 men and 200 women) were promoted to managerial positions last year from the pool of candidates (60% women and 40% men). It is known that women and men, on average, are equally capable of performing managerial positions. Based on this result, female workers of the company sued the company for discrimination against women. Let our outcome variable be 1 for women and 0 for men.

(1) Please explain why we need the Central Limit Theorem (CLT) to construct a 95% confidence interval for the population proportion for a binary outcome variable (women=1; men=0)? State clearly.

(2) Construct a 95% confidence interval for the population proportion. Briefly interpret the confidence interval.

(3) Please test whether the company, in general, discriminates against women in promotion. Construct the one-sided alternative hypothesis. Test at $\alpha = 0.01$ using the critical value. Interpret the test result.

7. Suppose that it is known that half of Korean women at age 30 were married in 2000. You want to know whether the marriage rate of Korean women at age 30 are still the same in 2010. Your sample size from the Korean census is 700 and your calculated sample proportion is 0.45. Construct the relevant hypotheses and show the test procedure at the 1% significance level. Interpret your test accordingly.

Chapter 3
Data Analysis for Social Science: Fundamental Methods

Examining the relationship between the two quantitative variables I: Correlation coefficient and introduction to the OLS regression analysis

Covarience and correlation coefficent

Until now, we have studied how to know something important using the sample mean. It is time to learn how to know whether one thing is related to another. There are basic to advanced methods to do so.

We often talk about whether one thing affects another in our daily lives, as well as political and economic issues. We may say that earning a college degree may lead to more earnings in the near future, or quitting smoking may lead to better health in the coming years. In the political and economic issues, we hear many news reports and opinions: "The interest rate hike by the Fed may cause the stock market meltdown"; "The law raising the tax on alcohol would reduce alcohol consumption"; "Sugar tax would lower the obesity rate."

However, it is hard to examine whether one thing truly affects another, which is called the causal relationship. On the other hand, it is relatively easy to show whether one thing is related to another using data. We start with studying how to examine a linear relationship between two variables in this chapter.

First, let's figure out how to measure the linear relationship between the two continuous variables, such as IQ and wage. We can think about the positive or negative linear relationship between two variables. In data analysis, as a basic step, covariance is used to recognize whether there is a positive or negative linear relationship between two variables.

Covariance is defined as follows, which is the population mean of the multiplication of the X deviation from its population mean and Y deviation from its population mean.

$$Cov(X,Y) = E\left((X - E(X))(Y - E(Y))\right)$$

The formula of the sample covariance is $\widehat{Cov(X,Y)} = \frac{\sum_{i=1}^{n}(X_i - \bar{X})(Y_i - \bar{Y})}{n-1}$ where n is the sample size, $\bar{X}$ is the sample mean of X, and $\bar{Y}$ is the sample mean of Y.

It looks complicated, but it is much easier to consider this definition using the X and Y coordinates below. Figure 3.1 below has four quadrants I, II, III, and IV. In quadrants I and III, the multiplication between the X deviation and the Y deviation is always positive since the X and Y deviations are all positive in quadrant I, and they are all negative in quadrant III. On the other hand, in quadrants II and IV, the multiplication between the X deviation and the Y deviation is always negative since the X and Y deviations are opposite signs in these quadrants.

Figure 3.1 X and Y coordinates in the population

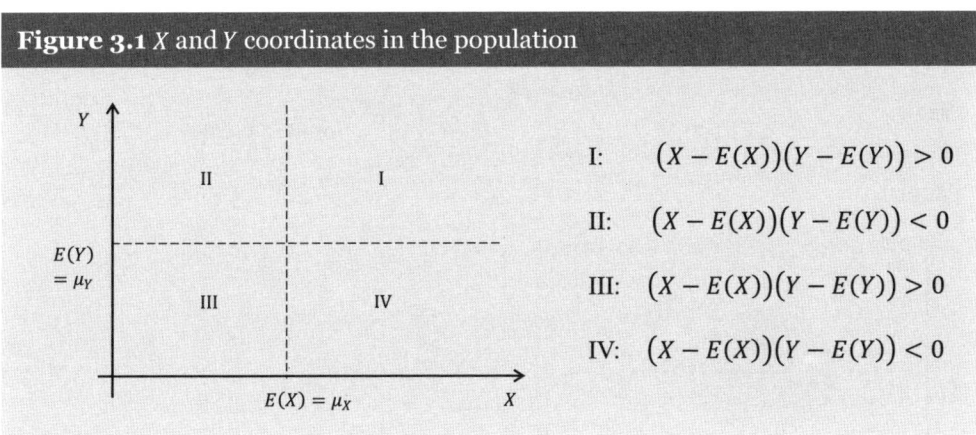

In Figure 3.2, let's see how this works in the sample. Assume that in the three panels of this figure, the data clouds indicate how the X and Y data points are scattered. In Panel A, it looks like as X increases, Y increases, which implies the positive linear relationship between X and Y. For Panel A, the formula of covariance turns out to be positive by having more data points in the first and third quadrants than in the second and fourth quadrants. In other words, dominating data points in the first and third quadrants make the sample covariance between X and Y, $\widehat{Cov(X,Y)} = \frac{\sum_{i=1}^{n}(X_i-\bar{X})(Y_i-\bar{Y})}{n-1}$, positive.

On the other hand, in Panel B, as X increases, Y decreases. Thus, it implies a negative linear relationship between X and Y. For this figure, the formula of covariance turns out to be negative by having more data points in the second and fourth quadrants than in the first and third quadrants. In other words, dominating data points in the second and fourth quadrants make the sample covariance between X and Y, $\widehat{Cov(X,Y)} = \frac{\sum_{i=1}^{n}(X_i-\bar{X})(Y_i-\bar{Y})}{n-1}$, negative.

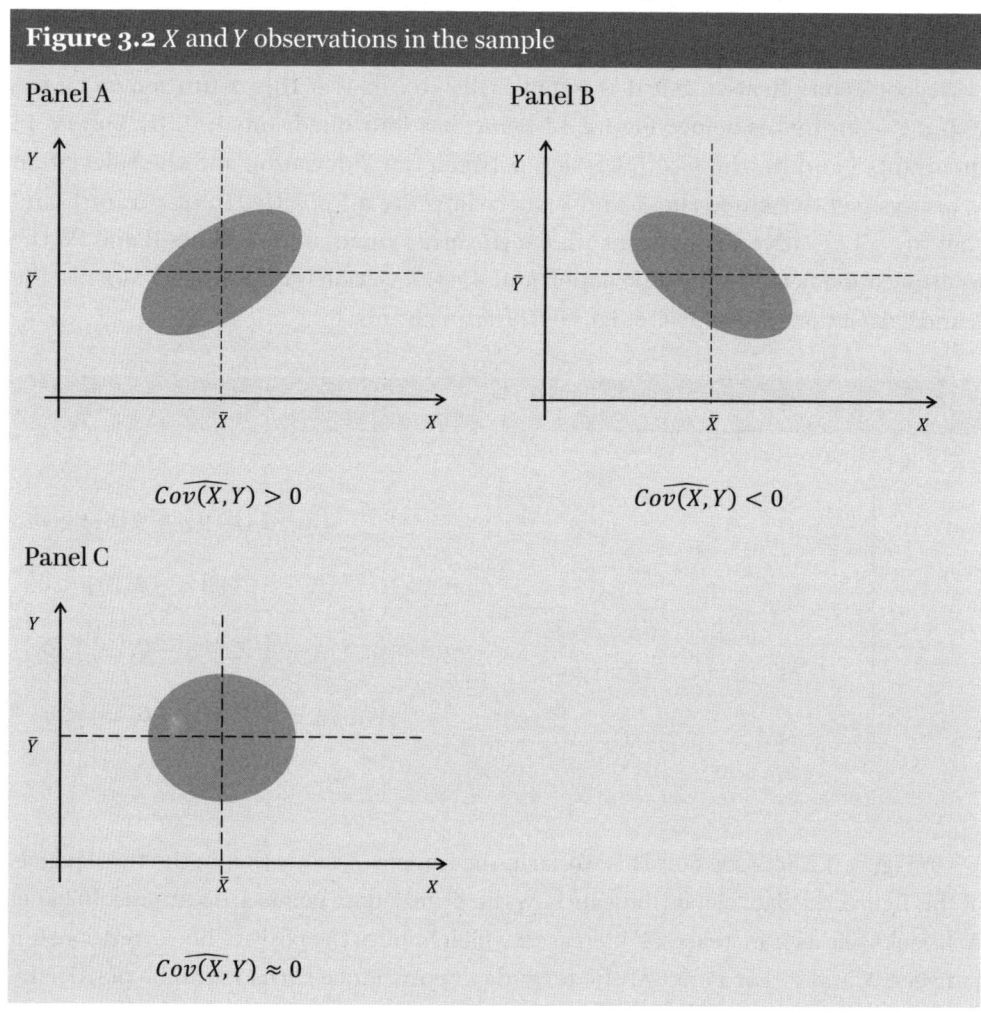

Figure 3.2 X and Y observations in the sample

The data cloud in Panel C implies no clear direction of the relationship between the two variables. The formula of covariance also turns out to be close to 0 since the data points are equally located in all four quadrants, which makes the sample covariance between X and Y, $\widehat{Cov}(X,Y) = \frac{\sum_{i=1}^{n}(X_i-\bar{X})(Y_i-\bar{Y})}{n-1}$, close to 0.

Figure 3.3 below shows two additional examples we may face when we examine the relationship between two variables. Panel A shows little variation in X values and wide variation in Y values, while panel B shows little variation in Y values and wide variation in X values. In both cases, it is impossible to see the linear relationship between X and Y since one of the variables only varies slightly. Therefore, the sample covariance in these cases is close to 0. For example, suppose that we would like to see the relationship between teachers' education in years and their teaching performance, and most teachers have 16 years of education. Then, it would be hard to examine the relationship between the two variables since there is little variation in teachers' education in years.

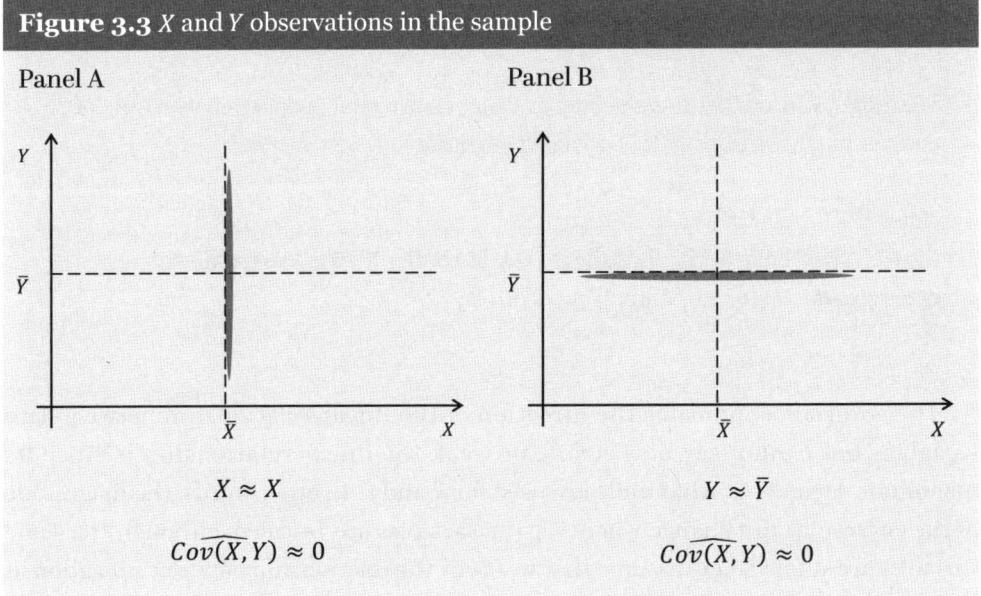

Figure 3.3 X and Y observations in the sample

Example 3.1

The figure below shows the scatter plot between years of education (X axis) and hourly wage (Y axis) in the year 1990 of the NLSY79 (National Longitudinal Survey of Youth - 1979 Cohort) data set.

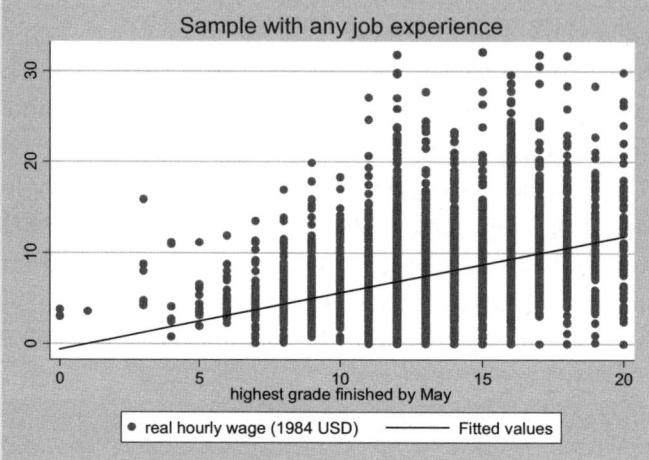

This figure implies that there seems to be a positive relationship between education and real hourly wage, even though it is quite noisy.

Notes:
the NLSY79 (National Longitudinal Survey of Youth - 1979 Cohort) data set
https://www.nlsinfo.org/content/cohorts/nlsy79

The covariance indicates the direction of the linear relationship between two variables but cannot say how strong or weak the linear relationship is since its magnitude depends on what units are used for X and Y. In other words, the magnitude of the covariance can change whenever the variables are rescaled, although the same variables are studied. Let's assume that we study the relationship between education in years and income. The covariance could be positive, but the magnitudes may decrease as we rescale the analysis unit of income from $10 to $100 to $1,000.

To resolve this issue in covariance, statisticians came up with the idea of standardizing the covariance as below.

Correlation coefficient: standardization of the covariance

$$\rho = Corr(X,Y) = \frac{Cov(X,Y)}{\sqrt{Var(X)}\sqrt{Var(Y)}} = \frac{Cov(X,Y)}{sd(X) \cdot sd(Y)}$$

$$-1 \leq \rho \leq 1$$

The formula of the sample correlation coefficient is $\hat{\rho} = \widehat{Corr}(X,Y) = (\frac{\sum_{i=1}^{n}(X_i-\bar{X})(Y_i-\bar{Y})}{n-1}) / (\sqrt{\frac{\sum_{i=1}^{n}(X_i-\bar{X})^2}{n-1}} \sqrt{\frac{\sum_{i=1}^{n}(Y_i-\bar{Y})^2}{n-1}})$ where n is the sample size, $\bar{X}$ is the sample mean of X, and $\bar{Y}$ is the sample mean of Y.

Therefore, the correlation coefficient is bounded between -1 and 1, which is not affected by unit changes. If the positive relationship gets stronger, the correlation coefficient becomes close to 1. On the other hand, if the negative relationship gets stronger, the correlation coefficient gets close to -1. If the linear relationship becomes weaker, the correlation coefficient gets close to 0. However, from the correlation coefficient, we cannot figure out a change rate of Y by a unit change of X.

In Figure 3.4, exemplary scatterplots of two variables, X and Y, in the sample present the different strengths of the positive linear relationships matched with the estimated correlation coefficients. As the scatterplots show a tighter linear pattern, the sample correlation coefficients become close to 1. As shown in this figure, when it is difficult to see a positive pattern in scatterplots, the correlation coefficient is 0. On the other hand, when there is a tight positive pattern in scatterplots, the correlation coefficient is 0.9.

Figure 3.4 Scatterplots with different sample correlation coefficients

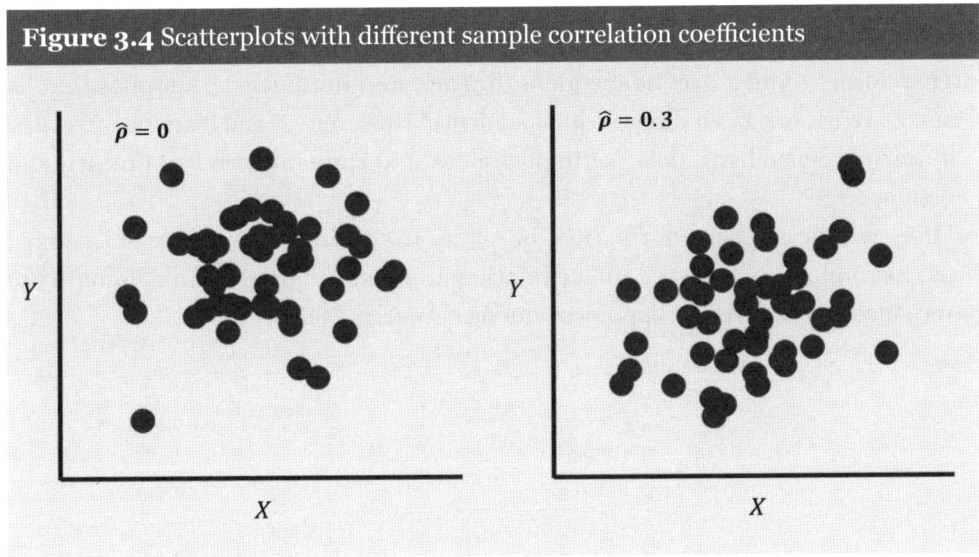

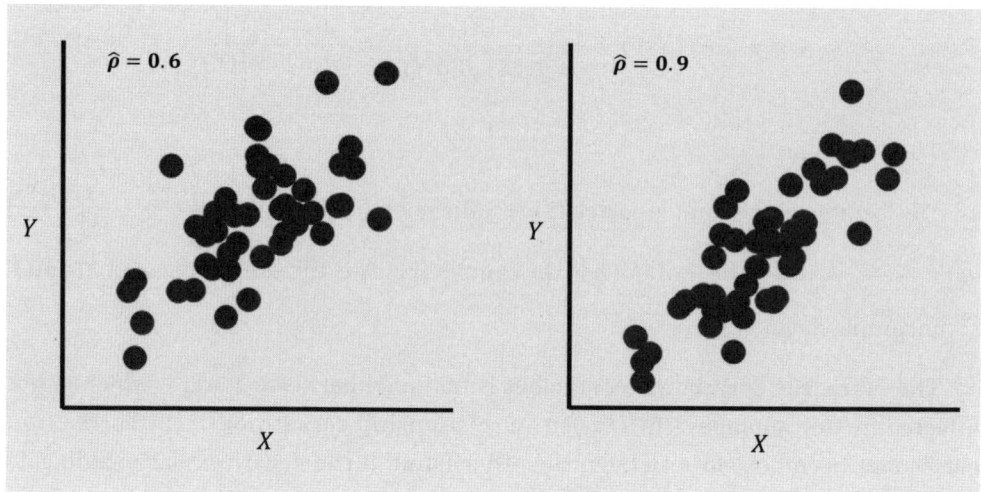

The relationships between the variables can be summarized as follows.

"X and Y are correlated (linearly dependent)" implies that "X and Y are dependent (linearly and nonlinearly)." However, "X and Y are dependent (linearly and nonlinearly)" does not imply that "X and Y are correlated (linearly dependent)."

- The correlation (linear dependency) between X and Y can be measured using covariance and correlation coefficient.
- The covariance indicates whether the linear dependence is positive or negative. However, it does not suggest the degree of linear dependency.
- The correlation coefficient indicates the degree of linear dependence between -1 (perfect negative linear dependence) and 1 (perfect positive linear dependence).
- Therefore, "X and Y are independent (linearly and nonlinearly)" implies that "X and Y are uncorrelated (linearly independent)." However, "X and Y are uncorrelated (linearly independent)" does not imply that "X and Y are independent (linearly and nonlinearly)."

How well the government runs may be related to citizens' happiness in the national level. Example 3.2 shows the linear relationship between the technical quality of governance and the average happiness among nations in 2006.

Example 3.2

Technical quality of governance and average happiness in nations in 2006

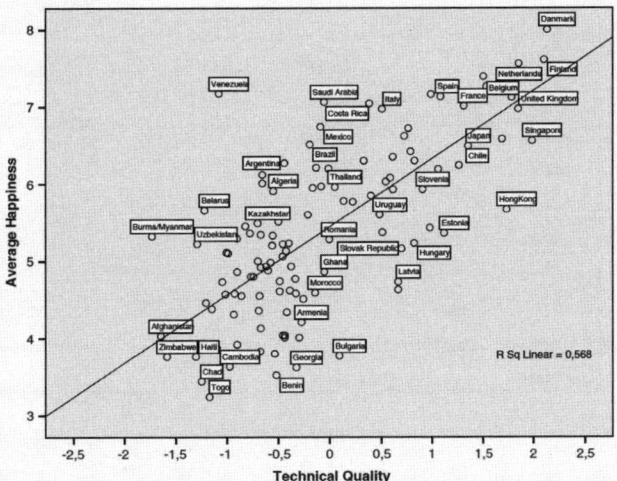

Ott, J. C. (2010). p. 360.
Ott, J. C. (2010). Good governance and happiness in nations: Technical quality precedes democracy and quality beats size. *Journal of Happiness Studies*, 11(3), 353-368.

This figure illustrates the connection between happiness and the technical quality of governance. A linear trend is evident. The correlations are noticeably weaker among the 43 countries with the lowest technical quality scores. In contrast, the correlations become stronger and more significant in nations with better technical governance. This implies that countries require a certain level of technical competence in their governance before any significant correlation with happiness can be observed.

As a policy maker, it should be important to know the relationship between education and democracy. Example 3.3 shows the correlation coefficient between schooling and democracy score.

Example 3.3

Schooling and growth of democracy 1960-2000

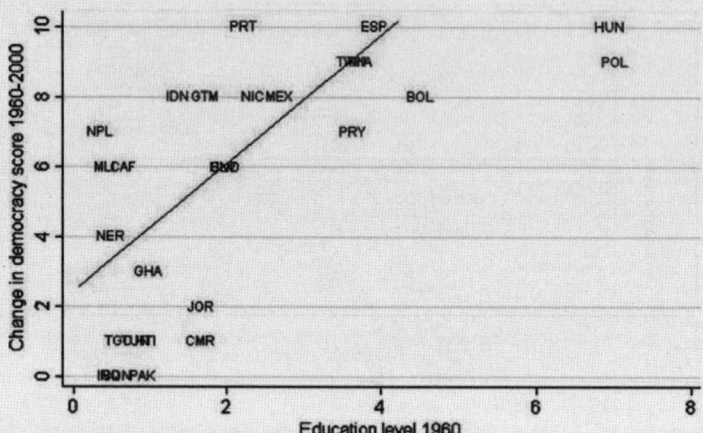

Glaeser, Ponzetto, & Shleifer. (2007). p. 80.
Glaeser, E. L., Ponzetto, G. A., & Shleifer, A. (2007). Why does democracy need education?. *Journal of economic growth*, 12(2), 77-99.

The graph illustrates a fairly strong correlation between education and democracy globally. Specifically, it presents the raw correlation coefficient between the change in the democracy score and the number of years of schooling in 1960 for countries with low democracy ratings (zero or one) in 1960, which is 0.66.

Introduction to the OLS regression analysis

There are more sophisticated ways to examine the relationships between variables. One of the most popular methods is linear regression analysis. Let's start with the two variables we are interested in, and we would like to know whether one variable affects the other. As discussed in the previous chapter, examining a causal relationship is much harder than just figuring out if there is a relationship. So, what is the best way to start? First, we can start with a functional structure that Y, the outcome variable (also called dependent variable), is affected by X, the explanatory variable (also called independent variable). Also, Y is explained by something other than X, which is called u, the unobserved variables (or the error term).

Then, we may make the following steps to develop the linear regression model for the population of our interest.

$Y = f(X, u)$ $f(X, u)$ is a generic function of X and u

X: observed variable

u: unobserved variables (or the error term)

$\Rightarrow Y = g(X) + u$ $g(X)$ is a generic function of X.

Assume that the error term is additive.

$\Rightarrow Y = \beta_0 + \beta_1 X + u$ Y is linear in parameters β_0 and β_1.

It is called the "population equation."

The second step above makes the unobserved characteristics, u, to be additive to the generic function of X. Then, the third equation implies that Y is explained by X in a functional form of $\beta_0 + \beta_1 X$. "linear" of the linear regression model comes from the fact that Y is linear in the parameters, β_0 and β_1. Creating this linear relationship between Y and the parameters and forcing the unobserved characteristics to be additive to the functional form of X is the first key assumption of the linear regression model. There must be many other ways to show how Y is explained by X and the error term, u, but the linear regression model decides to start with this way of explaining Y with X and u since it is easy and intuitive to explain the relationship between X and Y. In this regression model, the population parameters, β_0 and β_1, are key to explaining Y using X, but they are unknown.

Example 3.4

Suppose that we would like to know the impact of education on hourly wage: $Y = f(X, u)$ where Y is hourly wage, X is years of education, and u is other unknown or unobserved factors that affect hourly wage, such as family backgrounds and individual characteristics.

When we develop the simple regression model, $Y = \beta_0 + \beta_1 X + u$, we assume that β_1 indicates the slope of the linear relationship between X and Y and β_0 is the intercept (Y value when X is 0). The unknown or unobserved factors are combined in u in this regression model.

We don't know the true specification between X and Y. The population regression model in this example is based on practical and convenient assumptions to estimate the relationship between X and Y. We can make more sophisticated regression models later on.

How do we estimate these parameters? Also, what is the meaning of the estimators?

First, let's focus on how to estimate these parameters. There may be many ideas to estimate these parameters, but there is a scientific method that is commonly accepted by researchers. One of the most popular ways is to minimize the gaps between reality and the model prediction. This approach is quite intuitive. Then, let's see how we can implement this idea to estimation.

Suppose the following estimation equation is estimated using the random sample. This estimation equation is different from the population equation we discussed earlier. As shown below, we have the estimators for the parameters. Thus, the outcome variable, Y, is the summation of the estimated function of X, $\hat{\beta}_0 + \hat{\beta}_1 X$, and the left-over variation of Y called the residual, $\hat{u}$.

Estimation equation:

$Y = \hat{\beta}_0 + \hat{\beta}_1 X + \hat{u}$

$\hat{\beta}_0$ is an estimator for β_0.
$\hat{\beta}_1$ is an estimator for β_1.
$\hat{u}$: residual

$Y = \hat{Y} + \hat{u}$ $\qquad$ $\hat{Y} = \hat{\beta}_0 + \hat{\beta}_1 X$ $\qquad$ $\hat{u} = Y - \hat{Y}$

Therefore, the estimation equation, $Y = \hat{\beta}_0 + \hat{\beta}_1 X + \hat{u}$, can be decomposed into the prediction part, $\hat{Y} = \hat{\beta}_0 + \hat{\beta}_1 X$, and the residual part, $\hat{u}$. $\hat{u}$ is the gap between observed reality (Y) and the model prediction ($\hat{Y}$).

Before moving forward, let's discuss the key differences between the population equation and the estimation equation in the linear regression analysis.

Population equation	Estimation equation
$Y = \beta_0 + \beta_1 X + u$	$Y = \hat{\beta}_0 + \hat{\beta}_1 X + \hat{u}$
The population equation is conceptual. It is in our imagination and the true population parameters, β_0 and β_1, are unknown.	The estimation equation is tangible since it is estimated using a random sample.
The error term u, is part of Y.	The residual, $\hat{u}$, is the difference between Y and $\hat{Y}$, which is estimated in the OLS regression analysis. But the residual, $\hat{u}$, is not the unobserved, u.

Then, our goal in the estimation is to find the optimal numbers of $\hat{\beta}_0$ and $\hat{\beta}_1$ for β_0 and β_1 that minimizes the residual, $\hat{u}$, the difference between Y and $\hat{Y}$. This is the goal to minimize the gaps between reality and the model prediction.

As the sum of the deviations from the mean is 0, the sum of residuals is 0. However, the sum of squared residuals is not 0. Therefore, we can implement this idea by minimizing the sum of squared residuals, which is also called the residual sum of squares, $\sum_{i=1}^{n} \hat{u}_i^2$.

$$\min_{\hat{\beta}_0, \hat{\beta}_1} \sum_{i=1}^{n} \hat{u}_i^2$$

This idea can be explained using the figure below, too. In this figure, the upper-right oval shape of the X and Y data cloud seems to indicate a positive relationship between X and Y. Then, our goal is to find the best straight line through this data cloud. As we discussed earlier, one of the most scientific ways is to minimize the difference between Y (real data point) and $\hat{Y}$ (predicted value by the regression model). This unexplained part of Y is called the residual, $\hat{u}$. In other words, the regression line is the collection of all predicted values by the regression model, and the best fit is achieved by finding $\hat{\beta}_0$ and $\hat{\beta}_1$ for β_0 and β_1 that minimizes the sum of squared $\hat{u}$ (the residual sum of squares). Thus, this type of regression estimation is called the Ordinary Least Squares (OLS) regression analysis.

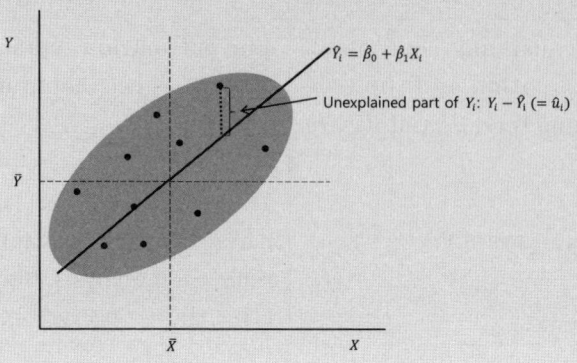

Figure 3.5 The estimated regression line

The mathematical process gives us the following formulas for $\hat{\beta}_0$ and $\hat{\beta}_1$.

$$\hat{\beta}_0 = \bar{Y} - \hat{\beta}_1 \bar{X} \text{ for } \beta_0$$

The estimated intercept coefficient can be shown as $\bar{Y} = \hat{\beta}_0 + \hat{\beta}_1 \bar{X}$, implying that the predicted regression line always goes through the sample mean of X and the sample mean of Y.

$$\hat{\beta}_1 = \frac{\sum_{i=1}^{n}(X_i - \bar{X})(Y_i - \bar{Y})}{\sum_{i=1}^{n}(X_i - \bar{X})^2} = \frac{\frac{\sum_{i=1}^{n}(X_i - \bar{X})(Y_i - \bar{Y})}{n-1}}{\frac{\sum_{i=1}^{n}(X_i - \bar{X})^2}{n-1}} = \frac{\sum_{i=1}^{n}(X_i - \bar{X})Y_i}{\sum_{i=1}^{n}(X_i - \bar{X})^2} = \frac{\sum_{i=1}^{n}X_i(Y_i - \bar{Y})}{\sum_{i=1}^{n}X_i(X_i - \bar{X})} \text{ for } \beta_1$$

Note: $\sum_{i=1}^{n}(X_i - \bar{X})(Y_i - \bar{Y}) = \sum_{i=1}^{n}(X_i - \bar{X})Y_i - (X_i - \bar{X})\bar{Y}$

$$= \sum_{i=1}^{n}(X_i - \bar{X})Y_i - \sum_{i=1}^{n}(X_i - \bar{X})\bar{Y}$$

$$= \sum_{i=1}^{n}(X_i - \bar{X})Y_i - \bar{Y}\sum_{i=1}^{n}(X_i - \bar{X})$$

$$= \sum_{i=1}^{n}(X_i - \bar{X})Y_i \text{ since } \sum_{i=1}^{n}(X_i - \bar{X}) = 0$$

In the same manner, $\sum_{i=1}^{n}(X_i - \bar{X})(Y_i - \bar{Y}) = \sum_{i=1}^{n}X_i(Y_i - \bar{Y})$.

The estimated slope coefficient, $\hat{\beta}_1$, could be shown in different forms, but they are all the same. Particularly, it could be considered to be the sample covariance between X and Y divided by the sample variance of X, as shown in the second form, $\frac{\frac{\sum_{i=1}^{n}(X_i - \bar{X})(Y_i - \bar{Y})}{n-1}}{\frac{\sum_{i=1}^{n}(X_i - \bar{X})^2}{n-1}}$.

Since the sample variance of X is always positive, the sample covariance of X and Y determines the sign of the estimated slope coefficient. Note that if the sample variance of X, $\frac{\sum_{i=1}^{n}(X_i-\bar{X})^2}{n-1}$, is 0, $\hat{\beta}_1$ is not defined. If the sample covariance between X and Y, $\frac{\sum_{i=1}^{n}(X_i-\bar{X})(Y_i-\bar{Y})}{n-1}$, is 0, $\hat{\beta}_1$ is 0. Also, $\hat{\beta}_1$ can be algebraically expressed in the third or fourth terms above, $\frac{\sum_{i=1}^{n}(X_i-\bar{X})Y_i}{\sum_{i=1}^{n}(X_i-\bar{X})^2} = \frac{\sum_{i=1}^{n}X_i(Y_i-\bar{Y})}{\sum_{i=1}^{n}X_i(X_i-\bar{X})}$.

There are three OLS properties we always have by running the OLS regression model. They are the results from the OLS computation. Be careful! Sometimes, there is some confusion between these properties and the OLS assumptions.

OLS property ①

$\sum_{i=1}^{n} \hat{u} = 0$

$\Rightarrow \frac{1}{n}\sum_{i=1}^{n} \hat{u} = 0$

OLS property ②

$\bar{Y} = \hat{\beta}_0 + \hat{\beta}_1 \bar{X}$

OLS property ③

$\sum_{i=1}^{n} \hat{u}_i X_i = 0$

$\Rightarrow \hat{u}_i \ \& \ X_i$: uncorrelated

$\widehat{Cov}(\hat{u}, X) = 0$

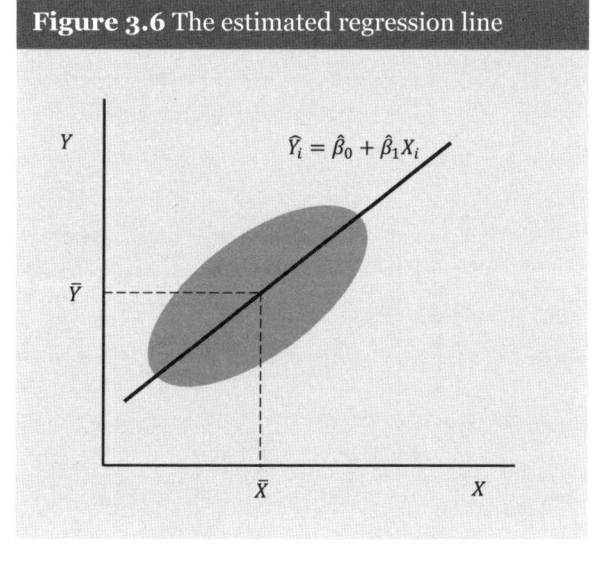

Figure 3.6 The estimated regression line

The first property says that the summation of the residual is 0, and its mean is 0, too. We already expected this property earlier since the residual is nothing but the deviation of Y from its predicted value. Thus, the residual can be positive or negative depending on the data points, and the sum of them should be 0. The second property indicates that the predicted regression line goes through the sample means of X and Y. We already mentioned this before when we introduced the estimated coefficient $\hat{\beta}_0$. The third property suggests that the sample covariance between X and the residual is 0. In other words, the independent variable and the residuals are not correlated all the time in the OLS regression analysis.

In the OLS regression analysis, we are particularly interested in $\hat{\beta}_1$ since it plays a key role in explaining the relationship between X and Y. As shown earlier, $\hat{\beta}_1 = \frac{\sum_{i=1}^{n}(X_i-\bar{X})Y_i}{\sum_{i=1}^{n}(X_i-\bar{X})^2}$ consists of X and Y information from the sample.

As we saw earlier, there seems to be a relationship between governance and happiness at the national level, and it is shown in Example 3.5. The straight line in this figure is created by the OLS estimation method we studied in this chapter.

Example 3.5

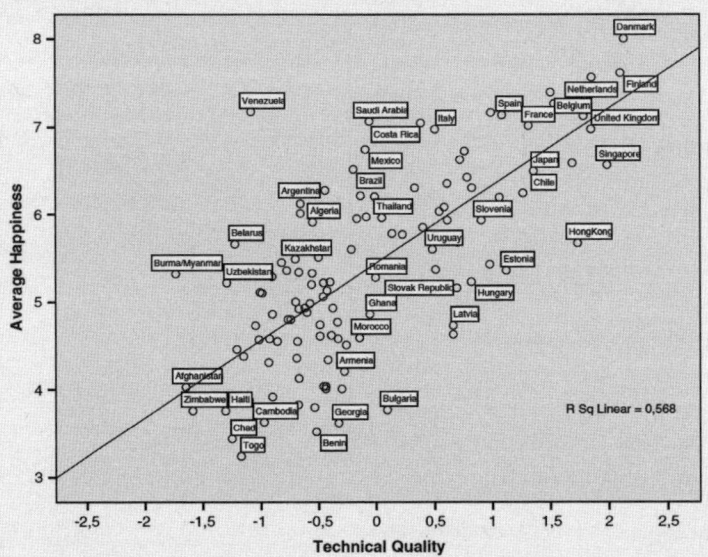

Technical quality of governance and average happiness in nations in 2006

Ott, J. C. (2010). p. 360.

Ott, J. C. (2010). Good governance and happiness in nations: Technical quality precedes democracy and quality beats size. *Journal of Happiness Studies*, 11(3), 353-368.

This figure illustrates the connection between happiness and the technical quality of governance. A linear trend is evident. The straight line indicates the estimated

> regression line by minimizing the residual sum of squares in this data set. The vertical distance between each data point and the straight line is the residual.

β_1 is unknown, and we obtain $\hat{\beta}_1$ from an idea of finding $\hat{\beta}_1$ that minimizes the sum of squared residuals. Then, we are wondering whether $\hat{\beta}_1$ is a valid, reliable, and sound estimator for β_1.

Before discussing this matter, let's talk about the sampling distribution of $\hat{\beta}_1$. When we studied the sample mean, $\bar{Y}$, for the population mean, μ, we examined the sampling distribution of $\bar{Y}$. In this case, the sample mean was an estimator to estimate the population mean, the unknown parameter we would like to know. In the same manner, the unknown parameter we would like to know is β_1 and the estimator for this parameter is $\hat{\beta}_1$. Thus, we can think about the sampling distribution of $\hat{\beta}_1$, assuming that infinitely many values of $\hat{\beta}_1$ can be obtained using infinitely many random samples with the sample size n. Of course, in reality, we only have one value of $\hat{\beta}_1$ we obtained from our random sample. The sampling distribution is in our imagination but useful to study the characteristics of $\hat{\beta}_1$.

There are two main criteria to determine whether the estimator, $\hat{\beta}_1$, is doing a good job. First, it is about whether $\hat{\beta}_1$ is unbiased for β_1. The first criterion is whether the average of all possible values in the sampling distribution of $\hat{\beta}_1$ is β_1. It does not mean that our estimated $\hat{\beta}_1$ is β_1. It simply means that if we estimated infinitely many $\hat{\beta}_1$ with infinitely many random samples, the average of them is β_1. Second, is $\hat{\beta}_1$ efficient? It is about whether the sampling distribution of $\hat{\beta}_1$ has a small variance. In other words, it is said that $\hat{\beta}_1$ is efficient when all possible values of $\hat{\beta}_1$ in the sampling distribution are more closely located in the center of the distribution.

First, let's carefully examine the unbiasedness of $\hat{\beta}_1$ for β_1. This ideal characteristic of $\hat{\beta}_1$ does not come for free. It takes several strict assumptions stated below.

Please see the four assumptions for the unbiased OLS estimator $\hat{\beta}_1 = \frac{\sum_{i=1}^{n}(X_i-\bar{X})Y_i}{\sum_{i=1}^{n}(X_i-\bar{X})^2}$ for β_1: $E(\hat{\beta}_1) = \beta_1$ (Wooldridge, 2012: 48).

① Linear in parameters & additive error term
② Random sample of X and Y
③ Variation in X
④ $E(u|X) = 0$

Figure 3.7 presents the sampling distribution of $\hat{\beta}_1$, where $E(\hat{\beta}_1) = \beta_1$ under the four

OLS assumptions.

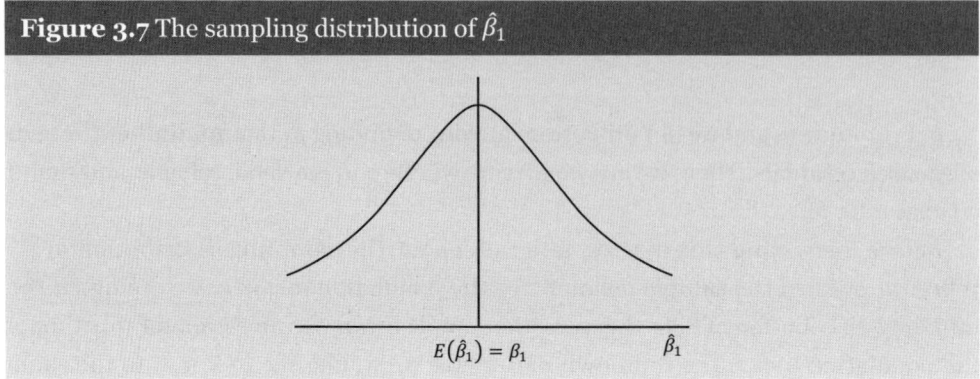

Figure 3.7 The sampling distribution of $\hat{\beta}_1$

The OLS assumptions are about the population. As we discussed earlier, the sample is tangible, while the population is in our imagination. Therefore, we are not able to examine whether the assumptions for the population hold, although it is possible to check the sample for possible violations or validations of the assumptions.

The first and third assumptions are easy to be understood since the first assumption gives the structure of the linear regression model we discussed earlier, and the third assumption is critical to studying the X variable. These two assumptions are fundamental to starting the regression analysis. The first assumption is the basic structure for the analysis and could be violated if the true structure is different from what is assumed. The third assumption is rather easily validated when the variation of X is not 0 in the sample. The second assumption is important, too. This assumption says that the individuals in the sample represent the population of interest. With this assumption, the OLS estimated coefficient would be legitimate for the population parameter. Also, the random sample assumption is fundamental for many statistical practices; particularly, the random sample assumption leads to an independent and identical distribution of all subjects in the study. In other words, all the individuals in the sample are not related, and they may have the same possible values of the outcome and explanatory variables. In practice, it is not easy to collect a random sample due to various reasons, such as the difficulty of having a complete list of subjects in the population and the nonresponses of subjects. The last assumption for the unbiasedness of $\hat{\beta}_1$ states that the conditional mean of the error term, u, given X is 0, which is called the conditional mean independence assumption. This assumption means that the population average of u is 0 regardless of the value of X, the included explanatory variable in the regression model. Loosely speaking, it is assumed that the unobserved variables in the regression model are not related to X, at least at the mean. This is the critical assumption to estimate the impact of X on Y. Also, assuming $E(u|X) = 0$ implies $E(u) = 0$ since X is not relevant anymore for the average of the error term. Intuitively, it is assumed that something that we cannot control for in the regression model is 0 on average. This assumption is crucial but hard to be validated since the error term is not observed. Also, when we think about the possible factors that are missed and not controlled for, they are easily related to the explanatory variable. For example, when we would like to know the impact of education on earnings, there are various unobserved factors, such as individuals' noncognitive ability or life experiences. Those unobserved factors are possibly related to their education choice. Then, this assumption could be violated.

$Y_i = \beta_0 + \beta_1 X_i + u_i$ -- population equation

Given four assumptions,

$$E(Y|X) = E(\beta_0 + \beta_1 X + u|X)$$
$$= \beta_0 + \beta_1 X + E(u|X)$$
$$= \beta_0 + \beta_1 X$$

$\frac{dE(Y|X)}{dX} = \beta_1$ 1 unit change in $X \Rightarrow \beta_1$ unit change in Y given X

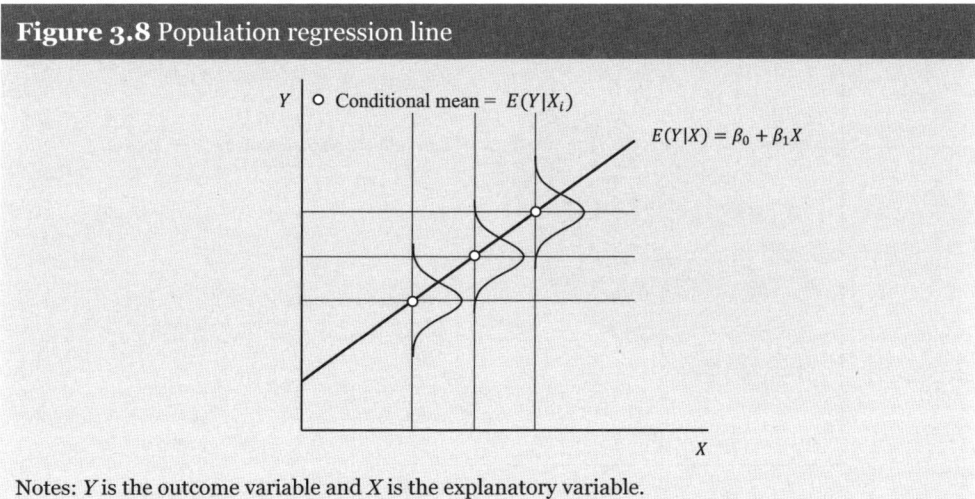

Figure 3.8 Population regression line

Notes: Y is the outcome variable and X is the explanatory variable.

As shown in Figure 3.8, the population regression line is conceptually the population mean of Y depending on X, $E(Y|X) = \beta_0 + \beta_1 X$. It is in our imagination. For each different X value, we can think about the possible distribution of Y. For example, suppose that Y is earnings and X is the years of education. For 9, 12, and 16 years of education in this figure, we can think about the possible distribution of earnings from low to high levels. The variation of Y at each X in the population is driven by the unobserved u. Such variations of Y driven by u are assumed to be equal and constant over the different levels of X for now. It is called homoscedasticity, the 5th assumption for the OLS regression model, which is needed later. The population regression line in this example is positively sloped. In other words, more years of education may lead to higher earnings on average.

The sample regression line, $\hat{Y}_i = \hat{\beta}_0 + \hat{\beta}_1 X_i$, can be shown below. Different from the population regression line, the sample regression line goes through the sample data points. The total variation of Y consists of the difference between Y and the sample mean, $\bar{Y}$, which is the full variation of Y in the sample. Some part of this full variation of Y is explained by the regression model, which is the explained variation of Y, consisting of $\hat{Y}_i - \bar{Y}$. The rest of the variation of Y after the explained part is called the unexplained variation of Y, consisting of $Y_i - \hat{Y}_i = \hat{u}_i$. When we square and sum those variations, we can come up with the equation below: the total sum of squares is the explained sum of squares plus the unexplained sum of squares.

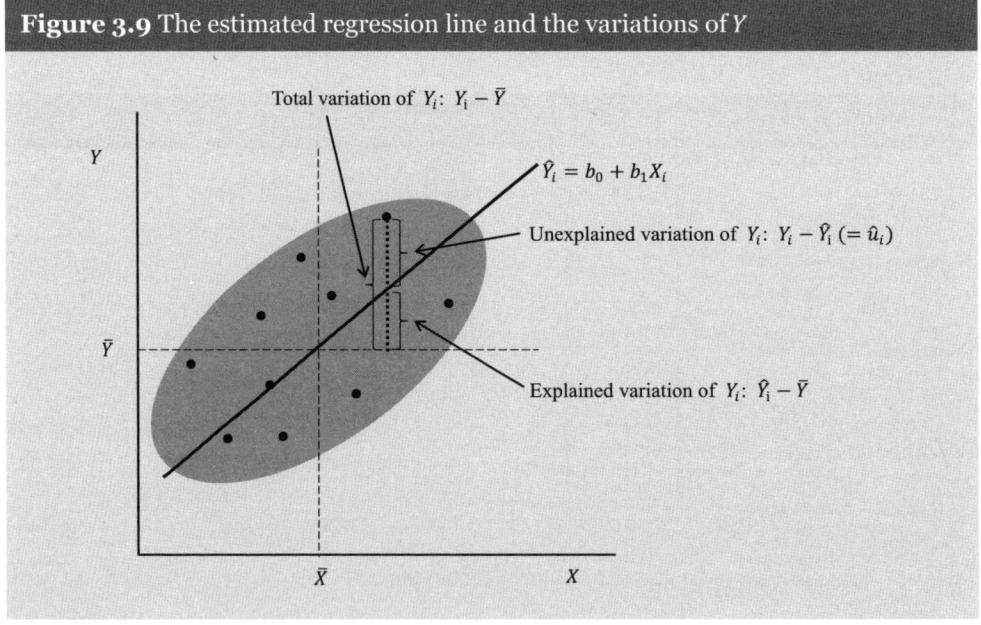

Figure 3.9 The estimated regression line and the variations of Y

$$\sum_{i=1}^{n}(Y_i - \bar{Y})^2 = \sum_{i=1}^{n}(\hat{Y}_i - \bar{Y})^2 + \sum_{i=1}^{n}(Y_i - \hat{Y}_i)^2$$

SST	SSE	SSR
(Total sum of squares)	(Explained sum of squares)	(Residual sum of squares or unexplained sum of squares)

Using this equation, we can measure how much of the total variation of Y is explained by the regression model as follows:

$$R^2 = \frac{SSE}{SST} = \frac{SST - SSR}{SST} = 1 - \frac{SSR}{SST}$$

$$0 \leq R^2 \leq 1$$

Close to 0: less explanatory power   Close to 1: more explanatory power

If R^2 is getting larger and closer to 1, the larger part of Y variation is explained by the regression model. However, larger R^2 says nothing about the unbiasedness of $\hat{\beta}_1$. The regression analysis is all about how to explain the variation of the outcome variable, Y, using the variation of the explanatory variable, X. If there is no variation of Y, there is no need to explain Y. Also, if there is no variation of X, Y cannot be explained. Thus, when the variations of Y and X are wider and more related, the regression analysis works better. R-squared is also called a measure of the goodness of fit of the OLS regression model.

Example 3.6

The regression result below is obtained using hourly wage in 1980 U.S. dollars (Y) and years of education (X) in the year 1990 of the NLSY79 (National Longitudinal Survey of Youth - 1979 Cohort) data set.

$$\hat{Y}_i = -0.587 + 0.62X_i$$
SE   (0.231)   (0.017)

SST (Total Sum of Squares) = 128911.008
SSE (Explained Sum of Squares) = 18083.2888

SSR (Residual Sum of Squares) = 110827.719

$R^2 = 0.1403$

The estimated coefficient of education indicates that a one-year increase in education implies 62 cents increase in real hourly wage. This association is not sufficient to claim the causation from education to real hourly wage because there are other factors to be controlled for, for example, demographic characteristics, actual job experience, and measure of ability. In this case, the fourth OLS assumption could be violated. As shown above, SST = SSE + SSR since 128911.008 = 18083.2888 + 110827.719 and R-squared = SSE/SST = 0.1403. This implies that education explains about 14% of the variation in real hourly wage for the sample.

Notes:
the NLSY79 (National Longitudinal Survey of Youth - 1979 Cohort) data set
https://www.nlsinfo.org/content/cohorts/nlsy79

Now, let's take a look at how to obtain the variance of $\hat{\beta}_1$ which measures the spreads of the sampling distribution of $\hat{\beta}_1$.

The additional assumption for the efficient standard error of the OLS estimator $\hat{\beta}_1$ is as below.

⑤ $Var(u|X) = Var(u) = \sigma^2$ -- Equal variance of u over any value of X

It is called "Homoscedasticity."

As discussed earlier, the variance of the error term reflects the variance of the outcome variable. Therefore, it is a good way to validate homoscedasticity by examining whether the outcome variable in the population has equal variance over the different values of X. For example, if we study the impact of education on earnings, it is important to ask whether earnings vary equally for individuals with a high school degree and a college degree. Earnings may vary much more at the college degree level than at the high school degree level if college degree holders show wider variations in earnings than high school degree holders. If so, this assumption could be violated.

With the four assumptions and the homoscedasticity assumption, the variance of $\hat{\beta}_1$ is as follows.

$$Var(\hat{\beta}_1) = \frac{\sigma^2}{\sum_{i=1}^{n}(X_i - \bar{X})^2}$$

The square root of the variance of $\hat{\beta}_1$ is the standard deviation of $\hat{\beta}_1$.

$$sd(\hat{\beta}_1) = \frac{\sigma}{\sqrt{\sum_{i=1}^{n}(X_i - \bar{X})^2}}$$

Since σ is unknown, it is estimated with $\hat{\sigma} = \sqrt{\frac{\sum \hat{u}_i^2}{n-k-1}}$.

Then, the standard error of $\hat{\beta}_1$ with $\hat{\sigma}$, $se(\hat{\beta}_1)$, is the estimator of $sd(\hat{\beta}_1)$:

$$se(\hat{\beta}_1) = \frac{\hat{\sigma}}{\sqrt{\sum_{i=1}^{n}(X_i - \bar{X})^2}} \quad \text{where } \hat{\sigma} = \sqrt{\frac{\sum \hat{u}_i^2}{n-k-1}} \quad \text{where } k = 1 \text{ in this case}$$

$$(k = \# \text{ of the explanatory variables})$$

Figure 3.10 presents the sampling distribution of $\hat{\beta}_1$, where $E(\hat{\beta}_1) = \beta_1$ under the four OLS assumptions and $se(\hat{\beta}_1) = \frac{\hat{\sigma}}{\sqrt{\sum_{i=1}^{n}(X_i - \bar{X})^2}}$ under the five OLS assumptions shown here.

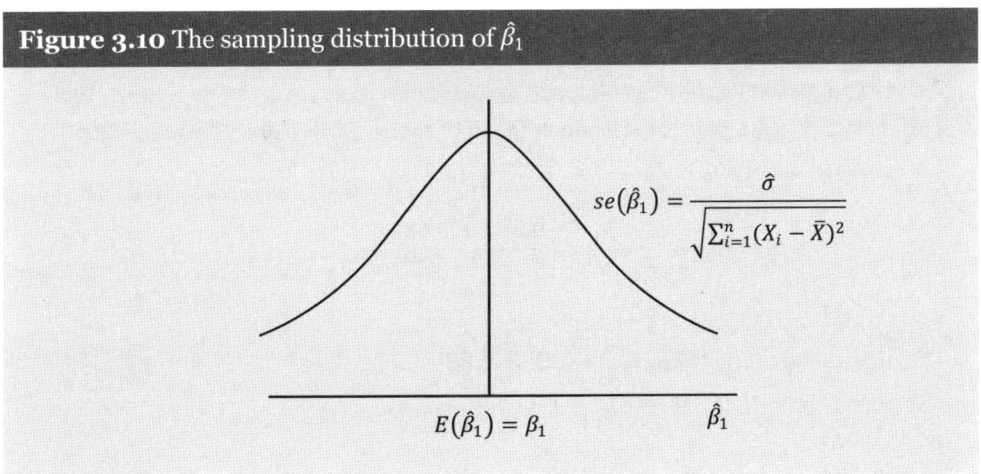

Figure 3.10 The sampling distribution of $\hat{\beta}_1$

$se(\hat{\beta}_1)$ is estimated using the sample. Understanding when $se(\hat{\beta}_1)$ is getting larger or smaller is important to understand what makes the distribution of $\hat{\beta}_1$ wider or narrower. Most importantly, the size of the test statistic for β_1 is determined partly by the size of $se(\hat{\beta}_1)$, as we studied in the test statistic for the population mean, u.

$\sum \hat{u}_i^2$ SSR (unexplained variation)   ↓ $\Rightarrow se(\hat{\beta}_1)$ ↓

n ↑ $\Rightarrow se(\hat{\beta}_1)$ ↓ $\hat{\beta}_1$: more efficient

$k = 1$

$\sum (X_i - \bar{X})^2$ Variation in X ↑ $\Rightarrow se(\hat{\beta}_1)$ ↓

As shown above, $\hat{\beta}_1$ has the smaller standard error as the residual sum of squares gets smaller (more Y is explained by the regression model), the sample size n gets larger (more information in the sample), and the variation of X gets larger (richer information in X). Also, note that the smaller residual sum of squares is equivalent to the larger R^2 since $R^2 = 1 - SSR/SST$.

Thus, if our $se(\hat{\beta}_1)$ is smaller or larger than expected, we can find possible reasons discussed above.

Example 3.7

As studied earlier, the regression result below is obtained using hourly wage in 1980 U.S. dollars (Y) and years of education (X) in the year 1990 of the NLSY79 (National Longitudinal Survey of Youth - 1979 Cohort) data set.

$$\hat{Y}_i = -0.587 + 0.62 X_i$$
$$SE \quad (0.231) \quad (0.017)$$

SST (Total Sum of Squares) = 128911.008
SSE (Explained Sum of Squares) = 18083.2888
SSR (Residual Sum of Squares) = 110827.719
$R^2 = 0.1403$
$n = 7,707$
$\sum (X_i - \bar{X})^2 = 47023.834$

The following regression result is from a subsample analysis for men and women aged 30 in the same sample of the earlier outcome.

$$\hat{Y}_i = -1.71 + 0.70X_i$$
$$\text{SE} \quad (0.672) \quad (0.051)$$

SST (Total Sum of Squares) = 15839.397
SSE (Explained Sum of Squares) = 2642.802
SSR (Residual Sum of Squares) = 13196.595
R^2 = 0.1668
n = 941
$\sum(X_i - \bar{X})^2$ = 5348.125

It is found that the R-squared of this regression, 0.1668, is greater than the previous one, 0.1403, implying that SSR relative to SST is smaller in this subsample. Thus, it may lead to a smaller standard error.

The sample size of this analysis is 941, which is smaller than that of the full sample analysis, 7,707. Thus, it may lead to a larger standard error.

$\sum(X_i - \bar{X})^2$ of this analysis, 5349.125, is smaller than $\sum(X_i - \bar{X})^2$ of the full sample analysis, 47023.834. Thus, it may lead to a larger standard error.

Therefore, the larger standard error of education, 0.051, in this subsample analysis than that of the full sample analysis, 0.017, is mainly driven by the smaller sample size and the smaller variation of X.

Notes:
the NLSY79 (National Longitudinal Survey of Youth - 1979 Cohort) data set
https://www.nlsinfo.org/content/cohorts/nlsy79

As mentioned earlier, the ideal estimator $\hat{\beta}_1$ for β_1 has been one of the main topics in the OLS regression analysis, which is summarized in the Gauss-Markov Theorem.
OLS estimator is BLUE by Gauss-Markov Theorem (Wooldridge, 2012: 102).

Best   Least variance of $\hat{\beta}_1$ (most efficient)

Linear $\hat{\beta}_1 = \frac{\sum_{i=1}^{n}(X_i-\bar{X})Y_i}{\sum_{i=1}^{n}(X_i-\bar{X})^2} = \beta_1 + \frac{\sum_{i=1}^{n}(X_i-\bar{X})u_i}{\sum_{i=1}^{n}(X_i-\bar{X})^2}$ $\hat{\beta}_1$ is linear in Y_i and u_i.

Unbiased $E(\hat{\beta}_1) = \beta_1$

Estimator

Under the five OLS assumptions below
① Linear in parameters and additive error term
② Random sample of X and Y
③ Variation in X
④ $E(u|X) = 0$
⑤ No heteroscedasticity $Var(u|X) = Var(u) = \sigma^2$

The Gauss-Markov Theorem states that the OLS estimator is the most efficient (Best) and unbiased estimator (Unbiased) for the population parameter under these five assumptions. In other words, among all the possible estimators, the OLS estimator is very useful and effective in estimating the population parameter. Also, under these assumptions, the OLS estimator is the linear function (Linear) of the outcome variable or the error term. The value of this property is not readily understood, but it is important to have a valid inference later.

Example 3.8

As shown before, the regression result below is obtained using hourly wage in 1980 U.S. dollars (Y) and years of education (X) in the year 1990 of the NLSY79 (National Longitudinal Survey of Youth - 1979 Cohort) data set.

$$\hat{Y}_i = -0.587 + 0.62 X_i$$
$$\text{SE} \quad (0.231) \quad (0.017)$$

SST (Total Sum of Squares) = 128911.008
SSE (Explained Sum of Squares) = 18083.2888
SSR (Residual Sum of Squares) = 110827.719
$R^2 = 0.1403$

$n = 7{,}707$

In this regression, the estimated coefficients are valid under OLS assumptions 1 to 4 above, and the standard errors are valid under OLS assumptions 1 to 5.

However, as mentioned in the earlier analysis, the fourth assumption, $E(u|X) = 0$, is likely to be violated since there are other factors to be controlled for, for example, demographic characteristics, actual job experience, and measure of ability.

Notes:
the NLSY79 (National Longitudinal Survey of Youth - 1979 Cohort) data set
https://www.nlsinfo.org/content/cohorts/nlsy79

Chapter Summary

How to measure the linear relationship between two variables	Covariance indicates the direction of the linear relationship, while the correlation coefficient measures its direction and magnitude within a bound of -1 and 1. As the positive relationship gets stronger, the correlation coefficient becomes close to 1. On the other hand, as the negative relationship gets stronger, the correlation coefficient gets close to -1. Also, as the linear relationship becomes weaker, the correlation coefficient gets close to 0.
Linear regression analysis	Linear comes from the first OLS assumption that the model is linear in parameters. The idea of estimating parameters in the model is to minimize the gaps (residuals) between the model prediction and the data points. Least Squares from the Ordinary Least Squares (OLS) come from minimizing the sum of residual squares. OLS assumptions are needed to make the regression model reliable in estimating the relationship between variables.
How to estimate the population parameter without bias	With the first to fourth OLS assumptions, the OLS estimator $\hat{\beta}_1$ is unbiased for β_1, the population parameter that we would like to know. That is, assuming the infinitely many OLS estimates from the infinitely many samples with the same sample size n, the average of them is the true population parameter, β_1. Particularly, the fourth OLS assumption (conditional mean independence assumption of the error term) is critical for the unbiased OLS estimator $\hat{\beta}_1$.

How to estimate the valid standard errors	With the first to fifth OLS assumption, the OLS estimation can provide the valid and most efficient standard errors. Particularly, the fifth assumption stating the equal variance of u over any value of X (Homoscedasticity) is critical to have the valid and most efficient standard errors.
How to precisely estimate the population parameter, β_1	More information (larger sample size), more explanation of the outcome variable by the regression model (smaller residual sum of squares), and more diverse characteristics of the explanatory variable (lager variance of the explanatory variable) lead to the narrower sampling distribution of the OLS estimator (the smaller standard error of the OLS estimator). This is helpful to precisely estimate the population parameter, β_1.
Addressing common misunderstandings and mistakes	Covariance and correlation coefficient do not suggest the causality between variables. There is no statistical estimation to directly indicate the causality. To argue the causality between variables, we need relevant assumptions and considerations. The validity of the first to fourth OLS assumptions is critical to estimate the causal relationship between X and Y. The three OLS properties should be understood separately from the OLS assumptions. Particularly, $\sum_{i=1}^{n} \hat{u} = 0$ and $\sum_{i=1}^{n} \hat{u}_i X_i = 0$ are nothing with the fourth OLS assumption, $E(u|X) = 0 \Rightarrow E(u) = 0$. An unbiased OLS estimator does not mean that the estimated coefficient, $\hat{\beta}_1$, from the sample is the population parameter, β_1.

Exercises

Chapter 3
Examining the relationship between the two continuous variables I: Correlation coefficient and introduction to the OLS regression analysis

1. Suppose that you would like to see the relationship between socio-economic measures and GDP per capita by analyzing 97 countries. It is found that the correlation between democracy index and GDP per capita is 0.72, the correlation between government trust and GDP per capita is 0.45, and the correlation between homicide rate and GDP per capita is -0.12.

(1) Please explain the implications of these three correlations.

(2) Please explain which one of socio-economic measures are strongest and weakest association with GDP per capita.

(3) Please evaluate the statement that increasing GDP is effective to improve democracy, government trust, and to suppress homicide rates.

2. Suppose that you examine the linear relationship between hourly wage in US dollars and cognitive skills measured by the AFQT score ranges from 1 and 100 (higher is better cognitive skills). The analysis sample is from the year of 1990 of the NLSY79 (National Longitudinal Survey of Youth - 1979 Cohort) data set. Please carefully answer the following questions.

(1) The covariance between hourly wage and the AFQT score is 48.80. Please explain what it means.

(2) You create the new AFQT score dividing the original value by 100. Then, the covariance between hourly wage and the new AFQT score is 0.488. Please explain why the covariance decreases and what it implies.

(3) Now, you find that the correlation coefficient between hourly wage and the original AFQT is the same as that between hourly wage and the new AFQT as below. Please explain why this happens and state the implications of the estimated correlation coefficients.

$$\text{Corr(hourly wage, AFQT)} = \text{Corr(hourly wage, new AFQT)} = 0.4135$$

3. Suppose that you investigate the impact of the campaign expenditure on winning a presidential election in South Korea and you have the following regression results.

$$\widehat{voteK} = 40.90 + 0.306 shareK$$
$$\text{SE} \quad (10.20) \quad (0.112)$$

$voteK$: the percentage of the vote received by Candidate K
$shareK$: the percentage of total campaign expenditures accounted for by Candidate K
$n = 82$

(1) Please interpret the estimated coefficient of $shareK$.

(2) Please state the OLS assumption to have the unbiased impact of the campaign expenditure on winning a presidential election

4. Suppose that for 180 nations in the world, the prediction equation relating Y = elderly poverty rate in 2010 to X = social expenditures as a percent of gross domestic product is

$$\hat{Y} = 22 - 2.1X$$
$$\text{SE} \quad (10) \quad (1.3)$$

where the standard errors are in parentheses. Y and X are valued in %.

We have SST (Total Sum of Squares) = 3,000.
SSE (Explained Sum of Squares) = 1,500; and
SSR (Residual Sum of Squares) = 1,500.

(1) Interpret the estimated coefficient of X. (5)

(2) Obtain R-squared and interpret it. (5)

5. Suppose that you are evaluating the causal impact of number of siblings on educational attainment. Suppose that your regression outcome is as follows.

$$\widehat{educ}_i = 14.139 - 0.228 sibs_i$$
$$\text{SE} \quad (0.113) \quad (0.030)$$

SSE = 258.055
SST = 4506.819
n = 935

(1) Please state the OLS assumption to have the unbiased impact of number of siblings on years of education.

(2) Interpret the estimated coefficient of $sibs_i$. Is it biased? If you are worried about other family characteristics that are not included but related to the number of siblings, which OLS assumption(s) is(are) violated?

6. There are some confusion between what we have with the OLS analysis (properties of the OLS analysis) and what we assume for the OLS analysis (OLS assumptions). Please carefully answer the following questions.

(1) Please explain what $\sum_{i=1}^{n} \hat{u}_i X_i = 0$ and $\sum_{i=1}^{n} \hat{u} = 0$ state.

(2) Please explain what $E(u|X) = 0 \Rightarrow E(u) = 0$ states.

(3) Please state the differences between the statements in (1) and (2).

7. Suppose that you would like to examine the impact of woman's education on fertility. The population of interest is women aged 40 to 67 in the 2007 Korean Longitudinal Survey of Women and Families (KLoWF). The outcome variable is the number of children while the explanatory variable is woman's education in years.

The regression result is as follows.

$$\hat{Y}_i = 3.445 - 0.109 X_i$$
$$\text{SE} \quad (0.037) \quad (0.004)$$

SST (Total Sum of Squares) = 6017.2828
SSE (Explained Sum of Squares) = 942.586497
SSR (Residual Sum of Squares) = 5074.6963
$R^2 = 0.1566$
$n = 5,046$
$\sum (X_i - \bar{X})^2 = 78720.3728$

The following regression result is from a subsample analysis for women whose mothers have completed at least high school.

$$\hat{Y}_i = 3.252 - 0.092 X_i$$
$$\text{SE} \quad (0.119) \quad (0.0097)$$

SST (Total Sum of Squares) = 525.674518
SSE (Explained Sum of Squares) = 85.9647818
SSR (Residual Sum of Squares) = 439.709736
$R^2 = 0.1635$
$n = 467$
$\sum (X_i - \bar{X})^2 = 10117.4218$

(1) Please state the population regression to estimate these two regressions and its implication.

(2) Please compare R-squared in these two regressions and explain why R-squared in the second regression is larger and its implication.

(3) Please explain the meaning of the estimated coefficients of education in years in these two regressions.

(4) Please state the OLS assumptions to have the unbiased estimates in these two regressions and the meaning of each assumption.

(5) Please compare the standard errors (SE) of the estimated coefficient of education in these two regressions and explain why the SE in the second regression is larger than that in the first one.

Chapter 4
Data Analysis for Social Science: Fundamental Methods

Examining the relationship between the two continuous variables II: Inference in the OLS regression analysis

The normally of the error term and the sampling distribution of the OLS estimator

Up to this point, we have covered how to construct the OLS estimator $\hat{\beta}_1$, and its standard error. However, we have yet to study how to develop confidence intervals and hypothesis tests for the population parameter β_1. To do so, we need to consider the shape and characteristics of the sampling distribution of the OLS estimator $\hat{\beta}_1$. As shown in the second section of the sample mean for the population mean, if the sampling distribution of the OLS estimator $\hat{\beta}_1$ is normally distributed, it is easy to develop confidence intervals and hypothesis tests for β_1.

By the Gauss-Markov Theorem, we learn that the OLS estimator $\hat{\beta}_1$ is the linear function of the error term under the five OLS assumptions:

$$\hat{\beta}_1 = \frac{\sum_{i=1}^{n}(X_i - \bar{X})Y_i}{\sum_{i=1}^{n}(X_i - \bar{X})^2} = \beta_1 + \frac{\sum_{i=1}^{n}(X_i - \bar{X})u_i}{\sum_{i=1}^{n}(X_i - \bar{X})^2},$$

Note that the linear function of a normally distributed variable also follows a normal distribution. Therefore, due to this property of the OLS estimator $\hat{\beta}_1$, if it is assumed that the error term, u_i, is normally distributed, the sampling distribution of the OLS estimator $\hat{\beta}_1$ follows the normal distribution. Thus, it is important to examine whether the normality assumption of the error term is reasonable and reliable in general. The error term in the regression model is the composite of all the unobserved factors that explain the outcome variable. Therefore, the characteristics of the population distribution of the error term follow the characteristics of the population distribution of the outcome variable. If the outcome variable is continuous and shows a bell-shaped symmetric distribution, it is reasonable to assume that the error term is normally distributed. However, there are plenty of exceptions: it is already well known that income and wage are not normally distributed (usually skewed to the right). Also, if the outcome variable is discrete ranking or binary, this assumption is easily violated. On the other hand, when the sample size gets larger, this normality assumption of the error term is not needed due to the Central Limit Theorem (CLT). Thus, when the sample size is small, extra attention is required to check whether the outcome variable is normally distributed.

The sixth assumption for inferences of a small sample OLS analysis is as follows.

$$u_i \sim N(0, \sigma^2)$$

This sixth assumption with the Gauss-Markov Theorem implies that

$$\hat{\beta}_1 \sim N\left(\beta_1, \frac{\sigma^2}{\sum_{i=1}^{n}(X_i - \bar{X})^2}\right).$$

This means that the OLS estimator $\hat{\beta}_1$ for β_1 follows the normal distribution with mean β_1 and variance $\frac{\sigma^2}{\sum_{i=1}^{n}(X_i - \bar{X})^2}$.

Under the six OLS assumptions, we now know the shape and main properties of the sampling distribution of $\hat{\beta}_1$ as shown in Figure 4.1. Using the properties of this sampling distribution, we can develop the confidence intervals and hypothesis tests for the population parameter, β_1.

Six OLS assumptions
① Linear in parameters and additive error term
② Random sample of X and Y
③ Variation in X
④ $E(u|X) = 0$
⑤ No heteroscedasticity $Var(u|X) = Var(u) = \sigma^2$
⑥ $u_i \sim N(0, \sigma^2)$

Figure 4.1 The sampling distribution of $\hat{\beta}_1$

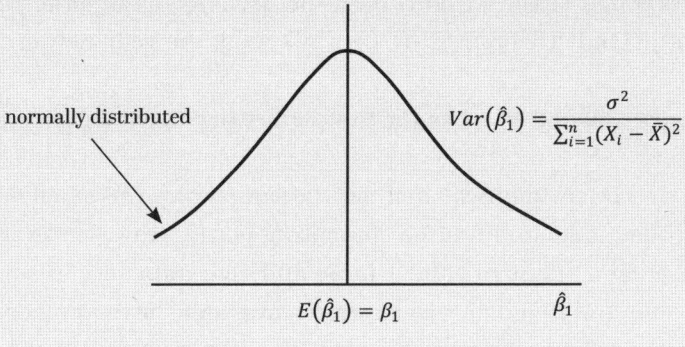

Under the six OLS assumptions,

$$\hat{\beta}_1 \sim N\left(\beta_1, \frac{\sigma^2}{\sum_{i=1}^n (X_i - \bar{X})^2}\right).$$

When we standardize the OLS estimator $\hat{\beta}_1$, then $\dfrac{\hat{\beta}_1 - \beta_1}{\left(\dfrac{\sigma}{\sqrt{\sum_{i=1}^n (X_i - \bar{X})^2}}\right)}$ follows the standard normal distribution.

Since σ is usually unknown, it is estimated using $\hat{\sigma} = \sqrt{\dfrac{\sum \widehat{u_i}^2}{n-k-1}}$.

Then, $\dfrac{\hat{\beta}_1 - \beta_1}{\left(\dfrac{\hat{\sigma}}{\sqrt{\sum_{i=1}^n (X_i - \bar{X})^2}}\right)}$ is the t-test statistic and follows the t distribution with the degree of freedom $= n-k-1$ where $\hat{\sigma} = \sqrt{\dfrac{\sum \widehat{u_i}^2}{n-k-1}}$.

In the degree of freedom $= n-k-1$, we have k to account for the number of the estimated coefficients of the explanatory variables and 1 to account for the estimated coefficient of the constant.

When n is large enough, $\dfrac{\hat{\beta}_1 - \beta_1}{\left(\dfrac{\hat{\sigma}}{\sqrt{\sum_{i=1}^n (X_i - \bar{X})^2}}\right)}$ approximately follows the standard normal distribution.

How large? Typically, if $n-k-1$ is larger than 100, it is safe to use the z distribution instead of the t distribution.

In summary, when the sample size n is small, we need to check the sixth OLS assumption, $u_i \sim N(0, \sigma^2)$, by examining the normality of the residuals or outcome variable to have valid confidence intervals and hypothesis tests. However, when the sample size n becomes larger, we don't need the sixth OLS assumption, $u_i \sim N(0, \sigma^2)$, due to the Central Limit Theorem (CLT). Let's talk about this right now in detail.

The linear regression model when the sample size becomes larger

During the early days of empirical analysis, the sample size was small due to limited resources to collect data and limited computing power. However, over time, more resources have been spent to collect large and rich data sets in social science. Nowadays, various and rich data sets have been available for researchers. One of the major advantages in OLS regression analysis with a large sample is that we don't need the normality assumption of the error term because of the Central Limit Theorem (CLT). Also, with a large random sample, the conditional independence assumption of the error term is loosened to assuming no correlation between the error term and the explanatory variables. Let's cover these two changes in detail. The summary of the OLS assumptions for the small sample and the large sample is shown below.

Small sample OLS analysis (Wooldridge, 2012: 120)

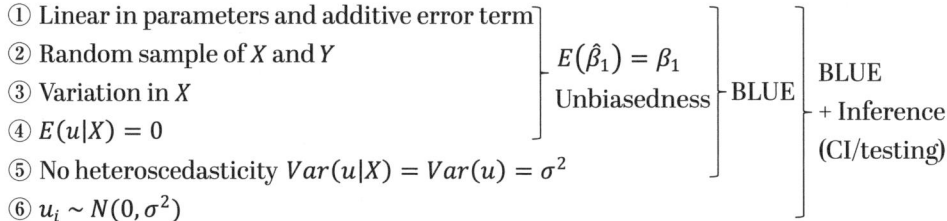

① Linear in parameters and additive error term
② Random sample of X and Y
③ Variation in X
④ $E(u|X) = 0$
⑤ No heteroscedasticity $Var(u|X) = Var(u) = \sigma^2$
⑥ $u_i \sim N(0, \sigma^2)$

$\left. \begin{array}{c} E(\hat{\beta}_1) = \beta_1 \\ \text{Unbiasedness} \end{array} \right\} \text{BLUE} \left. \begin{array}{c} \text{BLUE} \\ \text{+ Inference} \\ \text{(CI/testing)} \end{array} \right.$

Large sample OLS analysis (Wooldridge, 2012: 175)

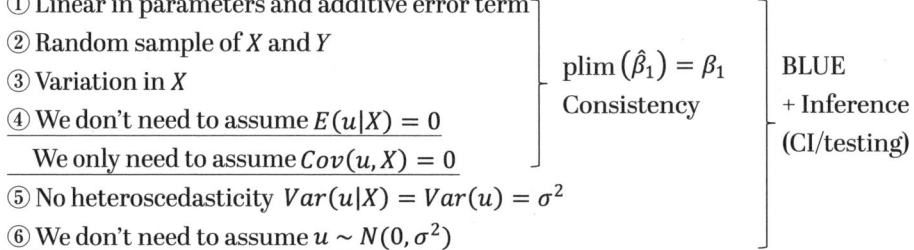

① Linear in parameters and additive error term
② Random sample of X and Y
③ Variation in X
④ We don't need to assume $E(u|X) = 0$
   We only need to assume $Cov(u, X) = 0$
⑤ No heteroscedasticity $Var(u|X) = Var(u) = \sigma^2$
⑥ We don't need to assume $u \sim N(0, \sigma^2)$

$\left. \begin{array}{c} \text{plim}(\hat{\beta}_1) = \beta_1 \\ \text{Consistency} \end{array} \right\} \begin{array}{c} \text{BLUE} \\ \text{+ Inference} \\ \text{(CI/testing)} \end{array}$

For the large sample analysis, the unbiasedness of OLS estimators is replaced by the consistency of OLS estimators. The main difference between unbiasedness and consistency of $\hat{\beta}_1$ for β_1 can be explained below.

1) Unbiasedness of $\hat{\beta}_1$ for β_1

$$E(\hat{\beta}_1) = \beta_1$$

Unbiasedness does not mean that the estimator $\hat{\beta}_1$ we get with a random sample is β_1 or even very close to β_1. It means that if we could draw infinitely many random samples from the population, compute an estimate $\hat{\beta}_1$ for each sample, and average these estimates, we would obtain β_1.

2) Consistency of $\hat{\beta}_1$ for β_1

$$\text{plim}(\hat{\beta}_1) = \beta_1$$

Consistency involves the behavior of the sampling distribution of $\hat{\beta}_1$ as the sample size n gets large. $\text{plim}(\hat{\beta}_1) = \beta_1$ means that as n gets larger and larger, the distribution of $\hat{\beta}_1$ becomes more and more concentrated around β_1. $Var(\hat{\beta}_1)$ gets close to 0 as n becomes larger. Thus, $\hat{\beta}_1$ becomes more likely to be close to β_1 for a large random sample.

Therefore, we may say that different from the unbiasedness of $\hat{\beta}_1$, the consistency of $\hat{\beta}_1$ is more informative about the location of $\hat{\beta}_1$ as the sample size gets larger. As a result, it gives more confidence to researchers.

Particularly, it is noticeable that the fourth OLS assumption for the unbiased estimator $\hat{\beta}_1$ is $E(u|X) = 0$, while the fourth OLS assumption for the consistent estimator $\hat{\beta}_1$ is $Cov(u, X) = 0$. $Cov(u, X) = 0$ is the weaker assumption than $E(u|X) = 0$. In other words, $Cov(u, X) = 0$ is easier to validate than $E(u|X) = 0$. Therefore, analyzing a large sample is more beneficial to researchers than analyzing a small sample.

Also, when the sample size is small, we need to assume $u \sim N(0, \sigma^2)$ to have the normally distributed sampling distribution of the OLS estimator $\hat{\beta}_1$. This condition enables the construction of valid confidence intervals and hypothesis tests for β_1. On the other hand, when the sample size is large enough, the five assumptions for large sample OLS analysis allow for Best Linear Unbiased Estimator (BLUE) and the normality of the OLS estimator $\hat{\beta}_1$, facilitating the construction of valid confidence intervals and hypothesis tests for β_1. As the sample size increases, the sixth OLS assumption, $u \sim N(0, \sigma^2)$, becomes unnecessary. Instead, the normality of the OLS estimator $\hat{\beta}_1$ is ensured as the distribution of $\frac{1}{\sqrt{n}} \sum X_i u_i$ asymptotically approaches the normal distribution, thanks to the Central Limit Theorem (CLT). However, it is important to note that the distribution of the error term does not tend to become close to the normal distribution as the sample size increases.

Form now on, let's assume the large sample OLS analysis in general.

Example 4.1

Suppose that we are interested in the relationship between hourly wage and education.

We are using hourly wage in 1980 U.S. dollars (Y) and years of education (X) in the year 1990 of the NLSY79 (National Longitudinal Survey of Youth - 1979 Cohort) data set.

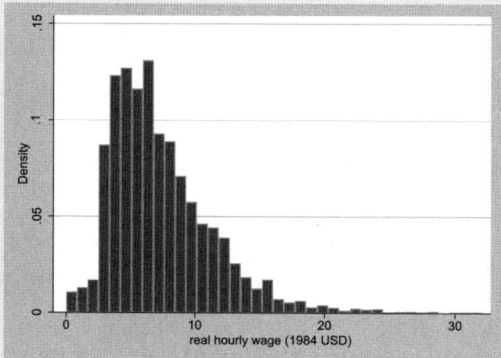

Sample mean = 7.46
Sample standard deviation = 4.09

As shown in this figure, we use the real hourly wage in 1984 U.S. dollars. It is obvious that it is not normally distributed, as shown here. It is skewed to the right and implies the violation of the sixth OLS assumption. However, since we have a large sample in this analysis, 7,707, it is valid to run the regression model and interpret the estimated results under the 1 to 5 OLS assumptions stated earlier. Under the five OLS assumptions with a large sample, the sampling distribution of the OLS estimator approximately follows the normal distribution, which allows BLUE and inference procedures, including confidence intervals and hypothesis tests.

The regression outcome is as follows.

$$\widehat{Y}_i = -0.587 + 0.62X_i$$
$$\text{SE} \quad (0.231) \quad (0.017)$$

SST (Total Sum of Squares) = 128911.008

SSE (Explained Sum of Squares) = 18083.2888

SSR (Residual Sum of Squares) = 110827.719

R^2 = 0.1403

n = 7,707

Under the five OLS assumptions with the large sample, we can say that the estimated coefficient of education is consistent for the true parameter β_1.

Notes:

the NLSY79 (National Longitudinal Survey of Youth -1979 Cohort) data set

https://www.nlsinfo.org/content/cohorts/nlsy79

Example 4.2

Suppose that we would like to examine whether education is related to cognitive ability.

We are using years of education (Y) and AFQT (X) in the year 1990 of the NLSY79 (National Longitudinal Survey of Youth - 1979 Cohort) data set. Like IQ, AFQT is the cognitive measure ranging from 1 to 100 in the sample.

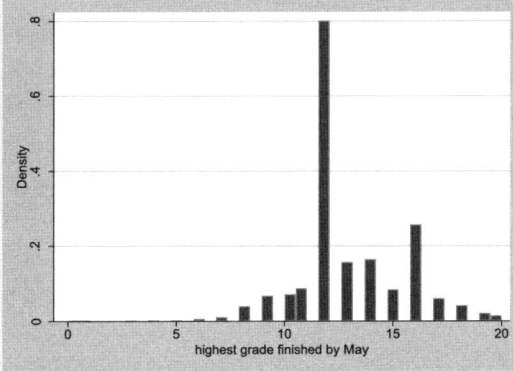

Sample mean = 12.97

Sample standard deviation = 2.47

As shown in this figure, we use the highest grade finished by May for the outcome variable to measure the level of education. This is the number of years of education that is a discrete variable ranging from 0 to 20. It is obvious that it is not normally distributed, as shown here. It suggests a violation of the sixth OLS assumption. However, since we have a large sample in this analysis, 7,707, it is valid to do the regression analysis with the confidence intervals and hypothesis tests. Under the five OLS assumptions with a large sample, the sampling distribution of the OLS estimator approximately follows the normal distribution, which allows BLUE and inference procedures, including confidence intervals and hypothesis tests.

The regression outcome is as follows.

$$\hat{Y}_i = 10.84 + 0.052 X_i$$
$$\text{SE} \quad (0.039) \quad (0.001)$$

SST (Total Sum of Squares) = 47023.834

SSE (Explained Sum of Squares) = 17404.914

SSR (Residual Sum of Squares) = 29618.92

$R^2 = 0.37$

$n = 7,707$

The estimated coefficient of AFQT implies that one more point increase in AFQT is associated with a 0.052 increase in years of education. In other words, a 10 more points increase in AFQT predicts a half-year increase in years of education.

Also, under the five OLS assumptions with the large sample, it is valid to say that the estimated coefficient of AFQT is consistent for the true parameter β_1.

R-squared indicates that AFQT explains about 37% of the total variation of education in this analysis.

Notes:

the NLSY79 (National Longitudinal Survey of Youth -1979 Cohort) data set

https://www.nlsinfo.org/content/cohorts/nlsy79

The Confidence Interval (CI) for the regression parameter β_1

Let's see how to develop the confidence interval starting with $\dfrac{\hat{\beta}_1 - \beta_1}{\left(\dfrac{\sigma}{\sqrt{\sum_{i=1}^{n}(X_i-\bar{X})^2}}\right)} \sim N(0,1)$ under the six OLS assumptions for small sample analysis.

$$P\left(-1.96 < \dfrac{\hat{\beta}_1 - \beta_1}{\left(\dfrac{\sigma}{\sqrt{\sum_{i=1}^{n}(X_i-\bar{X})^2}}\right)} < 1.96\right) = 0.95$$

$$\Rightarrow P\left(-1.96 * \left(\dfrac{\sigma}{\sqrt{\sum_{i=1}^{n}(X_i-\bar{X})^2}}\right) < \hat{\beta}_1 - \beta_1 < 1.96 * \left(\dfrac{\sigma}{\sqrt{\sum_{i=1}^{n}(X_i-\bar{X})^2}}\right)\right) = 0.95$$

$$\Rightarrow P\left(-\hat{\beta}_1 - 1.96 * \left(\dfrac{\sigma}{\sqrt{\sum_{i=1}^{n}(X_i-\bar{X})^2}}\right) < -\beta_1 < -\hat{\beta}_1 + 1.96 * \left(\dfrac{\sigma}{\sqrt{\sum_{i=1}^{n}(X_i-\bar{X})^2}}\right)\right) = 0.95$$

$$\Rightarrow P\left(\hat{\beta}_1 - 1.96 * \left(\dfrac{\sigma}{\sqrt{\sum_{i=1}^{n}(X_i-\bar{X})^2}}\right) < \beta_1 < \hat{\beta}_1 + 1.96 * \left(\dfrac{\sigma}{\sqrt{\sum_{i=1}^{n}(X_i-\bar{X})^2}}\right)\right) = 0.95$$

According to the first equation, with 95% chance, the random variable $Z = \dfrac{\hat{\beta}_1 - \beta_1}{\left(\dfrac{\sigma}{\sqrt{\sum_{i=1}^{n}(X_i-\bar{X})^2}}\right)}$ lies between -1.96 and 1.96. 1.96 can be found in the z table for the 2.5% tail probability.

Then, the second to third steps indicate how the terms are rearranged by algebra: the inequality terms should be held after multiplying, adding, or subtracting the same terms on both sides.

The last equation is what we want to use since the population parameter β_1, unknown truth, is bounded by the estimates that we can obtain from the sample. The left and right ends consist of $\hat{\beta}_1$, 1.96, and $\dfrac{\sigma}{\sqrt{\sum_{i=1}^{n}(X_i-\bar{X})^2}}$ that are fixed or can be estimated from the sample. Thus, although the true value of β_1 is unknown, it is possible to make a scientific estimation about it.

Thus,

95% CI for β_1: $\left[\hat{\beta}_1 - 1.96 * \left(\dfrac{\sigma}{\sqrt{\sum_{i=1}^{n}(X_i-\bar{X})^2}}\right), \hat{\beta}_1 + 1.96 * \left(\dfrac{\sigma}{\sqrt{\sum_{i=1}^{n}(X_i-\bar{X})^2}}\right)\right]$

99% CI for β_1: $\left[\hat{\beta}_1 - 2.58 * \left(\dfrac{\sigma}{\sqrt{\sum_{i=1}^{n}(X_i-\bar{X})^2}}\right), \hat{\beta}_1 + 2.58 * \left(\dfrac{\sigma}{\sqrt{\sum_{i=1}^{n}(X_i-\bar{X})^2}}\right)\right]$

As we covered in the earlier chapter, 2.58 can be found in the z table for the 0.5% tail probability.

Since σ is usually unknown, we use $\hat{\sigma} = \sqrt{\dfrac{\sum \widehat{u_i}^2}{n-k-1}}$ for σ and $k=1$ in the simple regression model with one explanatory variable.

Then, as shown below, the 95% and 99% confidence intervals can be constructed using the *t*-scores.

95% CI for β_1: $\left[\hat{\beta}_1 - t_{0.025,\,df=n-k-1} * se(\hat{\beta}_1), \hat{\beta}_1 + t_{0.025,\,df=n-k-1} * se(\hat{\beta}_1)\right]$

99% CI for β_1: $\left[\hat{\beta}_1 - t_{0.0005,\,df=n-k-1} * se(\hat{\beta}_1), \hat{\beta}_1 + t_{0.0005,\,df=n-k-1} * se(\hat{\beta}_1)\right]$

where $se(\hat{\beta}_1) = \dfrac{\hat{\sigma}}{\sqrt{\sum_{i=1}^{n}(X_i-\bar{X})^2}}$

The *t*-score ($t_{0.025,\,df=n-k-1}$) for the 95% CI corresponds to the z-score (1.96) for the 2.5% tail probability, while the *t*-score ($t_{0.005,\,df=n-k-1}$) for the 99% CI corresponds to the z-score (2.58) for the 0.5% tail probability. For instance, $t_{0.025,\,df=32-1-1} = 2.042$, larger than the z-score (1.96) for the 2.5% tail probability.

If we assume the large sample, it is fine to use the z distribution to have the confidence intervals instead of the *t* distribution since the *t* distribution converges to the z distribution as *n* gets larger. Also, the five OLS assumptions for large sample analysis is enough.

As we discussed earlier in the earlier chapter, when we interpret the estimated results of the 95% confidence interval, it is wrong to say that

with a 95% probability,

β_1 lies within the constructed interval, $\hat{\beta}_1 \pm 1.96 * \left(\dfrac{\sigma}{\sqrt{\sum_{i=1}^{n}(X_i-\bar{X})^2}}\right)$.

It is appropriate to say the following three statements for the 95% confidence interval for the OLS regression coefficient β_1.

(1) We are 95% confident that the constructed interval would contain the population parameter β_1 or the population parameter β_1 lies within the constructed interval.

(2) For 95% of all potential random samples, the constructed interval would contain the population parameter β_1.

(3) If we repeatedly selected random samples of size n and each time constructed a 95% confidence interval, then in the long run, about 95% of intervals would contain β_1.

Obviously, the first way of interpreting the CI is the most straightforward and popular in practice.

Example 4.3

As shown before, the regression result below is obtained using hourly wage in 1980 U.S. dollars (Y) and years of education (X) in the year 1990 of the NLSY79 (National Longitudinal Survey of Youth - 1979 Cohort) data set.

$$\hat{Y}_i = -0.587 + 0.62 X_i$$
$$\text{SE} \quad (0.231) \quad (0.017)$$

SST (Total Sum of Squares) = 128911.008
SSE (Explained Sum of Squares) = 18083.2888
SSR (Residual Sum of Squares) = 110827.719
R^2 = 0.1403
n = 7,707

From this analysis, the estimated coefficient of education indicates that a one-year increase in education implies around a $0.62 increase in real hourly wage. We stated that the estimated coefficients are valid under OLS assumptions 1 to 4 above, and the standard errors are valid under OLS assumptions 1 to 5. Additionally, under OLS assumptions 1 to 5 with the large sample, we can construct the 95% confidence interval for β_1 as below. Since the sample size is large, we can use the z-score, 1.96, for the 2.5% tail probability in the standard normal distribution in this confidence interval.

$$[0.62-1.96*0.017, 0.62-1.96*0.017] = [0.587, 0.653]$$

Therefore, we can say that we are 95% confident that the true parameter of education lies between 0.587 and 0.653.

Notes:
the NLSY79 (National Longitudinal Survey of Youth - 1979 Cohort) data set
https://www.nlsinfo.org/content/cohorts/nlsy79

Example 4.4

Also, we have the following regression using years of education (Y) and AFQT (X) in the year 1990 of the NLSY79 (National Longitudinal Survey of Youth - 1979 Cohort) data set. Like IQ, AFQT is the cognitive measure ranging from 1 to 100 in the sample.

$$\widehat{Y}_i = 10.84 + 0.052X_i$$
$$\text{SE} \quad (0.039) \quad (0.001)$$

SST (Total Sum of Squares) = 47023.834
SSE (Explained Sum of Squares) = 17404.914
SSR (Residual Sum of Squares) = 29618.92
R^2 = 0.37
n = 7,707

Under the five OLS assumptions with the large sample, the 95% confidence interval for the true coefficient of AFQT is as follows.

$$[0.052-1.96*0.001, 0.052+1.96*0.001] \rightarrow [0.05, 0.054]$$

Thus, we are 95% confident that the true coefficient of AFQT lies between 0.05 and 0.054.

Notes:
the NLSY79 (National Longitudinal Survey of Youth - 1979 Cohort) data set

https://www.nlsinfo.org/content/cohorts/nlsy79

Hypothesis test for the regression parameter β_1

It is time to talk about the hypothesis test. As we mentioned earlier, the coefficients of the explanatory variables imply the relationship between the explanatory variable and the outcome variable. When we start studying certain topics in social science, stories and anecdotal observations are structured into theories. For example, our story about more education and a better life is framed into the human capital theory. Also, another observation about typical complaints about buying a used car is framed into the information asymmetry theory. To test theories, we collect the representative data for the population of interest, develop the regression model, and test the hypothesis of the related coefficient.

Specifically, to construct the hypothesis test for β_1, we need to study the sampling distribution of $\hat{\beta}_1$. The sampling distribution of the OLS estimator $\hat{\beta}_1$ in Figure 4.2, is developed under the five OLS assumptions with the large sample stated earlier. The sampling distribution of the OLS estimator is the collection of possible values of the OLS estimator, which is conceptually defined for the population. To easily understand the sampling distribution, we can think about the infinitely many OLS estimates from the infinitely many large samples with the same sample size n. In this distribution under the five OLS assumptions, the OLS estimator is consistent for the population parameter, $\text{plim}(\hat{\beta}_j) = \beta_j$, and the variance is most efficient, smallest $Var(\hat{\beta}_j)$. Also, the distribution is normally distributed.

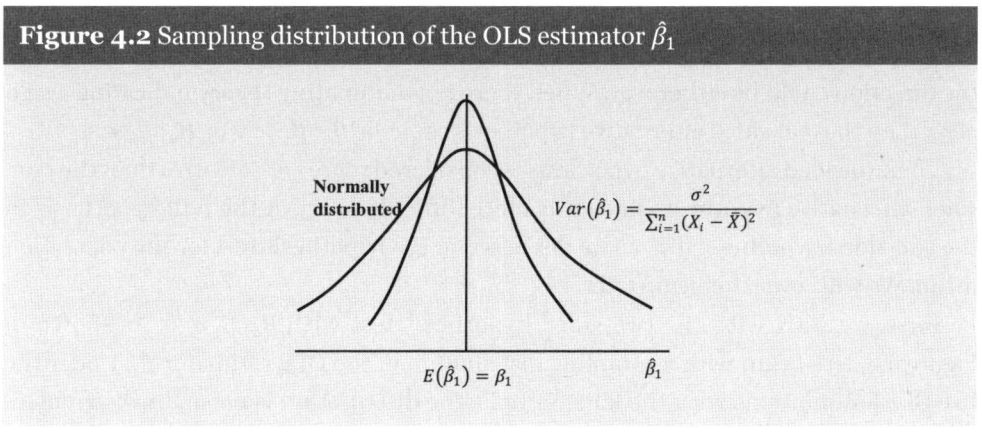

Figure 4.2 Sampling distribution of the OLS estimator $\hat{\beta}_1$

$$\hat{\beta}_1 \sim N\left(\beta_1, \frac{\sigma^2}{\sum_{i=1}^n (X_i - \bar{X})^2}\right)$$

$$\Rightarrow \frac{\hat{\beta}_1 - \beta_1}{\left(\frac{\sigma}{\sqrt{\sum_{i=1}^n (X_i - \bar{X})^2}}\right)} \sim N(0, 1)$$

Therefore, the standardized variable, $\frac{\hat{\beta}_1 - \beta_1}{\left(\frac{\sigma}{\sqrt{\sum_{i=1}^n (X_i - \bar{X})^2}}\right)}$, follows the standard normal distribution.

In the sampling distribution of $\hat{\beta}_1$, we don't know the true value of the population parameter β_1. The hypothesis test starts with setting β_1 to be a conventional value we would like to challenge. In other words, the hypothesis test is about whether the sample provides substantial evidence to challenge the conventional belief of the population parameter β_1. In the OLS analysis, the conventional belief of the population parameter β_1 is that the explanatory variable is not related to the outcome variable. That is, the population parameter β_1 is assumed to be 0.

Therefore, the null hypothesis is as follows:

$$H_o: \beta_1 = 0$$

Then, the alternative hypothesis is constructed to challenge the null hypothesis as follows:

$$H_a: \beta_1 \neq 0$$

This two-sided alternative hypothesis implies that it is possible that β_1 is not 0, but the direction could be either way. When there is a dominating theory indicating a sign of β_1, then the one-sided alternative hypothesis could be $H_a: \beta_1 > 0$ or $H_a: \beta_1 < 0$.

The two-sided alternative hypothesis is considered more conservative than the one-sided alternative hypothesis since it is more difficult to reject the null hypothesis in the two-sided hypothesis test, as we discussed in the hypothesis test for the population mean. We will cover this again later.

First, we start with the two-sided hypothesis test with $H_a: \beta_1 \neq 0$. As shown in Figure 4.3, let's begin with a sampling distribution of the OLS estimator $\hat{\beta}_1$. Under the five OLS assumptions with the large sample, the distribution is normally distributed, and $E(\hat{\beta}_1) = \beta_1$ is located in the center of the distribution. It is assumed that $\beta_1 = 0$ under the null hypothesis.

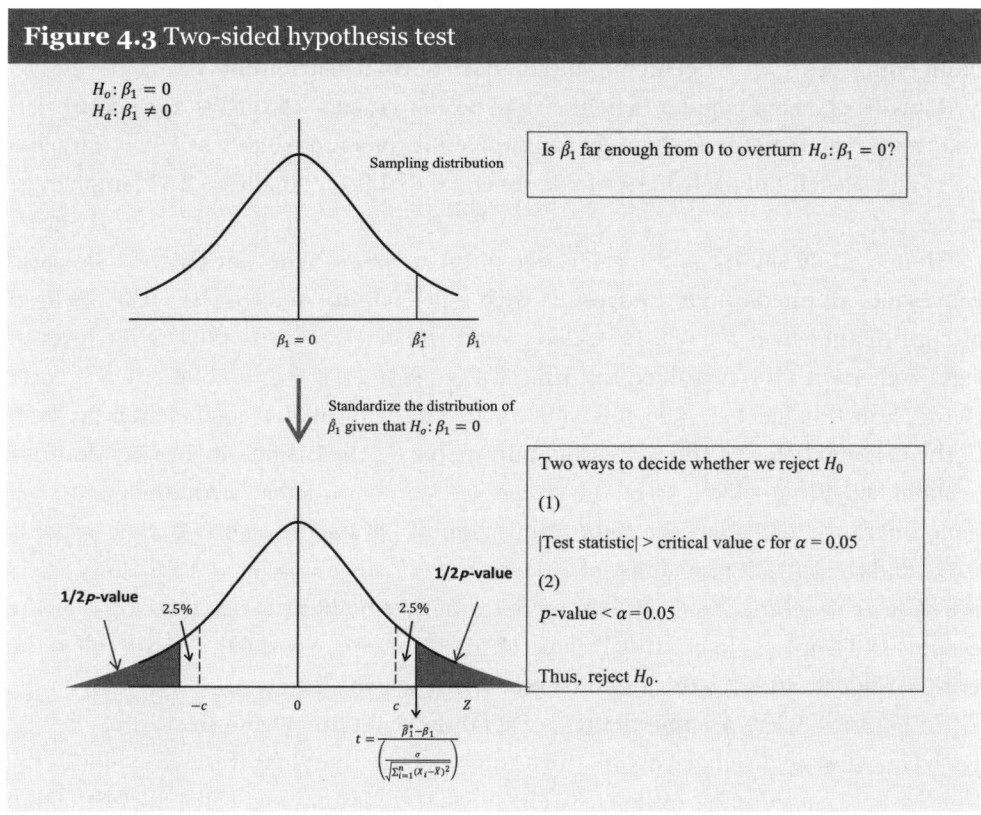

Figure 4.3 Two-sided hypothesis test

Then, suppose that $\hat{\beta}_1^*$ is the estimate we obtained from a sample and is located on the right side of the sampling distribution of $\hat{\beta}_1$. Under one of the OLS assumptions that the random sample for the study is well collected and represents the population of interest, we are wondering about the implication of the OLS estimate, $\hat{\beta}_1^*$, which is far away from $\beta_1 = 0$.

It is reasonable to think that the farther the OLS estimate is away from 0, the stronger the evidence from the OLS analysis is to challenge the null hypothesis. Then, how far is enough to reject the null hypothesis? To measure the distance between the OLS estimate and 0, we standardize the sampling distribution of the OLS estimator. As shown in Figure 4.3, the standardized variable of the OLS estimator is the test statistic, $\dfrac{\hat{\beta}_1 - \beta_1}{\left(\dfrac{\sigma}{\sqrt{\sum_{i=1}^{n}(X_i - \bar{X})^2}}\right)}$. Since the test statistic follows the standard normal distribution, it is easy to examine how far the test statistic estimated from the sample is from 0 using the z distribution table.

The alternative hypothesis indicates a possibility that the true population parameter can be smaller or greater than 0. Thus, the benchmark distance also should be on both sides from the center of the standard normal distribution, 0.

Usually, ±1.96 is a popular benchmark to be compared with the distance between 0 and the test statistic since the right tail probability of z-score equal to 1.96 or larger is 2.5%, and the left tail probability of z-score equal to -1.96 or smaller is 2.5%, implying a rare event.

Hence, ±1.96 serves as the reference point to assess whether the test statistic represents an uncommon occurrence with a probability of 5% or less (the 5% level of significance or $\alpha = 0.05$). It is also called the critical value for the 5% level of significance with the two-sided test (the two-tailed test). If the test statistic is greater than 1.96 or smaller than -1.96, it is safe to say that the estimated coefficient is far from 0, the original belief of the regression parameter β_1. Or it is possible to say that our original belief is less likely to be the true regression parameter β_1. Another well-used benchmark is ±2.58 since the right tail probability of z-score that is 2.58 or larger is 0.5%, and the left tail probability of z-score that is 2.58 or smaller is 0.5%. Thus, ±2.58 is a stricter benchmark since it is used to examine whether the test statistic is a rare event with 1% or less chance (the 1% level of significance or $\alpha = 0.01$). ±2.58 is called the critical value for the 1% level of significance with the two-sided test.

In Figure 4.3, let's assume that the test statistic obtained from the sample is 2.15. Based on what we discussed above, since 2.15 is greater than 1.96, it is reasonable to say that we have considerable evidence to challenge the conventional belief under the null hypothesis. Also, the chance that our argument is wrong is quite small, 5%, which is called the type I error (Reject the null hypothesis when it is true). As a result, we reject the null hypothesis with the 5% level of significance in the two-sided test.

We have another way to investigate whether the distance between the OLS estimate and the value of the regression parameter β_1, typically 0, under the null hypothesis is large enough to challenge the null hypothesis. It is possible to examine the tail probabilities of the critical value and the test statistic. When the tail probability of the test statistic is smaller than that of the critical value, it is evident that the test statistic is far enough from 0. Thus, we can reject the null hypothesis. In this examination, the tail probability of the test statistic is the "p-value." When we conduct the two-sided hypothesis test, the p-value equals twice the probability that the z-score matches the test statistic or is greater. When $P(Z>2.15) = 0.0158$, the p-value for the test statistic of 2.15 is 0.0316 since $0.0158 \times 2 = 0.0316$. As a result, it is reasonable to state that we reject the null hypothesis at the 5% level of significance since 3.16% is less than 5%.

Statistical software packages such as SAS, Stata, and R usually report the p-value in the two-sided hypothesis test as a default when they report the test statistics. Thus, it is easy to compare the p-value with our confidence level to determine whether our analysis rejects the null hypothesis or not.

Since σ is usually unknown, we use $\hat{\sigma} = \sqrt{\frac{\sum \hat{u}_i^2}{n-k-1}}$ for σ and $k=1$ in the simple regression model.

Then, the test statistic $t = \frac{\hat{\beta}_1 - \beta_1}{se(\hat{\beta}_1)} = \frac{\hat{\beta}_1 - \beta_1}{\left(\frac{\hat{\sigma}}{\sqrt{\sum_{i=1}^{n}(X_i - \bar{X})^2}}\right)} \sim t_{df = n-k-1}$

Since the test statistic follows the t distribution with the degree of freedom, $n-k-1$, the critical value for $\alpha = 0.05$ is $t_{df=n-k-1,\ 0.025}$. n is the sample size, and k is the number of explanatory variables in the model. This critical value from the t distribution is larger than ± 1.96 from the z distribution while it approaches to ± 1.96 as the degree of freedom, $n-k-1$, gets bigger. For example, $t_{df=30-1-1,\ 0.025} = 2.048$ and $t_{df=122-1-1,\ 0.025} = 1.98$.

Since large samples are common in modern data analysis, and we assume the large sample in the OLS analysis, it is safe to use the z distribution without worrying about the varying critical values under the t distribution with the degree of freedom.

Example 4.5

As shown before, the regression result below is obtained using hourly wage in 1980 U.S. dollars (Y) and years of education (X) in the year 1990 of the NLSY79 (National Longitudinal Survey of Youth - 1979 Cohort) data set.

$$\hat{Y}_i = -0.587 + 0.62 X_i$$
SE (0.231) (0.017)

SST (Total Sum of Squares) = 128911.008
SSE (Explained Sum of Squares) = 18083.2888
SSR (Residual Sum of Squares) = 110827.719
R^2 = 0.1403

$n = 7{,}707$

From this analysis, the estimated coefficient of education indicates that a one-year increase in education implies around a $0.62 increase in real hourly wage. We stated that the estimated coefficients are valid under OLS assumptions 1 to 4 above, and the standard errors are valid under OLS assumptions 1 to 5. Additionally, under OLS assumptions 1 to 5 with the large sample, we can conduct the two-sided hypothesis test with the 5% significance level ($\alpha = 0.05$) with the following null and alternative hypotheses.

$$H_o: \beta_1 = 0$$
$$H_a: \beta_1 \neq 0$$

$$t = \frac{\hat{\beta}_1 - \beta_1}{se(\hat{\beta}_1)} = \frac{0.62 - 0}{0.017} = 3.65$$

Since 3.65 is greater than 1.96 (the critical value for the 2.5% tail probability in the standard normal distribution), we can say that we reject the null hypothesis at the 5% significance level.

Therefore, it is likely that the true parameter of education is different from 0.

Notes:
the NLSY79 (National Longitudinal Survey of Youth - 1979 Cohort) data set
https://www.nlsinfo.org/content/cohorts/nlsy79

Example 4.6

Suppose that we have the following regression using years of education (Y) and AFQT (X) in the year 1990 of the NLSY79 (National Longitudinal Survey of Youth - 1979 Cohort) data set. Like IQ, AFQT is the cognitive measure ranging from 1 to 100 in the sample.

$$\hat{Y}_i = 10.84 + 0.052 X_i$$
$$\text{SE} \quad (0.039) \quad (0.001)$$

SST (Total Sum of Squares) = 47023.834
SSE (Explained Sum of Squares) = 17404.914
SSR (Residual Sum of Squares) = 29618.92
$R^2 = 0.37$
$n = 7,707$

Under the five OLS assumptions with the large sample, we do the hypothesis test for the coefficient of AFQT with the 1% significance level.

The null and alternative hypotheses for the two-sided hypothesis test are as follows.

$$H_o: \beta_1 = 0$$
$$H_a: \beta_1 \neq 0$$

$$t = \frac{\hat{\beta}_1 - \beta_1}{se(\hat{\beta}_1)} = \frac{0.052 - 0}{0.001} = 52$$

Since 52 is greater than 2.58 (critical value for the 0.5% tail probability in the standard normal distribution), we can say that we reject the null hypothesis at the 1% significance level.

Therefore, it is likely that the true parameter of AFQT is different from 0.

Notes:
the NLSY79 (National Longitudinal Survey of Youth - 1979 Cohort) data set
https://www.nlsinfo.org/content/cohorts/nlsy79

The first alternative hypothesis we studied earlier, $H_a: \beta_1 \neq 0$, is usually used for the hypothesis tests since it is compatible with our generic assumption that we don't know. Also, it is reliable when competing theories suggest the opposite directions in the relationship between X and Y.

The other two alternative hypotheses, such as $H_a: \beta_1 > 0$ and $H_a: \beta_1 < 0$, are used when there is a strong theory indicating one clear direction in the relationship between X and Y. In these one-sided alternative hypotheses, it is important to examine whether the true population parameter is greater than 0 for $H_a: \beta_1 > 0$ and smaller than 0 for $H_a: \beta_1 < 0$.

Figure 4.4 illustrates the case of the one-sided test(the one-tailed test) with the null hypothesis $H_o: \beta_1 = 0$ and the alternative hypothesis $H_a: \beta_1 > 0$.

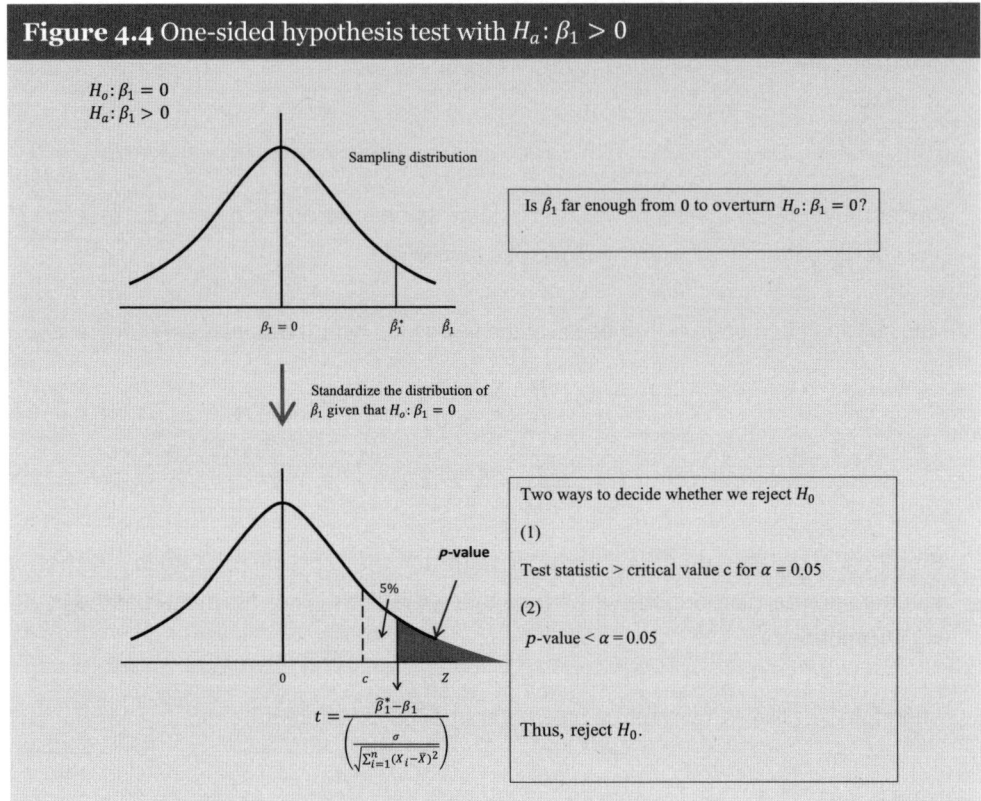

Figure 4.4 One-sided hypothesis test with $H_a: \beta_1 > 0$

Then, again, we need to set the benchmark distance from the center of the standard normal distribution, 0. This time, we only care about the positive side from 0.

For the 5% significance test with $H_a: \beta_1 > 0$, instead of using ±1.96, we use 1.645 as a benchmark to be compared with the distance between 0 and the test statistic since the right tail probability of z-score equal to 1.645 or larger is 5%, implying a rare event. 1.645 is called the critical value for the 5% level of significance with the one-sided test. If the test statistic is greater than 1.645, it is safe to say that the estimated coefficient is far enough from 0, the original belief of the regression parameter β_1. Or it is reasonable to say that 0 is less likely to be the true value of the regression parameter β_1. Further, 2.326 is used as a benchmark for the 1% significance test since the right tail probability of z-score that is 2.326 or larger is 1%. It is the critical value for the 1% level of significance with the one-sided test. For example, when the test statistic is 2, we reject the null hypothesis at the 5% level of significance, but we don't reject the null hypothesis at the 1% level of significance. As noted here, since the critical values with the one-sided test, 1.645 and 2.326, are smaller than those with the two-sided test, 1.96 and 2.58, in absolute values, it is easy to reject the null hypothesis in the one-sided test with the same test statistic. We can also use the p-value to do the hypothesis test: since $P(Z > 2) = 0.023$, the p-value of 2 is 0.023, which is smaller than 0.05 and greater than 0.01. Thus, we reject the null hypothesis at the 5% significance level but don't reject it at the 1% significance level.

Example 4.7

As shown before, the regression result below is obtained using hourly wage in 1980 U.S. dollars (Y) and years of education (X) in the year 1990 of the NLSY79 (National Longitudinal Survey of Youth - 1979 Cohort) data set.

$$\hat{Y}_i = -0.587 + 0.62 X_i$$
$$\text{SE} \quad (0.231) \quad (0.017)$$

SST (Total Sum of Squares) = 128911.008
SSE (Explained Sum of Squares) = 18083.2888
SSR (Residual Sum of Squares) = 110827.719
$R^2 = 0.1403$
$n = 7,707$

From this analysis, the estimated coefficient of education indicates that a one-year increase in education implies around a $0.62 increase in real hourly wage. We stated that the estimated coefficients are valid under OLS assumptions 1 to 4 above, and the standard errors are valid under OLS assumptions 1 to 5.

Under OLS assumptions 1 to 5 with the large sample, let's conduct the one-sided hypothesis test with 5% significance level ($\alpha = 0.05$) with the following null and alternative hypotheses.

$$H_o: \beta_1 = 0$$
$$H_a: \beta_1 > 0$$

$$t = \frac{\hat{\beta}_1 - \beta_1}{se(\hat{\beta}_1)} = \frac{0.62 - 0}{0.017} = 3.65$$

Since 3.65 is greater than 1.645 (the critical value for the 5% tail probability in the standard normal distribution), we can say that we reject the null hypothesis at the 5% significance level.

Therefore, it is likely that the true parameter of education is greater than 0.

The critical value, $z_{0.05}$ = 1.645, with the one-sided test is smaller than that, $z_{0.025}$ =1.96, with the two-sided test in Example 4.6. The significance level is the same as 5%, but the tail probability with the one-sided, 5%, is larger in the one-sided test than that in the two-sided test, 2.5%.

Notes:
the NLSY79 (National Longitudinal Survey of Youth - 1979 Cohort) data set
https://www.nlsinfo.org/content/cohorts/nlsy79

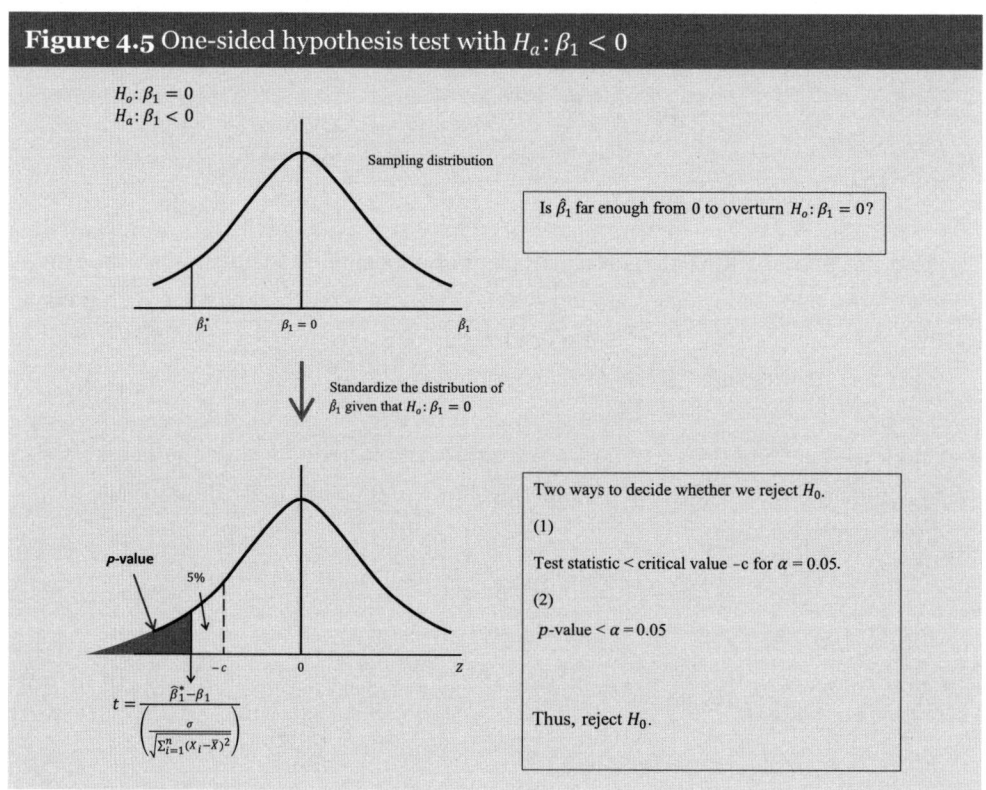

Figure 4.5 One-sided hypothesis test with $H_a: \beta_1 < 0$

Figure 4.5 illustrates the case of the one-sided test with the null hypothesis $H_o: \beta_1 = 0$ and the alternative hypothesis $H_a: \beta_1 < 0$. How to proceed with the test is the same as in the earlier case of the alternative hypothesis $H_a: \beta_1 > 0$. This time, -1.645 is a benchmark to be compared with the distance between 0 and the test statistic since the left tail probability of z-score equal to -1.645 or farther away from 0 is 5%, implying a rare event. In this case, -1.645 is called the critical value for the 5% level of significance with the one-sided test. Thus, if the test statistic is greater than 1.645 in absolute value (farther away from 0), it is evident that the estimated coefficient is far enough from 0, the original belief of the regression parameter β_1. Or it is fine to say that the true regression parameter β_1 is not likely to be 0. For the 1% significance test, -2.326 is used as a benchmark since the left tail probability of z-score that is -2.326 or farther away from 0 is 1%.

Suppose that the test statistic is -1.8. Then, we reject the null hypothesis at the 5% level of significance since -1.8 is greater than 1.645 in absolute value. Also, since P(Z -1.8) = 0.036, the p-value of -1.8 is 0.036, which is smaller than 0.05. Thus, we have the same conclusion that we reject the null hypothesis at the 5% level of significance.

In conclusion, the general steps of hypothesis tests of the population parameter in the OLS regression model are summarized below.

<Hypothesis tests of the population parameter β_1 in the OLS regression model>

(1) Think about a research question
(2) Develop H_o & H_a based on a research question: Two-sided test or one-sided test?
(3) Construct the relevant test statistic $t = ?$
(4) Choose the significance level $\alpha = 0.05$ or 0.01 (Prob of type I error: Prob of rejecting H_o when H_o is true)
(5) Find the critical value considering the chosen significance level based on whether you have a two-sided test or a one-sided test
c such that
$P(t > c \mid H_o) = \alpha$ One-sided test (e.g., $H_a: \beta_1 > 0$)
$P(t < c \mid H_o) = \alpha$ One-sided test (e.g., $H_a: \beta_1 < 0$)
$P(|t| > c \mid H_o) = \alpha$ Two-sided test (e.g., $H_a: \beta_1 \neq 0$)

(6) Compare the test statistic with the critical value

$$\left.\begin{array}{l}\text{Test statistic} > \text{critical value } c \ (H_a: \beta_1 > 0) \\ \text{Test statistic} < \text{critical value } c \ (H_a: \beta_1 < 0) \\ |\text{Test statistic}| > \text{critical value } c \ (H_a: \beta_1 \neq 0)\end{array}\right\} \quad \text{Reject } H_o$$

Or

(6) Compare your p-value with the significance level, $\alpha = 0.05$ or 0.01.
If p-value $< \alpha$, then reject H_o.
In a two-sided test, the p-value corresponds to double the tail probability of the test statistic.
In a one-sided test, the p-value corresponds to the tail probability of the test statistic.

Finally, it is useful to summarize the implications for confidence intervals and hypothesis tests when the OLS estimator $\hat{\beta}_1$ is more efficient.

- More efficient estimator $\hat{\beta}_1$ and its consequences in estimating the confidence interval for β_1

$se(\hat{\beta}_1)$ decreases ($\hat{\beta}_1$ becomes more efficient).

→ The 95% confidence interval $[\hat{\beta}_1 - 1.96 * se(\hat{\beta}_1), \hat{\beta}_1 + 1.96 * se(\hat{\beta}_1)]$ becomes narrower and more precise where $se(\hat{\beta}_1) = \frac{\hat{\sigma}}{\sqrt{\sum_{i=1}^{n}(X_i - \bar{X})^2}}$.

- More efficient estimator $\hat{\beta}_1$ and its consequences in the hypothesis test for β_1

$se(\hat{\beta}_1)$ decreases ($\hat{\beta}_1$ becomes more efficient) and $\hat{\beta}_1 - \beta_1$ becomes larger ($\hat{\beta}_1$ becomes bigger under $H_0: \beta_1 = 0$).

→ The test statistic $t = \frac{\hat{\beta}_1 - \beta_1}{se(\hat{\beta}_1)} = \frac{\hat{\beta}_1 - \beta_1}{\left(\frac{\hat{\sigma}}{\sqrt{\sum_{i=1}^{n}(X_i - \bar{X})^2}}\right)}$ increases and it is more likely to

reject $H_0: \beta_1 = 0$ when it is false.

Chapter Summary

Inference for the population parameter, β_1	The OLS estimator ($\hat{\beta}_1 = \frac{\sum_{i=1}^{n}(X_i-\bar{X})Y_i}{\sum_{i=1}^{n}(X_i-\bar{X})^2}$) represents a random variable, and it has its own distribution called the sampling distribution. With six OLS assumptions, the sampling distribution of the OLS estimator follows the normal distribution, enabling the construction of confidence intervals and hypothesis tests for the population parameter β_1. Particularly, the sixth assumption, the normality of the error term, is essential. For large sample analysis, we don't need the sixth OLS assumption for the inference because of the Central Limit Theorem(CLT). Therefore, with the first to fifth OLS assumptions for large sample analysis, we can employ the confidence intervals and the hypothesis tests for the population parameter β_1.
How to precisely estimate the population parameter β_1	More information (larger sample size), more explanation of the outcome variable by the regression model (smaller residual sum of squares), and more diverse information of the explanatory variable (large variance of the explanatory variable) lead to the narrower sampling distribution of the OLS estimator (the smaller standard error of the OLS estimator). This is helpful for the better estimation of the population parameter β_1 (smaller se($\hat{\beta}_1$)). Specifically, if se($\hat{\beta}_1$) is becoming smaller, we can have the narrower and more precise confidence intervals for β_1 and the hypothesis tests that are more likely to reject the null hypothesis when the null hypothesis ($\beta_1=0$) is false.
Large sample analysis	During the early days of the data analysis, the small sample analysis was common, and the more constrained OLS assumptions were carefully considered in the analysis. However, a large sample is common nowadays as

	the data collection is easy, and weaker OLS assumptions are allowed. Therefore, more information means greater flexibility in the OLS analysis.
Benefits of analyzing large samples	Large sample size → More efficient standard errors → larger test statistics → Easier to reject the null hypothesis when the null hypothesis is false. Instead of the unbiasedness of the OLS estimators, the consistency of the OLS estimators can be stated. A weaker OLS assumption is possible: $Cov(X,u)$ is enough to have consistent OLS estimators. The sixth assumption of the normality of the error term is not needed to have valid inferences of confidence intervals and hypothesis tests because of the Central Limit Theorem (CLT).
Addressing common misunderstandings and mistakes	The 95% confidence interval does not mean that the true parameter β_1 lies within the confidence interval with a 95% chance. The 95% confidence interval itself is an estimator, which implies that the true parameter is included in 95% of all possible 95% confidence intervals from the infinitely many random samples with the sample size n. Therefore, it is an accurate way to say that we are 95% confident that the true parameter lies within the confidence interval. When the sample size becomes larger, we don't need the sixth OLS assumption (normality of the error term) since the distribution of $\frac{1}{\sqrt{n}}\sum X_i u_i$ approximately follows the normal distribution because of the Central Limit Theorem (CLT). However, the distribution of the error term does not tend to becomes close to the normal distribution as the sample size increases.

Exercises

Chapter 4
Examining the relationship between the two continuous variables II: Inference in the OLS Regression Analysis

1. Suppose that you investigate the impact of the campaign expenditure on winning a presidential election in South Korea and you have the following regression results.

$$\widehat{voteA} = 40.90 + 0.206 shareA$$
$$\text{SE} \quad (10.20) \quad (0.112)$$

voteA: the percentage of the vote received by Candidate A
shareA: the percentage of total campaign expenditures accounted for by Candidate A
$n = 1,000$

(1) Please interpret the estimated coefficient of shareA.

(2) Test whether the coefficient of shareA is statistically different from 0 with a two-sided test at $\alpha = 0.05$. Discuss whether larger campaign expenditures are effective to gain more votes based on what you have in this analysis.

(3) The total sum of squares of this regression model is 4,100 and the explained sum of squares is 2,000. Please calculate and interpret R-squared.

(4) Please discuss possible issues with this study. What can be missing explanatory variables in this regression model?

2. Suppose that for 180 nations in the world, the prediction equation relating Y = elderly poverty rate in 2010 to X = social expenditures as a percent of gross domestic product is

$$\hat{Y} = 22 - 2.1X$$
$$\text{SE} \quad (10) \quad (1.3)$$

where the standard errors are in parentheses. Y and X are valued in %.
We have SST (Total Sum of Squares) = 3,000.
SSE (Explained Sum of Squares) = 1,500; and
SSR (Residual Sum of Squares) = 1,500.

(1) Obtain the 95% confidence interval for the coefficient of X and interpret it.

(2) A U.S. senator argues that U.S. government should increase social expenditures to reduce the elderly poverty. Test whether social expenditures reduce the elderly poverty with $\alpha = 0.05$ and make comments on this argument based on your findings. Show all steps with the null and alternative hypotheses and the test statistics.

3. Suppose that Korea University would like to evaluate whether frequent consultations with academic advisors help freshmen to improve their academic achievements. The regression results are as follows with $n = 2,000$.

$$\widehat{GPA} = 2.34 + 0.05 \, \text{Consultation}$$
$$\text{SE} \quad (1.52) \quad (0.025)$$

GPA = freshmen's first semester GPA (0 to 4)
Consultation = number of consultations with academic advisors per semester

(1) Please interpret the estimated coefficient of Consultation,

(2) Obtain and interpret the 95% confidence interval for the coefficient of Consultation

(3) Please test whether the coefficient of Consultation is statistically different from 0 with a two-sided test at $\alpha = 0.05$.

(4) Discuss whether frequent consultations with academic advisors are effective to improve the freshmen's GPA based on what you find in (1) to (3).

4. Human capital theory suggests that more education leads to higher earnings. Assume that you have real hourly wage (rhw1984) and education in years (edu) in your data.

(1) Construct the OLS regression model and the hypothesis to test this theory.

Now you have the following regression result.

$$\widehat{rhw1984} = -0.587 + 0.620\,edu$$
$$\text{SE} \qquad (0.231) \quad (0.017)$$

SST (Total Sum of Squares) = 128911.008
SSE (Explained Sum of Squares) = 18083.2888
SSR (Residual Sum of Squares) = 110827.719
$R^2 = 0.1403$
$n = 7,707$

(2) Please interpret the estimated coefficient of education.

(3) In order for this estimate to be unbiased, what assumptions are needed? Also, in order for the estimated standard error of this estimate to be valid, what additional assumptions are needed? Test your null hypothesis made in (1). In order for this test to be valid, what additional assumptions are needed? Write down your answers assuming that the sample size in this analysis is small for now.

(4) It seems that we have a large sample here, sample size $n = 7,707$, what assumptions can be modified and discarded? Is that good for you as a researcher? Why or why not?

(5) Show total sum of squares equals the regression sum of squares and residual sum of squares using the numbers provided in this result.

(6) Show how you calculate R-squared using numbers in this outcome. Name all components and show the details. Briefly interpret the R-squared you obtain.

(7) Construct a 99% confidence interval of the coefficient of education. Briefly interpret the 99% confidence interval you obtain.

Chapter 5
Data Analysis for Social Science: Fundamental Methods

Handling two or more explanatory variables in OLS regression analysis I: Multivariate Regression Analysis

Partialling out and multicollinearity in multivariate regression analysis

Suppose that we would like to expand the linear regression model by adding more explanatory variables. Then, it is important to ask why we want to add more explanatory variables to the regression model. There are two major reasons. First, having only one variable may lead to the violation of the conditional independence assumption for the unbiasedness of $\hat{\beta}_1$ for β_1. For example, suppose we would like to estimate the impact of participating in a public health program on individuals' health conditions. It is possible that program participants may be older and sicker compared with nonparticipants. Thus, to estimate the unbiased program impact, it is appropriate to control for individuals' age and health history. As a result, the ceteris paribus interpretation applies to the estimated coefficient of each variable in multivariate regression analysis. In other words, the estimated coefficient of each variable is interpreted with the other included variables held constant. Second, another purpose of adding relevant explanatory variables to the regression model is to improve the efficiency of the OLS estimators by taking more variations out of residuals (improving the explanatory power of the regression model), which makes the standard errors of the OLS estimators smaller. Improving the efficiency of the OLS estimators increases the probability of rejecting the null hypothesis when the null hypothesis is false.

Let's study how the linear regression model works when we add more explanatory variables to the model, starting with a conceptual explanation using the figure below. Assume that we would like to estimate the impact of education (X_{1i}) on earnings (Y_i). There are two more variables we would like to control for: one is job experience (X_{2i}) and the other is IQ (X_{3i}). It is found that education is correlated with job experience and IQ, which is illustrated as the overlapping variation in the figure below and is called multicollinearity. Multicollinearity is the linear dependence among included explanatory variables in OLS regression analysis. When OLS regression analysis estimates the coefficient of education, it only uses the pure variation of education that is not correlated with job experience or IQ. This is called a "partialling out" of OLS estimators. Due to multicollinearity, the pure variation of education for multivariate OLS analysis is smaller than the total variation of education, as shown in the figure below. If there is serious multicollinearity, the pure variation of education could be much smaller, and OLS analysis may not estimate the coefficient of education well.

* Conceptual explanation of a "partialling out" of OLS estimators

Population model: $Y_i = \beta_0 + \beta_1 X_{1i} + \beta_2 X_{2i} + \beta_3 X_{3i} + u_i$

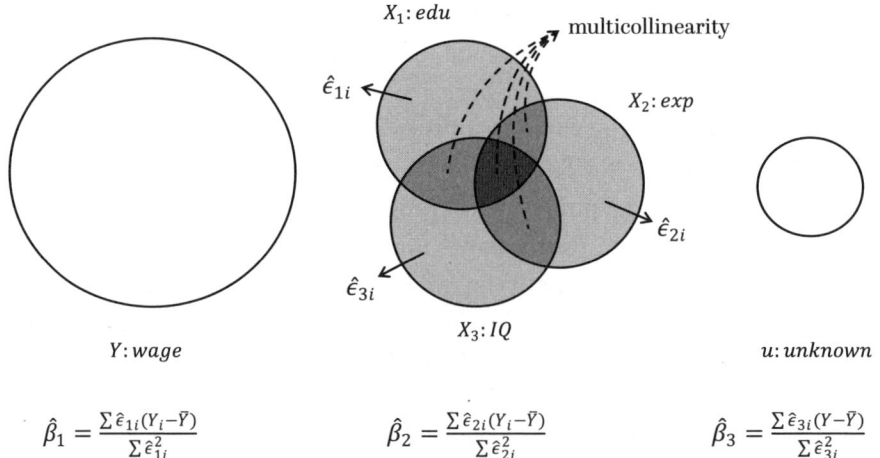

$$\hat{\beta}_1 = \frac{\sum \hat{\epsilon}_{1i}(Y_i - \bar{Y})}{\sum \hat{\epsilon}_{1i}^2} \qquad \hat{\beta}_2 = \frac{\sum \hat{\epsilon}_{2i}(Y_i - \bar{Y})}{\sum \hat{\epsilon}_{2i}^2} \qquad \hat{\beta}_3 = \frac{\sum \hat{\epsilon}_{3i}(Y - \bar{Y})}{\sum \hat{\epsilon}_{3i}^2}$$

where $\hat{\epsilon}_{1i}$ represents the residual variation of X_1 after accounting for its correlated variation with X_2 and X_3; $\hat{\epsilon}_{2i}$ represents the residual variation of after accounting for its correlated variation with X_1 and X_3; $\hat{\epsilon}_{3i}$ represents the residual variation of X_3 after accounting for its correlated variation with X_1 and X_2.

As shown above, the OLS estimator of education, $\hat{\beta}_1$, is using the pure variation of education in the OLS estimator, compared to the OLS estimator of education that uses the full variation of education when there are no other explanatory variables in the model below.

$$Y_i = \delta_0 + \delta_1 X_{1i} + u_i$$

$$\hat{\delta}_1 = \frac{\sum(X_{1i}-\bar{X})(Y_i-\bar{Y})}{\sum(X_{1i}-\bar{X})^2}$$

where $(X_{1i} - \bar{X})$ = full variation of X_{1i}

Multicollinearity is linear dependence among included right-hand side variables. Therefore, multicollinearity is not related to unbiasedness, but related to efficiency.

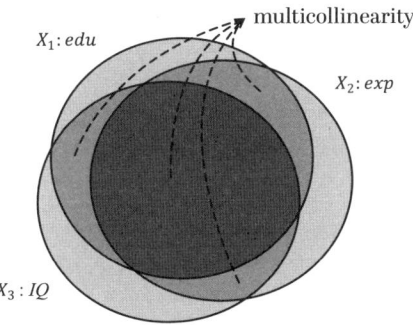

Intuitively, including more explanatory variables may take more variation out of the error term and lead to a smaller residual sum of squares, which makes standard errors smaller. On the other hand, adding more explanatory variables may generate more serious multicollinearity and lead to smaller pure variations to run the regression, which makes standard errors higher. The figure above shows an example of serious multicollinearity among three explanatory variables. In this example, little pure variation is left for each explanatory variable, which may lead to inefficient OLS estimation with larger standard errors. Thus, adding more explanatory variables to the regression model has trade-offs in terms of efficiency, as stated below.

# of explanatory ↑ → ⎡ Pure variation in X_1 ↓ → standard error ↑ → less efficient ⎤ Trade
variables   ⎣ → $\sum \hat{u}_i^2$ ↓ → standard error ↓ → more efficient ⎦ off

Suppose there is perfect multicollinearity, which is the complete overlapping of the explanatory variables. In that case, the OLS regression analysis cannot estimate the coefficients due to the lack of pure variations of the explanatory variables.

Perfect multicollinearity $\to$ no leftover variation (i.e., $\sum \hat{\epsilon}_{1i}^2 = 0$) $\to \hat{\beta}_1 = \frac{\sum \hat{\epsilon}_{1i}(Y_i - \bar{Y})}{\sum \hat{\epsilon}_{1i}^2}$ cannot be defined.

The mechanical process of multivariate OLS regression estimation is summarized below. Here, we focus on how to estimate the coefficient of X_{1i} when we control for X_{2i} and X_{3i} in the multivariate regression model.

The first step is running the regression of X_{1i} on X_{2i} and X_{3i}.

1st step:
Run $X_{1i} = \alpha_0 + \alpha_1 X_{2i} + \alpha_2 X_{3i} + \epsilon_{1i}$: sub-regression
Obtain $\hat{X}_{1i} = \hat{\alpha}_0 + \hat{\alpha}_1 X_{2i} + \hat{\alpha}_2 X_{3i}$
$\hat{\epsilon}_{1i} = X_{1i} - \hat{X}_{1i}$

$\hat{\epsilon}_{1i}$ is the pure variation of X_{1i}, the difference between X_{1i} and $\hat{X}_{1i}$ where $\hat{X}_{1i}$ indicates the multicollinearity between X_{1i} and the other control variables, X_{2i} and X_{3i}.

We know $\quad \frac{1}{n}\sum_{i=1}^{n} \hat{\epsilon}_{1i} = 0$

$\Rightarrow \bar{\hat{\epsilon}}_{1i} = 0$

Using R_1^2 obtained from the regression of the first step, we can decompose $\sum \hat{\epsilon}_{1i}^2$, the residual sum of squares that represents the sum of squares of the pure variation of X_{1i}.

$R_1^2 = 1 - \frac{SSR_1}{SST_1}$ where SSR_1 is the residual sum of squares and SST_1 is the total sum of squares of the regression in the first step

Then, $R_1^2 = 1 - \frac{\sum \hat{\epsilon}_{1i}^2}{\sum (X_{1i} - \bar{X}_1)^2}$

$\Rightarrow \frac{\sum \hat{\epsilon}_{1i}^2}{\sum (X_{1i} - \bar{X}_1)^2} = 1 - R_1^2$

$\Rightarrow \underbrace{\sum \hat{\epsilon}_{1i}^2}_{\text{Pure variation of } X_{1i}} = \underbrace{[\sum (X_{1i} - \bar{X}_1)^2]}_{\text{Total variation of } X_{1i}} \underbrace{(1 - R_1^2)}_{\text{Discount factor}}$

$\sum \hat{\epsilon}_{1i}^2$ is the pure variation of X_{1i} after excluding the multicollinearity. Thus, the pure variation of X_{1i} is the multiplication of the total variation of X_{1i} with the discount factor, $1 - R_1^2$, the degree of multicollinearity. If R_1^2 is 0, no multicollinearity, the pure variation of X_{1i} is the total variation of X_{1i} since the discount factor is 1. On the other hand, if R_1^2 is 1, perfect multicollinearity, the pure variation of X_{1i} is 0 since the discount factor is 0. Depending on the degree of multicollinearity, the discount factor may be between 0 and 1, and it determines the amount of the pure variation of X_{1i} that can be used to estimate the coefficient of X_{1i} in the multivariate regression. As multicollinearity decreases, the larger variation of X_{1i} can be used for the estimation.

2nd step:
Run $Y_i = \theta_0 + \theta_1 \hat{\epsilon}_{1i} + \eta_i$
$$\hat{\beta}_1 = \hat{\theta}_1 = \frac{\sum \hat{\epsilon}_{1i}(Y_i - \bar{Y})}{\sum \hat{\epsilon}_{1i}^2}$$

In this second step, we run the regression of Y_i on $\hat{\epsilon}_{1i}$, which is the pure variation of X_{1i} without the multicollinearity. $\hat{\beta}_2$ and $\hat{\beta}_3$ can be obtaned by the smilar steps.

As explained earlier, if there is no multicollinearity, then R_1^2 is 0 and $\sum \hat{\epsilon}_{1i}^2 = \sum (X_{1i} - \bar{X}_1)^2$. On the other hand, if multicollinearity is becoming serious, then R_1^2 is getting larger and $\sum \hat{\epsilon}_{1i}^2$ is getting smaller.

As shown here, if there is no multicollinearity in the education variable, estimating the coefficient of education with other control variables is equivalent to estimating it without control variables. In contrast, as multicollinearity in education with other control variables increases, the pure variation of education in the multivariate regression decreases.

When we run the multivariate regression using statistical packages such as SPSS, SAS, Stata, or R, the statistical computation goes through these two steps and gives us the estimation results. We are not doing these two steps separately in practice. However, it is good to understand what computational steps the multivariate regression works through.

For the multivariate regression model, there is no critical change in the classical linear model assumptions we covered in Chapter 5. The only noticeable addition is an assumption of no perfect collinearity for the unbiased OLS estimators.

For the multivariate regression, the OLS assumptions can be summarized below.

$$Y_i = \beta_0 + \beta_1 X_{1i} + \beta_2 X_{2i} + \cdots + \beta_k X_{ki} + u_i$$

For small sample OLS analysis
① Linear in parameters and additive error term
② Random sample of X and Y
③ Variation in X and no perfect multicollinearity
④ $E(u|X) = 0$
⑤ No heteroscedasticity $Var(u|X) = Var(u) = \sigma^2$
⑥ $u \sim N(0, \sigma^2)$

$\left. \begin{array}{l} E(\hat{\beta}_j) = \beta_j \\ j = 1, \ldots, k \\ \text{Unbiasedness} \end{array} \right\}$ BLUE $\left. \begin{array}{l} \text{BLUE} \\ + \text{ Inference} \\ \text{(CI/testing)} \end{array} \right.$

Therefore, there are no major changes except for including no perfect multicollinearity assumption in the third OLS assumption, compared with the simple regression model.

When the sample size becomes larger, we can have the following OLS assumptions as explained in the previous section. Therefore, we don't need the sixth OLS assumption anymore. Also, as discussed earlier, the fourth OLS assumption becomes weaker: $Cov(u, X) = 0$.

For large sample OLS analysis
① Linear in parameters and additive error term
② Random sample of X and Y
③ Variation in X and no perfect multicollinearity
④ We don't need to assume $E(u|X)$
  We only need to assume $Cov(u, X) = 0$
⑤ No heteroscedasticity $Var(u|X) = Var(u) = \sigma^2$
⑥ We don't need to assume $u \sim N(0, \sigma^2)$

$\left. \begin{array}{l} \text{plim}(\hat{\beta}_j) = \beta_j \\ \text{Consistency} \end{array} \right\}$ BLUE $\left. \begin{array}{l} \text{BLUE} \\ + \text{ Inference} \\ \text{(CI/testing)} \end{array} \right.$

Under the first to fourth OLS assumptions, the unbiasedness of OLS estimators is replaced by the consistency of OLS estimators. Also, as discussed earlier, for small sample OLS analysis, we need to validate the sixth OLS assumption, $u \sim N(0, \sigma^2)$, to ensure the normally distributed sampling distribution of the OLS estimator $\hat{\beta}_j$. This requirement enables the development of valid confidence intervals and hypothesis tests for the parameter β_j. However, when the sample size is large enough, the five assumptions for large sample OLS analysis allow for Best Linear Unbiased Estimator (BLUE) and the normality of the OLS estimator $\hat{\beta}_j$. It enables the construction of valid confidence intervals and hypothesis tests for β_j. The sixth OLS assumption, $u \sim N(0, \sigma^2)$, becomes unnecessary as the sample size increases.

Example 5.1

Suppose that we are interested in the relationship between wage and education. To control for individual cognitive ability, we add AFQT to the regression model.

The regression result below is obtained using hourly wage in 1980 US dollars (Y), years of education (X_1), and AFQT (X_2) in the year 1990 of the NLSY79 (National Longitudinal Survey of Youth - 1979 Cohort) data set.

$$\widehat{Y}_i = 1.556 + 0.323X_{1i} + 0.042X_{2i}$$
$$\text{SE} \quad (0.242) \quad (0.021) \quad (0.002)$$

SST (Total Sum of Squares) = 128911.008
SSE (Explained Sum of Squares) = 25135.902
SSR (Residual Sum of Squares) = 103775.106
R^2 = 0.195
n = 7,707

From this analysis, the estimated coefficient of education indicates that a one-year increase in education implies around a $0.323 increase in real hourly wage. It is also found that one more point increase in AFQT (ranging from 1 to 100 points) is associated with a $0.042 increase in real hourly wage. That is, a 10 more points increase in AFQT implies a $0.42 increase in real hourly wage.

R-squared = SSE/SST = 0.1905 implies that education and AFQT explain about 19% of the variation in real hourly wage for the sample.

We stated that the estimated coefficients are valid under OLS assumptions 1 to 4 above, and the standard errors are valid under OLS assumptions 1 to 5.

Under OLS assumptions 1 to 5 with the large sample, we can construct the confidence intervals and hypothesis tests.
For example, the 95% confidence interval for AFQT is

[0.042-1.96*0.002, 0.042-1.96*0.002] = [0.038, 0.046].

We can say that we are 95% confident that the true parameter of AFQT lies between

0.038 and 0.046. Also, it is likely that the true parameter of AFQT is greater than 0.

The two-sided hypothesis test with a 5% significance level ($\alpha = 0.05$) for the parameter of education can be done as follows.

$$H_o: \beta_1 = 0$$
$$H_a: \beta_1 \neq 0$$

$$t = \frac{\hat{\beta}_1 - \beta_1}{se(\hat{\beta}_1)} = \frac{0.323 - 0}{0.021} = 15.38$$

Since 15.38 is greater than 1.96 (the critical value for the 2.5% tail probability in the standard normal distribution), we can say that we reject the null hypothesis at a 5% significance level. Therefore, it is likely that the true parameter of education is different from 0.

Notes:
the NLSY79 (National Longitudinal Survey of Youth -1979 Cohort) data set
https://www.nlsinfo.org/content/cohorts/nlsy79

Example 5.2

Suppose that we would like to know the relationship between wage and education. To control for individuals' cognitive ability, we add AFQT on the right side of the regression.

The regression result below is obtained using hourly wage in 1980 U.S. dollars (Y), years of education (X_1), and AFQT (X_2) in the year 1990 of the NLSY79 (National Longitudinal Survey of Youth - 1979 Cohort) data set.

The estimation results are reported in the table below. The way of presentation of estimated coefficients in this table is commonly used. For each row of the corresponding independent variable, we report the estimated coefficient in the upper section and the standard error in parenthesis in the lower section. At the bottom of the table, we typically report R-squared and the number of observations, and the notes in the table state that statistically significant coefficients at $p<0.01$ (the 1% significance level), $p<0.05$ (the 5% significance level), and $p<0.1$ (the 10% significance level) bear three stars, two stars, and one star as shown in the table, respectively.

The first column reports the same results as we saw in Example 5.1. The second column includes a new variable that is dividing AFQT by 10 while the third column has a new variable that is the square of AFQT. As shown in column (2), the coefficient of AFQT/10 is not estimated since AFQT/10 is perfectly correlated with AFQT, which is perfect multicollinearity. On the other hand, the coefficient of the square of AFQT in column (3) is estimated and is statistically significant even at $p<0.01$ although the square of AFQT is seriously correlated with AFQT: the correlation coefficient between them is 0.9643. Therefore, it is found that serious multicollinearity does not lead to a critical issue in the OLS estimation if the sample size is big enough to provide a statistically significant estimate.

Estimated results using different AFQT variables

	(1)	(2)	(3)
Years of education	0.323***	0.323***	0.324***
	(0.021)	(0.021)	(0.021)
AFQT	0.042***	0.042***	0.026***
	(0.002)	(0.002)	(0.006)
AFQT/10		(dropped)	
AFQT squared			0.00017***
			(0.00006)
Constant	1.556***	1.556***	1.770***
	(0.242)	(0.242)	(0.253)
R^2	0.195	0.195	0.196
Number of observations	7,707	7,707	7,707

Notes: ***$p<0.01$, **$p<0.05$, *$p<0.1$; The outcome variable is hourly wage in 1980 US dollars in the year 1990 of the NLSY79 (National Longitudinal Survey of Youth - 1979 Cohort) data set.

> Notes:
> the NLSY79 (National Longitudinal Survey of Youth -1979 Cohort) data set
> https://www.nlsinfo.org/content/cohorts/nlsy79

Omitted variable bias in the linear regression model

One of the essential goals of data analysis is to estimate the causal impact of an explanatory variable on an outcome variable. It is particularly challenging in social science since we cannot set up a lab environment where researchers change one variable, such as drug doses, with other conditions constant, differently for the randomly assigned treatment and control groups and observe whether the outcome variable, such as health conditions, changes. This change in the main explanatory variable that is not related to any characteristics of individual subjects in the study is referred to "exogenous." In social science, when we would like to estimate the impact of a key explanatory variable on an outcome of our interest, a key explanatory variable is usually related to other unobserved variables. It is called "endogenous." This is typical because individual subjects, such as men, women, children, countries, and organizations, in the study made choices based on not only observed but also unobserved characteristics and hidden intentions. For example, in the study to estimate the impact of education on wages, education levels in the observed data are highly endogenous since individuals chose their educational attainment based on their family backgrounds, cognitive and non-cognitive abilities, and so on. If you recognize, measure, and include these characteristics in the regression model, you can minimize any estimation bias driven by endogeneity. However, even though you recognize these important characteristics in your study, some of them cannot be defined and measured thoroughly. For instance, it is difficult to define and measure noncognitive abilities, but they are important in the study of education and training. Thus, researchers have admitted that it is impossible to establish causality using multivariate regression analysis since we cannot control for all the key variables in the regression model. The estimation bias driven by excluded unobservables is called the omitted variable bias. Although we cannot avoid omitted variable bias in multivariate regression, we can state the bias direction by characterizing the omitted variable and its relationships with the outcome variable and the main explanatory variable in the regression model below.

Let's assume that we would like to estimate the impact of education on wages, and the true regression model includes education and IQ in the regression model. However, suppose that we cannot include IQ for some reason. Then, we may end up with a regression model with omitted variable bias in estimating the impact of education on wages. Therefore, it is useful to examine whether the estimated coefficient of education is positively or negatively biased by the omitted variable.

Let's see the example below for the omitted variable bias. Assume the small sample.

$\hat{\beta}_1$: OLS estimator in the true regression model
$$wage_i = \beta_0 + \beta_1 edu_i + \beta_2 IQ_i + u_i$$

-- true regression model with the six OLS assumptions, including the fourth assumption $E(u|edu, IQ) = 0$

$$wage_i = \beta_0 + \beta_1 edu_i + v_i \qquad (v_i = \beta_2 IQ_i + u_i)$$

$\tilde{\beta}_1$: OLS estimator in the model with the omitted variable

-- a model we are estimating

Then, the OLS estimator in the model with the omitted variable has the following consequences.

$E(\tilde{\beta}_1) \neq \beta_1$: $\tilde{\beta}_1$ biased since $E(v|edu) \neq 0$, the violation of the fourth OLS assumption.

Let's specifically study the omitted variable bias and its direction.

Assume that $IQ_i = \gamma_0 + \gamma_1 edu + \varepsilon_i$ and γ_1 is not 0.

Then, we can formalize the omitted variable bias in $\tilde{\beta}_1$ as below.

$$E(\tilde{\beta}_1) = \beta_1 + \underbrace{\beta_2 * \hat{\gamma}_1}_{} \neq \beta_1 \qquad \text{where } \beta_1 \text{ is the true value of the parameter.}$$

Omitted variable bias

Omitted variable bias is the multiplication of β_2 that indicates the linear relationship between the omitted variable (IQ) and the outcome variable (wage) and $\hat{\gamma}_1$ that indicates the linear relationship between the omitted variable (IQ) and the main explanatory variable (edu). Since we do not know the exact values of β_2 and $\hat{\gamma}_1$ in research, we cannot figure out the magnitude of omitted variable bias. On the other hand, we may know whether β_2 and $\hat{\gamma}_1$ are positive or negative based on previous studies and theories.

This idea can be presented as follows:
The direction of the omitted variable bias in the main explanatory variable = (the direction of the linear relationship between the omitted variable and the outcome variable) × (the direction of the linear relationship between the omitted variable and the main explanatory variable)

Thus, if these two relationships are in the same direction, then the omitted variable bias is positive. On the other hand, if these two relationships are in the opposite direction, then the omitted variable bias is negative.

Also, if one of these two relationships is 0, then the omitted variable bias is 0. First, if the linear relationship between the omitted variable and the outcome variable is 0, it means that the omitted variable is not relevant in the regression model. Thus, we don't have to consider this variable in the analysis. Second, if the linear relationship between the omitted variable and the main explanatory variable is 0, it means that the main explanatory variable is exogenous, but the omitted variable is still relevant to the outcome variable in the regression model. When the main explanatory variable is exogenous, we should include other relevant variables in the regression model since it can reduce the standard error of the main explanatory variable by increasing R-squared of the regression. As we discussed earlier, the lower standard error is helpful to increase the efficiency of the regression estimate of the main variable, which leads to a narrower confidence interval and a higher likelihood of rejecting the null hypothesis when the null hypothesis is false.

If IQ and wage are positively related while IQ and education are positively related, then the omitted variable bias in this example is positive. Thus, it is possible that the estimated impact of education on wage is positively biased (overstated).

Example 5.3

The following regression results illustrate the direction of omitted variable bias we covered earlier. The three regression results below are obtained using hourly wage in 1980 U.S. dollars (Y), years of education (X_1), and AFQT (X_2) in the year 1990 of the NLSY79 (National Longitudinal Survey of Youth - 1979 Cohort) data set. Like IQ, AFQT is the cognitive measure ranging from 1 to 100 in the sample.

<Regression 1>

$$\hat{Y}_i = -0.587 + 0.62X_{1i}$$
$$\text{SE} \quad (0.231) \quad (0.017)$$

SST (Total Sum of Squares) = 128911.008
SSE (Explained Sum of Squares) = 18083.2888
SSR (Residual Sum of Squares) = 110827.719
$R^2 = 0.1403$
$n = 7,707$

The estimated coefficient of education is 0.62, implying that one more year of education is associated with a $0.62 increase in real hourly wage.

<Regression 2>

$$\hat{Y}_i = 1.556 + 0.323X_{1i} + 0.042X_{2i}$$
$$\text{SE} \quad (0.242) \quad (0.021) \quad (0.002)$$

SST (Total Sum of Squares) = 128911.008
SSE (Explained Sum of Squares) = 25135.902
SSR (Residual Sum of Squares) = 103775.106
$R^2 = 0.195$
$n = 7,707$

When we add AFQT (cognitive measure) to the regression model, the estimated coefficient of education decreases from 0.62 to 0.323. It seems that the estimated coefficient of education in regression 1 was overstated (positively biased). It is what we anticipated, considering that AFQT is expected to be positively associated with education and real hourly wage.

<Regression 3>

$$\widehat{X_{2i}} = -51.291 + 7.106X_{1i}$$
$$\text{SE} \quad (1.395) \quad (0.106)$$

SST (Total Sum of Squares) = 6415376.89
SSE (Explained Sum of Squares) = 2374521.02
SSR (Residual Sum of Squares) = 4040855.86

$R^2 = 0.3701$
$n = 7{,}707$

Regression 3 result confirms that AFQT is positively associated with education.
It is important to note that this example is an illustration to show the direction of omitted variable bias. Although we examine whether the omitted variable (AFQT) is positively associated with the outcome variable (real hourly wage) and the included variable (education) in this example, we cannot examine an omitted variable in reality. Often, an omitted variable may be hard to measure. For example, individuals' motivation for the job market can be important when we study whether the number of children affects women's job market participation. However, it is not easy to measure women's motivation for the job market.

Notes:
the NLSY79 (National Longitudinal Survey of Youth -1979 Cohort) data set
https://www.nlsinfo.org/content/cohorts/nlsy79

Adding an explanatory variable and the efficiency of OLS estimators

In the multivariate regression analysis, we are often interested in whether the estimated coefficient of the main variable becomes statistically more or less significant when we add another explanatory variable to the regression model. Although we hope to have more significant estimates by adding another variable, the outcome can go either way. As we discussed earlier, containing another explanatory variable can bring two opposite consequences at the same time. First, including another variable may take more variations out of residuals (improving the explanatory power of the regression model). As a result, we may have a smaller standard error of the main estimate, which leads to a statistically more significant estimate. Second, adding a new variable may increase the degree of multicollinearity, which in turn raises the standard error of the main estimate and makes it statistically less significant. Therefore, whether the standard error of the main estimate increases or decreases depends on which one prevails over the other.

Let's examine these two opposite consequences step by step.

We start with the simple regression we covered earlier.

$$wage_i = \beta_0 + \beta_1 edu_i + v_i$$
$$\text{where } v_i = \beta_2 IQ_i + u_i$$

$$Var(\tilde{\beta}_1) = \frac{\sigma_v^2}{\Sigma(edu_i - \overline{edu})^2}$$

$$\widehat{Var}(\tilde{\beta}_1) = \frac{\hat{\sigma}_v^2}{\Sigma(edu_i - \overline{edu})^2} \text{ where } \hat{\sigma}_v^2 = \frac{\Sigma \hat{v}_i^2}{n-2} \text{ is the variance of}$$

the OLS estimator for education.

Then, $se(\tilde{\beta}_1) = \dfrac{\sqrt{\frac{\Sigma \hat{v}_i^2}{n-2}}}{\sqrt{\Sigma(edu_i - \overline{edu})^2}}$

After adding IQ to the regression model, we have

$$wage_i = \beta_0 + \beta_1 edu_i + \beta_2 IQ_i + u_i$$

$$\hat{\beta}_1 = \frac{\Sigma \hat{\epsilon}_{edu} \, wage_i}{\Sigma \hat{\epsilon}_{edu}^2} \qquad\qquad edu_i = \alpha_o + \alpha_1 IQ_i + \epsilon_{edu}$$

$$= \beta_1 + \frac{\Sigma \hat{\epsilon}_{edu} \cdot u_i}{\Sigma \hat{\epsilon}_{edu}^2} \qquad\qquad \hat{\epsilon}_{edu} = edu_i - \widehat{edu}_i$$

$$\qquad\qquad\qquad\qquad\qquad\qquad\quad = edu_i - (\hat{\alpha}_o + \hat{\alpha}_1 IQ_i)$$

$$Var(\hat{\beta}_1) = Var\left(\beta_1 + \frac{\Sigma \hat{\epsilon}_{edu} \cdot u_i}{\Sigma \hat{\epsilon}_{edu}^2}\right)$$

$$= Var\left(\frac{\Sigma \hat{\epsilon}_{edu} \cdot u_i}{\Sigma \hat{\epsilon}_{edu}^2}\right) = \frac{\sigma_u^2}{\Sigma \hat{\epsilon}_{edu}^2} \text{ is the the variance of the OLS estimator for}$$

education when we add IQ to the regression model.

$\Sigma \hat{\epsilon}_{edu}^2$ can be decomposed as follows.

$$R^2_{edu} = 1 - \frac{SSR_{edu}}{SST_{edu}} = 1 - \frac{\Sigma \hat{\epsilon}_{edu}^2}{\Sigma(edu_i - \overline{edu})^2}$$

$$\Rightarrow \Sigma \hat{\epsilon}_{edu}^2 = \left[\Sigma(edu_i - \overline{edu})^2\right] \underbrace{(1 - R^2_{edu})}_{\text{Discount factor}}$$

higher multicollinearity $\rightarrow R^2_{edu} \uparrow \rightarrow (1 - R^2_{edu}) \downarrow \rightarrow \Sigma \hat{\epsilon}_{edu}^2 \downarrow$

Therefore, higher multicollinearity by adding another variable may lead to a smaller pure variation of education in this case.

$$Var(\hat{\beta}_1) = \frac{\sigma_u^2}{[\Sigma(edu_i - \overline{edu})^2](1-R_{edu}^2)}$$

$$\Rightarrow \widehat{Var}(\hat{\beta}_1) = \frac{\hat{\sigma}_u^2}{[\Sigma(edu_i - \overline{edu})^2](1-R_{edu}^2)} \quad \text{where } \hat{\sigma}_u^2 = \frac{\Sigma \widehat{u_i}^2}{n-3}$$

Then, $se(\hat{\beta}_1) = \dfrac{\sqrt{\frac{\Sigma \widehat{u_i}^2}{n-3}}}{\sqrt{[\Sigma(edu_i - \overline{edu})^2](1-R_{edu}^2)}}$

As a result of adding IQ to the regression model, the following two consequences may happen to $se(\hat{\beta}_1)$.

<Consequence 1>

higher multicollinearity → $R_{edu}^2 \uparrow$ → $(1 - R_{edu}^2) \downarrow$

→ $\left[\Sigma(edu_i - \overline{edu})^2\right](1 - R_{edu}^2) \downarrow$ → $se(\hat{\beta}_1) \uparrow$

Therefore, higher multicollinearity by adding another variable may lead to a larger standard error.

<Consequence 2>

Taking more variation out of residuals → $\hat{\sigma}_u^2 = \frac{\Sigma \widehat{u_i}^2}{n-3} \downarrow$ → $se(\hat{\beta}_1) \downarrow$

Thus, taking more variation out of residuals by adding another variable may lead to a smaller standard error.

In summary, we can think about possible reasons of smaller $se(\hat{\beta}_1)$ as below:

$$se(\hat{\beta}_1) = \frac{\sqrt{\frac{\Sigma \widehat{u_i}^2}{n-3}}}{\sqrt{\left[\Sigma(edu_i - \overline{edu})^2\right](1 - R_{edu}^2)}}$$

$$\begin{array}{llll}
\sum \hat{u}_i^2 & \downarrow & \Rightarrow SE(\hat{\beta}_1) \downarrow & \\
n & \uparrow & \Rightarrow SE(\hat{\beta}_1) \downarrow & \\
\sum (edu_i - \overline{edu})^2 & \uparrow & \Rightarrow SE(\hat{\beta}_1) \downarrow & \\
R^2_{edu}: \text{multicollinearity} & \downarrow & \Rightarrow SE(\hat{\beta}_1) \downarrow &
\end{array} \Bigg\} \hat{\beta}_1 : \text{more efficient}$$

Therefore, the standard error is smaller, or the estimate is more efficient as there are less variation of residuals (more explanation by the regression model), a larger sample size, more variation of a variable, and less multicollinearity in the analysis.

Also, we can compare

$$\text{se}(\hat{\beta}_1) = \frac{\sqrt{\frac{\sum \hat{u}_i^2}{n-3}}}{\sqrt{\left[\sum(edu_i - \overline{edu})^2\right](1 - R^2_{edu})}} \text{ with } \text{se}(\tilde{\beta}_1) = \frac{\sqrt{\frac{\sum \hat{v}_i^2}{n-2}}}{\sqrt{\sum(edu_i - \overline{edu})^2}}.$$

Summary of consequence 1

$\sqrt{\left[\sum(edu_i - \overline{edu})^2\right](1 - R^2_{edu})}$ is usually smaller than $\sqrt{\sum(edu_i - \overline{edu})^2}$ since there is some level of multicollinearity driven by adding another variable to the model.

Summary of consequence 2
$\sum \hat{u}_i^2$ is usually smaller than $\sum \hat{v}_i^2$ since the additional variable explains some of the outcome variations.

Therefore, if consequence 1 overwhelms consequence 2, $\text{se}(\hat{\beta}_1) = \frac{\sqrt{\frac{\sum \hat{u}_i^2}{n-3}}}{\sqrt{\left[\sum(edu_i - \overline{edu})^2\right](1 - R^2_{edu})}}$ can be larger than $\text{se}(\tilde{\beta}_1) = \frac{\sqrt{\frac{\sum \hat{v}_i^2}{n-2}}}{\sqrt{\sum(edu_i - \overline{edu})^2}}$. On the other hand, if consequence 2 prevails over consequence 1, $\text{se}(\hat{\beta}_1) = \frac{\sqrt{\frac{\sum \hat{u}_i^2}{n-3}}}{\sqrt{\left[\sum(edu_i - \overline{edu})^2\right](1 - R^2_{edu})}}$ can be smaller than $\text{se}(\tilde{\beta}_1) = \frac{\sqrt{\frac{\sum \hat{v}_i^2}{n-2}}}{\sqrt{\sum(edu_i - \overline{edu})^2}}$.

Example 5.4

Whether the standard error of education becomes larger or smaller by adding AQFT to the regression model is illustrated in the following regression results.

The two regression results below are obtained using hourly wage in 1980 U.S. dollars (Y), years of education (X_1), and AFQT (X_2) in the year 1990 of the NLSY79 (National Longitudinal Survey of Youth - 1979 Cohort) data set. Like IQ, AFQT is the cognitive measure ranging from 1 to 100 in the sample.

<Regression 1>

$$\widehat{Y}_i = -0.587 + 0.62X_{1i}$$
$$\text{SE} \quad (0.231) \quad (0.017)$$

SST (Total Sum of Squares) = 128911.008
SSE (Explained Sum of Squares) = 18083.2888
SSR (Residual Sum of Squares) = 110827.719
R^2 = 0.1403
n = 7,707

<Regression 2>

$$\widehat{Y}_i = 1.556 + 0.323X_{1i} + 0.042X_{2i}$$
$$\text{SE} \quad (0.242) \quad (0.021) \quad (0.002)$$

SST (Total Sum of Squares) = 128911.008
SSE (Explained Sum of Squares) = 25135.902
SSR (Residual Sum of Squares) = 103775.106
R^2 = 0.195
n = 7,707

It is found that the standard error of education in regression 2, 0.021, is larger than that in regression 1, 0.017. This result is driven by the fact that the denominator of the standard error of education in regression 2 is smaller than that in regression 1 while the residual sum of squares in regression 2 is smaller than that in regression 1. In summary, consequence 1 prevails over consequence 2 in this case.

Notes:
the NLSY79 (National Longitudinal Survey of Youth -1979 Cohort) data set
https://www.nlsinfo.org/content/cohorts/nlsy79

Chapter Summary

How multivariate regression analysis works	When we have two or more explanatory variables in the regression model, the OLS estimation uses the pure variation of the explanatory variables that are not correlated with each other or one another. For the small sample OLS analysis under the six OLS assumptions, the OLS estimators are unbiased, and the confidence intervals and hypothesis tests are valid. The major addition to the OLS assumptions for the multivariate regression is the inclusion of no perfect multicollinearity in the third assumption. Some degree of multicollinearity is common in any multivariate regression and does not lead to biased OLS estimates. As studied before, for the large sample, the sixth assumption (the normality of the error term) is not needed, and the fourth assumption becomes weaker by assuming no correlation between explanatory variables and the error term.
Multicollinearity and its consequences	Higher multicollinearity may lead to a larger standard error, which may lower the significance of the estimate. Then, even if the null hypothesis is false, the chance to reject the null hypothesis becomes smaller.
Addressing common misunderstandings and mistakes	Multicollinearity does not lead to bias in OLS estimation, while it increases the standard error of the OLS estimator. The degree of multicollinearity is related to efficiency in the OLS estimation. It is often observed that OLS estimates are changed a lot with serious multicollinearity. It is not because of bias in estimation but because of less efficient estimates (larger standard errors).

Exercises

Chapter 5
Handling two or more explanatory variables in OLS regression analysis I: Multivariate Regression Analysis

1. Suppose that we want to test the human capital theory that more education leads to higher earnings or wages. The following outcome is from a multivariate OLS regression with real hourly wage in 1984 dollars (rhw1984) as the outcome variable and years of education (edu), afqt (AFQT score between 0 to 100; treated it as intelligence measure), and actual job experience in years (lcexpy) as the explanatory variables.

$$\widehat{rhw1984}_i = -1.384 + 0.390 edu_i + 0.031 afqt_i + 0.305 lcexpy_i$$
$$\text{SE} \quad (0.274) \quad (0.021) \quad\quad (0.002) \quad\quad (0.015)$$

SST (Total Sum of Squares) = 128911.008
SSE (Explained Sum of Squares) = 35723.3269
SSR (Residual Sum of Squares) = 98187.6811
$R^2 = 0.238$
$n = 7{,}707$

(1) Interpret the estimated coefficients of the explanatory variables in the regression model.

(2) What assumptions are needed to have unbiased estimates in this multivariate regression model for the small sample.

(3) When you use the large sample, what assumptions are needed to have consistent estimates in this multivariate regression model?

2. Supper that a study found that individuals who reported regular exercise had an average of half the number of doctor visits per year compared to those who reported not exercising regularly. In the results section of the article, the researchers examined whether age played a role as a confounding variable in this association.

As a researcher, you measure these three variables as follows;

Y = the annual number of doctor visits,
X_1 = the total minutes of exercise per week, and
X_2 = age in years.

Make any relevant assumptions.

(1) Please draw a figure to show possible relationships among these three variables and interpret your figure.

(2) Please construct an ideal regression model to estimate the impact of exercise on illness based on information given in this question and your figure in (1). Explain your regression model accordingly.

3. Suppose that Korea University would like to evaluate whether frequent consultations with academic advisors help freshmen to improve their academic achievements. The regression results are as follows with $n = 2,000$.

$$\widehat{GPA} = 2.34 + 0.05 \text{ Consultation}$$
$$\text{SE} \quad (1.52) \quad (0.025)$$

GPA = freshmen's first semester GPA (0 to 4)
Consultation = number of consultations with academic advisors per semester

Researchers thought that students' academic ability should be controlled in this regression model. Thus, they controlled for their high school GPA and had a following regression outcome.

$$\widehat{GPA} = 0.34 + 0.01 \text{ Consultation} + 0.9 \text{highschoolGPA}$$
$$\text{SE} \quad (0.12) \quad (0.02) \quad\quad\quad\quad (0.4)$$

High school GPA = high school GPA (0 to 4)

$R^2 = 0.21$

$n = 520$

(1) Please interpret the estimated coefficient of Consultation

(2) Please discuss what happened to the estimated coefficient of consultation after controlling for high school GPA.

4. Suppose that you are evaluating the causal impact of the number of siblings on educational attainment. Suppose that your true population model is $educ_i = \beta_0 + \beta_1 sibs_i + \beta_1 IQ_i + u_i$ where $educ_i$ is years of schooling, $sibs_i$ is the number of siblings, and IQ_i is an individual's IQ score. You run the following regression without IQ because you do not have it. Let's assume the small sample.

$$\widehat{educ_i} = 14.139 - 0.228 sibs_i$$
$$\text{SE} \quad (0.113) \quad (0.030)$$

SSE = 258.055
SST = 4506.819
$n = 935$

(1) Interpret the estimated coefficient of $sibs_i$. Is it biased? Which assumption(s) is(are) violated?

(2) Calculate R-squared using the numbers given in the outcome. Interpret the obtained R-squared.

Now you have an IQ score and include it in the model. You have the following outcome.

$$\widehat{educ}_i = 6.551 - 0.096 sibs_i + 0.071 IQ_i$$
$$\text{SE} \quad (0.464) \quad (0.028) \quad (0.004)$$

SSE = 1240.461
SST = 4506.819
n = 935

(3) Interpret the estimated coefficient of $sibs_i$ and IQ_i. Discuss the bias direction of the estimated coefficient of $sibs_i$ in the earlier regression.

5. Suppose that you would like to examine the impact of the child subsidy program on children's academic outcomes.

You develop the following regression model.

$$Y_i = \beta_0 + \beta_1 X_{1i} + \beta_2 X_{2i} + \beta_3 X_{3i} + u_i$$

Y_i : children's academic score measured in 1 to 100
X_{1i} : amount of child subsidy in U.S. dollars
X_{2i} : household income
X_{3i} : parents' education in years (higher one among parents)

The sample size is large enough and it is assumed that the five OLS assumptions for large sample OLS analysis are valid.

(1) If X_{1i} and X_{2i} are highly correlated, what could happen to your estimation in terms of multicollinearity?

(2) Suppose that you would like to include another variable, $X_{1i}/100$, in the regression model. Then, what could happen to your estimation in terms of multicollinearity?

(3) Suppose that you would like to include another variable, X_{2i}^2, in the regression model. Then, what could happen to your estimation in terms of multicollinearity?

6. You want to estimate the impact of a local job training program for single mothers that are qualified for the training program. Define that *part* is the number of months of the program participation. Also define *earn* as labor earnings in 100 dollars and *jskill* as job market skills. You want to run the following regression model. Let's assume that OLS assumptions for BLUE and Valid Inference are satisfied. (You do not need to state assumptions)

$$earn = \beta_0 + \beta_1 part + \beta_2 jskill + u$$

(1) Make the null and alternative hypotheses to test whether the local job training has a positive impact on single mothers' labor market earnings.

(2) Because you do not have *jskill* in your data, you run the regression of *earn* on *part* without controlling for *jskill*. Your regression outcome is as follows.

$$\widehat{earn}_i = 1.233 + 0.522 part_i$$
$$\text{SE} \quad (0.522) \quad (0.250)$$

$n = 122$

$R^2 = 0.123$

Interpret the estimated coefficient of *part* and use *t*-test with *df* and $\alpha = 0.05$ to test your hypotheses built in part (1).

(3) Because you do not have *jskill* in your data, you are worried about omitted variable bias. Please discuss the possible bias direction.

(4) What is your cautious policy recommendation to local policy makers based on your result?

Chapter 6
Data Analysis for Social Science: Fundamental Methods

Handling two or more explanatory variables in OLS regression analysis II: Hypothesis tests and more in Multivariate Regression Analysis

Hypothesis tests in multivariable regression analysis

In this chapter, we will study the different types of hypothesis tests in the multivariate regression model, depending on our research questions.

Suppose that we are estimating the regression model as follows:

$$Y_i = \beta_0 + \beta_1 X_{1i} + \beta_2 X_{2i} + \cdots + \beta_k X_{ki} + u_i$$

Generally, there are three types of hypothesis tests in a multivariate regression model. First, as we have seen earlier, if we are interested in the relationship between one specific explanatory variable and the outcome variable, we can set up the hypothesis test for β_j where j is 1 to k. It is a typical one-restriction hypothesis test as follows:

$$H_o: \beta_j = 0$$
$$H_a: \beta_j \neq 0$$

$$\text{Test statistic } t = \frac{\hat{\beta}_j - 0}{se(\hat{\beta}_j)}$$

The way of proceeding with the one-restriction hypothesis was explained in Chapter 4.

Also, we can test whether the parameter is different from a certain number, a. The only difference in the hypothesis test is replacing 0 with a.

$$H_o: \beta_j = a$$
$$H_a: \beta_j \neq a$$

$$\text{Test statistic } t = \frac{\hat{\beta}_j - a}{se(\hat{\beta}_j)}$$

The process after obtaining the test statistic is exactly the same as the typical hypothesis with 0 of the null hypothesis value.

Example 6.1

Suppose that we would like to know whether education is related to hourly wage controlling for cognitive ability and job experience.

The following regression result is obtained using hourly wage in 1980 U.S. dollars (Y), years of education (X_1), AFQT (X_2), years of job experience (X_3), in the year 1990 of the NLSY79 (National Longitudinal Survey of Youth - 1979 Cohort) data set.

$$\hat{Y}_i = -1.384 + 0.390 X_{1i} + 0.031 X_{2i} + 0.305 X_{3i}$$
$$\text{SE} \quad (0.274) \quad (0.021) \quad\quad (0.002) \quad\quad (0.015)$$

SST (Total Sum of Squares) = 128911.008
SSE (Explained Sum of Squares) = 30723.327
SSR (Residual Sum of Squares) = 98187.681
R^2 = 0.2383
n = 7,707

The estimated coefficient of education indicates that a one-year increase in education implies around a $0.390 increase in real hourly wage. Also, one more point increase in AFQT (ranging from 1 to 100 points) is associated with a $0.031 increase in real hourly wage. Lastly, one more year of job experience is associated with a $0.305 increase in real hourly wage.

R-squared = SSE/SST = 0.2383 implies that education, AFQT, and job experience explain about 24% of the variation in real hourly wage in this analysis.

We stated that the estimated coefficients are valid under OLS assumptions 1 to 4 above, and the standard errors are valid under OLS assumptions 1 to 5.

Under OLS assumptions 1 to 5 with the large sample, we construct the two-sided hypothesis test with 5% significance level ($\alpha = 0.05$) for the parameter of job experience. For an illustration, we suppose that β_3 is 0.3 under the null hypothesis.

$$H_o: \beta_3 = 0.3$$
$$H_a: \beta_3 \neq 0.3$$

$$t = \frac{\hat{\beta}_3 - \beta_3}{se(\hat{\beta}_3)} = \frac{0.305 - 0.3}{0.015} = 0.33$$

Since 0.33 is smaller than 1.96 (critical value for the 2.5% tail probability in the standard normal distribution), we can say that we don't reject the null hypothesis at the 5% significance level.

Therefore, it is unlikely that the true parameter of job experience is different from 0.3.

Notes:
the NLSY79 (National Longitudinal Survey of Youth -1979 Cohort) data set
https://www.nlsinfo.org/content/cohorts/nlsy79

Second, if we are interested in the relationship between a linear combination of the two coefficients and the outcome variable in the regression model, we can set up the hypothesis test as explained below.

Suppose that we would like to test whether β_1 and β_2 are the same.
Then, we can define $\theta = \beta_1 - \beta_2$ and the hypothesis test is for θ.

$$H_o: \theta = 0 \text{ and } H_a: \theta \neq 0$$

This is equivalent to the null and alternative hypotheses below:

$$H_o: \beta_1 - \beta_2 = 0 \text{ and } H_a: \beta_1 - \beta_2 \neq 0$$

The test statistic is

$$t = \frac{\hat{\theta} - 0}{se(\hat{\theta})} = \frac{(\hat{\beta}_1 - \hat{\beta}_2) - 0}{se(\hat{\beta}_1 - \hat{\beta}_2)}.$$

The way of proceeding with this one-restriction hypothesis is the same as the first type of hypothesis tests explained earlier.

$\hat{\beta}_1 - \hat{\beta}_2$ is the difference between two estimated coefficients. The only thing that we need to be careful about is $se(\hat{\beta}_1 - \hat{\beta}_2)$, which is not the difference between $se(\hat{\beta}_1)$ and $se(\hat{\beta}_2)$. It is the standard error of $\hat{\beta}_1 - \hat{\beta}_2$.

It can be computed as below.

$$se(\hat{\beta}_1 - \hat{\beta}_2) = \sqrt{\widehat{Var}(\hat{\beta}_1 - \hat{\beta}_2)} = \sqrt{\widehat{Var}(\hat{\beta}_1) + \widehat{Var}(\hat{\beta}_2) - 2\widehat{Cov}(\hat{\beta}_1, \hat{\beta}_2)}$$

$$= \sqrt{\left(se(\hat{\beta}_1)\right)^2 + \left(se(\hat{\beta}_2)\right)^2 - 2\widehat{Cov}(\hat{\beta}_1, \hat{\beta}_2)}$$

since

$$Var(aX + bY) = a^2 Var(X) + b^2 Var(Y) + 2ab Cov(X, Y) \text{ when } a \text{ and } b \text{ are real numbers.}$$

Most statistical analysis packages, such as SPSS, Stata, SAS, and R, provide the test statistics related to this test.

Example 6.2

Suppose that we would like to know whether education is related to hourly wage controlling for cognitive ability and job experience.

The following regression result is obtained using hourly wage in 1980 U.S. dollars (Y), years of education (X_1), AFQT (X_2), years of job experience (X_3), in the year 1990 of the NLSY79 (National Longitudinal Survey of Youth - 1979 Cohort) data set.

$$\hat{Y}_i = -1.384 + 0.390X_{1i} + 0.031X_{2i} + 0.305X_{3i}$$
$$\text{SE} \quad (0.274) \quad (0.021) \quad (0.002) \quad (0.015)$$

SST (Total Sum of Squares) = 128911.008
SSE (Explained Sum of Squares) = 30723.327
SSR (Residual Sum of Squares) = 98187.681
R^2 = 0.2383
n = 7,707
$\widehat{Cov}(\hat{\beta}_1, \hat{\beta}_3)$ = 0.00005

The estimated coefficient of education indicates that a one-year increase in education implies around a $0.390 increase in real hourly wage. Also, one more point increase in AFQT (ranging from 1 to 100 points) is associated with a $0.031 increase in real hourly wage. Lastly, one more year of job experience is associated with a $0.305 increase in real hourly wage.

R-squared = SSE/SST = 0.2383 implies that education, AFQT, and job experience explain about 24% of the variation in real hourly wage in this analysis.

We stated that the estimated coefficients are valid under OLS assumptions 1 to 4 above, and the standard errors are valid under OLS assumptions 1 to 5.

Under OLS assumptions 1 to 5 with the large sample, we test whether the parameters of education and job experience are the same. We construct the two-sided hypothesis test with a 5% significance level ($\alpha = 0.05$). The null and alternative hypotheses are as follows.

$$H_o: \beta_1 - \beta_3 = 0$$
$$H_a: \beta_1 - \beta_3 \neq 0$$

$$t = \frac{\hat{\beta}_1 - \hat{\beta}_3}{se(\hat{\beta}_1 - \hat{\beta}_3)} = \frac{\hat{\beta}_1 - \hat{\beta}_3}{\sqrt{(se(\hat{\beta}_1))^2 + (se(\hat{\beta}_3))^2 - 2\widehat{Cov}(\hat{\beta}_1, \hat{\beta}_3)}} = \frac{0.390 - 0.305}{\sqrt{(0.021)^2 + (0.014)^2 - 2*0.00005}} = 3.67$$

Since 3.67 is larger than 1.96 (critical value for the 2.5% tail probability in the standard normal distribution), we can say that we reject the null hypothesis at the 5% significance level.

> Therefore, it is likely that the true parameters of education and job experience are different from each other.
>
> Notes:
> the NLSY79 (National Longitudinal Survey of Youth -1979 Cohort) data set
> https://www.nlsinfo.org/content/cohorts/nlsy79

Third, if we want to test whether a group of two or more explanatory variables is statistically significant in the regression model, we can set up the hypothesis test with multiple restrictions, as shown below.

The regression model with all the explanatory variables is called an unrestricted model.

$$Y_i = \beta_0 + \beta_1 X_{1i} + \beta_2 X_{2i} + \cdots + \beta_k X_{ki} + u_i \qquad \text{-- Unrestricted model}$$

Suppose that we want to test whether the first three variables, X_{1i}, X_{2i}, and X_{3i}, are statistically significant as a group. The null and alternative hypotheses related to this research question are as follows.

$$\begin{cases} H_o: \beta_1 = 0, \ \beta_2 = 0 \text{ and } \beta_3 = 0 \\ H_a: otherwise \end{cases} \equiv \quad \beta_1 = \beta_2 = \beta_3 = 0 \qquad \text{(3 restrictions)}$$

Then, we can come up with a regression model excluding these three variables under the null hypothesis, which is called a restricted model.

$$Y_i = \beta_0 + \beta_4 X_{4i} + \cdots + \beta_k X_{ki} + v_i \qquad \text{-- Restricted model}$$

Different from the previous two hypothesis tests, the null hypothesis includes three restrictions. The test statistic for the hypothesis test with multiple restrictions is developed as the F-test statistic.

The test statistic

$$F = \frac{(SSR_r - SSR_{ur})/q=3}{SSR_{ur}/(n-k-1)}) \quad q: \# \text{ of restrictions}$$

$$\sim F_{df_n=q, df_{dn}=n-k-1} \quad k: \# \text{ of independent variables in the unrestricted model}$$

The numerator of the F test statistic is the difference between the residual sum of squares (SSR) of the restricted and unrestricted models. Since SSR is the variation of the outcome that cannot be explained by the regression model, the smaller SSR indicates the better model. Thus, it is expected that the SSR of the restricted model will be larger than or as large as the SSR of the unrestricted model, depending on the contribution of the three variables to the unrestricted model. Thus, the larger this difference becomes, the stronger the evidence is to challenge the null hypothesis that the three variables do not contribute to the unrestricted regression model. The denominator of the F test statistic consisting of the SSR of the unrestricted model works as the base for the test statistic. The F test statistic follows the F distribution with df_n (numerator degree of freedom) and df_{dn} (denominator degrees of freedom). The degree of freedom by the numerator ($df_n = q$) is the number of restrictions while the degree of freedom by the denominator ($df_{dn} = n - k - 1$) is the degree of freedom of the unrestricted model. The F distribution below has a positive value only, and its table shows the critical values from 0.5% to 10% levels of significance with different degrees of freedom of numerator and denominator: $df_1 = df_n$ and $df_2 = df_{dn}$ in this F distribution table.

Appendix F of the textbook: critical values of the F distribution

df_2	a	df_1 1	2	3	4	5	6	7	8	9
1	.100	39.86	49.50	53.59	55.83	57.24	58.20	58.91	59.44	59.86
	.050	161.4	199.5	215.7	224.6	230.2	234.0	236.8	238.9	240.5
	.025	647.8	799.5	864.2	899.6	921.8	937.1	948.2	956.7	963.3
	.010	4052	4999.5	5403	5625	5764	5859	5928	5982	6022
	.005	16211	20000	21615	22500	23056	23437	23715	23925	24091
2	.100	8.53	9.00	9.16	9.24	9.29	9.33	9.35	9.37	9.38
	.050	18.51	19.00	19.16	19.25	19.30	19.33	19.35	19.37	19.38
	.025	38.51	39.00	39.17	39.25	39.30	39.33	39.36	39.37	39.39
	.010	98.50	99.00	99.17	99.25	99.30	99.33	99.36	99.37	99.39
	.005	198.5	199.0	199.2	199.2	199.3	199.3	199.4	199.4	199.4
3	.100	5.54	5.46	5.39	5.34	5.31	5.28	5.27	5.25	5.24
	.050	10.13	9.55	9.28	9.12	9.01	8.94	8.89	8.85	8.81
	.025	17.44	16.04	15.44	15.10	14.88	14.73	14.62	14.54	14.47
	.010	34.12	30.82	29.46	28.71	28.24	27.91	27.64	27.49	27.35
	.005	55.55	49.80	47.47	46.19	45.39	44.84	44.43	44.13	43.88
4	.100	4.54	4.32	4.19	4.11	4.05	4.01	3.98	3.95	3.94
	.050	7.71	6.94	6.59	6.39	6.26	6.16	6.09	6.04	6.00
	.025	12.22	10.65	9.98	9.60	9.36	9.20	9.07	8.98	8.90
	.010	21.20	18.00	16.69	15.98	15.52	15.21	14.98	14.80	14.66
	.005	31.33	26.28	24.26	23.15	22.46	21.97	21.62	21.35	21.14

5	.100	4.06	3.78	3.62	3.52	3.45	3.40	3.37	3.34	3.32
	.050	6.61	5.79	5.41	5.19	5.05	4.95	4.88	4.82	4.77
	.025	10.01	8.43	7.76	7.39	7.15	6.98	6.85	6.76	6.68
	.010	16.26	13.27	12.06	11.39	10.97	10.67	10.46	10.29	10.16
	.005	22.78	18.31	16.53	15.56	14.94	14.51	14.20	13.96	13.77
6	.100	3.78	3.46	3.29	3.18	3.11	3.05	3.01	2.98	2.96
	.050	5.99	5.14	4.76	4.53	4.39	4.28	4.21	4.15	4.10
	.025	8.81	7.26	6.60	6.23	5.99	5.82	5.70	5.60	5.52
	.010	13.75	10.92	9.78	9.15	8.75	8.47	8.26	8.10	7.98
	.005	18.63	14.54	12.92	12.03	11.46	11.07	10.79	10.57	10.39
7	.100	3.59	3.26	3.07	2.96	2.88	2.83	2.78	2.75	2.72
	.050	5.59	4.74	4.35	4.12	3.97	3.87	3.79	3.73	3.68
	.025	8.07	6.54	5.89	5.52	5.29	5.12	4.99	4.90	4.82
	.010	12.25	9.55	8.45	7.85	7.46	7.19	6.99	6.84	6.72
	.005	16.24	12.40	10.88	10.05	9.52	9.16	8.89	8.68	8.51
8	.100	3.46	3.11	2.92	2.81	2.73	2.67	2.62	2.59	2.56
	.050	5.32	4.46	4.07	3.84	3.69	3.58	3.50	3.44	3.39
	.025	7.57	6.06	5.42	5.05	4.82	4.65	4.53	4.43	4.36
	.010	11.26	8.65	7.59	7.01	6.63	6.37	6.18	6.03	5.91
	.005	14.69	11.04	9.60	8.81	8.30	7.95	7.69	7.50	7.34
9	.100	3.36	3.01	2.81	2.69	2.61	2.55	2.51	2.47	2.44
	.050	5.12	4.26	3.86	3.63	3.48	3.37	3.29	3.23	3.18
	.025	7.21	5.71	5.08	4.72	4.48	4.32	4.20	4.10	4.03
	.010	10.56	8.02	6.99	6.42	6.06	5.80	5.61	5.47	5.35
	.005	13.61	10.11	8.72	7.96	7.47	7.13	6.88	6.69	6.54

F **distribution**

The *F* distribution, sometimes referred to as the Fisher-Snedecor distribution, is a statistical probability distribution that is frequently used in the field of statistics. It is widely employed for conducting hypothesis tests and performing analyses related to variance. This distribution is symbolically represented as $F_{df_n, df_{dn}}$. The *F*-test statistic that follows the *F* distribution is always positive.

The shape of the *F* distribution depends on the values assigned to two degrees of freedom, df_n (degree of freedom by the numerator) and df_{dn} (degree of freedom by the denominator). It consistently exhibits a positive skew, but its specific appearance varies based on the degrees of freedom. As both df_n and df_{dn} increase, the *F* distribution gradually becomes more symmetrical.

As shown below, the *F*-test statistics also can be expressed using *R*-squared. The numerator of the *F*-test statistic can be the difference between the *R*-squared of the restricted and unrestricted models. Since *R*-squared is how much the model explains the outcome variable, the *R*-squared of the unrestricted model is larger than or as large as the *R*-squared of the restricted model, depending on the contribution of the three variables to the restricted model. Therefore, as explained earlier, the larger this difference becomes, the stronger the evidence is to challenge the null hypothesis that the three variables do not contribute to the unrestricted regression model.

$$F = \frac{(SSR_r - SSR_{ur})/q=3}{SSR_{ur}/(n-k-1)} \quad q: \text{\# of restrictions}$$

$$k: \text{\# of independent variables in the unrestricted model}$$

$$= \frac{(R_{ur}^2 - R_r^2)/q=3}{(1-R_{ur}^2)/(n-k-1)}$$

$$\sim F_{df_n=q, df_{dn}=n-k-1}$$

It is from

$$F = \frac{(R_{ur}^2 - R_r^2)/q}{(1-R_{ur}^2)/(n-k-1)} \quad \text{where}$$

$$R_{ur}^2 = 1 - \frac{SSR_{ur}}{SST}, \; R_r^2 = 1 - \frac{SSR_r}{SST}, \text{ and } SST = \sum(Y_i - \bar{Y})^2$$

Then, $F = \dfrac{\left(\left(1-\frac{SSR_{ur}}{SST}\right)-\left(1-\frac{SSR_r}{SST}\right)\right)/q}{\left(1-\left(1-\frac{SSR_{ur}}{SST}\right)\right)/(n-k-1)}$

$$= \frac{\left(-\frac{SSR_{ur}}{SST}+\frac{SSR_r}{SST}\right)/q}{\left(\frac{SSR_{ur}}{SST}\right)/(n-k-1)}$$

$$= \frac{(SSR_r - SSR_{ur})/q}{SSR_{ur}/(n-k-1)}$$

$$\sim F_{df_n=q, df_{dn}=n-k-1}$$

Example 6.3

Suppose that we would like to know whether education is related to hourly wage controlling for cognitive ability and job experience.

Suppose that we would like to test whether AFQT and job experience are important in explaining the real hourly wage.

The null and alternative hypotheses are as follows.

$H_o: \beta_2 = 0$ and $\beta_3 = 0$ $\equiv$ $\beta_2 = \beta_3 = 0$
$H_a: otherwise$

Let's test with the 1% significance level.
The regression outcomes from the restricted and unrestricted regressions are as follows.

Unrestricted model:
The unrestricted regression result is obtained using hourly wage in 1980 U.S. dollars (Y), years of education (X_1), AFQT (X_2), years of job experience (X_3), in the year 1990 of the NLSY79 (National Longitudinal Survey of Youth - 1979 Cohort) data set.

$$\hat{Y}_i = -1.384 + 0.390X_{1i} + 0.031X_{2i} + 0.305X_{3i}$$
$$\text{SE} \quad (0.274) \quad (0.021) \quad\quad (0.002) \quad\quad (0.015)$$

SST (Total Sum of Squares) = 128911.008
SSEur (Explained Sum of Squares) = 30723.327
SSRur (Residual Sum of Squares) = 98187.681
$R_{ur}^2 = 0.2383$
$n = 7,707$

Restricted model:
The restricted regression result below is obtained using hourly wage in 1980 U.S. dollars (Y) and years of education (X) in the year 1990 of the NLSY79 (National Longitudinal Survey of Youth - 1979 Cohort) data set.

$$\hat{Y}_i = -0.587 + 0.62X_i$$
$$\text{SE} \quad (0.231) \quad (0.017)$$

SST (Total Sum of Squares) = 128911.008
SSEr (Explained Sum of Squares) = 18083.2888
SSRr (Residual Sum of Squares) = 110827.719
$R_r^2 = 0.1403$
$n = 7,707$

q: 2 of restrictions
k: 3 of explanatory variables in the unrestricted model

We find that the number of restrictions is 2 since the excluded variables in the restricted model are AFQT and job experience. Also, the number of explanatory variables in the unrestricted model is 3, as shown above.

Using the given information from the unrestricted and restricted models, we compute the F-test statistic as follows. One way is using the Residual Sum of Squares (SSR), and the other is using the R-squared. Their outcomes are practically the same.

$$F = \frac{(SSR_r - SSR_{ur})/q}{SSR_{ur}/(n-k-1)} = \frac{(110827.719 - 98187.681)/2}{98187.681/(7707-3-1)} = 495.82$$

$$F = \frac{(R^2_{ur} - R^2_r)/q}{(1-R^2_{ur})/(n-k-1)} = \frac{(0.2383 - 0.1403)/2}{(1-0.2383)/(7707-3-1)} = 495.53$$

Since 495 is larger than 4.60 ($F_{\alpha=0.01, df_n=2, df_{dn}=7703}$, the critical value of the 1% significance level with $df_n = 2$ and $df_{dn} = 7703$ in the F distribution), we reject the null hypothesis at $p<0.01$. Thus, it is likely that AFQT and job experience are important enough to explain the real hourly wage in the regression model.

Notes:
the NLSY79 (National Longitudinal Survey of Youth -1979 Cohort) data set
https://www.nlsinfo.org/content/cohorts/nlsy79

The third type of hypothesis test can be used to test whether all the explanatory variables are statistically significant as a group. In other words, this test is to examine whether all the explanatory variables fully contribute to the regression model to explain the outcome variable.

The null and alternative hypotheses are as follows.

$H_o: \beta_1 = 0, \beta_2 = 0, \beta_3 = 0 \dots$ and $\beta_k = 0$

$\equiv \beta_1 = \beta_2 = \dots = \beta_k = 0$

(k restrictions)

H_a: otherwise

The restricted regression model includes the intercept only as below.

$Y_i = \beta_0 + u_i$ -- Restricted model

Thus, the R-squared of the restricted model is 0.

Then, the F-test statistic can be expressed as below.

$$F = \frac{(R_{ur}^2 - R_r^2)/q=k}{(1-R_{ur}^2)/(n-k-1)}$$

$$= \frac{R_{ur}^2/q=k}{(1-R_{ur}^2)/(n-k-1)} \quad \text{since } R_r^2 = 0$$

$$\sim F_{df_n=k, df_{dn}=n-k-1}$$

Also, it is useful to know that the square of the t-test statistic is the F-test statistic when we have one restriction in the hypothesis test. This is why some statistical packages provide the F-test statistic instead of the t-test statistic even when the number of restrictions of the hypothesis test is one.

Example 6.4

Suppose that we would like to know whether education is related to hourly wage controlling for cognitive ability and job experience.

We would like to test whether all the explanatory variables are important in explaining the real hourly wage.

The null and alternative hypotheses are as follows.

$H_o: \beta_1 = 0, \beta_2 = 0,$ and $\beta_3 = 0 \quad \equiv \quad \beta_1 = \beta_2 = \beta_3 = 0$ (3 restrictions)
H_a: otherwise

Let's test at the 1% level of significance.

The regression outcomes from the restricted and unrestricted regressions are as follows.

Unrestricted model:
The unrestricted regression result is obtained using hourly wage in 1980 U.S. dollars (Y), years of education (X_1), AFQT (X_2), years of job experience (X_3), in the year 1990 of the NLSY79 (National Longitudinal Survey of Youth - 1979 Cohort) data set.

$$\hat{Y}_i = -1.384 + 0.390X_{1i} + 0.031X_{2i} + 0.305X_{3i}$$
$$\text{SE} \quad (0.274) \quad (0.021) \quad (0.002) \quad (0.015)$$

SST (Total Sum of Squares) = 128911.008
SSEur (Explained Sum of Squares) = 30723.327
SSRur (Residual Sum of Squares) = 98187.681
$R_{ur}^2 = 0.2383$
$n = 7,707$

Restricted model:
The restricted regression result below is obtained using hourly wage in 1980 U.S. dollars (Y) with no explanatory variable in the year 1990 of the NLSY79 (National Longitudinal Survey of Youth - 1979 Cohort) data set.

$$\hat{Y}_i = 7.46$$
$$\text{SE} \quad (0.0.047)$$

SST (Total Sum of Squares) = 128911.008
SSEr (Explained Sum of Squares) = 0
SSRr (Residual Sum of Squares) = 128911.008
$R_r^2 = 0$
$n = 7,707$

q: 3 of restrictions
k: 3 of explanatory variables in the unrestricted model

We find that the number of restrictions is 3 since all the explanatory variables are excluded in the restricted model. Also, the number of explanatory variables in the unrestricted model is 3, as shown above.

Using the given information from the unrestricted and restricted models, we compute the F-test statistic as follows. One way is using the Residual Sum of Squares (SSR), and the other is using the R-squared. Their outcomes are practically the same.

$$F = \frac{(R_{ur}^2 - R_r^2)/q=k}{(1-R_{ur}^2)/(n-k-1)} = \frac{R_{ur}^2/q=k}{(1-R_{ur}^2)/(n-k-1)} = \frac{0.2383/3}{(1-0.2383)/(7707-3-1)} = 803.30$$

Since 803.3 is larger than 3.79 ($F_{\alpha=0.01, df_n=3, df_{dn}=7703}$, the critical value of the 1% significance level with $df_n = 3$ and $df_{dn} = 7703$ in the F distribution), we reject the null hypothesis at $p < 0.01$.

Thus, it is likely that all three variables are important enough to explain the real hourly wage in the regression model.

Notes:
the NLSY79 (National Longitudinal Survey of Youth -1979 Cohort) data set
https://www.nlsinfo.org/content/cohorts/nlsy79

Adjusted R-squared

Adjusted R-squared is a version of R-squared that takes into account the number of variables in a model and may decrease using the formula as follows.

$$\bar{R}^2 = 1 - \frac{SSR/(n-k-1)}{SST/(n-1)}$$

Remember that

$$R^2 = \frac{SSE}{SST} = \frac{SST - SSR}{SST} = 1 - \frac{SSR}{SST}$$

$$0 \leq R^2 \leq 1$$

As more explanatory variables are added to the OLS regression model, R^2 automatically increase. On the other hand, as the number of explanatory variables (k) increases, $\bar{R}^2$ decreases if SSR (Residual Sum of Squares, which is an unexplained variation of Y) is not reduced by including more explanatory variables. In other words, if we include unnecessary variables in the OLS regression model, the formula of the adjusted R-squared puts a penalty on this move.

However, as we discussed earlier, increasing R-squared and adjusted R-squared may not be our main goal in data analysis, although it may lead to more efficient estimates by reducing standard errors. The main purpose of data analysis in social science is to estimate the causal relationship between the outcome variable and the explanatory variable. Therefore, choosing the appropriate variables in the OLS regression should be based on theory and common sense, not based on increasing R-squared and adjusted R-squared.

Example 6.5

The regression result below is obtained using hourly wage in 1980 U.S. dollars (Y), years of education (X_1), AFQT (X_2), years of job experience (X_3), in the year 1990 of the NLSY79 (National Longitudinal Survey of Youth - 1979 Cohort) data set.

$$\widehat{Y}_i = -1.384 + 0.390X_{1i} + 0.031X_{2i} + 0.305X_{3i}$$
$$\text{SE} \quad (0.274) \quad (0.021) \quad\quad (0.002) \quad\quad (0.015)$$

SST (Total Sum of Squares) = 128911.008
SSE (Explained Sum of Squares) = 30723.327
SSR (Residual Sum of Squares) = 98187.681
R^2 = 0.2383
Adjusted R^2 = 0.2380
n = 7,707

In this analysis, adjusted R^2 is 0.2380, which is slightly smaller than R^2, 0.2383. It is driven by the adjusted computation we discussed earlier. Since the difference is negligible, the included explanatory variables seem not overstate R^2.

Notes:
the NLSY79 (National Longitudinal Survey of Youth -1979 Cohort) data set
https://www.nlsinfo.org/content/cohorts/nlsy79

Chapter Summary

Hypothesis tests when there are multiple explanatory variables	Depending on our research question, we can develop different hypothesis tests. If we want to test one restriction or condition related to the parameters, we can use the t-tests. On the other hand, if we would like to test multiple restrictions or conditions related to the parameters, we can use the F-tests.
Addressing common misunderstandings and mistakes	We cannot say that one regression model is better than the other by comparing R-squared and adjusted R-squared since our quantitative analysis mainly focuses on consistently estimating the causal relationship between X and Y. Also, a small R-squared does not indicate that the regression model is poor or unreliable. It is more important to yield efficient estimates that have smaller standard errors. With efficient estimates, we can easily reject the null hypothesis when the null hypothesis is false.

Exercises

Chapter 6
Handling two or more explanatory variables in OLS regression analysis II: Hypothesis tests and more in Multivariate Regression Analysis

1. We want to test the human capital theory that more education leads to higher earnings or wages. The following outcome is from a multivariate OLS regression with real hourly wage in 1984 dollars (rhw1984) as the outcome variable and years of education (edu), afqt (AFQT score between 0 to 100; treated it as intelligence measure), and actual job experience in years (lcexpy) as the explanatory variable.

$$\widehat{rhw1984}_i = -1.384 + 0.390 edu_i + 0.031 afqt_i + 0.305 lcexpy_i$$
$$\text{SE} \quad\quad (0.274) \quad (0.021) \quad\quad (0.002) \quad\quad (0.015)$$

SST (Total Sum of Squares) = 128911.008
SSE (Explained Sum of Squares) = 35723.3269
SSR (Residual Sum of Squares) = 98187.6811
$R^2 = 0.238$
$n = 7,707$

(1) Construct the null and two-sided alternative hypotheses to test whether there is a significant relationship between each independent variable and real hourly wage. What do you learn from these significance tests? Explain briefly.

(2) Explain what BLUE stands for and what assumptions we need to have BLUE. Let's assume the small sample.

(3) What additional assumption do we need to conduct valid inference procedures with BLUE? Let's assume the small sample.

(4) It seems that the sample size of this study is large. If it is, then which assumption is unnecessary for the inference and why?

(5) Find the following components, and explain what each component stands for in both mathematical and intuitive terms: SST, SSE, and SSR. Check that SST = SSE + SSR using provided results.

(6) Calculate R^2 and Interpret it. Explain or show how to calculate it using SST, SSE, and SSR.

2. Suppose that Korea University would like to evaluate whether frequent consultations with academic advisors help freshmen to improve their academic achievements. Researchers thought that students' academic ability should be controlled in this regression model. Thus, they controlled for their high school GPA and had a following regression outcome.

$$\widehat{GPA} = 0.34 + 0.01 \text{ Consultation} + 0.9 \text{highschoolGPA}$$
$$\text{SE} \quad (0.12) \quad (0.02) \quad\quad\quad\quad\quad (0.4)$$

High school GPA = highschool GPA (0 to 4)
$R^2 = 0.275$
$n = 2,000$

(1) Please test whether the coefficient of Consultation is statistically different from 0 with the two-sided test at $\alpha = 0.05$.

(2) Please interpret the coefficient of high school GPA and test whether it is statistically different from 0 with the two-sided test at $\alpha = 0.05$.

(3) Construct the null and alternative hypotheses to test whether all explanatory variables collectively explain the outcome variable. Explain and show how to

calculate the *F* statistic using *R*-squared.

3. Human capital theory suggests that more education leads to higher wage. Assume that you have real hourly wage (rhw1984) and education in years (edu) in your data.

Now you have the following regression result

$$\widehat{rhw1984} = -0.587 + 0.620 \ edu$$
$$\text{SE} \quad\quad (0.231) \quad (0.017)$$

SST (Total Sum of Squares) = 128911.008
SSE (Explained Sum of Squares) = 18083.2888
SSR (Residual Sum of Squares) = 110827.719
$R^2 = 0.1403$
$n = 7,707$

(1) Some of your colleagues argue that your model is limited and naïve because you do not include cognitive skills measured by AFQT in your model. What problems does this exclusion cause for your estimated coefficient of education? Is it biased? If it is, which direction is bias?

Now we add one more variable, AFQT score from 0 to 100 (afqt), to this data. Assume that this measures individuals' cognitive skills.

$$\widehat{rhw1984}_i = 1.556 + 0.323 edu_i + 0.042 afqt_i$$
$$\text{SE} \quad\quad (0.242) \quad (0.021) \quad\quad (0.002)$$

SST (Total Sum of Squares) = 128911.008
SSE (Explained Sum of Squares) = 25135.902
SSR (Residual Sum of Squares) = 103775.106
$R^2 = 0.195$
$n = 7,707$

(2) In this new regression outcome, please explain the difference in the estimated coefficient of education compared to that presented in the earlier output.

(3) Construct the null hypothesis to test statistically whether education and AFQT score explains real hourly wage in this model. Calculate the F-test statistic using numbers provided in this output.

(4) Your colleagues also want to know whether the impact of one additional year of education and one point increase in AFQT is a 35 cent increase in real hourly wage. Construct and test the hypothesis to test this remark using numbers provided in this Stata outcome. Assume that covariance between the two coefficients is 0.

(5) Is there evidence of near multicollinearity between education and AFQT score? Why or why not?

4. Suppose that you want to investigate whether having a job training affects individuals' earnings.

Y is yearly earnings in \$. X_1 and X_2 are education and job experience in years, respectively. X_3 is the number of months of the program participation in the past three years.

The estimated equation (with standard errors in parentheses below estimates) is:
$$\hat{Y} = 45.08 + 200.083\,X_1 + 150.215\,X_2 + 50.1\,X_3$$
$$\text{SE} \quad (3.93) \quad (43.38) \quad (50.37) \quad (10.5)$$

$n = 1{,}730$, $R^2 = 0.332$

(1) Please interpret the estimated coefficient of X_3 and test whether it is statistically significant at $\alpha=5\%$ using the two-sided test. Please also construct the null and alternative hypotheses and interpret your results.

(2) Suppose that you would like to test whether the estimated coefficient of job experience is the same as three times of the estimated coefficient of job training. Construct and test the hypothesis to test this remark using numbers provided in this outcome. Assume that covariance between the two coefficients is 0.

(3) Construct the null and alternative hypotheses to test whether all explanatory variables collectively explain the outcome variable. Explain and show how to calculate the F statistic using R-squared.

(4) Suppose that the estimated equation with the job training program only is as follows:

$$\hat{Y} = 35.08 + 70.1\, X_4$$
$$\text{SE} \quad (3.93) \quad (10.5)$$

$n = 1{,}730,\ R^2 = 0.154$

Please test whether education and job experience are important in the original regression.

5. Suppose that you are evaluating the causal impact of number of siblings on educational attainment. Suppose that your true population model is $educ_i = \beta_0 + \beta_1 sibs_i + \beta_1 IQ_i + u_i$ where $educ_i$ is years of schooling, $sibs_i$ is number of siblings, and IQ_i is individual's IQ score.

You have the following outcome.

$$\widehat{educ_i} = 6.551 - 0.096 sibs_i + 0.071 IQ_i$$
$$\text{SE} \quad (0.464) \quad (0.028) \quad (0.004)$$

SSE = 1240.461
SST = 4506.819
$n = 935$
$Cov(\hat{\beta}_1, \hat{\beta}_2) = 0.0000335$

(1) Calculate R-squared using numbers given in the outcome. Interpret the obtained R-squared.

(2) Test whether more siblings lead to less educational attainment. Construct the null and alternative hypotheses and calculate the test statistics.

(3) Calculate the 95% and 99% confidence intervals for the true parameter of IQ_i and interpret it.

(4) Test whether the positive impact of one point increase in IQ offsets the negative impact of additional sibling in the family. The covariance between OLS estimates of $sibs_i$ and IQ_i is .0000335.

(5) Based on this outcome, a politician argues that birth control policies are effective in improving educational attainment. Make your comment on this argument.

Chapter 7
Data Analysis for Social Science: Fundamental Methods

The OLS regression analysis when comparing the outcomes of the two or more groups:
Use of binary explanatory variables

Typical introductory data analysis textbooks cover the hypothesis test of the group difference using the t-test that compares the sample means. However, this textbook did not study this topic until now because it is much easier to deal with examining group differences using regression analysis. In this chapter, we will study how to test various group differences in an outcome variable.

A binary variable is a variable that takes on the value 1 or 0, which is popular to present qualitative events or characteristics. For example, a man is 1 and a woman is 0; Monday is 1 and other days are 0; college education or more is 1 and 0 for otherwise. Binary variables are also called dummy variables or indicator variables. Instead of using the other two numbers, such as 1 and 2, 2 and 3, or 1 and 100, using 1 or 0 is useful mathematically since 1 stands for 100% and 0 for 0%. When the outcome variable is binary, with 1 for men and 0 for women, the sample mean of the outcome variable indicates what percent of individuals are men.

Estimating group differences in an outcome variable

Suppose that we would like to study the difference in college GPA by gender and different years of study in college.

Assume that Y is college GPA (0 to 4.5) and W is 1 for women and 0 for men.

Let's start with a difference between the two groups. Consider a simple model with the continuous outcome variable (Y) and one dummy variable (W).

$$Y = \beta_0 + \delta_0 W + u$$

This model can be interpreted as allowing an intercept change.

If $W = 0$, then $Y = \beta_0 + u$. In this case, β_0 is the population mean for the base group consisting of men ($W = 0$).

If $W = 1$, then $Y = (\beta_0 + \delta_0) + u$. For the comparison group consisting of women ($W = 1$), $\beta_0 + \delta_0$ is the population mean.

Therefore, δ_0 is the population mean difference in college GPA between men and women.

Suppose that the estimated regression is as follows:

$$\hat{Y}_i = 2.9 + 0.5 W_i$$
$$\text{SE} \quad (1.2) \quad (0.1)$$

Then, since β_0 and δ_0 are estimated to be 2.9 and 0.5, we can say that men's college GPA is 2.9 and women's college GPA is higher than men's by 0.5. The difference between men and women is also statistically significant at $p<0.01$ (the 1% level of significance) since the test statistic for the null hypothesis $\delta_0 = 0$ is $5 = 0.5/0.1$, and it is larger than 2.58 (critical value of the two-sided test with the 1% level of significance).

We can easily expand this regression model to examine the differences among more than two groups. Suppose that we are interested in the difference in college GPA among different years of study in college. Then, we have the four groups of men and women: freshmen, sophomores, juniors, and seniors.

We can develop the following dummy variables to include all four groups of men and women.

$D_0 = 1$ for freshmen and 0 otherwise
$D_1 = 1$ for sophomores and 0 otherwise
$D_2 = 1$ for juniors and 0 otherwise
$D_3 = 1$ for seniors and 0 otherwise

$$Y = \beta_0 + \delta_1 D_1 + \delta_2 D_2 + \delta_3 D_3 + u$$

The base group consists of freshmen.
This model can be interpreted as allowing an intercept change.
If D_1 to D_3 are all 0, then $Y = \beta_0 + u$. In this case, β_0 is the population mean for the base group consisting of freshmen.

If $D_1 = 1$, then $Y = (\beta_0 + \delta_1) + u$. For sophomores, $\beta_0 + \delta_1$ is the population mean. Thus, δ_1 is the population mean difference in college GPA between the base group (freshmen) and sophomores.

In the same manner, thus, δ_2 is the population mean difference in GPA between the base group (freshmen) and juniors. Also, δ_3 is the population mean difference in GPA between the base group (freshmen) and seniors.

Suppose that we would like to examine the population mean difference between sophomores and juniors.

If $D_1 = 1$ then $Y = \beta_0 + \delta_1 + u$.
If $D_2 = 1$ then $Y = \beta_0 + \delta_2 + u$.
Then, the population mean difference between the two groups is $\delta_2 - \delta_1$.

Suppose that we have the following estimated result:

$$\widehat{Y}_i = 2.3 + 0.3 D_{1i} + 0.2 D_{2i} + 0.09 D_{3i}$$
SE (1.1) (0.15) (0.05) (0.11)

From this, it is found that compared to freshmen (base group), the GPAs of sophomores, juniors, and seniors are higher by 0.3, 0.2, and 0.09, respectively. The estimated differences are statistically significant for sophomores and juniors at least at $p<0.05$ (the 5% significance level), while it is not statistically significant for seniors even at $p<0.05$. Under the conventional null hypothesis, their test statistics are $0.3/0.15 = 2$, $0.2/0.05 = 4$, and $0.09/0.11 = 0.82$, respectively.

Now, let's think about the differences in GPA by gender and different years of study in college. It is possible to develop the regression model by introducing the interaction terms between gender and different years of study in college as follows.

$$Y = \beta_0 + \delta_0 W + \delta_1 D_1 + \delta_2 D_2 + \delta_3 D_3 + \gamma_1 W \times D_1 + \gamma_2 W \times D_2 + \gamma_3 W \times D_3 + u$$

In this case, if $W = 0$ and all three D_1 to D_3 are 0, then

$y = \beta_0 + u$ where β_0 is the average GPA for male freshmen.

If $W = 1$ and $D_1 = 1$, then

$Y = \beta_0 + \delta_0 + \delta_1 + \gamma_1 + u$ where $\beta_0 + \delta_0 + \delta_1 + \gamma_1$ is the average GPA for female sophomores. Thus, the population mean difference between the base group (male freshmen) and this group is $\delta_0 + \delta_1 + \gamma_1$.

In the same manner, we can examine the difference between any gender and years of study in college. For example, if we would like to compare the population mean difference between men and women in the senior class, we can compare the following two regression equations.

When $W = 0$ and $D_3 = 1$ for men of seniors,
$Y = \beta_0 + \delta_3 + u$.
When $W = 0$ and $D_3 = 1$ for women of seniors,
$Y = \beta_0 + \delta_0 + \delta_3 + \gamma_3 + u$.

Thus, the population mean difference between the two groups is measured by $\delta_0 + \gamma_3$.

In another example, if we would like to examine the difference between male seniors and male sophomores, then we can do so in the following manner:

When $W = 0$ and $D_1 = 1$ for men of sophomores,
$Y = \beta_0 + \delta_1 + u$.
When $W = 0$ and $D_3 = 1$ for men of seniors,
$Y = \beta_0 + \delta_3 + u$.

Thus, the population mean difference between the two groups is measured by $\delta_3 - \delta_1$.

Example 7.1

Suppose that we would like to examine whether there is a wage difference between men and women.

The regression outcome is obtained using hourly wage in 1980 US dollars (Y_i), female dummy variable ($W_i = 1$ for women and 0 for otherwise) in the year 1990 of the NLSY79 (National Longitudinal Survey of Youth - 1979 Cohort) data set.

$$\widehat{Y}_i = 8.304 - 1.652 W_i$$
$$\text{SE} \quad (0.065) \quad (0.091)$$

SST (Total Sum of Squares) = 128911.008
SSE (Explained Sum of Squares) = 5252.3703
SSR (Residual Sum of Squares) = 123658.638
R^2 = 0.0407
n = 7,707

The estimated coefficient of the female dummy variable suggests that women's wage is lower than men's wage by $1.652. The estimated constant, $8.304, indicates the average wage level for men in the sample. According to R^2, the regression model explains the variation of real hourly wage by about 4.1%. We test the wage difference by gender under the following null and alternative hypotheses.

$$H_o: \beta_w = 0$$
$$H_a: \beta_w \neq 0$$

Under the default null and alternative hypotheses above, it is statistically significant even at the 1% level of significance since the test statistic computed below is 3.65 greater than 2.58 (the critical value of the 0.05% tail probability in the standard normal distribution).

$$t = \frac{\widehat{\beta_w} - \beta_w}{se(\widehat{\beta_w})} = \frac{1.652 - 0}{0.017} = 3.65$$

Therefore, it seems that women's wage is lower than men's.

Notes:
the NLSY79 (National Longitudinal Survey of Youth -1979 Cohort) data set
https://www.nlsinfo.org/content/cohorts/nlsy79

Example 7.2

Suppose that we would like to examine the wage differences by ethnic groups such as black, Hispanic, and others (non-black and non-Hispanic).

To yield the regression outcome below, we use hourly wage in 1980 U.S. dollars (Y_i) and two ethnic group dummy variables indicating black and Hispanic ($D_{1i} = 1$ for black and 0 for otherwise; $D_{2i} = 1$ for Hispanic and 0 for otherwise) in the year 1990 of the NLSY79 (National Longitudinal Survey of Youth - 1979 Cohort) data set.

$$\widehat{Y}_i = 7.939 - 1.565 D_{1i} - 0.597 D_{2i}$$
$$\text{SE} \quad (0.060) \quad (0.111) \quad (0.128)$$

SST (Total Sum of Squares) = 128911.008
SSE (Explained Sum of Squares) = 3289.34502
SSR (Residual Sum of Squares) = 125621.663
$R^2 = 0.0255$
$n = 7{,}707$

The estimated constant, 7.939, indicates the average wage of non-black and non-Hispanic workers. Also, according to the estimated coefficients of the two dummy variables, black and Hispanic workers earn $1.565 and $0.597 lower than non-black and non-Hispanic workers since they are indicating the wage difference between the particular group and the base group (non-black and non-Hispanic workers). These differences are statistically significant even at 1% under the default null and alternative hypotheses since the test statistics for black and Hispanic coefficients are -14.16 and -4.65 greater than 2.58 in absolute values (the critical value of the 0.05% tail probability in the standard normal distribution). Thus, it seems that black and Hispanic workers earn less than other workers.

Also, suppose that we are wondering whether black workers earned less than Hispanic workers. Then, we can test whether the coefficients of D_{1i} and D_{2i} are different as constructing the null and alternative hypotheses below. Let's set the 1% significance level, $\alpha = 0.01$, for the test.

$$H_o: \beta_1 - \beta_2 = 0$$
$$H_a: \beta_1 - \beta_2 \neq 0$$

$$t = \frac{\widehat{\beta_1} - \widehat{\beta_2}}{se(\widehat{\beta_1} - \widehat{\beta_2})} = 6.60$$

Since 6.60 is larger than 2.58 (the critical value of the 0.05% tail probability in the standard normal distribution), we can say that we reject the null hypothesis at the 1% significance level.

Therefore, it is likely that the true parameters of black and Hispanic workers are different from each other. Further, it implies that black workers are likely to earn less than Hispanic workers.

Notes:
the NLSY79 (National Longitudinal Survey of Youth -1979 Cohort) data set
https://www.nlsinfo.org/content/cohorts/nlsy79

Example 7.3

Suppose that we would like to examine the wage differences by gender and ethnic groups such as black, Hispanic, and others (non-black and non-Hispanic).

To yield the regression outcome below, we use hourly wage in 1980 U.S. dollars (Y_i), female dummy variable ($W_i = 1$ for women and 0 for otherwise), and two ethnic group dummy variables indicating black and Hispanic ($D_{1i} = 1$ for black and 0 for otherwise; $D_{2i} = 1$ for Hispanic and 0 for otherwise) in the year 1990 of the NLSY79 (National Longitudinal Survey of Youth - 1979 Cohort) data set. We also add the interaction terms between gender and ethnic groups to examine whether gender and ethnic groups play a role together in wage differences.

$$\widehat{Y}_i = 8.972 - 2.015 W_i - 2.102 D_{1i} - 0.983 D_{2i} + 1.074 W_i \times D_{1i} + 0.689 W_i \times D_{2i}$$
SE (0.084) (0.117)   (0.1567)   (0.176)   (0.127)   (0.251)

SST (Total Sum of Squares) = 128911.008
SSE (Explained Sum of Squares) = 8877.692
SSR (Residual Sum of Squares) = 120033.316
R^2 = 0.0689

$n = 7,707$

The estimated constant, 8.972, indicates the average wage of the base group (non-black and non-Hispanic male workers).

The estimated coefficient of W_i indicates the wage difference between non-black and non-Hispanic female workers and the base group since D_{1i} and D_{2i} are 0 for this estimation.

For example, if we would like to know the wage difference between black women and Hispanic women.
For black women ($W_i=1$ and $D_{1i}=1$), $\widehat{Y_i} = 8.972 - 2.015 - 2.102 + 1.074$.
For Hispanic women ($W_i=1$ and $D_{2i}=1$), $\widehat{Y_i} = 8.972 - 2.015 - 0.983 + 0.689$.
Thus, the difference is $(-2.102 + 1.074) - (-0.983 + 0.689) = -0.734$ since the first two coefficients are the same.

Thus, black women's wage is lower than Hispanic women's.

We can test whether the difference between the two groups is statistically significant at the 1% level of significance, $p<0.01$, with the following null and alternative hypotheses.

$$H_o: \beta_2 + \beta_4 - (\beta_3 + \beta_5) = 0$$
$$H_a: \beta_2 + \beta_4 - (\beta_3 + \beta_5) \neq 0$$

$$t = \frac{\widehat{\beta_2} + \widehat{\beta_4} - (\widehat{\beta_3} + \widehat{\beta_5})}{se(\widehat{\beta_2} + \widehat{\beta_4} - (\widehat{\beta_3} + \widehat{\beta_5}))} = 3.63$$

Since 3.63 is larger than 2.58 (critical value at the 0.5% tail probability in the z distribution), in absolute values, the difference is statistically significant at $p<0.01$. Thus, it is likely that black women's wage is lower than Hispanic women.

Notes:
the NLSY79 (National Longitudinal Survey of Youth -1979 Cohort) data set
https://www.nlsinfo.org/content/cohorts/nlsy79

Estimating group differences in an outcome variable without the constant

As we covered earlier, suppose that we are interested in the difference in college GPA among different years of study in college. Then, we have the four groups of men and women: freshmen, sophomores, juniors, and seniors.

We can develop the following dummy variables to include all four groups of men and women.

$D_0 = 1$ for freshmen
$D_1 = 1$ for sophomores
$D_2 = 1$ for juniors
$D_3 = 1$ for seniors

$$Y = \delta_0 D_0 + \delta_1 D_1 + \delta_2 D_2 + \delta_3 D_3 + u$$

In this regression model, we exclude the constant and include the dummy variable for the base group consisting of freshmen.

This model can be interpreted as allowing an intercept change. If $D_0 = 1$, then $Y = \delta_0 + u$. Thus, δ_0 is the average GPA for freshmen. Also, if $D_1 = 1$, then $Y = \delta_1 + u$. Thus, δ_1 is the average GPA for sophomores. In the same manner, δ_2 and δ_3 are the average GPAs for juniors and seniors. Thus, the coefficients in this regression represent the average GPA for related groups. This is different from what we saw in the earlier model.

Example 7.4

Suppose that we would like to examine the wage differences by ethnic groups such as black, Hispanic, and others (non-black and non-Hispanic).

<Regression 1>
In regression 1, to yield the regression outcome below, we use hourly wage in 1980 U.S. dollars (Y_i) and two ethnic group dummy variables indicating black and Hispanic ($D_{1i} = 1$ for black and 0 for otherwise; $D_{2i} = 1$ for Hispanic and 0 for otherwise) in the year 1990 of the NLSY79 (National Longitudinal Survey of Youth - 1979 Cohort) data set.

$$\hat{Y}_i = 7.939 - 1.565 D_{1i} - 0.597 D_{2i}$$
$$\text{SE} \quad (0.060) \quad (0.111) \quad (0.128)$$

SST (Total Sum of Squares) = 128911.008
SSE (Explained Sum of Squares) = 3289.34502
SSR (Residual Sum of Squares) = 125621.663
R^2 = 0.0255
n = 7,707

<Regression 2>
Compared with the result from regression 1, we construct another regression model including all three dummy variables for ethnic groups without the constant term. Therefore, we have three ethnic group dummy variables: non-black & non-Hispanic, black, and Hispanic (D_{0i} = 1 for non-black & non-Hispanic and 0 for otherwise; D_{1i} = 1 for black and 0 for otherwise; D_{2i} = 1 for Hispanic and 0 for otherwise). Thus, each estimated coefficient is for the average wage of each ethnic group.

$$\hat{Y}_i = 7.939 D_{0i} + 6.374 D_{1i} + 7.342. D_{2i}$$
$$\text{SE} \quad (0.060) \quad (0.093) \quad (0.113)$$

SST (Total Sum of Squares) = 128911.008
SSE (Explained Sum of Squares) = 431847.735
SSR (Residual Sum of Squares) = 125621.663
R^2 = 0.7747
n = 7,707

7.939, 6.374, and 7.342 are the average wages of non-black & non-Hispanic workers, black workers, and Hispanic workers, respectively. They are all statistically significant even at $p<0.01$ with the default null and alternative hypotheses. In regression 2, it is easy to obtain the average wage of all three groups, but we need to get a difference of the estimated coefficients to examine the wage difference between groups. For example, the wage difference between non-black & non-Hispanic workers and black workers is 7.939 − 6.374 = 1.565. Thus, black workers' wage is lower than non-black & non-Hispanic workers by $1.565. This is the estimated coefficient for black workers in regression 1.

It is notable that R^2 in regression 2, 0.7747, is much larger than that in regression

1, 0.0255. This does not mean that regression 2 is much better than regression 1. These two models have different specifications for the different research questions, depending on whether they focus on the group differences or averages.

Notes:
the NLSY79 (National Longitudinal Survey of Youth -1979 Cohort) data set
https://www.nlsinfo.org/content/cohorts/nlsy79

Estimating group differences using an interval variable

Suppose that we would like to examine whether household income is positively associated with children's academic outcomes in elementary schools.

Sometimes, the yearly household income is recorded as an interval variable as below to minimize nonresponses in survey.

	Yearly household income in the U.S. dollars in 2020
1	0 ~ 20,000
2	20,000 ~ 50,000
3	50,000 ~ 70,000
4	70,000 ~ 100,000
5	100,000 ~

Then, we cannot include this variable as it is. Although there is a ranking in this variable, 1 to 5 in this variable are not meaningful in our analysis. 2 is higher than 1, and 5 is higher than 4 in terms of household income, while one more unit increase from 1 to 2 is not the same as one more unit increase from 4 to 5.

To make a meaningful analysis, we need to change this variable into dummy variables as below.

H_1 = 1 for 0 ~ 20,000 and 0 otherwise
H_2 = 1 for 20,000 ~ 50,000 and 0 otherwise
H_3 = 1 for 50,000 ~ 70,000 and 0 otherwise
H_4 = 1 for 70,000 ~ 100,000 and 0 otherwise
H_5 = 1 for 100,000 ~ and 0 otherwise

Suppose that Y is a 4th-grade student's math score.

$$Y = \beta_0 + \delta_1 H_1 + \delta_2 H_2 + \delta_3 H_3 + \delta_4 H_4 + u$$

In this regression model, the base group consists of the highest household income group (100,000 ~).

As mentioned earlier, this model also can be interpreted as allowing an intercept change.

If H_1 to H_4 are all 0, then $Y = \beta_0 + u$. In this case, β_0 is the population mean for the base group consisting of the highest household income group.

If $H_2 = 1$, then $Y = (\beta_0 + \delta_2) + u$. For the household income group of 20,000 ~ 50,000, $\beta_0 + \delta_2$ is the population mean. Thus, δ_2 is the population mean difference in students' math scores between this income group and the base group (highest income group).

Therefore, δ_1 is the population mean difference in students' math scores between the lowest household income group (0~20,000) and the base group.

Example 7.5

Suppose that we would like to examine the wage differences by education level.

We use hourly wage in 1980 U.S. dollars (Y) and years of education in the year 1990 of the NLSY79 (National Longitudinal Survey of Youth - 1979 Cohort) data set.

We create new dummy variables for the different education levels, using years of education in the data, as shown below.

$E_0 = 1$ for 0 to 11 years of education (equivalent to less than a high school graduate) and 0 otherwise

$E_1 = 1$ for 12 years of education (equivalent to high school graduate) and 0 otherwise

$E_2 = 1$ for 13 to 15 years of education (equivalent to some college) and 0 otherwise

$E_3 = 1$ for 16 years of education or more (equivalent to college graduate or more) and 0 otherwise

$$\hat{Y}_i = 5.678 + 0.879 E_{1i} + 2.089 E_{2i} + 4.600 E_{3i}$$
SE (0.109) (0.128) (0.143) (0.144)

SST (Total Sum of Squares) = 128911.008
SSE (Explained Sum of Squares) = 19367.428
SSR (Residual Sum of Squares) = 109543.58
R^2 = 0.1502
n = 7,707

It is found that the estimated constant is 5.678, the average wage of workers with less than a high school graduate (the base group of this analysis). 0.879 suggests that workers with high school diplomas earn more hourly wage than the base group by $0.879, which is statistically significant at $p<0.01$ under the default null and alternative hypotheses. The wage difference between workers with some college education and the base group is $2.089, while the wage difference between workers with a college diploma or more and the base group is $4.6. They are all statistically significant at $p<0.01$ under the default null and alternative hypotheses.

Notes:
the NLSY79 (National Longitudinal Survey of Youth -1979 Cohort) data set
https://www.nlsinfo.org/content/cohorts/nlsy79

Estimating group differences in a slope coefficient

We can extend this model with dummy variables by including continuous explanatory variables. Suppose that we want to study whether college GPA is related to high school GPA and whether gender matters in that relationship.

Let's consider a simple model with college GPA in percentage (continuous Y), high school GPA in percentage (continuous variable X), and women (dummy variable W).

$$Y = \beta_0 + \delta_0 W + \beta_1 X + u$$

This model is constructed to allow an intercept shift while the slope of X, β_1, is assumed to be the same for men and women.

If $W = 0$, then $Y = \beta_0 + \beta_1 X + u$.
If $W = 1$, then $Y = (\beta_0 + \delta_0) + \beta_1 X + u$.

Figure 7.1 Intercept difference between men and women

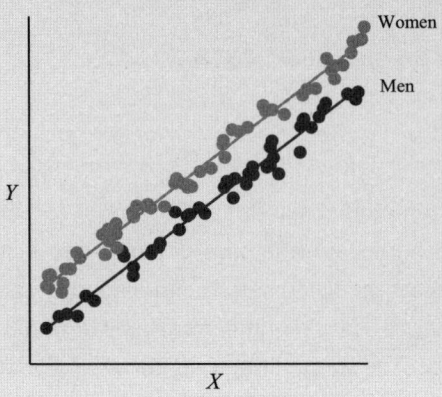

Notes: Y is the outcome variable and X is the explanatory variable.

The case of $W = 0$ is the base group indicating men.

Thus, δ_0 indicates the intercept difference between men and women in college GPA. If δ_0 is positive, upper and lower regression lines in Figure 7.1 may indicate women's and men's regression lines, respectively.

We can extend this model further by interacting a dummy variable, W, with a continuous variable, X, as follows.

$$Y = \beta_0 + \delta_0 W + \beta_1 X + \delta_1 W \times X + u$$

If $W = 0$ (men), then $Y = \beta_0 + \beta_1 X + u$.
If $W = 1$ (women), then $= (\beta_0 + \delta_0) + (\beta_1 + \delta_1) X + u$.

δ_1 in this modification is interpreted as a change in the slope of the relationship between men and women.

Thus, δ_0 indicates the intercept difference between men and women in college GPA, while δ_1 is the slope difference between men and women in the relationship between high school GPA and college GPA. If δ_0 is negative and δ_1 is positive, the upper regression line is for women and the lower regression line is for men in Figure 7.2.

Figure 7.2 Intercept and slope differences between men and women

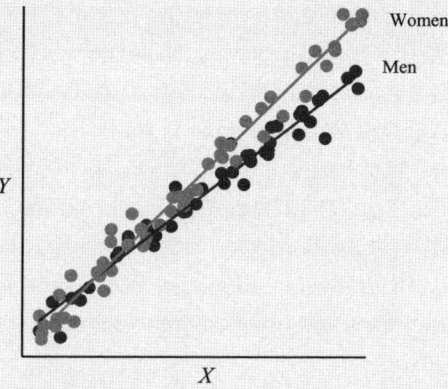

Notes: Y is the outcome variable and X is the explanatory variable.

Example 7.6

Suppose that we would like to know whether the relationship between education and wage are different by ethnic groups.

The two regression results below are yielded using hourly wage in 1980 U.S. dollars (Y_i), years of education (X_{1i}) and two ethnic group dummy variables indicating black and Hispanic (D_{1i} = 1 for black and 0 for otherwise; D_{2i} = 1 for Hispanic and 0 for otherwise) in the year 1990 of the NLSY79 (National Longitudinal Survey of Youth - 1979 Cohort) data set.

<Regression 1>

$$\widehat{Y}_i = -0.148 + 0.611X_{1i} - 1.314D_{1i} - 0.024D_{2i}$$
$$\text{SE} \quad (0.238) \quad (0.017) \quad (0.103) \quad (0.120)$$

SST (Total Sum of Squares) = 128911.008
SSE (Explained Sum of Squares) = 20520.582
SSR (Residual Sum of Squares) = 108390.427
R^2 = 0.1592
n = 7,707

In regression 1, we examine whether there are wage differences among ethnic groups, controlling for education level. In this analysis, we assume that the slope coefficient of education is the same for all ethnic groups. The estimated coefficient of education indicates that one more year of education leads to $0.611 more in real hourly wage, controlling for ethnic groups. When controlling for education, the wage difference between black workers and the base group of non-black & non-Hispanic workers is $1.314 and statistically significant at $p<0.01$, while the wage difference between Hispanic workers and the base group is only 0.024 and statistically insignificant even at $p<0.05$. Therefore, with the same education level, black workers' wage is lower than the base group, but Hispanic workers seem to earn as much as the base group.

<Regression 2>

$$\hat{Y}_i = -0.823 + 0.662X_{1i} - 0.755D_{1i} + 2.959D_{2i} - 0.042X_{1i} \times D_{1i} - 0.239X_{1i} \times D_{2i}$$
SE (0.294) (0.022)   (0.613)   (0.591)   (0.047)   (0.046)

SST (Total Sum of Squares) = 128911.008
SSE (Explained Sum of Squares) = 20894.891
SSR (Residual Sum of Squares) = 108016.117
R^2 = 0.1621
n = 7,707

In regression 2, we test whether there are wage differences among ethnic groups and whether the slope coefficient of education is different among ethnic groups. The estimated coefficient of education, 0.662, suggests that one more year of education leads to $0.662 more hourly wage for the base group (non-black and non-Hispanic workers). The estimated coefficients of D_{1i} and D_{2i} indicate the wage differences between the particular ethnic groups and the base group. It is found that the wage difference between black workers and the base group is small, 0.755, and statistically insignificant at $p<0.05$, while Hispanic workers' wage is larger than that of the base group by $2.959 and statistically significant at $p<0.01$. The estimated coefficient of the interaction term between education and black workers indicates that the slope difference in education between black workers and the base group is negligible, -0.042, and statistically insignificant at $p<0.05$. On the other hand, the estimated coefficient of the interaction term between education and Hispanic workers is large, -0.239, and statistically significant at $p<0.01$.

It seems that compared with the base group, black workers earn as much as the base group and their wage increase by education is similar to the base group. In contrast, Hispanic workers earn more hourly wage than the base group, but their wage increase by education is lower than the base group.

Notes:
the NLSY79 (National Longitudinal Survey of Youth -1979 Cohort) data set
https://www.nlsinfo.org/content/cohorts/nlsy79

Estimating group differences in all explanatory variables

Assume that we want to test whether men and women follow the same regression model for yearly earnings. The restricted model is an inflexible regression model, assuming that the regression model for yearly earnings is the same for men and women. Thus, there are no slope and intercept differences by gender. However, the unrestricted model is flexible to allow the slope and intercept differences between men and women. We compare these two regression models to test whether men and women follow the same regression model for yearly earnings.

Restricted: $Earnings = \beta_0 + \beta_1 Edu + \beta_2 Jobexp + u$
Unrestricted: $Earnings = \beta_0 + \delta_0 Women + \beta_1 Edu + \beta_2 Jobexp + \delta_1 Women \times Edu + \delta_2 Women \times Jobexp + u$

$Earnings$ = yearly earnings in U.S. dollars; Edu = education in years; $Jobexp$ = job experience in years; $Women$ = 1 for women and 0 for men

Then, we can use the following F-test to examine the intercept and slope differences between men and women in the regression model.

$$H_0: \delta_0 = 0, \delta_1 = 0, \delta_2 = 0$$
$$H_a: otherwise$$

Also, a separate t-test for δ_0 to δ_2 can be useful to examine whether there is any difference in the intercept or slopes in the regression model.

Example 7.7

Suppose that we would like to test whether different ethnic groups have distinct relationships between education and wage.

The restricted and unrestricted regression models are estimated as below using hourly wage in 1980 U.S. dollars (Y_i), years of education (X_{1i}) and two ethnic group dummy variables indicating black and Hispanic ($D_{1i} = 1$ for black and 0 for otherwise; $D_{2i} = 1$ for Hispanic and 0 for otherwise) in the year 1990 of the NLSY79 (National Longitudinal Survey of Youth - 1979 Cohort) data set.

<Restricted regression model>

$$\widehat{Y}_i = -0.587 + 0.62X_{1i}$$
$$\text{SE} \quad (0.231) \quad (0.017)$$

SST (Total Sum of Squares) = 128911.008
SSE (Explained Sum of Squares) = 18083.2888
SSR (Residual Sum of Squares) = 110827.719
$R_r^2 = 0.1403$
$n = 7,707$

<Unrestricted regression model>

$$\widehat{Y}_i = -0.823 + 0.662X_{1i} - 0.755D_{1i} + 2.959D_{2i} - 0.042X_{1i} \times D_{1i} - 0.239X_{1i} \times D_{2i}$$
$$\text{SE} \quad (0.294) \quad (0.022) \quad (0.613) \quad (0.591) \quad (0.047) \quad (0.046)$$

SST (Total Sum of Squares) = 128911.008
SSE (Explained Sum of Squares) = 20894.891
SSR (Residual Sum of Squares) = 108016.117
$R_{ur}^2 = 0.1621$
$n = 7,707$

The null and alternative hypotheses are as follows:

H_0: the coefficients of $D_{1i}, D_{2i}, X_{1i} \times D_{1i}$, and $X_{1i} \times D_{2i}$ are 0.
H_a: otherwise

F-test statistic is computed as follows.

$$F = \frac{(R_{ur}^2 - R_r^2)/q}{(1 - R_{ur}^2)/(n - k - 1)} = \frac{(0.1621 - 0.1403)/4}{(1 - 0.1621)/(7707 - 5 - 1)} = 50.09$$

Since 50.09 is larger than 3.32 ($F_{\alpha=0.01, df_n=4, df_{dn}=7701}$, the critical value of the 1% significance level with $df_n = 4$ and $df_{dn} = 7701$ in the F distribution), we reject the null hypothesis at $p<0.01$.

Thus, it is likely that different ethnic groups have distinct relationships between education and wage.

Notes:
the NLSY79 (National Longitudinal Survey of Youth -1979 Cohort) data set
https://www.nlsinfo.org/content/cohorts/nlsy79

Estimating the nonlinear relationship between an explanatory variable and an outcome variable

There are some complex nonlinear relationships between an explanatory variable and an outcome variable that cannot be accommodated using a functional specification. Constructing dummy variables using continuous or discrete explanatory variables can be useful for capturing and examining unusual nonlinear relationships. Let's see the example below.

Example 7.8

Suppose that we employ the flexible way of capturing the relationship between education and wage by generating multiple dummy variables for different years of education. We use hourly wage in 1980 U.S. dollars (Y) and years of education (X_1) in the year 1990 of the NLSY79 (National Longitudinal Survey of Youth - 1979 Cohort) data set. Using years of education, we generate the following dummy variables.

$E_0 = 1$ for 0 to 6 years of education and 0 otherwise
$E_7 = 1$ for 7 years of education and 0 otherwise

E_8 = 1 for 8 years of education and 0 otherwise
E_9 = 1 for 9 years of education and 0 otherwise
E_{10} = 1 for 10 years of education and 0 otherwise
E_{11} = 1 for 11 years of education and 0 otherwise
E_{12} = 1 for 12 years of education (equivalent to a high school diploma) and 0 otherwise
E_{13} = 1 for 13 years of education and 0 otherwise
E_{14} = 1 for 14 years of education and 0 otherwise
E_{15} = 1 for 15 years of education and 0 otherwise
E_{16} = 1 for 16 years of education (equivalent to a college diploma) and 0 otherwise
E_{17} = 1 for 17 years of education and 0 otherwise
E_{18} = 1 for 18 years of education and 0 otherwise
E_{19} = 1 for 19 years of education and 0 otherwise
E_{20} = 1 for 20 years of education and 0 otherwise

With the base group of 0 to 6 years of education, we include E_7 to E_{20} as explanatory variables and present the regression coefficients in the table below.

Estimated coefficients of the regression

	OLS
7 years of education	−0.251
	(0.751)
8 years of education	0.003
	(0.590)
9 years of education	0.110
	(0.560)
10 years of education	0.458
	(0.558)
11 years of education	0.504
	(0.549)
12 years of education	1.158**
	(0.516)
13 years of education	1.926***
	(0.533)

14 years of education	2.605***
	(0.532)
15 years of education	2.734***
	(0.551)
16 years of education	4.604***
	(0.525)
17 years of education	5.038***
	(0.565)
18 years of education	5.481***
	(0.588)
19 years of education	5.400***
	(0.652)
20 years of education	6.488***
	(0.700)
Constant	5.398***
	(0.512)
Adjusted R^2	0.153
Number of observations	7,707

Notes: ***$p<0.01$, **$p<0.05$, *$p<0.1$; The outcome variable is hourly wage in 1980 U.S. dollars in the year 1990 of the NLSY79 (National Longitudinal Survey of Youth - 1979 Cohort) data set.

As shown in this table, compared with the base group (workers with up to 6 years of education), workers with 7 to 11 years of education show no considerable difference in hourly wage, which is not statistically significant even at $p<0.1$. Workers with 12 years of education earn more hourly wage than the base group by $1.158, and it is statistically significant at $p<0.05$. It implies the importance of a high school diploma in the job market.

Between 13 to 15 years of education, one more year of education increases hourly wage by less than one dollar. Then, workers with 16 years of education seem to earn more than one dollar than those with 15 years of education. The exact difference is $1.87, which is statistically significant at $p<0.01$. It also implies how important the college diploma is in hourly wage.

Therefore, the relationship between education and hourly wage may not be linear, and education has some noticeable thresholds, such as 12 and 16 years of education in increasing hourly wage.

Notes:
the NLSY79 (National Longitudinal Survey of Youth -1979 Cohort) data set
https://www.nlsinfo.org/content/cohorts/nlsy79

Subsample analysis based on exogenous explanatory variables

To examine the heterogeneous relationship between the main explanatory variables and the outcome variable, we can conduct the subsample analyses by the different groups of interest. We can run separate regressions for the different groups of interest with the same regression model. It is possible without estimation bias if the subsamples are based on exogenous explanatory variables. If the subsample analysis is based on endogenous explanatory variables or outcome variables, the resulting estimates are biased or inconsistent since the fourth OLS assumption, $E(u|X)$ for the small sample or $Cov(u, X)$ for the large sample, is violated. It is called the sample selection bias.

Example 7.9

Suppose the subsample analysis is based on ethnic groups to examine whether the relationship between hourly wage and education is different by ethnic groups. We use hourly wage in 1980 U.S. dollars (Y), years of education (X_1) in the year 1990 of the NLSY79 (National Longitudinal Survey of Youth - 1979 Cohort) data set.

The four analyses for all workers, non-black & non-Hispanic workers, black workers, and Hispanic workers are shown in the table below.

Estimated coefficients by ethnic groups

	All	Non-black & Non-Hispanic	Black	Hispanic
Years of education	0.620***	0.662***	0.620***	0.424***
	(0.017)	(0.023)	(0.034)	(0.042)
Constant	−0.587**	−0.823***	−1.578***	2.136***
	(0.231)	(0.311)	(0.443)	(0.522)
Adjusted R-squared	0.140	0.153	0.149	0.075
Number of observations	7,707	4,552	1,888	1,267

Notes: ***$p<0.01$, **$p<0.05$, *$p<0.1$; The outcome variable is hourly wage in 1980 U.S. dollars in the year 1990 of the NLSY79 (National Longitudinal Survey of Youth - 1979 Cohort) data set.

The estimated coefficients of education for all workers, non-black & non-Hispanic workers, and black workers are similar. However, Hispanic workers have a smaller coefficient, which is compatible with our previous analysis in Example 7.6.

If the subsample analysis is based on the outcome variable, hourly wage, and the separate regressions are run for low-wage and high-wage groups, it leads to the sample selection bias. Thus, please avoid such a mistake.

Notes:
the NLSY79 (National Longitudinal Survey of Youth -1979 Cohort) data set
https://www.nlsinfo.org/content/cohorts/nlsy79

Chapter Summary

The usefulness of binary variables	A binary or dummy variable is a variable that takes on the value 1 or 0, which is popular to present qualitative events or characteristics that are nominal and cannot be shown in computational numbers. Binary variables can be used to examine the group differences in an outcome variable. Also, the interaction term between a binary variable and a continuous variable can be used to see the group differences in a slope coefficient. The transforming of a continuous or district explanatory variable into multiple dummy variables can be useful to capture the unusual nonlinear relationship between an explanatory variable and an outcome variable.
Addressing common misunderstandings and mistakes	Including categorical variables indicating nominal values, such as ways of commuting to work and geographical regions, does not give any meaningful estimation results in the regression model. It is best to change them to dummy variables and include them in the regression analysis. When the dummy variables are included to examine the group differences in the outcome, the coefficient of a dummy variable indicates the difference between the base group and the group of the particular dummy variable. Thus, to get the average outcome of the group of interest, we need to add the constant coefficient to the coefficient of a dummy variable. When the dummy variables are included to examine the group differences in the outcome, including the dummy variables of all the groups with the constant in the regression model leads to perfect multicollinearity since the constant accounts for the base group. This is called the dummy variable trap.

Exercises

Chapter 7
The OLS regression analysis when comparing the outcomes of the two or more groups: Use of binary explanatory variables

1. Suppose that Korea University would like to evaluate whether frequent consultations with academic advisors (at least 5 times for the first semester) help freshmen to improve their academic achievements. The regression results are as follows with n =2,000.

$$\widehat{GPA} = 2.34 + 0.33 \text{ Consultation}$$
$$\text{SE} \quad (1.52) \quad (0.11)$$

GPA = freshmen's first semester GPA (0 to 4)
Consultation = 1 for students who have frequent consultations with academic advisors (at least 5 times for the first semester) and 0 otherwise.

(1) Please interpret the estimated coefficient of Consultation.

(2) Obtain the 95% confidence interval for the coefficient of Consultation and state its implication.

(3) Please test whether the coefficient of Consultation is statistically different from 0 with a two-sided test at.

(4) Discuss whether frequent consultations with academic advisors are effective in improving the freshmen's GPA based on what you find in (1) to (3).

(5) Please discuss a possible estimation bias of this study. What is missing in this regression model? What can you do to improve this regression model?

2. A study of pay rates in a company concludes that "white men are likely to be paid more than men with other ethnic origins." The study goes on to observe that the disparity between white men's and other men's pay rates are "in excess of two standard errors and thus allows one to rule out a chance occurrence." Constructing the regression model to analyze this case and make relevant discussions. Also, discuss the possible omitted variable bias in your regression model.

3. Suppose that you test whether hourly wages are different among high school dropouts, high school graduates, and persons with more than high school education. You have the following two regression results.

   rhw1984: hourly wage in 1984
   lesshsg: less than high school = 1; otherwise = 0
   highg: high school graduate = 1; otherwise = 0
   mhgs: more than high school = 1; otherwise = 0
   afqt: a cognitive measure from 0 to 100

   Regression 1:
   $$\widehat{rhw1984} = 5.67 + 0.88 highg + 3.33 mhgs$$
   $$\text{SE} \quad (0.11) \quad (0.13) \quad\quad (0.13)$$

   $n = 7707, R^2 = 0.110$

   Regression 2:
   $$\widehat{rhw1984} = 4.98 - 0.02 highg + 1.27 mhgs + 0.05 afqt$$
   $$\text{SE} \quad (0.11) \quad (0.13) \quad\quad (0.15) \quad\quad (0.002)$$

   $n = 7707, R^2 = 0.189$

   (1) Please interpret estimated coefficients of *highg* and *mghs* in the two regression results and discuss why estimates are different in these two models.

(2) In the first regression, please test whether hourly wages are different among high school dropouts, high school graduates, and persons with more than high school education at $\alpha = 0.01$.

4. Suppose that you would like to examine the impact of education on women's fertility. Using the analysis sample of women aged 40 to 67 from the 2007 Korean Longitudinal Survey of Women and Families (KLoWF), you have the regression outcome below.

Table 7.1

	(1)	(2)	(3)
Education in years	-0.109***	-0.066***	-0.020***
	(0.004)	(0.004)	(0.007)
Aged 50-59 = 1		0.331***	1.165***
		(0.033)	(0.102)
Aged 60-69 = 1		0.901***	1.503***
		(0.046)	(0.104)
Education in years × Aged 50-59 = 1			-0.080***
			(0.009)
Education in years × Aged 60-69 = 1			-0.056***
			(0.011)
Constant	3.445***	2.758***	2.213***
	(0.037)	(0.053)	(0.084)
R^2	0.157	0.217	0.228
Number of observations	5,046	5,046	5,046

Notes: ***$p<0.01$, **$p<0.05$, *$p<0.1$; The outcome variable is the number of children of women aged 40 to 67.

(1) Please interpret the estimated coefficient of education in column (2) compared with that in column (1). Also, please explain its implications with their statistical significance.

(2) Please interpret the estimated coefficients of two age dummies in column (2) and examine their statistical significance (2).

(3) Please interpret the estimated coefficients of two interaction terms between age dummies and education in column (3).

(4) Please test whether the intercepts and slopes of education are different by three age groups using R-squared in columns (1) to (3). Please indicate the unrestricted and restricted models among three regressions.

Suppose that the following regression results are from the subsample analyses of women aged 40-49, 50-59, and 60-69.

Table 7.2

	Women aged 40-49	Women aged 50-59	Women aged 60-69
Education in years	-0.020***	-0.100***	-0.076***
	(0.005)	(0.007)	(0.012)
Constant	2.213***	3.378***	3.716***
	(0.067)	(0.060)	(0.086)
R^2	0.006	0.112	0.045
Number of observations	2,334	1,879	833

Notes: ***$p<0.01$, **$p<0.05$, *$p<0.1$; The outcome variable is the number of children.

(5) Please interpret the estimated coefficients of education in Table 7.2.

(6) Please discuss the implications of estimated coefficients in these subsample analyses in Table 7.2 compared with the estimated coefficients in column (3) of Table 7.1 above.

5. Suppose that you would like to examine whether attending college affects women's fertility. Using the analysis sample of women aged 40 to 67 from the 2007 Korean Longitudinal Survey of Women and Families (KLoWF), you have the regression outcome below.

	OLS (1)	OLS (2)	OLS (3)
Some college or more = 1	-0.585***	-0.273***	-0.125***
	(0.043)	(0.042)	(0.047)
Aged 50-59 = 1		0.502***	0.567***
		(0.032)	(0.033)
Aged 60-69 = 1		1.225***	1.277***
		(0.041)	(0.042)
Some college or more = 1 × Aged 50-59 = 1			-0.623***
			(0.106)
Some college or more = 1 × Aged 60-69 = 1			-0.723***
			(0.213)
Constant	2.475***	2.042***	2.006***
	(0.016)	(0.023)	(0.023)
Adjusted R^2	0.034	0.184	0.190
Number of observations	5,046	5,046	5,046

Note: ***$p<0.01$, **$p<0.05$, *$p<0.1$; The outcome variable is the number of children.

(1) Please interpret the estimated coefficient of some college dummy variable in column (2) compared to column (1).

(2) Please interpret the estimated coefficients and their statistical significance of two age dummies in column (2).

(3) Please interpret the estimated coefficients of two interaction terms between age dummies and some college dummy variables and their statistical significance in column (3).

(4) Please compare the difference in the number of children between women aged 50-59 with some college education and those aged 40-49 without some college education using estimates in column (3).

Chapter 8
Data Analysis for Social Science: Fundamental Methods

Developing and completing the OLS regression analysis by using rescaling and functional specifications

Depending on the field of study and related theories, we can rescale the outcome and explanatory variables. Also, we can develop various functional relationships between the outcome and explanatory variables to accommodate theories and different data conditions by time and place. In this chapter, we will study rescaling and functional specifications and then cover general rules and criteria related to them.

Rescaling of the outcome and explanatory variables

In social science, analysis units of explanatory variables are important when we interpret the estimation results. If we choose irrelevant units in explanatory variables, the estimated coefficients could be meaningless. For example, when we study the impact of import and export of countries on their economic growth, the typical unit of study is a billion U.S. dollars. If we use U.S. dollars, it is inconvenient to interpret the meaning of estimated coefficients. Thus, it is usual to rescale the units of explanatory and outcome variables for our research purpose in the data analysis.

So, what happens when we change the scale of explanatory and outcome variables? Rescaling the units of variables changes the magnitudes of estimated coefficients and standard errors at the same time. As a result, the t-statistic and its statistical significance shown by p-values does not change. In other words, rescaling the units of variables does not change the statistical significance of the estimated results. However, we need to pay attention to the new units of explanatory and outcome variables when we interpret the estimation results after rescaling them.

Standardization of explanatory or outcome variables is one kind of rescaling, which is useful when the units of variables in the data are unfamiliar or difficult to compare across studies. Therefore, standardization is particularly popular in the field of education and environmental studies since it is easy to interpret and compare their estimated results in academic outcomes or environmental improvements across studies in different times and places.

As shown below in Case 1, when we standardize all the explanatory and outcome variables in the analysis at the same time, the new regression model with standardized variables has no constant since it is removed by standardization. The coefficients in this full standardized analysis are called beta coefficients.

On the other hand, as shown in Cases 2 and 3, the standardization of some of the explanatory and outcome variables does keep the constant in the OLS analysis. The interpretation of estimated coefficients should be based on what variables we standardize. See the details below.

Case 1: Standardization of X and Y

$$Y_i = \hat{\beta}_0 + \hat{\beta}_1 X_{1i} + \hat{\beta}_2 X_{2i} + \cdots + \hat{\beta}_k X_{ki} + \hat{u}_i$$

$$\bar{Y} = \hat{\beta}_0 + \hat{\beta}_1 \bar{X}_1 + \hat{\beta}_2 \bar{X}_2 + \cdots + \hat{\beta}_k \bar{X}_k + \bar{\hat{u}}_i$$

$$(Y_i - \bar{Y}) = \hat{\beta}_1 (X_{1i} - \bar{X}_1) + \hat{\beta}_2 (X_{2i} - \bar{X}_2) + \cdots + \hat{\beta}_k (X_{ki} - \bar{X}_k) + \hat{u}_i$$

$$\frac{(Y_i - \bar{Y})}{\hat{\sigma}_Y} = \frac{\hat{\beta}_1}{\hat{\sigma}_Y}(X_{1i} - \bar{X}_1) + \frac{\hat{\beta}_2}{\hat{\sigma}_Y}(X_{2i} - \bar{X}_2) + \cdots + \frac{\hat{\beta}_k}{\hat{\sigma}_Y}(X_{ki} - \bar{X}_k) + \frac{\hat{u}_i}{\hat{\sigma}_Y}$$

$$\frac{(Y_i - \bar{Y})}{\hat{\sigma}_Y} = \frac{\hat{\beta}_1 \cdot \hat{\sigma}_1}{\hat{\sigma}_Y}\frac{(X_{1i} - \bar{X}_1)}{\hat{\sigma}_1} + \frac{\hat{\beta}_2 \cdot \hat{\sigma}_2}{\hat{\sigma}_Y}\frac{(X_{2i} - \bar{X}_2)}{\hat{\sigma}_2} + \cdots + \frac{\hat{\beta}_k \cdot \hat{\sigma}_k}{\hat{\sigma}_Y}\frac{(X_{ki} - \bar{X}_k)}{\hat{\sigma}_k} + \frac{\hat{u}_i}{\hat{\sigma}_Y}$$

$\tilde{Y}_i = \hat{\delta}_1 \tilde{X}_{1i} + \hat{\delta}_2 \tilde{X}_{2i} + \cdots + \hat{\delta}_k \tilde{X}_{ki} + \tilde{\hat{u}}_i$ where $\frac{\hat{\beta}_j \cdot \hat{\sigma}_j}{\hat{\sigma}_Y} = \hat{\delta}_j$ and $\frac{(X_{ji} - \bar{X}_j)}{\hat{\sigma}_j} = \tilde{X}_{ji}$ with no constant

Therefore, 1 SD (standard deviation) increase in $X_j \Rightarrow \hat{\delta}_j$ SD change in Y.

$\hat{\delta}_j$ is called a beta coefficient.

Example 8.1

Suppose that we would like to examine whether education and cognitive skills are associated with wages. We use hourly wage in 1980 U.S. dollars (Y), years of education (X_1), and AFQT (X_2) in the year 1990 of the NLSY79 (National Longitudinal Survey of Youth - 1979 Cohort) data set. AFQT is the cognitive measure ranging from 1 to 100 in the sample.

This time, we are also interested in the standardized magnitudes of estimated coefficients of education and cognitive skills. We report the two regression results below. The first one is from the regression using the original values of wage in US dollars, education in years, and AFQT score from 1 to 100. The second regression is using the standardized wage, education, and AFQT score: SY_i, SX_{1i}, and SX_{2i}, respectively.

<Regression 1>

$$\hat{Y}_i = 1.556 + 0.323 X_{1i} + 0.042 X_{2i}$$
$$\text{SE} \quad (0.242) \quad (0.021) \quad (0.002)$$
$$t\text{-stat} \quad\quad\quad\quad [15.16] \quad [22.88]$$

SST (Total Sum of Squares) = 128911.008
SSE (Explained Sum of Squares) = 25135.902
SSR (Residual Sum of Squares) = 103775.106
R^2 = 0.195
n = 7,707

It is found that one more year of education leads to a $0.323 increase in real hourly wage. Also, one more point of AFQT is related to a $0.042 increase in real hourly wage. The test statistics are reported under the default null and alternative hypotheses. Those for education and AFQT are greater than 2.58 (critical value for the 0.5% tail probability in the standard normal distribution). Thus, they are statistically significant at $p<0.01$.

<Regression 2>

$$\widehat{SY}_i = 0.000 + 0.195 SX_{1i} + 0.295 SX_{2i}$$
$$\text{SE} \quad (0.010) \quad (0.013) \quad (0.013)$$
$$t\text{-stat} \quad \quad \quad [15.16] \quad [22.88]$$

SST (Total Sum of Squares) = 7706
SSE (Explained Sum of Squares) = 1502.566
SSR (Residual Sum of Squares) = 6203.434
R^2 = 0.195
n = 7,707

One more standard deviation (SD) of education leads to a 0.195 SD increase in real hourly wage, while one more SD increase of AFQT is related to a 0.295 SD increase in real hourly wage. It seems that in terms of SD, an increase in AFQT leads to a greater increase in hourly wage than that of education. Their difference is statistically significant at $p<0.01$: test statistic $t = \frac{\hat{\beta}_1 - \hat{\beta}_2}{se(\hat{\beta}_1 - \hat{\beta}_2)} = 4.31$ under the following null and alternative hypotheses, $H_o: \beta_1 - \beta_2 = 0$ and $H_a: \beta_1 - \beta_2 \neq 0$.

It is noticeable that the reported test statistics for education and AFQT are the same as those in regression 1. Therefore, as studied earlier, the standardization of variables in the OLS analysis does not change the statistical significance of the estimated coefficients.

Notes:
the NLSY79 (National Longitudinal Survey of Youth -1979 Cohort) data set
https://www.nlsinfo.org/content/cohorts/nlsy79

Case 2: Standardization of Y only

$$Y_i = \hat{\beta}_0 + \hat{\beta}_1 X_{1i} + \hat{\beta}_2 X_{2i} + \cdots + \hat{\beta}_k X_{ki} + \hat{u}_i$$
$$\bar{Y} = \hat{\beta}_0 + \hat{\beta}_1 \bar{X}_1 + \hat{\beta}_2 \bar{X}_2 + \cdots + \hat{\beta}_k \bar{X}_k + \bar{\hat{u}}_i$$
$$(Y_i - \bar{Y}) = \hat{\beta}_1(X_{1i} - \bar{X}_1) + \hat{\beta}_2(X_{2i} - \bar{X}_2) + \cdots + \hat{\beta}_k(X_{ki} - \bar{X}_k) + \hat{u}_i$$

$$\frac{(Y_i-\bar{Y})}{\hat{\sigma}_Y} = \frac{\hat{\beta}_1}{\hat{\sigma}_Y}(X_{1i}-\bar{X}_1) + \frac{\hat{\beta}_2}{\hat{\sigma}_Y}(X_{2i}-\bar{X}_2) + \cdots + \frac{\hat{\beta}_k}{\hat{\sigma}_Y}(X_{ki}-\bar{X}_k) + \frac{\hat{u}_i}{\hat{\sigma}_Y}$$

$$\frac{(Y_i-\bar{Y})}{\hat{\sigma}_Y} = -\underbrace{\left(\frac{\hat{\beta}_1}{\hat{\sigma}_Y}\bar{X}_1 + \frac{\hat{\beta}_2}{\hat{\sigma}_Y}\bar{X}_2 + \cdots + \frac{\hat{\beta}_k}{\hat{\sigma}_Y}\bar{X}_k\right)}_{\text{intercept}} + \frac{\hat{\beta}_1}{\hat{\sigma}_Y}X_{1i} + \frac{\hat{\beta}_2}{\hat{\sigma}_Y}X_{2i} + \cdots + \frac{\hat{\beta}_k}{\hat{\sigma}_Y}X_{ki} + \frac{\hat{u}_i}{\hat{\sigma}_Y}$$

$\tilde{Y}_i = \hat{a}_o + \hat{a}_1 X_{1i} + \hat{a}_2 X_{2i} + \cdots + \hat{a}_k X_{ki} + \tilde{\hat{u}}_i$ where $-\left(\frac{\hat{\beta}_1}{\hat{\sigma}_Y}\bar{X}_1 + \frac{\hat{\beta}_2}{\hat{\sigma}_Y}\bar{X}_2 + \cdots + \frac{\hat{\beta}_k}{\hat{\sigma}_Y}\bar{X}_k\right) = \hat{a}_o$ and $\frac{\hat{\beta}_j}{\hat{\sigma}_Y} = \hat{a}_j$

Therefore, 1 unit increase in $X_j \Rightarrow \hat{a}_j$ SD change in Y.

Futher, when we would like to change the unit of Y on different occasions, we can use the same way of transformation as we have seen here. The only difference is whether we replace $\bar{Y}$ and $\hat{\sigma}_Y$ with other fixed numbers for transformation. For example, if Y is price in U.S. dollars and we want to change this to price in 100 U.S. dollars, we can replace $\bar{Y}$ and $\hat{\sigma}_Y$ with 0 and 100, respectively, in the transformation shown above.

Case 3: Standardization of X_1 only

$$Y_i = \hat{\beta}_0 + \hat{\beta}_1 X_{1i} + \hat{\beta}_2 X_{2i} + \cdots + \hat{\beta}_k X_{ki} + \hat{u}_i$$

$$Y_i = \hat{\beta}_0 + \hat{\beta}_1(X_{1i}-\bar{X}_1) + \hat{\beta}_1\bar{X}_1 + \hat{\beta}_2 X_{2i} + \cdots + \hat{\beta}_k X_{ki} + \hat{u}_i$$

$$Y_i = (\hat{\beta}_0 + \hat{\beta}_1\bar{X}_1) + \hat{\beta}_1\hat{\sigma}_1\frac{(X_{1i}-\bar{X}_1)}{\hat{\sigma}_1} + \hat{\beta}_2 X_{2i} + \cdots + \hat{\beta}_k X_{ki} + \hat{u}_i$$

$Y_i = \hat{\gamma}_0 + \hat{\gamma}_1\tilde{X}_{1i} + \hat{\beta}_2 X_{2i} + \cdots + \hat{\beta}_k X_{ki} + \tilde{\hat{u}}_i$ where $(\hat{\beta}_0 + \hat{\beta}_1\bar{X}_1) = \hat{\gamma}_0$, $\hat{\beta}_1\hat{\sigma}_1 = \hat{\gamma}_1$, and $\frac{(X_{1i}-\bar{X}_1)}{\hat{\sigma}_1} = \tilde{X}_{1i}$

Therefore, 1 SD increase in $X_1 \Rightarrow \hat{\gamma}_1$ unit change in Y.

Also, if we want to change the unit of X_1 on other occasions, we can use the same way of transformation as we have seen here. To do so, we can replace $\bar{X}_1$ and $\hat{\sigma}_1$ with other fixed numbers for transformation. For instance, if X is the number of sales in millions and we want to rescale this to the number of sales in thousands, we can replace $\bar{X}_1$ and $\hat{\sigma}_1$ with 0 and 1/1000, respectively, in the transformation shown above.

Example 8.2

Suppose that we would like to examine whether education and cognitive skills are associated with wage, using hourly wage in 1980 U.S. dollars (Y), years of education (X_1), and AFQT (X_2) in the year 1990 of the NLSY79 (National Longitudinal Survey of Youth - 1979 Cohort) data set. AFQT is the cognitive measure ranging from 1 to 100 in the sample.

We report the three regression results below. The first one is from the regression using the original values of wage in U.S. dollars, education in years, and AFQT score from 1 to 100. The second regression is using the standardized wage (SY_i), education in years (X_{1i}), and AFQT score (X_{2i}). The third regression is using hourly wage in 1980 US dollars (Y_i), education in years (X_{1i}), and the standardized AFQT score (SX_{2i}).

<Regression 1>

$$\hat{Y}_i = 1.556 + 0.323 X_{1i} + 0.042 X_{2i}$$
$$\text{SE} \quad (0.242) \quad (0.021) \quad (0.002)$$
$$t\text{-stat} \quad \quad \quad [15.16] \quad [22.88]$$

SST (Total Sum of Squares) = 128911.008
SSE (Explained Sum of Squares) = 25135.902
SSR (Residual Sum of Squares) = 103775.106
R^2 = 0.195
n = 7,707

According to regression 1, one more year of education leads to a $0.323 increase in real hourly wage. Also, one more point of AFQT is related to a $0.042 increase in real hourly wage. The test statistics of education and AFQT are greater than 2.58 (critical value for the 0.5% tail probability in the standard normal distribution). Thus, they are statistically significant at $p<0.01$.

<Regression 2>

$$\widehat{SY}_i = -1.443 + 0.079 X_{1i} + 0.010 X_{2i}$$
$$\text{SE} \quad (0.059) \quad (0.005) \quad (0.0004)$$
$$t\text{-stat} \quad \quad \quad [15.16] \quad [22.88]$$

SST (Total Sum of Squares) = 7706
SSE (Explained Sum of Squares) = 1502.566
SSR (Residual Sum of Squares) = 6203.434
R^2 = 0.195
n = 7,707

Since the outcome variable is standardized, we can interpret accordingly. Therefore, one more year of education leads to a 0.079 standard deviation (SD) increase in real hourly wage, and one more point of AFQT is associated with a 0.01 SD increase in real hourly wage. The test statistics of education and AFQT are the same as those in regression 1. Therefore, there is no change in the statistical significance of the estimated coefficients of explanatory variables.

<Regression 3>

$$\widehat{Y}_i = 3.264 + 0.323X_{1i} + 1.20SX_{2i}$$
SE (0.280) (0.021) (0.053)
t-stat   [15.16]   [22.88]

SST (Total Sum of Squares) = 128911.008
SSE (Explained Sum of Squares) = 25135.902
SSR (Residual Sum of Squares) = 103775.106
R^2 = 0.195
n = 7,707

In regression 3, the AFQT score is standardized. Thus, we can interpret the estimated coefficients accordingly. The estimated coefficient of education is the same as that in regression 1. On the other hand, the estimated coefficient of the standardized AFQT is different from that in regression 1. Thus, one more standard deviation (SD) of AFQT leads to a $1.20 increase in real hourly wage. As in regression 2, the test statistics of education and AFQT are the same as those in regression 1.

Notes:
the NLSY79 (National Longitudinal Survey of Youth -1979 Cohort) data set
https://www.nlsinfo.org/content/cohorts/nlsy79

Linearity in the OLS analysis

In the OLS analysis, linearity appears on many occasions and generates some confusion. They can be summarized as the three critical linearity concepts. The first concept is from the first OLS assumption, stating that the outcome is linear in parameters and has an additive error term, which makes the terminology of the linear regression model. The second linearity concept is from the Best Linear Unbiased Estimator of the Gauss-Markov Theorem, stating that the OLS estimator is linear in the outcome variable or error term, which helps the normality assumption of the error term lead to the normality of the OLS estimator. The third linearity concept indicates the linear relationship between X and Y, which is one of the functional specifications we can construct in the regression model. From time to time, some people misunderstand that this linear specification is the meaning of "linear" in the linear regression model. However, "linear" in the linear regression model is about the first OLS assumption, stating that the outcome variable is linear in parameters.

Linearity in OLS
① OLS assumption: Y_i is linear in parameters and has an additive error term.
② BLUE of Gauss-Markov Theorem: $\hat{\beta}_1$ is linear in Y_i and u_i.
③ Linear relationship between X and Y.

Linear and nonlinear specifications in the OLS analysis

To accommodate theories and data contexts, we can think about linear and nonlinear relationships between the outcome and explanatory variables. Let's talk about the possible functional specifications between X and Y in the OLS regression model.

There is ambiguity about what functional relationship (or specification) is the best for the relationship between X and Y in the OLS regression model. At least in social science, there are two major considerations for the right choice of specification. First, the specification depends on the theories or conventions in the related field. For example, it is common to use the log of earnings and the number of years in school to examine the impact of education on earnings. In the field of education, it is popular to use standardized academic scores for the standard deviation interpretation of empirical results. Second, the specification depends on the data or sample researchers have. Depending on times and places, the data collected might have more or less variations in the key variables. Even some data may have legitimate but erratic patterns due to the sample's socio-economic environments. Thus, by examining the patterns within a particular sample's data, researchers can introduce unique nonlinear specifications to fit the data and explain contextual details.

Assume that we are studying the continuous variables X and Y.

(1) Regresson of Y on X

Typically, when we have the continuous variables X and Y in the OLS regression model like below, β_1 indicate that one unit increase in X leads to β_1 unit change in Y. If the coefficient is positive or negative, then it means an increase or decrease in Y. It is a linear function of specification between X and Y.

$$Y = \beta_0 + \beta_1 X + u$$

$$\beta_1 = \frac{\Delta Y}{\Delta X}$$

$$\Rightarrow \Delta Y = \beta_1 \cdot \Delta X$$

When we have a more complicated and nonlinear relationship between X and Y, we can introduce the following four specifications, which are some of the most popular ones in social science.

(2) Regresson of ln Y on X

When we want to capture the increasing marginal relationship of X on Y as below, we can introduce the log of Y and X in the OLS regression model, equivalent to that Y is the exponential function of $\beta_0 + \beta_1 X + u$. This implies that the marginal change of Y per unit of X is increasing as X is increasing.

$$\ln Y = \beta_0 + \beta_1 X + u$$

$$\Rightarrow Y = \exp(\beta_0 + \beta_1 X + u)$$

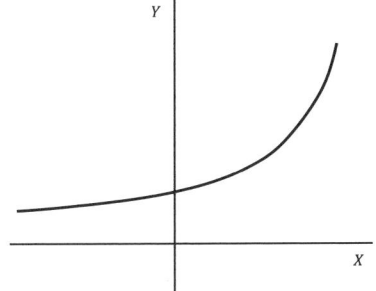

Increasing marginal effect of X on Y

The interpretation of β_1 in this regression analysis is different from the typical regression model. As shown below, 1 unit change in X leads to $(100 \cdot \beta_1)\%$ change in Y. Therefore, the example below shows that a one-year increase in education leads to an 7.9 percent (100*0.079) increase in hourly wage. This is sometimes called the semi-elasticity interpretation.

$$\ln Y = \beta_0 + \beta_1 X + u$$

$$\beta_1 = \frac{d \ln Y}{dX} = \frac{\frac{dY}{Y}}{dX} \quad \text{from} \quad \frac{d \ln Y}{dY} = \frac{1}{Y} \Rightarrow d \ln Y = \frac{dY}{Y}$$

$$\Rightarrow \frac{dY}{Y} = \beta_1 \cdot dX$$

Thus, $\frac{\Delta Y}{Y} = \beta_1 \cdot \Delta X$ and

$$\left(100 \cdot \frac{\Delta Y}{Y}\right) = (100 \cdot \beta_1)\Delta X$$

1 unit change in $X \Rightarrow (100 \cdot \beta_1)\%$ change in Y

As an example,
$$\widehat{hourlywage} = 0.782 + 0.079\, education$$

(3) Regresson of Y on $\ln X$

The third regression model includes the continuous Y and the log of X. As shown in the figure below, this specification captures the decreasing marginal relationship of X on Y. Therefore, the marginal change of Y per unit of X decreases as X increases.

$$Y = \beta_0 + \beta_1 \ln X + u$$

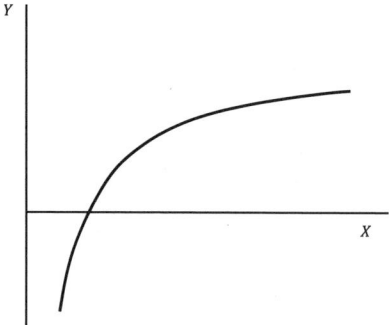

Decreasing marginal effect of X on Y

In this specification, the interpretation of β_1 is that a 1% increase in X leads to $\frac{\beta_1}{100}$ unit change in Y as explained below. The estimated coefficient in the example below suggests that a 1% change in hourly wage leads to a 0.376-hour increase in work hours. This is also called the semi-elasticity interpretation.

$$Y = \beta_0 + \beta_1 \ln X + u$$

$$\beta_1 = \frac{dY}{d \ln X} = \frac{dY}{\frac{dX}{X}}$$

Thus, $dY = \beta_1 \cdot \frac{dX}{X}$ and

$$\Delta Y = \beta_1 \cdot \frac{\Delta X}{X} = \frac{\beta_1}{100} \cdot \left(\frac{\Delta X}{X} \cdot 100\right)$$

1% increase in $X \Rightarrow \frac{\beta_1}{100}$ unit change in Y

As an example,

$$\widehat{hours} = 35 + 37.6 \ln wage$$

(4) Regresson of $\ln Y$ on $\ln X$

The fourth specification includes the log of Y and the log of X, implying that the log of Y is a linear function of the log of X. The interpretation is that a 1% increase in X leads to β_1% change in Y. The example below indicates that a 1% increase in price predicts a 0.677% decrease in consumption. This is also called the elasticity interpretation.

$$\ln Y = \beta_0 + \beta_1 \ln X + u$$

$$\beta_1 = \frac{d \ln Y}{d \ln X} = \frac{\frac{dY}{Y}}{\frac{dX}{X}} \Rightarrow \frac{dY}{Y} = \beta_1 \cdot \frac{dX}{X}$$

Thus, $\frac{\Delta Y}{Y} = \beta_1 \cdot \frac{\Delta X}{X}$ and

$$\left(100 \cdot \frac{\Delta Y}{Y}\right) = \beta_1 \left(100 \cdot \frac{\Delta X}{X}\right)$$

$$\%\Delta Y = \beta_1 \%\Delta X$$

1% increase in $X \Rightarrow \beta_1$% change in Y

As an example,

$\ln(\widehat{consumption}) = 10.01 - 0.677 \ln(price)$

(5) Regresson of Y on X and X^2
$Y = \beta_0 + \beta_1 X + \beta_2 X^2 + u$

Some of the theoretical relationships may be more complicated than positive or negative relationships. The U shape (convex) or inverse U shape (concave) relationships are popular ones adopted by social science theories, which can be captured using the quadratic functions in Figure 8.1. One of the most popular environmental theories

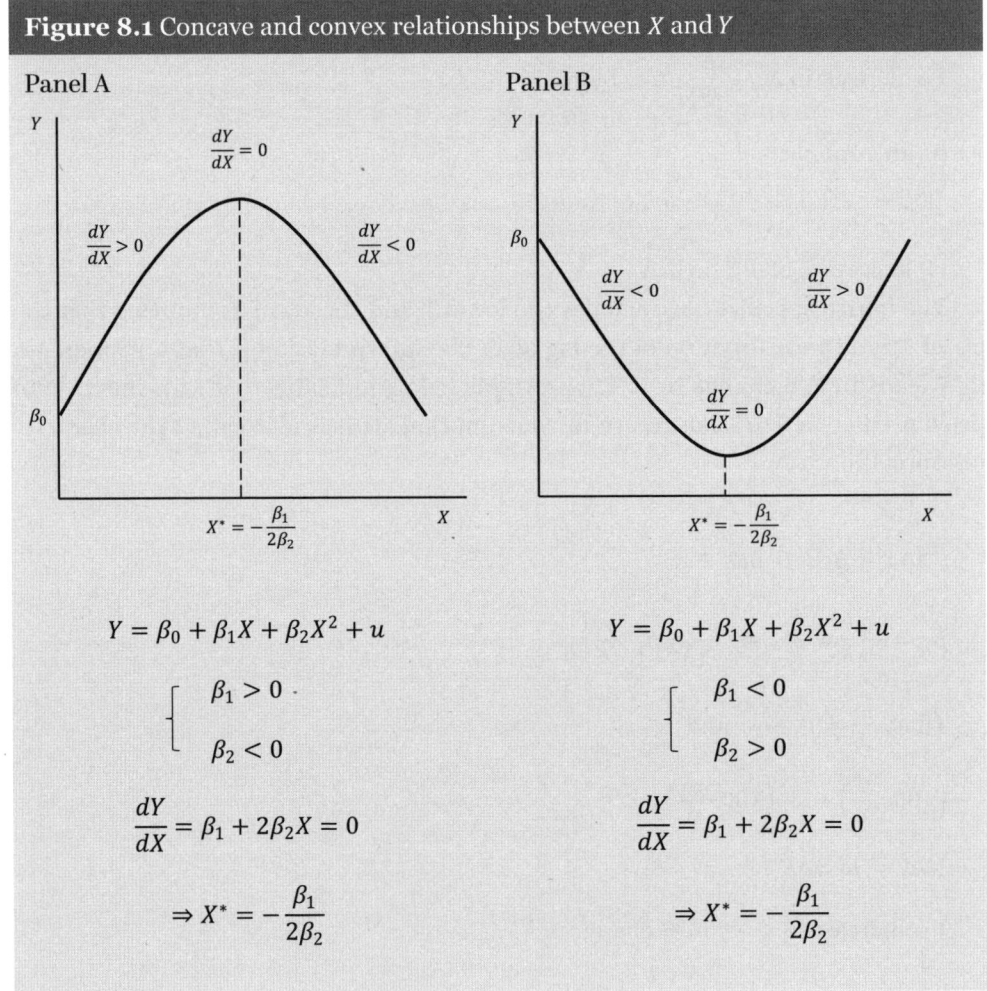

Figure 8.1 Concave and convex relationships between X and Y

is the environmental Kuznets curve, which is the inverse U shape between economic development and environmental outcomes.

Specifically, the concave relationship in Panel A of Figure 8.1 suggests that Y increases to the maximum value as X increases in the beginning, while after passing by the maximum value, Y decreases as X increases. In this case, the coefficient of X is positive, the coefficient of X square is negative, and the maximum point of Y is obtained at $X^* = -\frac{\beta_1}{2\beta_2}$. On the other hand, the convex relationship in Panel B of Figure 8.1 captures the opposite case where Y decreases to the minimum value as X increases in the beginning, while after passing by the minimum value, Y increases as X increases. The coefficients of X and X square are negative and positive, respectively, and the minimum point of Y is obtained at $X^* = -\frac{\beta_1}{2\beta_2}$.

Example 8.3

Suppose that we analyze the sample of men to estimate the impact of education on hourly wage. We are using hourly wage in 1980 US dollars (Y_i), years of education (X_{1i}), and AFQT (X_{2i}) in the year 1990 of the NLSY79 (National Longitudinal Survey of Youth - 1979 Cohort) data set. AFQT is the cognitive measure ranging from 1 to 100 in the sample.

We report the four regression results in columns 1 to 4 below. The first one is from the regression using hourly wage in U.S. dollars, education in years, and AFQT score from 1 to 100. The second regression is using the log of wage (lnY_i), education in years (X_{1i}), and AFQT score (X_{2i}). The third regression is using hourly wage in 1980 U.S. dollars (Y_i), education in years (X_{1i}), and the log of AFQT score (lnX_{2i}). The fourth regression is using the log of hourly wage in 1980 U.S. dollars (Y_i), education in years (X_{1i}), and the log of AFQT score (lnX_{2i}).

	(1) Wage	(2) Log of wage	(3) Wage	(4) Log of wage
Education in years	0.260***	0.027***	0.338***	0.031***
	(0.032)	(0.005)	(0.030)	(0.004)
AFQT	0.049***	0.006***		
	(0.003)	(0.000)		

Log of AFQT			1.059***	0.147***
			(0.066)	(0.010)
Constant	3.013***	1.392***	0.595*	1.107***
	(0.352)	(0.052)	(0.321)	(0.047)
R^2	0.208	0.140	0.195	0.143
Number of observations	3,755	3,755	3,755	3,755

Notes: ***$p<0.01$, **$p<0.05$, *$p<0.1$

As shown below, we interpret the estimated coefficients in the four columns. They are all statistically significant at $p<0.01$ under the conventional two-sided hypothesis test.

Column (1)
One more year of education → $0.26 increase in hourly wage
One unit increase in AFQT → $0.049 increase in hourly wage

Column (2)
One more year of education → 2.7% (0.027*100) increase in hourly wage
One unit increase in AFQT → 0.6% (0.006*100) increase in hourly wage

Column (3)
One more year of education → $0.338 increase in hourly wage
One percent increase in AFQT → $0.0159 (1.059/100) increase in hourly wage

Column (4)
One more year of education → 3.1% (0.031*100) increase in hourly wage
One percent increase in AFQT → 0.147% increase in hourly wage

Notes:
the NLSY79 (National Longitudinal Survey of Youth -1979 Cohort) data set
https://www.nlsinfo.org/content/cohorts/nlsy79

Example 8.4

Suppose that we would like to examine the nonlinear relationship between women's age and their monthly household income per person. To do this analysis, we use the analysis sample from the 2007 Korean Longitudinal Survey of Women and Families (KLoWF). The outcome variable (Y_i) is women's monthly household income per person in 10,000 Korean won (about $8), and the explanatory variables are age (X_{1i}) and age squared (X_{1i}^2).

$$\hat{Y}_i = 11.151 + 4.384 X_{1i} - 0.058 X_{1i}^2$$
$$\text{SE} \quad (12.143) \quad (0.596) \quad (0.007)$$

SST (Total Sum of Squares) = 86453716.9
SSE (Explained Sum of Squares) = 1045829.19
SSR (Residual Sum of Squares) = 85407887.7
R^2 = 0.0121
n = 9,469

The estimated coefficients of age and age squared are statistically significant at $p<0.01$. Particularly, the estimated coefficient of age squared is negative. Therefore, it is likely that the relationship between monthly household income and age for women is concave. To obtain the maximized monthly income, we set the marginal relation between monthly income and age to be 0 as follows.

$$\frac{\widehat{dY}}{dX_1} = \hat{\beta}_1 + 2\hat{\beta}_2 X_1 = 0$$

$$\Rightarrow X_1^* = -\frac{\hat{\beta}_1}{2\hat{\beta}_2} = -\frac{4.384}{2 \times (-0.058)} = 37.793$$

Thus, the monthly family income per person of women is maximized at about age 38 in this analysis.

Notes:
The Korean Longitudinal Survey of Women and Families (KLoWF)
https://gsis.kwdi.re.kr/klowf/portal/eng/introSummaryPage.do

Choosing specifications by considering three different types of causal paths

When we estimate the impact of a main explanatory variable on the outcome variable, there are three types of causal paths we need to consider in the multivariate regression model.

First, a spurious relationship can be found when there are confounding variables between the key explanatory variable and the outcome variable, as shown in Figure 8.2. A confounder affects the outcome variable and the main explanatory variable that is believed to affect the outcome variable. As a result, without controlling for confounders, the estimated impact of the key explanatory variable on the outcome variable can be overstated even if there is no relationship between them. Confounders are endogenous variables that usually happened before the main explanatory variable. For example, when we are interested in the impact of education on an hourly wage, an individual's parents' education level or earnings could be confounders. When we control for those confounders, the estimated causal relationship between the main explanatory variable and the outcome variable could become weaker.

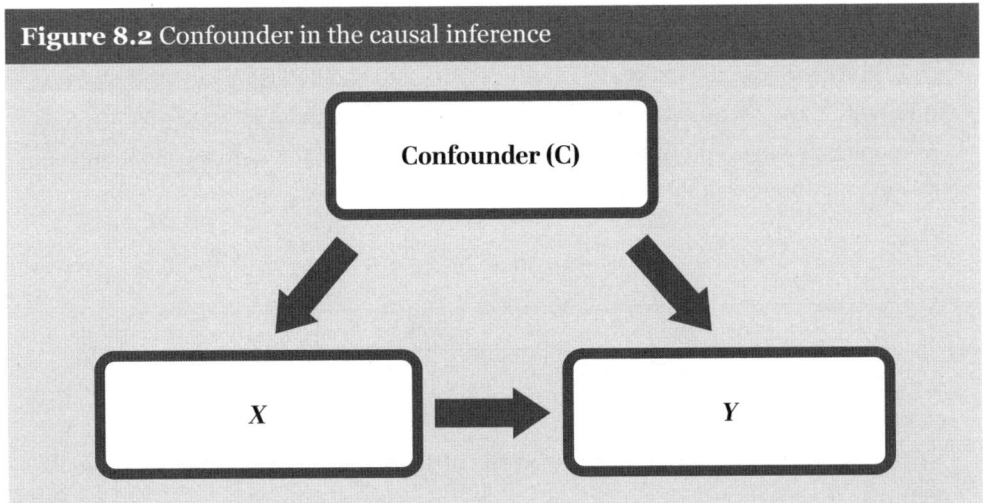

Figure 8.2 Confounder in the causal inference

Example 8.5

In Chapter 5, we studied the omitted variable bias. The omitted variable is a confounder in the OLS regression analysis. Suppose that we would like to estimate the impact of education on wages.

We come back to our analysis example that explained the omitted variable bias. The following two regression results are using hourly wage in 1980 U.S. dollars (Y_i), years of education (X_{1i}), and AFQT (X_{2i}) in the year 1990 of the NLSY79 (National Longitudinal Survey of Youth - 1979 Cohort) data set. AFQT is the cognitive measure ranging from 1 to 100 in the sample.

Let's assume that we don't have AFQT even though it is an important confounding variable. Then, we have the following regression outcome in regression 1.

<Regression 1>

$$\widehat{Y}_i = -0.587 + 0.62X_{1i}$$
$$\text{SE} \quad (0.231) \quad (0.017)$$

SST (Total Sum of Squares) = 128911.008
SSE (Explained Sum of Squares) = 18083.2888
SSR (Residual Sum of Squares) = 110827.719
R^2 = 0.1403
n = 7,707

The estimated coefficient of education is 0.62, suggesting that one more education is associated with a $0.62 increase in real hourly wage.

Let's include AFQT, a confounding variable, in the new regression model. The regression outcome is as follows in regression 2.

<Regression 2>

$$\widehat{Y}_i = 1.556 + 0.323X_{1i} + 0.042X_{2i}$$
$$\text{SE} \quad (0.242) \quad (0.021) \quad (0.002)$$

SST (Total Sum of Squares) = 128911.008
SSE (Explained Sum of Squares) = 25135.902
SSR (Residual Sum of Squares) = 103775.106

$R^2 = 0.195$

$n = 7,707$

After adding AFQT (cognitive measure) to the regression model, the estimated coefficient of education changes from 0.62 to 0.323. It implies that the estimated coefficient of the main variable (education) without controlling for a confounding variable (AFQT) is positively biased (overstated).

Notes:
the NLSY79 (National Longitudinal Survey of Youth -1979 Cohort) data set
https://www.nlsinfo.org/content/cohorts/nlsy79

Second, as shown in Figure 8.3, the impact of a main explanatory variable on the outcome variable may vary by the different levels of a particular exogenous variable that is called a moderator. For example, when we would like to estimate the impact of job training on labor earnings, age can be a moderator. The impact of job training can change depending on a person's age.

It is possible to develop a regression model with interaction terms between continuous variables to examine whether one explanatory variable affects the outcome differently by a moderating variable.

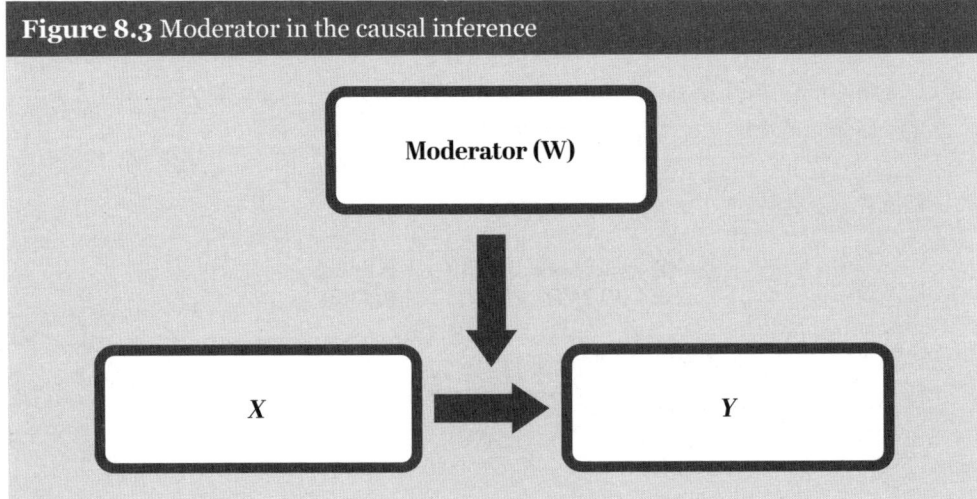

Figure 8.3 Moderator in the causal inference

Assume that we are interested in the impact of X_1 (continues variable) on Y and X_2 is a moderator in theory. Then, we can develop the regression model as follows.

$$Y = \beta_0 + \beta_1 X_1 + \beta_2 X_2 + \beta_3 X_1 \times X_2 + u.$$

In this case, when we interpret the impact of X_1 on Y, we need to take into account not only β_1 but also β_3 since $\frac{\partial Y}{\partial X_1} = \beta_1 + \beta_3 X_2$.

To summarize the effect of X_1 on Y we typically evaluate $\beta_1 + \beta_3 \overline{X_2}$ by replacing X_2 with its mean when X_2 is a continuous variable. Then, we can obtain the fixed marginal effect of X_1 on Y at the mean of X_2. Also, we can impute the lower or higher value of X_2 to examine the effect of X_1 on Y at a lower or higher value of a moderator. On the other hand, when X_2 is a binary variable, the marginal effect of X_1 on Y when $X_2 = 1$ is $\beta_1 + \beta_3$ while the marginal effect of X_1 on Y when $X_2 = 0$ is β_1.

Example 8.6

Suppose that we would like to know whether education affects hourly wage by ethnic groups, which work as modeators in the OLS regression analysis.

We use hourly wage in 1980 U.S. dollars (Y_i) and years of education (X_i) in the year 1990 of the NLSY79 (National Longitudinal Survey of Youth - 1979 Cohort) data set. We use two ethnic group dummy variables indicating black and Hispanic ($D_{1i} = 1$ for black and 0 for otherwise; $D_{2i} = 1$ for Hispanic and 0 for otherwise) with non-black & non-Hispanic workers as the base group.

$\widehat{Y_i} = -0.823 + 0.662 X_{1i} - 0.755 D_{1i} + 2.959 D_{2i} - 0.042 X_{1i} \times D_{1i} - 0.239 X_{1i} \times D_{2i}$
SE   (0.294) (0.022)   (0.613)   (0.591)   (0.047)   (0.046)

SST (Total Sum of Squares) = 128911.008
SSE (Explained Sum of Squares) = 20894.891
SSR (Residual Sum of Squares) = 108016.117
R^2 = 0.1621
n = 7,707

In this regression, the estimated coefficient of education, 0.662, implies that one more year of education leads to $0.662 more hourly wage for the base group (non-black and non-Hispanic workers). The wage differences between the particular ethnic groups and the base group are captured by the estimated coefficients of D_{1i} and D_{2i}. According to the estimated coefficient of the interaction term between education and black workers, the slope difference in education between black workers and the base group is negligible, -0.042, and statistically insignificant at $p<0.05$. In contrast, the estimated coefficient of the interaction term between education and Hispanic workers is considerable, -0.239, and statistically significant at $p<0.01$. It seems that ethnic groups partially work as moderators in this analysis.

This time, suppose that we want to examine whether the effect of education on hourly wage depends on cognitive ability, AFQT, which works as a moderator in the OLS regression analysis. We use hourly wage in 1980 U.S. dollars (Y_i), years of education (X_{1i}), and AFQT (X_{2i}) in 1990 of the NLSY79 (National Longitudinal Survey of Youth - 1979 Cohort) data set. AFQT is the cognitive measure ranging from 1 to 100 in the sample.

$$\hat{Y}_i = 3.788 + 0.144X_{1i} - 0.015X_{2i} + 0.004X_{1i} \times X_{2i}$$
$$\text{SE} \quad (0.383) \quad (0.032) \quad (0.008) \quad (0.001)$$

SST (Total Sum of Squares) = 128911.008
SSE (Explained Sum of Squares) = 25890.0853
SSR (Residual Sum of Squares) = 103020.923
$R^2 = 0.200$
$n = 7{,}707$
The sample mean of AFQT ($\overline{X_2}$) = 40.887

It is found that the estimated coefficients of education and the interaction term between education and AFQT are statistically significant at $p<0.01$, whereas that of AFQT is statistically significant only at $p<0.1$.

To summarize the effect of education on hourly wage, we evaluate $\hat{\beta}_1 + \hat{\beta}_3 \overline{X_2}$ by replacing X_2 with its mean. Thus, the fixed marginal effect of education on hourly wage at the mean of AFQT is 0.144 + 0.004*40.877 = 0.308. It implies that one more year of education leads to $0.308 more hourly wage at the mean of AFQT. Further, if we put 80 into AFQT, $\hat{\beta}_1 + \hat{\beta}_3 \overline{X_2}$ = 0.144 + 0.004*80 = 0.464. On the other hand, if we put 20 into AFQT, $\hat{\beta}_1 + \hat{\beta}_3 \overline{X_2}$ = 0.144 + 0.004*20 = 0.224. Therefore, we find that as AFQT increases, the impact of education on hourly wage increases.

Notes:
the NLSY79 (National Longitudinal Survey of Youth -1979 Cohort) data set
https://www.nlsinfo.org/content/cohorts/nlsy79

Third, as shown in Figure 8.4, the impact of a main explanatory variable on the outcome variable can be fully or partially through a particular variable that is called a mediator. Mediators are typically variables that happen after the main explanatory variable. It is advised not to control for mediators when we would like to estimate the full impact of a main explanatory variable on the outcome variable. If we control for mediators in the causal study, it is called "over-controlling." Over-controlling may understate the full impact of a main explanatory variable. For example, when we are interested in the impact of education on an hourly wage, controlling for marriage or the number of children may block or distort the full impact of education.

Figure 8.4 Mediator in the causal inference

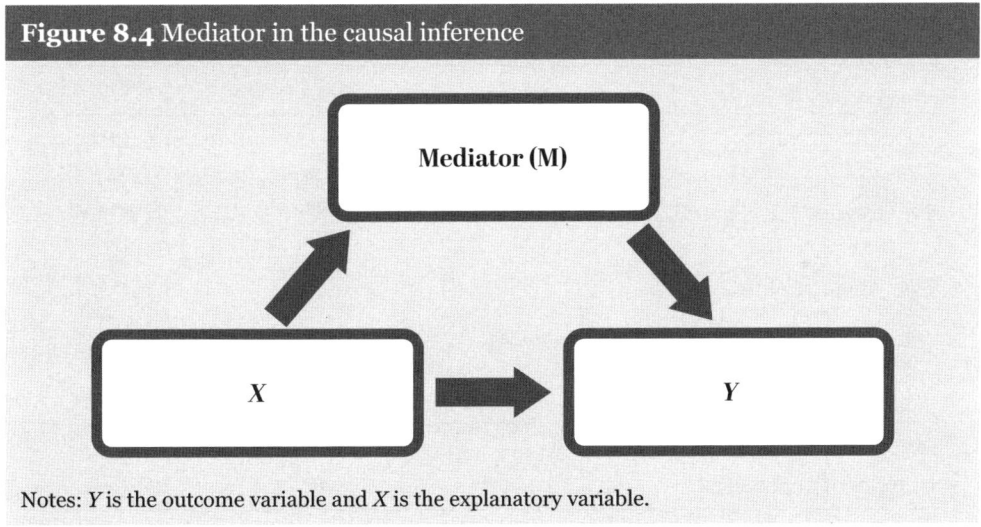

Notes: Y is the outcome variable and X is the explanatory variable.

Example 8.7

Suppose that we would like to examine the impact of education on women's fertility.

To do this analysis, we use the analysis sample of women aged 40 or more from the 2007 Korean Longitudinal Survey of Women and Families (KLoWF). We use women's number of children as the outcome variable and their years of education as the main explanatory variable. As mediators that happened between education and the number of children, we use ever-married (1 for ever-married and 0 for otherwise) and ever-worked (1 for ever-worked before and 0 for otherwise). The first column reports the regression estimates without mediators, and the second column presents the estimation results with mediators.

It is found that one more year of education leads to 0.109 fewer children in column (1). It is statistically significant at $p<0.01$. The estimate of education in column (2) after controlling for mediators is modestly smaller than that in column (1). The estimates of whether ever married and whether ever worked imply that ever-married women have 2.129 more children and ever-worked women have 0.201 fewer children, which are statistically significant at $p<0.01$.

Estimated results

	(1)	(2)
Education in years	-0.109***	-0.100***
	(0.004)	(0.004)
Ever married = 1		2.129***
		(0.119)
Ever worked before = 1		-0.201***
		(0.033)
Constant	3.445***	1.408***
	(0.037)	(0.127)
Adjusted R^2	0.156	0.212
Number of observations	5,046	5,046

Notes: ***$p<0.01$, **$p<0.05$, *$p<0.1$; The outcome is the number of children for women aged 40 or more.

Notes:
The Korean Longitudinal Survey of Women and Families (KLoWF)
https://gsis.kwdi.re.kr/klowf/portal/eng/introSummaryPage.do

When we consider these three types of causal paths in our analysis, we can have the following general rules to select relevant explanatory variables for the multivariate regression model.

General rules for including additional variables and making specifications in multivariate regression analysis

Assume that we focus on estimating the causal impact of a main explanatory variable on the outcome variable.

1. It is preferable to include the explanatory variables stated in the theory or hypothesis.
2. It is preferable to come up with the appropriate functional forms of the outcome variable and the explanatory variables based on theories and conventions in the related field.
3. If the research question involues the role of the moderator in theory, it is better to include interaction terms between the main explanatory variable and the moderator.
4. It is recommended to create dummy variables that correspond to those categories in the nominal variable instead of including nominal variables whose numbers have no meaning.
5. The base group for dummy variables should be based on theories or research questions. If there is no particular guidance on theory or research question, it is better to choose the largest group as the base group to increase the efficiency of estimates.
6. It is recommended to control for the explanatory variables that occurred and were recorded before the main explanatory variables: for example, gender, ethnic groups, where individuals were born and raised, and what family and community backgrounds they had.
7. It is advisable not to control for the variables that occurred after the main explanatory variable and could affect the outcome variable.
8. It is better to run the OLS regression model and assess estimated coefficients by gradually adding explanatory variables. If there are any sudden changes in the estimates of the main explanatory variables, it is recommended to examine the outliers (extreme values in the outcome and explanatory unables) and multicollinearity.

Chapter Summary

Rescaling variables	For various analytical purposes, it is common to rescale the outcome and explanatory variables. Interpreting the estimation results should be based on rescaled variables.
What is the model specification?	The model specification involves designing and defining the nature of the relationship between the outcome variable and the explanatory variables. This includes choosing the relevant variables and determining the specific ways in which they are included in the model equation by selecting the appropriate functional form. The model specification considers related theories, analytical contexts, and data.
Addressing common misunderstandings and mistakes	Rescaling the outcome and explanatory variables does not change the significance of the estimates. The linear regression model means that the model is linear in parameters. "Linear" in the linear regression model does not mean that the outcome is linearly related to the explanatory variables.

Exercises

Chapter 8
Developing and completing the OLS regression analysis by using rescaling and functional specifications

1. Suppose you collect data from a survey on wages, education, experience, and gender. In addition, you ask for information about marijuana usage. The original question is: "On how many separate occasions last week did you smoke marijuana?"

(1) Please write an equation that would allow you to estimate the effects of marijuana usage on wage, while controlling for other factors. You should be able to make statements such as, "One more time of smoking marijuana per week is estimated to (   ) percentage change in wage."

(2) Suppose that you would like to know the relationship between number of smoking marijuana per day and wage. To do so, please suggest the new regression model.

(3) Suppose you think it is better to measure marijuana usage by putting people into one of three categories: nonuser, light user (1 to 2 times per week) and heavy user (3 or more times per week). Now please write a model that allows you to estimate the effects of marijuana usage on wage.

(4) Using the model in part (3), explain in detail how to test the null hypothesis that marijuana usage has no effect on wage. Please be specific and include a careful listing of degrees of freedom.

(5) Suppose you think it is better to measure marijuana usage by putting people into one of two categories: nonuser and user. Please write a model that would allow you to test whether drug usage has different effects on wages for people with different

education, job experience, and gender. Explain a way to test that there are no differences in the effects of drug usage over different education, job experience, and gender.

2. Suppose that in order to determine the demand for tulips in 150 small districts in Seoul in South Korea, we estimate the following model.

$$\widehat{lnY_i} = 0.627 - 1.274 lnX_{1i} + 0.937 lnX_{2i} + 1.713 lnX_{3i}$$
$$\text{SE} \quad (6.148) \quad (0.527) \quad\quad (0.659) \quad\quad (1.201)$$

$$R^2 = 0.128 \quad\quad n = 150$$

where lnY = log of quantity of tulips sold, dozens
lnX_1 = log of average wholesale price of tulips, \$/dozen
lnX_2 = log of average wholesale price of carnations, \$/dozen
lnX_3 = log of average weekly family disposable income

(1) Interpret all estimated coefficients of explanatory variables.

(2) Test whether higher sale price of tulips lowers the demand of tulips. Construct hypotheses and use relevant test statistics.

(3) You would like to capture the regional differences in the demand of tulips. Suppose there are four regional areas in Seoul, such as North West, North East, South West, and South East. Please write a new regression model by adding appropriate dummy variables to capture the regional differences in the demand of tulips.

(4) Please explain the meaning of the coefficients of the new variables in (3).

3. You want to know whether more years of education lead to higher wage. Your variables are as follows:

"lnrhw1984" = log of real hourly wage in 1984,
"edu" = years in school,
"afqt" = a cognitive measure from 0 to 100, and
"lcexpy" = a job experience in years.

We have the following regression results.

Regression 1

$\ln(\widehat{rhw1984})_i = 0.826 + 0.079 edu_i$
SE   (0.036)   (0.003)

SST (Total Sum of Squares) = 3032.46553
SSE (Explained Sum of Squares) = 295.46488
SSR (Residual Sum of Squares) = 2737.00065
$R^2 = 0.097$
$n = 7{,}707$

Regression 2

$\ln(\widehat{rhw1984})_i = 0.606 + 0.054 edu_i + 0.003 afqt_i + 0.05 lcexpy_i$
SE   (0.044)   (0.003)   (0.000)   (0.002)

SST (Total Sum of Squares) = 3032.46553
SSE (Explained Sum of Squares) = 552.95244
SSR (Residual Sum of Squares) = 2479.51308
$R^2 = 0.182$
$n = 7{,}707$

---

(1) Please write down population regression models for these two regression outcomes.

(2) Please interpret estimated coefficient of education in these two models and discuss why the estimated coefficients of education are different.

(3) Using the results in Regression 2, please test whether education leads to higher wage using the one-sided test with $\alpha = 0.01$.

(4) Please test whether afqt and lcexpy should be controlled for in Regression 2 using the F-test with $\alpha = 0.05$. Discuss your test results.

4. You want to know the impact of education on real hourly wage. In your data, hwg is real hourly wage (in dollars), edu is years of schooling, $afqt$ is the cognitive score (1 to 100), fml is a dummy variable equal to 1 for woman and 0 otherwise, and $black$ is a dummy variable equal to 1 for black and 0 otherwise. You have the following estimated regression output for all. Let's assume that OLS assumptions for BLUE and Valid Inference are satisfied.

$$\widehat{\ln(hwg)} = 1.0955 + 0.045 edu + 0.0046 afqt - 0.0534 black$$
$$\text{SE} \quad\quad (0.0376) \quad (0.0034) \quad\quad (0.0003) \quad\quad (0.0163)$$

$$N = 8{,}223 \quad\quad R^2 = 0.1298 \quad\quad SSR_r = 2754.8839$$

(1) Please interpret the estimated coefficients in this regression.

(2) You would like to test whether the coefficients in this model are different for men and women. Suggest the new regression model to test this hypothesis; construct the null and alternative hypotheses and the F-test statistic. Obtain the critical F-value with dfs and $\alpha = 0.05$.

5. Suppose that you would like to examine the impact of education on hourly wage and employs different regression models by changing functional forms of X and Y.

	(1) Hourly wage in dollars	(2) Log of hourly wage	(3) Hourly wage in cents	(4) Log of hourly wage
Education in years	0.323***	0.043***	40.988***	0.049***
	(0.021)	(0.003)	(2.091)	(0.003)
AFQT	0.042***			
	(0.002)			
Standardized AFQT		0.148***		
		(0.008)		
ln(AFQT)			84.059***	0.119***
			(4.782)	(0.008)
Constant	1.556***	1.299***	-64.136***	0.818***
	(0.242)	(0.045)	(22.649)	(0.036)
Adjusted R^2	0.195	0.132	0.173	0.126
Number of observations	7,707	7,707	7,707	7,707

Notes: ***$p<0.01$, **$p<0.05$, *$p<0.1$; Armed Forces Qualification Test (AFQT) is a cognitive measure that ranges from 1 to 100.

(1) Please examine the difference in the estimated coefficients of education in columns (1) and (2).

(2) Please examine the difference in the estimated coefficients of AFQT in columns (1) and (2).

(3) Please interpret the estimated coefficients of education and log of AFQT in column (4).

(4) Please interpret the estimated coefficient of log of AFQT in columns (3) and (4) and explain their difference.

6. Suppose that you would like to examine the impact of education on women's household income per person. The regression results are below.

	OLS (1)	OLS (2)	OLS (3)	OLS (4)
Education in years	7.059***	6.643***	6.226***	6.159***
	(0.389)	(0.400)	(0.404)	(0.410)
Age	7.976***	8.078***	7.832***	7.884***
	(1.183)	(1.181)	(1.190)	(1.192)
Age squared	-0.074***	-0.076***	-0.070***	-0.071***
	(0.013)	(0.013)	(0.013)	(0.013)
Father: some college or more =1		20.291***	19.120***	-5.837
		(4.584)	(4.576)	(25.955)
Ever married = 1			-9.256	-9.041
			(6.863)	(6.867)
Number of children			-7.122***	-7.180***
			(1.277)	(1.278)
Education in years × Father: some college or more =1				1.714
				(1.754)
Constant	-195.989***	-193.779***	-165.343***	-165.739***
	(26.952)	(26.925)	(27.242)	(27.246)
R^2	0.054	0.056	0.061	0.062
Number of observations	7,980	7,980	7,980	7,980

Notes: ***$p<0.01$, **$p<0.05$, *$p<0.1$; The outcome variable is women's monthly household income per person in 10,000 Korea won (about $8).

(1) Please interpret the estimated coefficient of age and age squared in column (1). Also find their implications.

(2) Suppose that to control for women's family background (confounding factors), you control for whether women's fathers have attended college. Please examine the estimated coefficient of education between columns (1) and (2).

(3) In column (3), ever-married and number of children are controlled for as mediators. Please interpret the estimated coefficient of education in this analysis and provide its implications.

(4) Please interpret the estimated coefficient of education and its interaction with father's college education in column (4).

7. Suppose that you would like to study the high school student's standardized college entrance exam score with mean 0 and standard deviation 1 in South Korea in 2019:

$$strscore_i = \beta_0 + \beta_1 lnfinc_i + \beta_2 female_i + \beta_3 lnpulspen_i + \beta_4 qschool + \beta_5 tpartliv_i + u_i$$

where *stscore* is student's standardized score, *lnfinc* is log of family income, *female* is 1 if a student is female and 0 if otherwise, *lnpulspen* is log of school spending per pupil per year, *qschool* the quality of school surveyed by parents (or caregivers) as 1 for very bad, 2 for bad, 3 for neutral, 4 for good, 5 for very good, and *tpartliv* is 1 if a student lives with two parents and 0 if otherwise. Suppose that you have a large sample and the five OLS assumptions for the consistent and efficient estimators hold.

(1) Suppose that you want to know the impact of family income on those students from low-income families. So, your new sample includes students whose family income is less than the median. If you use OLS on such a subsample, do we get consistent estimators of the β_j? Why or why not?

(2) Suppose that you want to know the impact of school spending on students whose score is less than the average. Thus, your new sample includes students whose strscore is less than 0. If you use OLS on such a subsample, do we get consistent estimators of the β_j?

(3) Suppose that you use the full sample to know the impact of school quality on student's score. Interpret β_4. What is an assumption you need for this interpretation? Also, please suggest a better way to measure the impact of school quality on student's score using the dummy variables.

8. Suppose that you would like to study whether an increase in sales leads to higher CEO salary in fortune 500 companies in South Korea.

$$\widehat{\ln(salary)} = 4.822 + 0.257 \ln(sales)$$
$$\text{SE} \quad\quad (2.222) \quad (0.124)$$

$\ln$(salary) = log of CEO salary
$\ln$(sales) = log of firm sales
$n = 500$

We have SST (Total Sum of Squares) = 900.
SSE (Explained Sum of Squares) = 300; and
SSR (Residual Sum of Squares) = 600.

(1) Please interpret the estimated coefficient of $\ln$(sales).

(2) Obtain R^2 and interpret it.

(3) Obtain and interpret the 99% confidence interval for the coefficient of ln(sales).

(4) Test whether the coefficient of ln(sales) is statistically different from 0 with a two-sided test at $\alpha = 0.01$. Discuss whether increase in sales leads to higher CEO salary based on what you have in this analysis.

(5) Please discuss possible issues with this study. What is missing in this regression model? What can you do to improve this regression model?

Chapter 9
Data Analysis for Social Science: Fundamental Methods

The OLS regression analysis when the variance of the error term depends on the explanatory variables: Heteroscedasticity

Valid and efficient standard errors are critical for inference in OLS regression analysis. One of the important assumptions for valid standard errors is homoscedasticity, which assumes the equal variance of the error term regardless of included explanatory variables in the regression model.

The assumption of homoscedasticity cannot be fully validated since it is about the error term that is not observed. However, the theories and sample studies can provide strong arguments for possible violations of homoscedasticity. The violation of the homoscedasticity assumption is the unequal variance of the error term depending on included explanatory variables, which is called heteroscedasticity. The next question is what consequences heteroscedasticity brings to the OLS regression analysis and how researchers can handle the consequences.

If we estimate the typical standard errors assuming homoscedasticity, when in fact there is heteroscedasticity, the estimated standard errors are invalid and cannot be used for inference. However, the violation of homoscedasticity does not affect the unbiasedness or consistency of the OLS estimator.

The natural question is how to obtain valid and efficient standard errors under heteroscedasticity. There are two popular solutions to this problem. First, if we do not know the source of heteroscedasticity and have a large sample, we can use the "robust standard errors" by incorporating heteroscedasticity into the computation of standard errors. The robust standard errors are not the most efficient but are valid under any type of unknown heteroscedasticity if the large sample is analyzed. Second, if we know the source of heteroscedasticity, we can remove heteroscedasticity and estimate the standard errors with homoscedasticity. They will be valid and the most efficient standard errors. The method is Weighted Least Squares (WLS).

First of all, let's study the specifics of heteroscedasticity.

For simplicity, suppose the following regression model with one explanatory variable and the small sample.

$$Y_i = \beta_0 + \beta_1 X_i + u_i$$

The most common way to express heteroscedasticity is $Var(u|X) = \sigma^2 h(X)$, indicating that the variance of the error term, $Var(u|X)$, depends on some function of X, $h(X)$, and σ^2 is an unknown constant. On the other hand, homoscedasticity is stated as $Var(u|X) = \sigma^2$, indicating that the variance of the error term, $Var(u|X)$, is an unknown constant, σ^2.

At the population level, homoscedasticity in the error term is shown in Figure 9.1, while heteroscedasticity is conceptualized in Figure 9.2. In Figure 9.1, the distributions of the error term are drawn at the different values of X around the population

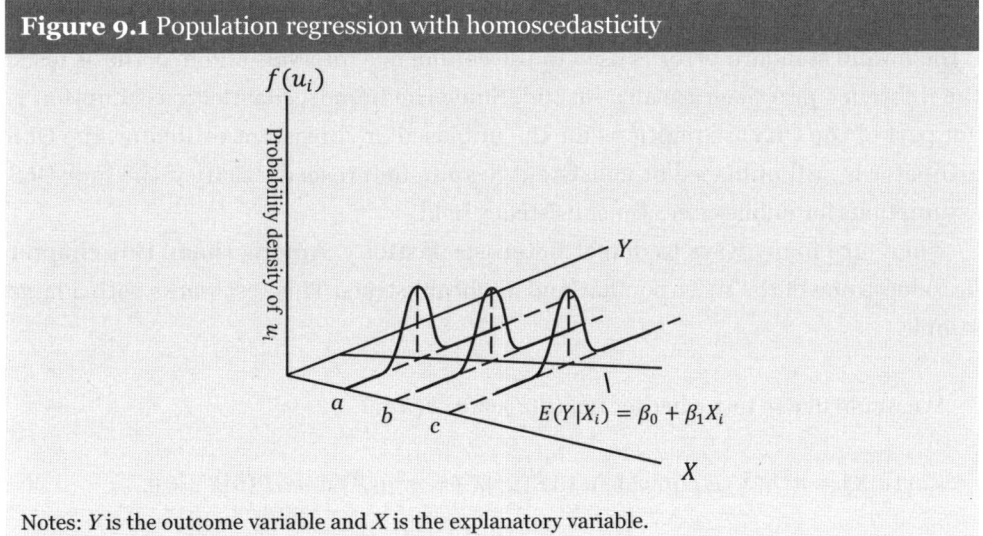

Figure 9.1 Population regression with homoscedasticity

Notes: Y is the outcome variable and X is the explanatory variable.

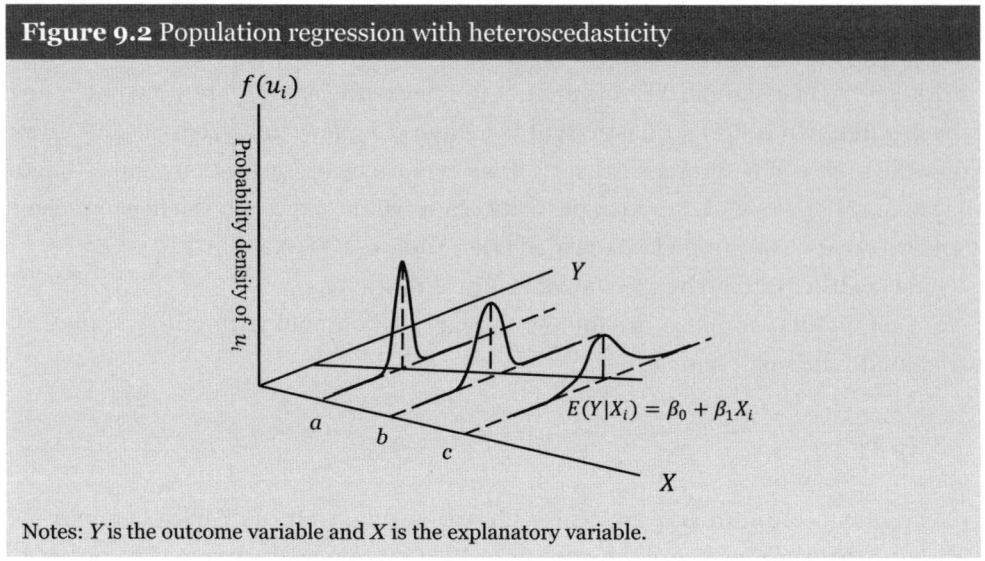

Figure 9.2 Population regression with heteroscedasticity

Notes: Y is the outcome variable and X is the explanatory variable.

regression line, and the variances of the distributions are the same. In contrast, in Figure 9.2, the variances of the distributions of the error term are different depending on the values of the explanatory variable X.

Under homoscedasticity, the formula to compute the standard error is $se(\hat{\beta}_{OLS}) = \frac{\hat{\sigma}}{\sqrt{\sum(X_i - \bar{X})^2}}$ as we studied earlier. Therefore, if we use this formula to obtain the standard error under heteroscedasticity, the estimated standard error is not valid. If the invalid standard error is used in the confidence intervals and hypothesis tests, the inference practices are also invalid. Since the homoscedasticity assumption is not part of the OLS assumptions for the unbiased or consistent estimator, the OLS estimator is still unbiased or consistent despite heteroscedasticity if the four OLS assumptions for unbiasedness or consistency hold.

There are many ways to detect heteroscedasticity. Among them, this chapter introduces one of the most popular and applicable tests. This test works with a large sample.

We would like to test whether $Var(u|X) = \sigma^2 h(X)$.

$Var(u|X) = \sigma^2 h(X)$ is equivalent to $E(u^2|X) = \sigma^2 h(X)$ since $E(u|X) = 0$.

The first idea is as follows.

We assume the large sample and the population regression model below with the five OLS assumptions for the large sample OLS analysis.

$$Y_i = \beta_0 + \beta_1 X_{1i} + \beta_2 X_{2i} + \cdots + \beta_k X_{ki} + u_i$$

① By running $u_i^2 = \delta_0 + \delta_1 X_1 + \delta_2 X_2 + \cdots + \delta_k X_k + v_i$

Test $\begin{cases} H_o: \delta_1 = 0 \ \& \ \delta_2 = 0 \ \& \ \ldots \ \& \ \delta_k = 0 \quad \text{-- homoscedasticity} \\ H_a: otherwise \end{cases}$

⇒ Use the F-test statistics

If H_0 is not rejected, we may conclude that there is no heteroscedasticity.

However, this test cannot detect the nonlinear relationship between u_i^2 and X variables since the regression model does not include the nonlinear functions of explanatory variables.

Thus, the second idea is as follows.

② By running $u_i^2 = \delta_0 + \delta_1 X_1 + \delta_2 X_2 + \cdots + \delta_k X_k + \delta_{k+1} X_1^2 + \cdots + \delta_{k+k} X_k^2 + \cdots + v_i$

This model includes the nonlinear functions of the explanatory variables, but it is too complicated and takes up too many degrees of freedom. We also do not have u_i^2 in our analysis.

Instead, it is suggested to run $\hat{u}_i^2 = \delta_0 + \delta_1 \hat{Y}_i + \delta_2 \hat{Y}_i^2 + v_i$ where $\hat{Y}_i$ and $\hat{Y}_i^2$ are the linear and nonlinear functions of X variables, respectively.

Then, use the F-test statistics to test the following null hypothesis.

$\begin{cases} H_o: \delta_1 = 0 \ \& \ \delta_2 = 0 \quad \text{-- homoscedasticity} \\ H_a: otherwise \end{cases}$

If H_0 is not rejected, it is likely that $\hat{u}_i^2$ is not any function of explanatory variables. As a result, we may conclude that there is no heteroscedasticity.

This is called the White test.

Example 9.1

Suppose that we would like to examine the impact of education on wage controlling for AFQT and job experience. We use hourly wage in 1980 U.S. dollars (Y), years of education (X_1), AFQT (X_2), years of job experience (X_3), in the year 1990 of the NLSY79 (National Longitudinal Survey of Youth - 1979 Cohort) data set.

Suppose that we would like to examine whether there is heteroscedasticity in the error term of this analysis.

$$\widehat{Y}_i = -1.384 + 0.390X_{1i} + 0.031X_{2i} + 0.305X_{3i}$$
$$\text{SE} \quad (0.274) \quad (0.021) \quad (0.002) \quad (0.015)$$

$R^2 = 0.2383$
$n = 7{,}707$

From this regression, we create the square of residuals ($\hat{u}_i^2$), the predicted outcome ($\widehat{Y}_i$), and the square of the predicted outcome ($\widehat{Y}_i^2$). Then, we conduct the White test using these variables as follows.

$$\widehat{\hat{u}_i^2} = 19.629 - 5.137\widehat{Y}_i + 0.527\widehat{Y}_i^2$$
$$\text{SE} \quad (4.004) \quad (1.107) \quad (0.074)$$

$R^2 = 0.0329$
$n = 7{,}707$

The null and alternative hypotheses of this test are as follows.

$H_o: \delta_1 = 0 \ \& \ \delta_2 = 0$ -- homoscedasticity
$H_a: otherwise$

Test statistic $F = \dfrac{R^2/k}{(1-R^2)/(n-k-1)} = \dfrac{0.0329/2}{(1-0.0329)/(7707-2-1)} = 131.032$, and its p-value is close to 0. Therefore, we reject the null hypothesis even at $p<0.01$. Therefore, it is likely that there is heteroscedasticity in this analysis. However, we don't know the structure of heteroscedasticity. In other words, we don't know what $h(X)$ is in $Var(u|X) = \sigma^2 h(X)$.

Notes:

the NLSY79 (National Longitudinal Survey of Youth -1979 Cohort) data set
https://www.nlsinfo.org/content/cohorts/nlsy79

If we find that there is possible heteroscedasticity, then what should we do to get valid standard errors?

There are two most popular ways to obtain valid standard errors when there is heteroscedasticity in the error term. First, we can use robust standard errors when we do not know the source and structure of heteroscedasticity. The robust standard error is estimated using the new formula assuming heteroscedasticity. It is valid under any kind of heteroscedasticity, but it is only valid with a large sample.

Suppose that there is heteroscedasticity and we don't know the structure of $h(X)$. We know that under homoscedasticity,

$$Var(\hat{\beta}_1) = \frac{\sigma^2}{\Sigma(X_i-\bar{X})^2}$$

$$\Rightarrow \widehat{Var}(\hat{\beta}_1) = \frac{\hat{\sigma}^2}{\Sigma(X_i-\bar{X})^2}$$

$$\Rightarrow se(\hat{\beta}_1) = \frac{\hat{\sigma}}{\sqrt{\Sigma(X_i-\bar{X})^2}}$$

where $\hat{\sigma}^2 = \frac{\Sigma \hat{u}_i^2}{n-k-1}$

Thus, $se(\hat{\beta}_1) = \frac{\hat{\sigma}}{\sqrt{\Sigma(X_i-\bar{X})^2}}$, which is not valid under heteroscedasticity.

On the other hand, by incorporating heteroscedasticity into the computation,

$$Var(\hat{\beta}_1) = \frac{\Sigma(X_i-\bar{X})^2 \sigma_i^2}{[\Sigma(X_i-\bar{X})^2]^2}$$

$$\Rightarrow \widehat{Var}(\hat{\beta}_1) = \frac{\Sigma(X_i-\bar{X})^2 \hat{u}_i^2}{[\Sigma(X_i-\bar{X})^2]^2} \text{ by using } \hat{u}_i^2 \text{ for } \sigma_i^2.$$

We can show that plim $\widehat{Var}(\hat{\beta}_1) = \frac{\Sigma(X_i-\bar{X})^2 \sigma_i^2}{[\Sigma(X_i-\bar{X})^2]^2}$ because of the Central Limit Theorem (CLT).

Thus, robust se is

$$se(\hat{\beta}_1)_{robust} = \sqrt{\frac{\sum(X_i-\bar{X})^2 \hat{u}_i^2}{[\sum(X_i-\bar{X})^2]^2}} \text{ by using } \hat{u}_i^2.$$

This is only valid with a large sample since it is based on the CLT.

The second way to obtain the valid standard error under heteroscedasticity is the Weighted Least Squares (WLS), which is one kind of the Generalized Least Squares (GLS). The GLS typically refers to a statistical technique used to estimate the valid standard errors in the OLS regression model when heteroscedasticity or autocorrelation is present in the error term.

We assume that we know the source and structure of heteroscedasticity, $h(X)$.

Then, we can do the following steps to remove the sources of heteroscedasticity in the error term.

$$Var(u|X) = \sigma^2 h(X)$$

$$\Rightarrow \frac{Var(u|X)}{h(X)} = \frac{\sigma^2 h(X)}{h(X)}$$

$$\Rightarrow Var\left(\frac{u}{\sqrt{h(X)}} \bigg| X\right) = \frac{\sigma^2 h(X)}{h(X)} = \sigma^2 \quad \text{-- homoscedasticity}$$

Thus, after this step, we have the error term with homoscedasticity.

To do so, we need to transform the population regression equation as follows:

$$\frac{Y_i}{\sqrt{h(X)}} = \beta_0 \frac{1}{\sqrt{h(X)}} + \beta_1 \frac{X_{1i}}{\sqrt{h(X)}} + \beta_2 \frac{X_{2i}}{\sqrt{h(X)}} + \cdots + \beta_k \frac{X_{ki}}{\sqrt{h(X)}} + \frac{u_i}{\sqrt{h(X)}}$$

$$\rightarrow \tilde{Y}_i = \beta_0 \frac{1}{\sqrt{h(X)}} + \beta_1 \tilde{X}_{1i} + \beta_2 \tilde{X}_{2i} + \cdots + \beta_k \tilde{X}_{ki} + \tilde{u}_i$$

If we run this transformed regression model without a constant and with the new explanatory variables, $\beta_0 \frac{1}{\sqrt{h(X)}}, \tilde{X}_{1i}, \tilde{X}_{2i}, \ldots$, and $\tilde{X}_{ki}$ that were transformed, we can obtain valid and efficient standard errors that are free from heteroscedasticity. This method is valid under any sample size, but we need to know the source of heteroscedasticity to obtain valid standard errors. In practice, it is very hard to know the source and structure of heteroscedasticity, $h(X)$. Therefore, this method is not widely used.

Example 9.2

Suppose that we would like to examine the impact of education on wages, controlling for cognitive skills and job experience. We are worried about a violation of the homoscedasticity assumption in the OLS analysis. The table below reports the default OLS results, the OLS results with robust standard errors, and the WLS results. For WLS, we assume that $h(X) = edu$ in $Var(u|X) = \sigma^2 h(X)$.

The estimated coefficients of education, AFQT, and job experience in OLS and OLS with robust standard errors in columns (1) and (2) are the same. The only difference is the reported standard errors. If the homoscedasticity assumption is violated, the standard errors in the first column are wrong since they are estimated under the homoscedasticity assumption. On the other hand, the standard errors in the second column are valid with the large sample under heteroscedasticity.

The third column reports the estimation results of WLS assuming that $Var(u|X) = \sigma^2 h(X) = \sigma^2 edu$. The estimated coefficients of three variables are different from the first two regressions, implying that the estimation is not stable with the transformed data when dividing all the variables by $\sqrt{h(X)}$. It is typical in WLS and implies that the specification of the regression model is not reliable. The estimated standard errors are valid, assuming that WLS removes heteroscedasticity driven by $h(X) = edu$. If $h(X)$ is not edu, the estimated standard errors are not valid.

Estimated results

	OLS	OLS with Robust SE	WLS
Years of education	0.390***	0.390***	0.317***
	(0.021)	(0.023)	(0.019)
AFQT	0.031***	0.031***	0.031***
	(0.002)	(0.002)	(0.002)
Years of job experience	0.305***	0.305***	0.295***
	(0.015)	(0.013)	(0.014)
Constant	-1.384***	-1.384***	-0.373
	(0.274)	(0.282)	(0.247)

Adjusted R^2	0.238	0.238	0.227
Number of observations	7,707	7,707	7,705

Notes: ***$p<0.01$, **$p<0.05$, *$p<0.1$; The outcome variable is hourly wage in 1980 U.S. dollars in the year 1990 of the NLSY79 (National Longitudinal Survey of Youth - 1979 Cohort) data set.

Notes:
the NLSY79 (National Longitudinal Survey of Youth -1979 Cohort) data set
https://www.nlsinfo.org/content/cohorts/nlsy79

There is an extended method of the Generalized Least Squares, which is called the Feasible Generalized Least Squares (F-GLS). When the functional form of $h(X)$ is unknown, the F-GLS is to estimate the flexible form of $h(X)$. Since the approaches to estimate $h(X)$ is somewhat arbitrary and unpopular nowadays, this book does not cover the F-GLS in detail.

Chapter Summary

What is heteroscedasticity?	Heteroscedasticity is the unequal variance of the error term depending on included explanatory variables. This is a violation of the fifth OLS assumption of homoscedasticity. Heteroscedasticity is common in any social science studies.
Consequences of heteroscedasticity	When there is heteroscedasticity, the default standard errors of the OLS estimates under the homoscedasticity assumption are invalid. As a result, the confidence intervals and hypothesis tests are also invalid.
What can be the best way to resolve present heteroscedasticity?	When we do not know the structure of heteroscedasticity and the sample size is large, it is better to use the robust standard errors. When we do know the structure of heteroscedasticity, it is possible to use the Weighted Least Squares (WLS). Generally, since it is hard to know the structure of heteroscedasticity and the sample sizes are large in modern data sets, it is popular to use robust standard errors.
Addressing common misunderstandings and mistakes	Analyzing large samples does not automatically resolve heteroscedasticity. We need to estimate the robust standard errors using the large sample when there is heteroscedasticity.

Exercises

Chapter 9
The OLS regression analysis when the variance of the error term depends on the explanatory variables: Heteroscedasticity

1. Suppose that in order to determine the demand for tulips in small 150 districts in Seoul in South Korea, we estimate the following model.

$$\widehat{lnY_i} = 0.627 - 1.274 lnX_{1i} + 0.937 lnX_{2i} + 1.713 lnX_{3i}$$
$$\text{SE} \quad (6.148) \quad (0.527) \quad\quad (0.659) \quad\quad (1.201)$$

$$R^2 = 0.128 \quad\quad n = 150$$

where lnY = log of quantity of tulips sold, dozens
lnX_1 = log of average wholesale price of tulips, $/dozen
lnX_2 = log of average wholesale price of carnations, $/dozen
lnX_3 = log of average weekly family disposable income

(1) You are wondering whether there is heteroscedasticity in the model. Please suggest the test to check whether there is heteroscedasticity.

(2) Suppose that the variance of error term is linear function of lnX_3. Please transform the regression model appropriately to have homoscedasticity.

2. Suppose that you want to investigate whether having a job training affects individuals' earnings.

Y is yearly earnings in $. X_1 and X_2 are education and job experience in years, respectively. X_3 is a dummy variable equal to 1 if an individual had at least one month of job training in the past year and equal to 0 otherwise. The estimated equation is:

$$\hat{Y}_i = 45.08 + 200.083\, X_{1i} + 150.215\, X_{2i} + 500.1\, X_{3i}$$
$$\text{SE} \quad (3.93) \quad (43.38) \quad\quad (50.37) \quad\quad (100.5)$$
$$n = 1{,}730 \quad\quad R^2 = 0.332.$$

(1) Now construct the White test using all the explanatory variables and their squared and interaction terms. Also, construct the F statistic. You are not required to calculate the F statistic. One of your colleagues said that in White test, the square term of X_3 should not be included. Is he right or wrong? Explain.

(2) Construct the alternative form of the White test using the predicted outcome and its squared term. Again construct the F statistic form. You are not required to calculate the F statistic.

(3) Suppose that $Var(u|X) = \sigma^2 X_2$. Please construct the WLS regression model to have homoscedasticity.
Hint: Transform the following population regression model:
$$Y_i = \beta_0 + \beta_1 X_{1i} + \beta_2 X_{2i} + \beta_3 X_{3i} + u_i$$

3. Suppose that you would like to examine what affects women's educational attainment in South Korea. The three regression results are as below. Since you are worried about possible heteroscedasticity in the regression model, you have the OLS result in column (1) and the OLS result with robust SEs in column (2). The third column includes the Weighted Least Squares(WLS) result assuming that $h(X) =$ age in $Var(u|X) = \sigma^2 h(X)$.

	(1) OLS	(2) OLS Robust SE	(3) WLS
Age	-0.238***	-0.238***	-0.229***
	(0.003)	(0.004)	(0.003)
Father: high school graduate = 1	1.543***	1.543***	1.431***
	(0.096)	(0.091)	(0.088)

	(1)	(2)	(3)
Father: some college or more = 1	2.697***	2.697***	2.584***
	(0.148)	(0.143)	(0.137)
Not having father = 1	-0.353***	-0.353***	-0.328***
	(0.113)	(0.125)	(0.109)
Mother: high school graduate = 1	0.188	0.188	0.109
	(0.123)	(0.116)	(0.111)
Mother: some college or more = 1	1.022***	1.022***	0.905***
	(0.278)	(0.275)	(0.250)
Not having mother = 1	-1.458***	-1.458***	-1.434***
	(0.192)	(0.219)	(0.192)
Number of brothers woman has	-0.057**	-0.057**	-0.067***
	(0.026)	(0.028)	(0.025)
Number of sisters woman has	-0.048**	-0.048**	-0.043**
	(0.022)	(0.022)	(0.021)
Constant	21.601***	21.601***	21.253***
	(0.162)	(0.158)	(0.152)
Adjusted R^2	0.516	0.516	0.506
Number of observations	7,976	7,976	7,976

Notes: ***$p<0.01$, **$p<0.05$, *$p<0.1$; Women aged 30 to 67; The outcome variable is education in years.

(1) Please state the large sample OLS assumptions for the valid estimated standard errors in column (1).

(2) Please compare the estimated coefficients and SEs in columns (1) and (2) and their implications.

(3) Please explain how to get the transformed regression model for the WLS in column (3).

(4) Please explain the advantages and disadvantages of robust SEs and SEs by the WLS when there is heteroscedasticity.

Chapter 10
Data Analysis for Social Science: Fundamental Methods

The regression analysis when the outcome variable is binary: LPM, Logit, and Probit

We may face many research questions that ask the impact of explanatory variables on binary qualitative outcomes, such as employed or not, college degree or not, married or not, ever divorced or not, having a private pension or not, and so on. Since an outcome variable in these studies is binary, there is some confusion about what analysis methods should be chosen. In this chapter, we will study the three main analysis methods, such as the Linear Probability Model (LPM), probit model, and logit model, and their advantages and disadvantages.

Linear Probability Model (LPM): Using OLS when the outcome variable is binary

When the outcome variable is binary, it is common to ask whether the OLS regression analysis is still valid and useful. The answer is "Yes" with caution.

There are three major concerns when we use the OLS regression for the binary outcome variable. The first concern is that the normality assumption of the error term is violated when the outcome variable is binary. However, if we use a large sample to do the OLS regression analysis, the normality assumption is not needed.

The second concern is that the predicted outcome is not bounded between 0 and 1 when the OLS regression is used for the binary outcome variable. However, if the analysis focuses on consistently estimating the impact of the explanatory variable on the outcome variable and we are interested in the marginal relations between the outcome and explanatory variables, predicting the values of the outcome variable is not critical.

The third concern is that the standard errors in the OLS analysis are not valid due to heteroscedasticity driven by the binary outcome variable. However, if the sample size is large enough, then robust standard errors could be used and are valid.

Let's study the Linear probability models (LPM) in detail.

Binary dependent variable $Y \begin{cases} = 1 \\ = 0 \end{cases}$

If we use LPM, we can have the population regression line as follows.

$E(Y|X) = \beta_0 + \beta_1 X$

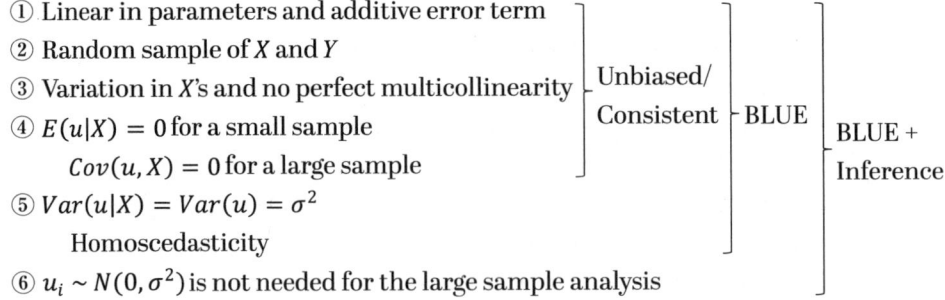

Thus, $E(Y|X)$ can be > 1 or < 0. When our analysis is to consistently estimate the impact of the explanatory variable on the outcome variable, and we are interested in the marginal relations between X and Y, predicting the values of the outcome variable is not important.

The OLS assumptions for the valid inference (confidence intervals, hypothesis tests) can be stated below.

① Linear in parameters and additive error term
② Random sample of X and Y
③ Variation in X's and no perfect multicollinearity
④ $E(u|X) = 0$ for a small sample
   $Cov(u, X) = 0$ for a large sample
⑤ $Var(u|X) = Var(u) = \sigma^2$
   Homoscedasticity
⑥ $u_i \sim N(0, \sigma^2)$ is not needed for the large sample analysis

{①②③ → Unbiased/Consistent}
{①②③④⑤ → BLUE}
{①②③④⑤⑥ → BLUE + Inference}

If our sample size is small, we need the sixth assumption (the normality of the error term) for the valid confidence intervals and hypothesis tests. However, as we studied earlier, we don't need the sixth assumption for a large sample.

Another limitation of LPM is that homoscedasticity is always violated since $Var(u|X)$ is a function of X as shown below.

$$Var(u|X) = Var(Y|X) = \underbrace{E(Y|X)(1 - E(Y|X))}_{\text{Function of } X}$$

Thus, $Var(u|X) \neq Var(u)$

Then, how can we yield valid standard errors?

It is popular to use robust SE when the sample size is large. Also, we can use the Weighted Least Squares (WLS) given that we know the structure of $Var(u|X) = E(Y|X)(1 - E(Y|X))$. However, if we do not know other possible sources and structures of heteroscedasticity in the analysis, the WLS based on $Var(u|X) = E(Y|X)(1 - E(Y|X))$ may not give valid standard errors. Therefore, it is popular to use robust standard errors in LPM when the sample size is large.

In summary, it is fine to use LPM to estimate the marginal relationship between X and Y when the sample size is large and robust standard errors are used.

Example 10.1

Suppose that we would like to examine the impact of education on being a high-wage earner. We define a high-wage earner as workers who earned $10 or more per hour in the year 1990 of the NLSY79 (National Longitudinal Survey of Youth - 1979 Cohort) data set. The sample mean of hourly wage is 6.53, and the standard deviation is 4.09. About 21.49% of workers earn $10 or more in the analysis sample. The outcome variable is 1 for workers who earn $10 or more and 0 for otherwise. From columns 1 to 4, we gradually control for years of job experience, standardized AFQT score, female dummy variable (=1 for female and 0 for male), black dummy variable (=1 for black and 0 for otherwise), and Hispanic dummy variable (=1 for Hispanic and 0 for otherwise). We use robust standard errors since using the OLS regression model for the binary outcome variable always has heteroscedasticity in the error term. The sample size is large enough, 7,707, to have valid robust standard errors.

Linear Probability Model (LPM) estimation results

	(1)	(2)	(3)	(4)
Years of education	0.051***	0.029***	0.030***	0.030***
	(0.002)	(0.002)	(0.002)	(0.002)
Standardized AFQT		0.086***	0.089***	0.091***
		(0.006)	(0.006)	(0.007)
Years of job experience		0.018***	0.014***	0.014***
		(0.001)	(0.001)	(0.001)
Female = 1			-0.132***	-0.131***
			(0.009)	(0.009)
Black = 1				0.002
				(0.011)
Hispanic = 1				0.038***
				(0.013)
Constant	-0.444***	-0.312***	-0.225***	-0.233***
	(0.025)	(0.033)	(0.034)	(0.034)
Adjusted R^2	0.093	0.150	0.174	0.175
Number of observations	7,707	7,707	7,707	7,707

Notes: ***$p<0.01$, **$p<0.05$, *$p<0.1$; Robust standard errors are used; The outcome variable is 1 for workers who earn $10 or more and 0 for otherwise.

We can interpret the estimated coefficients as we do for the other OLS analyses. Changes in the outcome variable are percentage point increases or decreases since the outcome variable is binary, and its value moves between 0 and 1 (between 0% and 100% by multiplying 100). In our analysis example, the probability of being high-wage workers may move between 0 (0%) and 1 (100%) by changes in explanatory variables.

When we control for more variables, the estimated coefficient of education changes from 0.051 to 0.029 and 0.03. It seems that AFQT and job experience are key confounding variables to be controlled for. The full regression model in column (4) suggests that one more year of education leads to a 3 percentage point increase in the probability of being high-wage workers, which is statistically significant at $p<0.01$. Since high-wage workers are about 21.49% of the sample, a 3 percentage point increase is considerable. One standard deviation increase in AFQT increases the probability of being high-wage workers by 9.1 percentage points, and it is statistically significant at $p<0.01$, while a one-year increase in job experience raises the chance of being high-wage workers by 1.4 percentage points, statistically significant at $p<0.01$. Women are less likely to be high-wage workers by 13.1 percentage points than men, statistically significant at $p<0.01$. It seems that there is no considerable and statistically significant difference in being high-wage workers between black workers and non-black & non-Hispanic workers: 0.2 percentage point difference and statistically insignificant. On the other hand, Hispanic workers are more likely to be high-wage workers by 3.8 percentage points than non-black & non-Hispanic workers, statistically significant at $p<0.01$.

Notes:
the NLSY79 (National Longitudinal Survey of Youth -1979 Cohort) data set
https://www.nlsinfo.org/content/cohorts/nlsy79

The estimation of logit and probit models

Since the predicted outcome in LPM is not bounded between 0 and 1, statisticians wanted to develop a new regression model that is designed to predict outcome values between 0 and 1. As a result, the logit regression model was introduced and has been popular to analyze the binary outcome variable for a long time since it was originally designed to make the predicted outcome variable be bounded between 0 and 1. It is also easy to handle a computation in estimating parameters, and this advantage had been critical until the computer was well advanced to do complex computations. Nowadays, the probit model has become popular to replace the logit model since the data generating progress for the binary outcome variable is more aligned to the normal distribution assumption for the probit model than the logistic distribution assumption for the logit model. Also, the advanced computation makes the probit estimation easier than before.

The population regression model for the logit model is constructed as follows:

$$E(Y|X) = G(\delta_0 + \delta_1 X_1 + \delta_2 X_2)$$
$$= \frac{1}{1+\exp(-(\delta_0+\delta_1 X_1+\delta_2 X_2))}$$
$$= \frac{\exp(\delta_0+\delta_1 X_1+\delta_2 X_2)}{1+\exp(\delta_0+\delta_1 X_1+\delta_2 X_2)}$$

The population average of Y conditional on X is the cumulative distribution function (CDF) of logit, which represents the population regression depicted here. Different from the OLS regression model, where the outcome variable is linear in parameters, $E(Y|X)$ is nonlinear in parameters in this logit model. That is why it is called the nonlinear regression model.

The CDF shows the shape below in Figure 10.1. Due to the CDF, the predicted average of Y conditional on X is bounded between 0 and 1. Also, it is important to note that the population regression line is convex at the lower value of $\beta_0 + \beta_1 X$ and concave at the higher value of $\beta_0 + \beta_1 X$, fixating the nonlinear relationship between $E(Y|X)$ and $\beta_0 + \beta_1 X$.

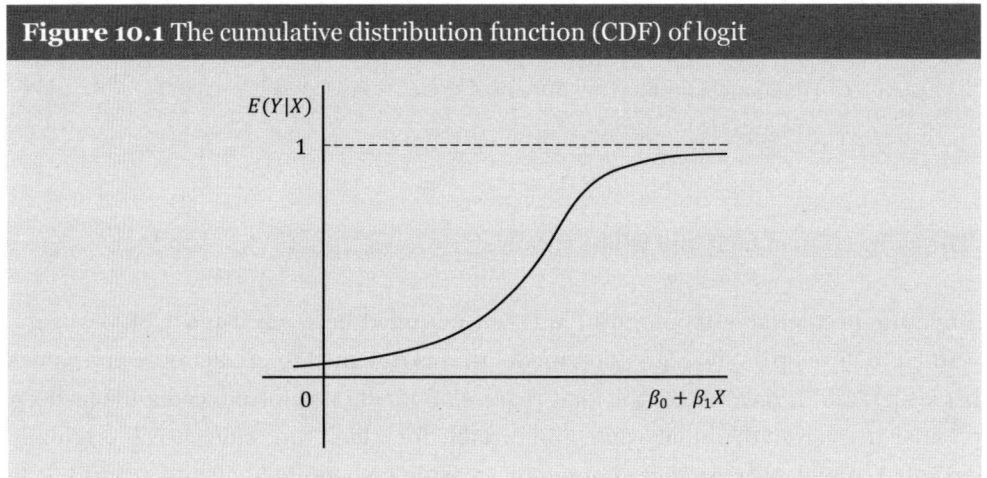

Figure 10.1 The cumulative distribution function (CDF) of logit

> Cumulative distribution function (CDF)
>
> The Cumulative Distribution Function (CDF) is a fundamental concept in statistics and probability theory. It describes the probability that a real-valued random variable X is less than or equal to a certain value a as shown below. In the illustration of the probability density function (PDF) and the cumulative distribution function (CDF), the CDF in the second figure gives the cumulative probability associated with a probability distribution presented by the PDF in the first figure.
>
> Let's define the cumulative distribution function to be $F(x)$ and

$F(a) = P(X \leq a) = \int_{-\infty}^{a} f(x)dx.$

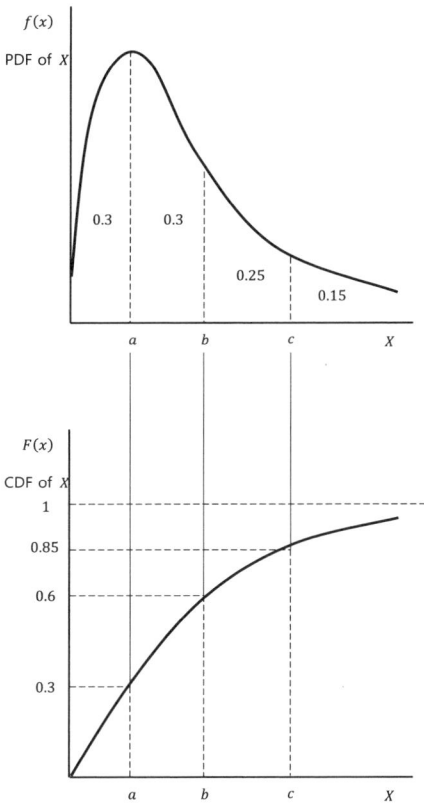

$F(x)$ presents probability.
$F(x)$ is a non-decreasing function.
Thus, $F(a) \leq F(b)$ if $a \leq b$ and $0 \leq F(x) \leq 1$.

In this example, it can be obtained below.

$F(a) = P(X \leq a) = P(X < a) = 0.3$
$F(b) = P(X \leq b) = P(X < b) = 0.6$
$F(c) = P(X \leq c) = P(X < c) = 0.85$

Also, it can be shown below.
$P(a < X < b) = P(X < b) - P(X < a) = F(b) - F(a)$
$P(X > c) = 1 - P(X \leq c) = 1 - F(c)$

The CDF of the probit model also shows a similar shape to the CDF of the logit model. $E(Y|X)$ of the probit model is shown below.

$$E(Y|X) = \Phi(\beta_0 + \beta_1 X_1 + \beta_2 X_2)$$

$$= \int_{-\infty}^{\beta_0 + \beta_1 X_1 + \beta_2 X_2} \frac{1}{\sqrt{2\pi}} \exp\left(-\frac{1}{2} z^2\right) dz$$

Example 10.2

Suppose that we would like to examine the impact of education on the probability of being high-wage workers, controlling for AFQT, job experience, gender, and ethnic groups. We use hourly wage in 1980 U.S. dollars (Y), years of education (X_1), standardized AFQT (SX_2), years of job experience (X_3), in the year 1990 of the NLSY79 (National Longitudinal Survey of Youth - 1979 Cohort) data set. We also control for the female dummy variable ($W = 1$ for women and 0 for otherwise) and two ethnic group dummy variables of black and Hispanic ($D_1 = 1$ for black and 0 for otherwise; $D_2 = 1$ for Hispanic and 0 for otherwise).

We can construct the following three regression equations for LPM, probit, and logit analyses. As mentioned earlier, LPM is the linear regression model since the relationship between the outcome variable and the parameters of explanatory variables is linearly modeled. The probit and logit models are called the nonlinear regression model since the relationship between the outcome variable and the parameters of explanatory variables is nonlinearly modeled.

Regression equation of LPM
$$Y = \beta_0 + \beta_1 X_1 + \beta_2 SX_2 + \beta_3 X_3 + \beta_4 W + \beta_5 D_1 + \beta_6 D_2 + u_i$$

Regression equation of the probit model
$$E(Y|X) = \Phi(\alpha_0 + \alpha_1 X_1 + \alpha_2 SX_2 + \alpha_3 X_3 + \alpha_4 W + \alpha_5 D_1 + \alpha_6 D_2)$$

Regression equation of the logit model
$$E(Y|X) = G(\delta_0 + \delta_1 X_1 + \delta_2 X_2 + \delta_3 X_3 + \delta_4 W + \delta_5 D_1 + \delta_6 D_2)$$

$$= \frac{\exp(\delta_0 + \delta_1 X_1 + \delta_2 X_2 + \delta_3 X_3 + \delta_4 W + \delta_5 D_1 + \delta_6 D_2)}{1 + \exp(\delta_0 + \delta_1 X_1 + \delta_2 X_2 + \delta_3 X_3 + \delta_4 W + \delta_5 D_1 + \delta_6 D_2)}$$

The coefficients of LPM, probit, and logit analyses are different from one another since they stand for different meanings depending on the models. The predicted outcome of LPM is not bounded between 0 and 1, while that of the probit and logit models always lies between 0 and 1 due to its use of cumulative distribution function (CDF).

Notes:
the NLSY79 (National Longitudinal Survey of Youth -1979 Cohort) data set
https://www.nlsinfo.org/content/cohorts/nlsy79

It is possible to understand the nonlinear regression model with the latent variable model. For illustration, we will study how to develop the probit regression model using the latent variable model.

Suppose that the outcome variable is binary below.

$$Y = \begin{cases} 1 & \text{choose} \\ 0 & \text{not choose} \end{cases}$$

Examples: going to college, getting married, having a baby, and getting a job

Thus, we observe the individuals' choice or outcome indicating one side or the other. Suppose that there is a continuous index as below that determines the observed outcome. Figure 10.2 below indicates that when Y^* is greater than 0, then the observed outcome Y is 1, while when Y^* is less than 0, then the observed outcome Y is 0. It captures how our binary decisions or outcomes work. In reality, there is no perfect decision. Our binary decisions or outcomes are based on imperfect information and incomplete preferences. Thus, we may make binary choices or outcomes when we are leaning more toward one side or the other.

Figure 10.2 Determination of the binary variable Y by the latent variable Y*

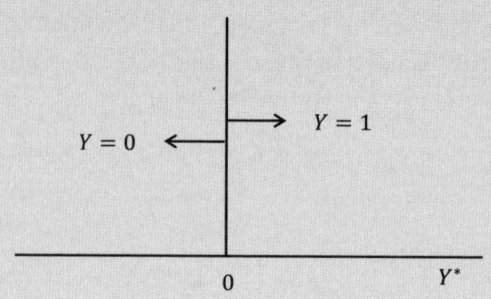

Using the latent variable, Y^*, we can construct the following regression equation. We assume that the error term follows the standard normal distribution, which is plausible since the latent variable, Y^*, could be assumed to have a variance of 1. Y^* is in our imagination, and we can standardize its distribution for our needs.

Suppose that $Y^* = \beta_0 + \beta_1 X_1 + \beta_2 X_2 + u$ \qquad $u \sim N(0,1)$

$$\begin{cases} Y^* \geq 0 \Rightarrow Y = 1 \\ Y^* < 0 \Rightarrow Y = 0 \end{cases}$$

Based on the latent variable equation above, we can derive $E(Y|X)$ in terms of the CDF of the standard normal distribution below.

$$E(Y|X) = P(Y^* \geq 0|X)$$
$$= P(\beta_0 + \beta_1 X_1 + \beta_2 X_2 + u \geq 0|X)$$
$$= P(u \geq -(\beta_0 + \beta_1 X_1 + \beta_2 X_2)|X)$$
$$= P(u \leq \beta_0 + \beta_1 X_1 + \beta_2 X_2|X)$$
$$= \Phi(\beta_0 + \beta_1 X_1 + \beta_2 X_2)$$

Then, $P(Y = 1|X)$ and $P(Y = 0|X)$ can be shown below.

$$P(Y = 1|X) = E(Y|X)$$
$$= \Phi(\beta_0 + \beta_1 X_1 + \beta_2 X_2)$$

$$P(Y = 0|X) = 1 - E(Y|X)$$
$$= 1 - \Phi(\beta_0 + \beta_1 X_1 + \beta_2 X_2)$$

As a result, $E(Y|X) = P(Y = 1|X)$ can be between 0 and 1 and can be shown in the figure below.

$$0 < E(Y|X) = P(Y = 1|X) = \Phi(\beta_0 + \beta_1 X_1 + \beta_2 X_2) < 1$$

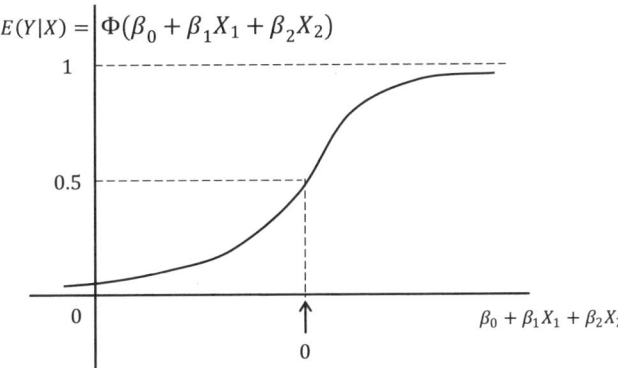

Thus, the marginal effect ($\partial E(Y|X) / \partial X_j$) changes as X changes.

Generally speaking, the marginal effect (slope of $E(Y|X)$) is the largest when $\beta_0 + \beta_1 X_1 + \beta_2 X_2 = 0$.

Different from the linear regression model that uses the least squares estimation method to estimate the parameters, the nonlinear regression model usually uses the maximum likelihood estimation (MLE) method to estimate the parameters. Since explaining all the working steps of the MLE is beyond the scope of this textbook, I would like to provide an intuitive explanation as follows.

The key idea of the OLS estimation is to find the OLS estimators for parameters that minimize the gap (residuals) between the data points and the predicted regression line. In practice, the OLS estimators are obtained by minimizing the residual sum of squares.

On the other hand, the MLE estimation is to obtain the optimal MLE estimators for parameters that maximize the chance of fitting the formatted likelihood function to the data. In other words, the maximum likelihood estimator is obtained to make the analysis sample most likely conform to the distribution assumption of the regression model. The likelihood function is nothing but the joint probability function of whether the outcome variable, Y, can happen to be 1 or 0, which is driven by using $P(Y = 1|X) = E(Y|X)$ and $P(Y = 0|X) = 1 - E(Y|X)$ as mentioned above.

The MLS estimation for the probit model is based on the normality assumption of the outcome variable and the error term. Thus, if this assumption is violated, the MLS estimation is invalid. Under the valid distribution assumption of the outcome variable and the error term, the MLE estimation is mathematically proven to be the most efficient estimation method.

The only difference between the probit and logit models is the distribution assumption of the latent variable. For the logistic regression model, we assume that the error term follows the logistic distribution as below. The logistic distribution is also symmetric but has wider tails than the standard normal distribution. Then, the important and sensitive question is whether the error term should be assumed to follow the logistic distribution or the standard normal distribution. The answer is "We don't know." As mentioned earlier, the logistic distribution was popular in the early time of the nonlinear regression analysis since its computation was relatively easier and was handled well with limited computing power. In recent years, more and more researchers have used the probit model, arguing that nature is more likely to follow the normal distribution than the logistic distribution. Also, the improved computing power has made the use of probit analysis easier and more accessible to most of the researchers.

As shown below, the standard normal distribution has a higher value of the probability density function (PDF) at 0 and thinner tails than the logistic distribution.

Probit: $u \sim N(0, 1)$

Logit: $u \sim logistic(0, \frac{\pi^2}{3})$

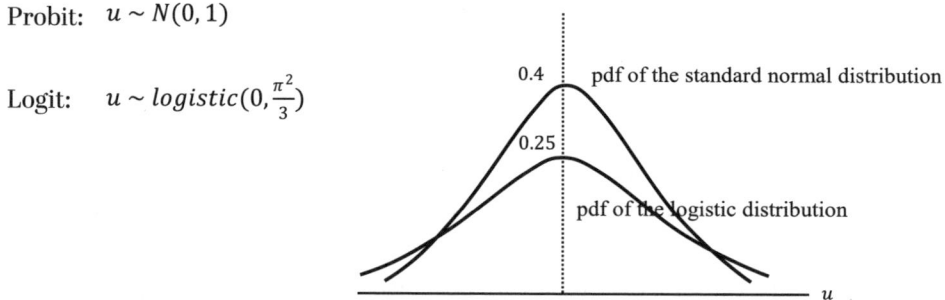

In summary, the probit and logit regression equations can be written as follows. It is also important to note that the probit and logit regression equations are presented as the function of $P(Y = 1|X) = E(Y|X)$ without the error term.

Probit: $P(Y = 1|X) = E(Y|X) = \Phi(\beta_0 + \beta_1 X_1 + \beta_2 X_2)$

$$= \int_{-\infty}^{\beta_0+\beta_1 X_1+\beta_2 X_2} \frac{1}{\sqrt{2\pi}} \exp\left(-\frac{1}{2}z^2\right) dz$$

Logit: $P(Y = 1|X) = E(Y|X) = G(\delta_0 + \delta_1 X_1 + \delta_2 X_2)$

$$= \frac{1}{1+\exp\left(-(\delta_0+\delta_1 X_1+\delta_2 X_2)\right)}$$

$$= \frac{\exp(\delta_0+\delta_1 X_1+\delta_2 X_2)}{1+\exp(\delta_0+\delta_1 X_1+\delta_2 X_2)}$$

Example 10.3

We use the probit and logit models with the same explanatory variables in column 4 in Example 10.1. We present the estimated coefficients from LPM, probit, and logit analyses in the table below.

It is noticeable that the estimated coefficients of probit and logit are quite different from those of LPM. Also, the estimated coefficients of probit and logit are different from each other. As mentioned earlier, the estimated coefficients of LPM are directly interpretable in terms of marginal changes or outcome differences between groups. However, the estimated coefficients of the probit and logit analyses are for parameters in the model, and they cannot be directly interpretable like those in LPM.

Estimation results of LPM, probit, and logit analyses

	LPM	probit	logit
Years of education	0.030***	0.131***	0.239***
	(0.002)	(0.009)	(0.017)
Standardized AFQT	0.091***	0.304***	0.515***
	(0.007)	(0.025)	(0.044)
Years of job experience	0.014***	0.085***	0.160***
	(0.001)	(0.007)	(0.013)
Female = 1	-0.131***	-0.511***	-0.886***
	(0.009)	(0.036)	(0.064)
Black = 1	0.002	-0.018	-0.020
	(0.011)	(0.051)	(0.093)

Hispanic = 1	0.038***	0.154***	0.262***
	(0.013)	(0.051)	(0.091)
Constant	-0.233***	-3.122***	-5.670***
	(0.034)	(0.154)	(0.284)
Adjusted R^2/ Pseudo R^2	0.175	0.182	0.183
Number of observations	7,707	7,707	7,707

Notes: ***$p<0.01$, **$p<0.05$, *$p<0.1$; Robust standard errors are used for LPM; The outcome variable is 1 for workers who earn $10 or more and 0 for otherwise.

Notes:
the NLSY79 (National Longitudinal Survey of Youth -1979 Cohort) data set
https://www.nlsinfo.org/content/cohorts/nlsy79

After the estimation of the parameters in the probit and logit models, the next important task is how to interpret the estimated results. First, we focus on the marginal effect interpretation, which is interested in the magnitude change of the outcome Y by the one-unit increase of continuous variable X.

As shown in Table 10.1 below, the marginal effect in LPM is straightforward since the outcome variable is the linear function of parameter. Assume that X_1 and X_2 are continuos. For the estimated regression model, $\widehat{E(Y|X)} = \hat{\beta}_0 + \hat{\beta}_1 X_1 + \hat{\beta}_2 X_2$, the one-unit increase in X_1 leads to $\hat{\beta}_1$ change in Y, which indicates $\hat{\beta}_1*100$ percentage point changes (changes in probability).

The marginal effect in the logit and probit regression models is more complicated. As shown below, the estimated parameters do not directly indicate the marginal effect. For the probit and logit models, the marginal change in Y by the one-unit increase in X_1 is not fixed but depends on the different values of X_1 and X_2.

For the probit model, $\frac{\partial \widehat{E(Y|X)}}{\partial X_1} = \Phi'(\hat{\alpha}_0 + \hat{\alpha}_1 X_1 + \hat{\alpha}_2 X_2)\hat{\alpha}_1 = \phi(\hat{\alpha}_0 + \hat{\alpha}_1 X_1 + \hat{\alpha}_2 X_2)\hat{\alpha}_1$ where $\phi(\hat{\alpha}_0 + \hat{\alpha}_1 X_1 + \hat{\alpha}_2 X_2)$ is the pdf of the standard normal distribution.

For the logit model, $\frac{\partial \widehat{E(Y|X)}}{\partial X_1} = G'(\hat{\delta}_0 + \hat{\delta}_1 X_1 + \hat{\delta}_2 X_2)\hat{\delta}_1 = g(\hat{\delta}_0 + \hat{\delta}_1 X_1 + \hat{\delta}_2 X_2)\hat{\delta}_1 = G(\hat{\delta}_0 + \hat{\delta}_1 X_1 + \hat{\delta}_2 X_2)\left(1 - G(\hat{\delta}_0 + \hat{\delta}_1 X_1 + \hat{\delta}_2 X_2)\right)\hat{\delta}_1$ where $g(\hat{\delta}_0 + \hat{\delta}_1 X_1 + \hat{\delta}_2 X_2)$ is the pdf of the logistic distribution.

Let's get into more specifics of the marginal effect of probit models. Logit models are the same as we explain here.

Table 10.1 How to interpret LPM/probit/logit coefficients

	LPM	Probit	Logit
$E(Y\|X)$	$E(Y\|X) = \beta_0 + \beta_1 X_1 + \beta_2 X_2$	$E(Y\|X) = \Phi(\alpha_0 + \alpha_1 X_1 + \alpha_2 X_2)$	$E(Y\|X) = G(\delta_0 + \delta_1 X_1 + \delta_2 X_2)$
How to interpret the estimated coefficients (ME)	$\widehat{E(Y\|X)} = \hat{\beta}_0 + \hat{\beta}_1 X_1 + \hat{\beta}_2 X_2$ $\frac{\partial \widehat{E(Y\|X)}}{\partial X_1} = \hat{\beta}_1$	$\widehat{E(Y\|X)} = \Phi(\hat{\alpha}_0 + \hat{\alpha}_1 X_1 + \hat{\alpha}_2 X_2)$ $\frac{\partial \widehat{E(Y\|X)}}{\partial X_1}$ $= \Phi'(\hat{\alpha}_0 + \hat{\alpha}_1 X_1 + \hat{\alpha}_2 X_2)\hat{\alpha}_1$ $= \phi(\hat{\alpha}_0 + \hat{\alpha}_1 X_1 + \hat{\alpha}_2 X_2)\hat{\alpha}_1$ Marginal effects (ME) depend on X variables	$\widehat{E(Y\|X)} = G(\hat{\delta}_0 + \hat{\delta}_1 X_1 + \hat{\delta}_2 X_2)$ $\frac{\partial \widehat{E(Y\|X)}}{\partial X_1}$ $= G'(\hat{\delta}_0 + \hat{\delta}_1 X_1 + \hat{\delta}_2 X_2)\hat{\delta}_1$ $= g(\hat{\delta}_0 + \hat{\delta}_1 X_1 + \hat{\delta}_2 X_2)\hat{\delta}_1$ $= G(\hat{\delta}_0 + \hat{\delta}_1 X_1 + \hat{\delta}_2 X_2)$ $(1 - G(\hat{\delta}_0 + \hat{\delta}_1 X_1 + \hat{\delta}_2 X_2))\hat{\delta}_1$ Marginal effects (ME) depend on X variables Note: $G(\cdot) = \frac{\exp(\cdot)}{1+\exp(\cdot)}$ $g(\cdot) = \frac{\exp(\cdot)}{(1+\exp(\cdot))^2}$ $= G(\cdot)(1 - G(\cdot))$

Notes: Suppose that X_1 and X_2 are continuous.

In practice, there are four ways of estimating the marginal effect explained below. Each of them has its own advantages.

① Marginal effects (ME) at the mean of X's

$$\frac{\partial \widehat{E(Y|X)}}{\partial X_1} = \phi(\hat{\alpha}_0 + \hat{\alpha}_1 \bar{X}_1 + \hat{\alpha}_2 \bar{X}_2) \cdot \hat{\alpha}_1$$

The marginal effect at the mean of X's provides the convenient fixed marginal effect at the mean values of the explanatory variables, which may indicate the average individual of the sample.

② Marginal effects (ME) at the representative values of X_j^*

At $X_1 = X_1^*$, $X_2 = X_2^*$

$$\frac{\partial E(\widehat{Y|X^*})}{\partial X_1} = \phi(\hat{\alpha}_0 + \hat{\alpha}_1 X_1^* + \hat{\alpha}_2 X_2^*) \cdot \hat{\alpha}_1$$

The marginal effect at some specified values of X's provides the convenient fixed marginal effect at the designated values of the explanatory variables, which could be of interest to researchers or readers.

③ Average marginal effects (AME): obtain AME across all values of explanatory variables, X_1 and X_2

$$\frac{1}{n}\sum_{i=1}^{n} \frac{\partial E(\widehat{Y|X_i})}{\partial X_1} = \frac{1}{n}\sum_{i=1}^{n} \phi(\hat{\alpha}_0 + \hat{\alpha}_1 X_{1i} + \hat{\alpha}_2 X_{2i}) \cdot \hat{\alpha}_1$$

The average marginal effect has become popular since it is the mean of the marginal effect of all possible values of the explanatory variables in the sample. The representativeness of this interpretation seems to provide a strong advantage.

④ Marginal effects (ME) at $\phi(0) = 0.4$ or $g(0) = 0.25$ → The biggest marginal effects

Probit: $\left.\dfrac{\partial E(\widehat{Y|X})}{\partial X_1}\right|_{at\ \phi(0)} = \phi(0) * \hat{\alpha}_1 = 0.4 * \hat{\alpha}_1$

Logit: $\left.\dfrac{\partial E(\widehat{Y|X})}{\partial X_1}\right|_{at\ g(0)} = g(0) * \hat{\delta}_1 = 0.25 * \hat{\delta}_1$

This marginal effect at the greatest value of the pdf function is convenient in calculation and interpretation. Since the maximum value of the pdf of the standard normal distribution and the logistic distribution are 0.4 and 0.25, respectively, we can easily calculate the biggest magnitude in the marginal effect by imputing those values in the marginal effect equation of the probit and logit regression results. This effect could be the largest marginal change in Y by the one unit increase of X.

When the explanatory variable is binary, we can obtain the probability difference between the two groups by calculating $E(Y|\widehat{X, X_k} = 1) - E(Y|\widehat{X, X_k} = 0)$.

In the OLS analysis, we made an interaction term between the continuous variable and the dummy variable to estimate the changing amount of slope coefficient by the change in the dummy variable.

Suppose that we have the following regression model:

$$Y = \delta_0 + \delta_1 X_1 + \delta_2 D_1 + \delta_3 X_1 D_1 + \delta_4 X_2 + u$$

Then, $\frac{\partial E(Y|X)}{\partial X_1} = \delta_1 + \delta_3 D_1$

Thus, the difference in the impact of X_1 on Y between $D_1 = 1$ and $D_1 = 0$ is δ_3.

However, it is not straightforward in nonlinear regression models, such as logit and probit models.

Let's introduce the interaction term between the continuous variable and the dummy variable to a logit model below:

$$E(Y|X) = G(\delta_0 + \delta_1 X_1 + \delta_2 D_1 + \delta_3 X_1 D_1 + \delta_4 X_2)$$

Then, $\frac{\partial E(Y|X)}{\partial X_1} = g(\delta_0 + \delta_1 X_1 + \delta_2 D_1 + \delta_3 X_1 D_1 + \delta_4 X_2) \times (\delta_1 + \delta_3 D_1)$

For $D_1 = 1$ (at $X_1 = X_1^*$, $X_2 = X_2^*$)

$$\frac{\partial E(Y|X^*)}{\partial X_1} = g(\delta_0 + \delta_1 X_1^* + \delta_2 + \delta_3 X_1^* + \delta_4 X_2^*) \times (\delta_1 + \delta_3) \quad \text{-- (1)}$$

For $D_1 = 0$ (at $X_1 = X_1^*$, $X_2 = X_2^*$)

$$\frac{\partial E(Y|X^*)}{\partial X_1} = g(\delta_0 + \delta_1 X_1^* + \delta_4 X_2^*) \times \delta_1 \quad \text{-- (2)}$$

Therefore, the difference in the impact of X_1 on Y between $D_1 = 1$ and $D_1 = 0$ is (1) – (2), which gives the slope change (premium) of X_1 given $D_1 = 1$.

Thus, in the logit and probit models, the direct interpretation of the estimated coefficient of the interaction term does not give the interpretation of the slope change of the continuous variable between the two groups.

Example 10.4

In the table below, we report the LPM estimates and the average marginal effects (AME) estimates of the probit and logit models. Different from the estimated coefficients in Example 10.3, the estimated coefficients of the probit and logit models are similar to those of LPM. As mentioned earlier, the AME estimate of each variable is the mean of the marginal effects of all possible values of the explanatory variables in the sample. The AME estimates are popular because of their representativeness.

LPM estimates and average marginal effects (AME) estimates of the probit and logit analyses

	LPM	Probit AME	Logit AME
Years of education	0.030***	0.031***	0.032***
	(0.002)	(0.002)	(0.002)
Standardized AFQT	0.091***	0.072***	0.070***
	(0.007)	(0.006)	(0.006)
Years of job experience	0.014***	0.020***	0.022***
	(0.001)	(0.002)	(0.002)
Female = 1	-0.131***	-0.123***	-0.122***
	(0.009)	(0.009)	(0.009)
Black = 1	0.002	-0.004	-0.003
	(0.011)	(0.012)	(0.013)
Hispanic = 1	0.038***	0.038***	0.037***
	(0.013)	(0.013)	(0.013)
Adjusted R^2/ Pseudo R^2	0.175	0.182	0.183
Number of observations	7,707	7,707	7,707

Notes: ***$p<0.01$, **$p<0.05$, *$p<0.1$; Robust standard errors are used for LPM; The outcome variable is 1 for workers who earn $10 or more and 0 for otherwise.

The table below presents the LPM estimates and the marginal effect (ME) estimates at the mean of explanatory variables. Compared with the estimated coefficients in Example 10.3, the estimated coefficients of the probit and logit models are similar to those of LPM. ME estimates in this example provide the fixed marginal effect at the mean values of the explanatory variables, and they are useful if we would like to show the marginal relations between explanatory variables and the outcome for the average subject of the analysis sample.

LPM estimates and marginal effects (ME) estimates at the mean of all explanatory variables of the probit and logit analyses

	LPM	Probit ME	Logit ME
Years of education	0.030***	0.033***	0.032***
	(0.002)	(0.002)	(0.002)
Standardized AFQT	0.091***	0.076***	0.069***
	(0.007)	(0.006)	(0.006)
Years of job experience	0.014***	0.021***	0.021***
	(0.001)	(0.002)	(0.002)
Female = 1	-0.131***	-0.129***	-0.120***
	(0.009)	(0.009)	(0.009)
Black = 1	0.002	-0.004	-0.003
	(0.011)	(0.013)	(0.012)
Hispanic = 1	0.038***	0.040***	0.037***
	(0.013)	(0.014)	(0.014)
Adjusted R^2/ Pseudo R^2	0.175	0.182	0.183
Number of observations	7,707	7,707	7,707

Notes: ***$p<0.01$, **$p<0.05$, *$p<0.1$; Robust standard errors are used for LPM; The outcome variable is 1 for workers who earn $10 or more and 0 for otherwise.

As we discussed earlier, the marginal estimates of the probit and logit models change depending on the values of explanatory variables. In the following table of the probit model, the first column reports the marginal effect (ME) estimates at the mean of explanatory variables in the first column, and the second to fourth columns present the ME estimates at 6, 12, and 16 years of education of male Hispanic workers with 2 standardized AFQT and 10 years of job experience. We also report the predicted outcomes of all four estimates in the last row of the table. As we notice, the ME estimates of education are largest in the third column when the predicted outcome probability presented in the last row of this table is close to 0.5 and becomes smaller in the first, second, and fourth columns as it is far away from 0.5. The biggest estimate of education is 0.052 in the third column, while the smallest estimate of education is 0.033 in the first column.

Marginal effects (ME) estimates of the probit model

	Probit ME (1)	Probit ME (2)	Probit ME (3)	Probit ME (4)
Years of education	0.033***	0.040***	0.052***	0.044***
	(0.002)	(0.002)	(0.004)	(0.004)
Standardized AFQT	0.076***	0.093***	0.121***	0.102***
	(0.006)	(0.015)	(0.010)	(0.007)
Years of job experience	0.021***	0.026***	0.034***	0.029***
	(0.002)	(0.003)	(0.003)	(0.003)
Female = 1	-0.129***	-0.126***	-0.198***	-0.192***
	(0.009)	(0.016)	(0.014)	(0.014)
Black = 1	-0.004	-0.005	-0.007	-0.006
	(0.013)	(0.015)	(0.020)	(0.018)
Hispanic = 1	0.040***	0.044***	0.061***	0.054***
	(0.014)	(0.016)	(0.020)	(0.017)
Adjusted R^2/ Pseudo R^2	0.182	0.182	0.182	0.182
Number of observations	7,707	7,707	7,707	7,707
Predicted outcome probability	0.167	0.234	0.523	0.719

Notes: ***$p<0.01$, **$p<0.05$, *$p<0.1$; The outcome variable is 1 for workers who earn $10 or more and 0 for otherwise; ME (1) is estimated at the mean of all explanatory variables of the probit and logit analyses; ME (2) to (4) are estimated at 6, 12, and 16 years of education of male Hispanic workers with 2 standardized AFQT and 10 years of job experience.

Notes:
the NLSY79 (National Longitudinal Survey of Youth -1979 Cohort) data set
https://www.nlsinfo.org/content/cohorts/nlsy79

Statistical inference and goodness of it for probit and logit models

It is time to study the methods for conducting hypothesis tests on the estimated coefficients of probit and logit models. There are two popular tests: the Wald test and the Likelihood Ratio Test (LRT). Both tests are valid when the sample size is large. For hypothesis tests and confidence intervals on estimated coefficients to be valid in logit and probit analyses, it is essential to use large samples. Therefore, similar to the Linear Probability Model (LPM), logit and probit analyses should use large samples.

The hypothesis test with one restriction can be done with the Wald test. This test is valid for large samples and asymptotically follows $\chi^2_{df=1}$ (Chi-square distribution with 1 degree of freedom). The Wald test is similar in practice to the t-test we are familiar with. The statistical packages provide the p-value to check whether we reject the null hypothesis or not.

For nonlinear maximum likelihood estimators,

$$W = \frac{(\hat{\beta}_k - \beta_k)^2}{Var(\hat{\beta}_k)} \overset{a}{\sim} \chi^2_{df=1}$$

$$\rightarrow \sqrt{W} = t = \frac{\hat{\beta}_k - \beta_k}{se(\hat{\beta}_k)} \overset{a}{\sim} Z$$

The square root of the Wald statistic with 1 degree of freedom is the test statistic that asymptotically follows the standard normal distribution (Cameron & Trivedi, 2005: 137). Therefore, in practice, it is common to report the asymptotic z statistics based on the standard normal distribution and the related confidence intervals and hypothesis tests for the estimated coefficients in the probit and logit regression results.

When we have two or more restrictions in the null hypothesis, we can expand the Wald test with q (number of restrictions) dimensions. We do not cover the exact form of this Wald test since it uses matrix algebra (Cameron & Trivedi, 2005: 136).

Chi-square distribution

The Chi-square distribution is a statistical probability distribution that is used frequently in the field of statistics. It finds extensive application in tasks, including hypothesis testing. This distribution is symbolically represented as χ^2_{df}. The Chi-square statistic that follows the Chi-square distribution is always positive.

The shape of the Chi-square distribution depends on the degrees of freedom (df). As df increases, the distribution becomes more symmetric and approaches a normal distribution. When df is small, the distribution is right-skewed.

There is another popular test statistic when we have two or more restrictions in the null hypothesis, which is the Likelihood Ratio Test (LRT). The idea is to compare the log-likelihood values of the unrestricted and restricted models. If its differences are large enough, it is possible to say that the unrestricted model is better. This is similar to how the *F*-test statistic works for the OLS analysis. The LRT is valid with large samples.

Assume that we want to test whether black and Hispanic variables are important in the unrestricted model below.

$$H_0: \beta_2 = 0 \ \& \ \beta_3 = 0$$
$$H_0: otherwise$$

Unrestricted model:
$E(Y|X) = \Phi(\beta_0 + \beta_1 afqt + \beta_2 black + \beta_3 hisp + \beta_4 female)$
We can obtain the log-likelihood of the unrestricted model (ln L_{UR}).

Restricted model:
$E(Y|X) = \Phi(\beta_0 + \beta_1 afqt + \beta_4 female)$
We can obtain the log-likelihood of the restricted model (ln L_R).

We expect that ln $L_{UR} \geq$ ln L_R since the log-likelihood of a more flexible model is greater than that of a less flexible model.

The Likelihood Ratio Test (LRT) can be constructed below, and it asymptotically follows the Chi-square distribution with q (number of restrictions in the test) degrees of freedom.

Then, the test statistic is

$$LR = 2(\ln L_{UR} - \ln L_R) \overset{a}{\sim} \chi^2_{df=q} \#$$

$$df = \# \text{ of restrictions}$$

The likelihood ratio (*LR*) test for the nonlinear regression model is analogous to the *F*-test for the linear regression model, while it is only valid for large samples. The statistical packages report the *p*-value for the hypothesis test to examine whether we reject the null hypothesis or not.

In the probit and logit analyses, there is no *R*-squared that measures the goodness of fit of the regression model. Instead, pseudo *R*-squared is constructed to mimic *R*-squared in the OLS analysis, using the ratio of log likelihood values of the full regression model and the regression model without any explanatory variables as follows.

$$\text{Pseudo } R\text{-squared} = \frac{\ln L_N - \ln L_F}{\ln L_N} = 1 - \frac{\ln L_F}{\ln L_N}$$

Where $\ln L_F$ is the log likelihood value of the full regression model and $\ln L_N$ is the log likelihood value of the regression model without any explanatory variables (Cameron & Trivedi, 2005: 474).

By design, it is bounded between 0 and 1. However, different from R-squared in the OLS analysis, it is not a measure of the proportion of variance of the outcome variable explained by the model.

Example 10.5

In the table below, we report the LPM estimates and the average marginal effects (AME) estimates of the probit and logit models. The estimated coefficients of the probit and logit models in the second and third columns are comparable to those in LPM in the first column. In the second and third columns, the AME estimate of each variable is the mean of the marginal effects of all possible values of the explanatory variables in the sample. The standard errors are reported in the parentheses in the second and third columns for the probit and logit models as those in the first column for LPM. The reported statistical significance (*** $p<0.01$, ** $p<0.05$, * $p<0.1$) in the second and third columns are based on the asymptotic z statistics studied earlier for the probit and logit analyses. The statistical significances of all explanatory variables in the probit and logit analyses are the same as those in LPM.

LPM estimates and average marginal effects (AME) estimates of the probit and logit analyses

	LPM	Probit AME	Logit AME
Years of education	0.030***	0.031***	0.032***
	(0.002)	(0.002)	(0.002)
Standardized AFQT	0.091***	0.072***	0.070***
	(0.007)	(0.006)	(0.006)
Years of job experience	0.014***	0.020***	0.022***
	(0.001)	(0.002)	(0.002)

Female = 1	-0.131***	-0.123***	-0.122***
	(0.009)	(0.009)	(0.009)
Black = 1	0.002	-0.004	-0.003
	(0.011)	(0.012)	(0.013)
Hispanic = 1	0.038***	0.038***	0.037***
	(0.013)	(0.013)	(0.013)
Adjusted R^2/ Pseudo R^2	0.175	0.182	0.183
Number of observations	7,707	7,707	7,707

Notes: ***$p<0.01$, **$p<0.05$, *$p<0.1$; The outcome variable is 1 for workers who earn $10 or more and 0 for otherwise.

For example, the estimated coefficient of education implies that one more year of education leads to about a 3 to 3.2 percentage point increase in being high-wage workers, which is statistically significant at $p<0.01$. The test statistic for the probit estimate is $t = \frac{\hat{\beta}_k - \beta_k}{se(\hat{\beta}_k)} = \frac{0.031 - 0}{0.002} = 15.5$, while the test statistic for the logit estimate is $t = \frac{\hat{\beta}_k - \beta_k}{se(\hat{\beta}_k)} = \frac{0.032 - 0}{0.002} = 16$. They are large enough to reject the default null hypothesis ($H_o: \beta_{edu} = 0$) at $p<0.01$. The 95% confidence interval for the education parameter can be easily constructed for the probit and logit analyses as follows. Using 1.96 for the 2.5% tail probability in the standard normal distribution, [0.031-1.96*0.002, 0.031-1.96*0.002] = [0.027, 0.035] for the probit analysis and [0.032-1.96*0.002, 0.032-1.96*0.002] = [0.028, 0.036] for the logit analysis. Thus, we are 95% confident that the true parameter of education lies between 0.027 and 0.035 in the probit analysis.

In this regression analysis, suppose that we would like to test whether the dummy variables of female, black, and Hispanic are statistically significant at $p<0.01$. The null and alternative hypotheses are as follows.

$H_o: \beta_{female} = 0$, $\beta_{black} = 0$, and $\beta_{Hispanic} = 0$
$H_a: otherwise$

For the probit model, the Wald test statistic that follows the Chi-square distribution with $df=3$ is 212.97, and its p-value is close to 0. As a result, we reject the null hypothesis at $p<0.01$.

For the logit model, the Wald test statistic that follows the Chi-square distribution with $df=3$ is 203.91, and its p-value is close to 0. Therefore, we reject the null hypothesis at $p<0.01$.

For the probit model, the likelihood ratio (LR) test statistic that follows the Chi-square distribution with $df=3$ is $LR = 2(\ln L_{UR} - \ln L_R) = 217.87$, and its p-value is close to 0. Thus, we reject the null hypothesis at $p<0.01$.

For the logit model, the likelihood ratio (LR) test statistic that follows the Chi-square distribution with $df=3$ is $LR = 2(\ln L_{UR} - \ln L_R) = 212.46$, and its p-value is close to 0. Therefore, we reject the null hypothesis at $p<0.01$.

The pseudo R-squared is 0.182 and 0.183 for the probit and logit models, respectively. They are similar to the R-squared of the LPM in the first column.

Notes:
the NLSY79 (National Longitudinal Survey of Youth -1979 Cohort) data set
https://www.nlsinfo.org/content/cohorts/nlsy79

Which methods are better or worse with a binary outcome is summarized in Table 10.2 below. It is found that there is no clear reason why one method is much better than the other. Which methods should be used with a binary outcome depends on what methods the field of study prefers in practice. In particular, as discussed earlier, due to the functional relationship illustrated in the cumulative distribution function (CDF) of the logit and probit models, the marginal effect of the explanatory variable on the outcome variable is highest at the midpoint of the CDF and diminishes as it moves away from the center. This pattern is commonly observed in probit and logit models. If the theoretical expectations do not align with such changes in the marginal effect, researchers should be cautious in determining the suitability of probit and logit models for their studies.

Table 10.2 Strength and weakness of three analytical methods when an outcome variable is binary

	OLS regression model: The regression model is linear in parameters.	Nonlinear regression model: The regression model is nonlinear in parameters.	
	Linear probability model (LPM)	Logit regression model	Probit regression model
Strength	Easy to interpret the estimated coefficient. If the four OLS assumptions for the consistent estimators are valid, the estimated coefficients suggest the causal relationship.	Predicted Y is bounded between 0 and 1. It was popular during the early period of data analysis since computation is easy.	Predicted Y is bounded between 0 and 1. The data-generating process (DGP) is based on the standard normal distribution.
Weakness	Predicted Y is not bounded between 0 and 1. The fifth OLS assumption of homoscedasticity is violated all the time since the variance of the error term is a function of the explanatory variables. The sixth OLS assumption of the normality of the error term is violated all the time since the outcome is binary.	The data-generating process (DGP) is based on the logistic distribution. If the DGP does not follow the logistic distribution, the estimated coefficient is not consistent. It is difficult for the general audience to understand odds ratio interpretations typically used with logit regression. The marginal relationship between X and Y should be recalculated using the	Computation is difficult. If the DGP does not follow the standard normal distribution, the estimated coefficient is not consistent. The marginal relationship between X and Y should be recalculated using the estimated coefficient, and it varies depending on X values. The estimated coefficients of the interaction terms between the

		estimated coefficient, and it varies depending on X values.

The estimated coefficients of the interaction terms between the explanatory variables and the square and cubic terms of the explanatory variables do not suggest the same meaning in the OLS regression model. | explanatory variables and the square and cubic terms of the explanatory variables do not suggest the same meaning in the OLS regression model. |
| Guidance in practice | LPM coefficient estimates are only valid when the sample size is large.

In LPM analysis, robust standard errors should be used under the condition that the sample size is large.

LPM analysis is preferred for causal inference. | For hypothesis tests and confidence intervals on estimated coefficients to be valid in logit and probit analyses, it is essential to use large samples.

Please recalculate the estimated coefficients to get the marginal estimates.

Do not use the interaction terms and square terms as you use them in the OLS regression model.

The Logit model has been preferred when we predict the outcome. | For hypothesis tests and confidence intervals on estimated coefficients to be valid in logit and probit analyses, it is essential to use large samples.

Please recalculate the estimated coefficients to get the marginal estimates.

Do not use the interaction terms and square terms as you use them in the OLS regression model.

Recently, the Probit model has become more preferred when we predict the outcome as the computation power of personal computers increases. |

Chapter Summary

Linear regression model vs. Nonlinear regression model	The Linear Probability Model (LPM) is the linear regression model since the model is linear in parameters. The probit and logit models are called the nonlinear regression model since the model is nonlinear in parameters.
The latent variable model behind the probit and logit models	We assume that the unobservable latent variable is assumed to be continuous, and it determines the observed binary outcome. Specifically, it is assumed that the latent variable follows the logistic distribution for the logit model and adheres to the standard normal distribution for the probit model.
Addressing common misunderstandings and mistakes	Using the OLS regression model, the linear probability model (LPM) for a binary outcome variable is valid when the sample size is large and robust standard errors are used. Particularly, if our analysis focuses on the marginal impact of the explanatory variables on the outcome variable, the OLS regression model has more advantages in the flexible model specifications and the interpretation of the estimation results. The probit and logit models can be useful for predicting the outcome variable since the predicted outcomes are bounded between 0 and 1 in these models. For analyzing a binary outcome variable, nonlinear regression models, such as the probit and logit models, are not superior or inferior to the OLS regression model. Three regression models are different in analysis assumptions, and they have their own advantages and disadvantages.

Exercises

Chapter 10
The regression analysis when the outcome variable is binary: LPM, Logit, and Probit

1. Suppose that you want to know the impact of education on the employability of an individual. Your true population model is $emp_i = \beta_0 + \beta_1 edu_i + \beta_2 afqt_i + \beta_3 lcexpy_i + u_i$ for each i. emp_i equals 1 if an individual is currently working and 0 if an individual is currently not working. edu_i represents the number of years in school and $afqt_i$ indicates the individuals' cognitive score from 0 to 100. $lcexpy_i$ indicates the job experience in years.

   (1) One of your colleagues argues that because the dependent variable is binary, your OLS estimates are not consistent for the true parameters. What do you think? Respond to the criticism.

   (2) One of your colleagues argues that because the dependent variable is binary, you always have heteroskedasticity in the error term. What do you think? Respond to the criticism.

   (3) One of your colleagues said that your inference procedures (t-test and F-test) are always invalid even if you have valid SE because the error term is not normally distributed in your OLS model. What do you think? Respond to the criticism.

2. Suppose that as part of the government of Pakistan's commitment to the reduction of gender disparity in education, it initiated a conditional cash transfer program targeted to female students in Punjab. The program was announced in 2003. The government did not consider randomization politically feasible and therefore used district-level literacy rates for citizens aged 10 and above, according to the 1998

census (the most recent census at the time), to determine which districts would be eligible to receive the stipend program. Districts with literacy levels below 40 percent were deemed eligible for receipt of the stipend program. Those districts with literacy rates equal to or higher than 40 percent were ineligible. Implementation of the program reportedly did not begin in full until the second quarter of 2004. Suppose that you have the 2006 data for girls that are enrolled in grades 6 to 8 in eligible and ineligible provinces.

(1) Construct the OLS regression model to estimate the impact of Pakistan's conditional cash transfer program on girls' school enrollment. You know whether they were enrolled during 2006 in eligible and ineligible provinces. You also know their families' labor income.

(2) Based on the OLS regression model you develop, please state the OLS assumption to have the consistent OLS estimators. What is the problem concerning eligible and ineligible districts in this analysis?

(3) Based on the OLS regression model you develop, show whether the standard error of the estimator of the policy impact is valid. What assumptions are needed? Explain how you can obtain the valid standard error when you have a large sample. How about when you have a small sample? (15)

(4) There are some characteristics of districts you cannot control for. Some districts may be liberal and others conservative. Determine the bias direction of the policy estimator when you cannot control for this characteristic.

3. Suppose that you want to measure the impact of the college preparation program in Indiana public high schools ($D = 1$ for participation in programs and 0 for otherwise during the last academic year) on students' college enrollment ($Y = 1$ for college enrollment and 0 for otherwise) in 2008. You control for parents' income in $1,000 per year ($X$). Suppose that you have a large random sample and there is variation in

all variables.

(1) The logit model for this study is as follows; $E(Y|D,X) = G(\beta_0 + \beta_1 D + \beta_2 X)$ where G ( ) is the CDF of logistic distribution. Explain why researchers prefer this nonlinear model to the linear probability model (LPM) when they predict the outcome variable.

(2) The estimated coefficients using the logit model are as follows.

	Estimated Coefficient (Standard Error)
College preparation program	0.05 (0.012)
Parents' income per year ($1,000)	0.005 (0.002)
Constant	0.02 (0.005)

What is the estimated impact of the college preparation program on the college enrollment when the parents' annual income is $40,000? Please show all the steps.

(3) What is the estimated impact of parents' income on the college enrollment among the program nonparticipants with parents' income of $50,000.

4. Suppose that you want to measure the impact of the job training programs in Seoul ($D = 1$ for participation in programs and 0 for otherwise) on women's labor market participation ($Y = 1$ for employment and 0 for otherwise) in 2018. You control for their education in years. Suppose that you have a large random sample and there is variation in all variables.

(1) Is it possible to have unbiased estimates of D and X and valid test statistics using the OLS? Please state relevant assumptions and remedies.

(2) Please show how to derive the probit model using the latent variable model. Also, discuss the intuition behind this modeling. (15)

(3) Suppose that you decide to employ the logit model to examine the research question. Please discuss the advantages and limitations of the logit model compared with the LPM. (10)

(4) What is the estimated impact of the training program on the probability of being employed when women's education is 16? Please show all the steps.

(5) What is the estimated impact of education on the probability of being employed among the program participants with 12 years of education.

5. Suppose that you would like to examine the impact of parents' education on women's college degree attainment (1 for Yes and 0 for No) using linear probability model (LMP), probit model, and logit model. Please answer the following questions.

Binary outcome analysis

	(1) LPM	(2) Probit	(3) Logit
Age	-0.007***	-0.041***	-0.074***
	(0.000)	(0.002)	(0.005)
father: high school graduate = 1	0.176***	0.631***	1.100***
	(0.016)	(0.050)	(0.086)
father: some college or more = 1	0.356***	1.169***	2.016***
	(0.026)	(0.073)	(0.123)
Not having father = 1	-0.007	-0.016	-0.019
	(0.012)	(0.075)	(0.140)
mother: high school graduate = 1	0.081***	0.170***	0.248**
	(0.022)	(0.060)	(0.102)
mother: some college or more = 1	0.311***	0.893***	1.506***
	(0.043)	(0.151)	(0.274)
Not having mother = 1	-0.067***	-0.599***	-1.243***
	(0.014)	(0.182)	(0.395)
Number of brothers	-0.017***	-0.086***	-0.162***
	(0.003)	(0.018)	(0.034)
Number of sisters	-0.012***	-0.054***	-0.099***
	(0.003)	(0.014)	(0.026)
Constant	0.503***	0.833***	1.620***
	(0.021)	(0.103)	(0.189)
R^2/ Pseudo R^2	0.213	0.217	0.214
Number of observations	7,976	7,976	7,976

Notes: ***$p<0.01$, **$p<0.05$, *$p<0.1$; The outcome variable is 1 for women with college degree or more and 0 for otherwise; The analysis sample consists of women aged 30 or older from the 2007 Korean Longitudinal Survey of Women and Families (KLoWF); The base group for father's education consists of fathers with less than high school education; The base group for mother's education includes mothers with less than high school education;

(1) Please explain why the coefficients in LPM, probit, and logit models differ.

(2) Please interpret the estimated coefficients of father's education dummies in column (1).

(3) Please calculate the maximum level of marginal relations between the number of brothers women have and women's college degree attainment in the probit and logit models. Compare them with the estimated coefficient of the number of brothers in the LPM and interpret them.

6. Suppose that you would like to examine the impact of parents' education on women's college degree attainment (1 for Yes and 0 for No) using linear probability model (LMP), probit model, and logit model. The probit and logit estimates are transferred to the average marginal effect (AME) estimates. Please answer the following questions.

	LPM	Probit AME	Logit AME
Age	-0.007***	-0.009***	-0.009***
	(0.000)	(0.001)	(0.001)
father: high school graduate = 1	0.176***	0.162***	0.161***
	(0.016)	(0.014)	(0.013)
father: some college or more = 1	0.356***	0.322***	0.318***
	(0.026)	(0.021)	(0.020)
Not having father = 1	-0.007	-0.004	-0.002
	(0.012)	(0.016)	(0.017)
mother: high school graduate = 1	0.081***	0.040***	0.032**
	(0.022)	(0.014)	(0.014)
mother: some college or more = 1	0.311***	0.239***	0.229***
	(0.043)	(0.045)	(0.047)
Not having mother = 1	-0.067***	-0.110***	-0.124***
	(0.014)	(0.026)	(0.030)
Number of brothers woman has	-0.017***	-0.019***	-0.020***
	(0.003)	(0.004)	(0.004)
Number of sisters woman has	-0.012***	-0.012***	-0.012***
	(0.003)	(0.003)	(0.003)
R^2/ Pseudo R^2	0.213	0.217	0.214
Number of observations	7,976	7,976	7,976

Notes: ***$p<0.01$, **$p<0.05$, *$p<0.1$; The outcome variable is 1 for women with college degree or more and 0 for otherwise

(1) Please compare the reported coefficients in LPM, probit, and logit models and explain their implications.

(2) Please interpret the estimated coefficients of mother's education dummies of the probit model in column (2).

(3) Please compare *R*-squared for the LPM and Pseudo *R*-squared for the probit and logit models and explain their implications.

(4) Please test whether the number of brothers and the number of sisters are important in the probit and logit models using the reported results below.

Probit:
Log likelihood of the unrestricted model with all the variables including these two variables = -2900.8186
Log likelihood of the restricted model without all the variables except for these two variables = -2917.3883

Logit:
Log likelihood of the unrestricted model with all the variables including these two variables = -2910.7972
Log likelihood of the restricted model without all the variables except for these two variables = -2927.299

(5) Please estimate the 95% confidence intervals for the coefficient of "not having mother=1" in three regression models of the table and interpret their implications.

Appendix

Appendix A
Software programs for data analysis: SPSS, SAS, Stata, R

There are many software programs for data analysis. Among them, some of the most popular programs in social science are SPSS, SAS, Stata, and R. SPSS is a software program with menus that researchers can choose to do the data analysis. On the other hand, SAS, Stata, and R are software programs with a command file that researchers can write the list of commands to do the data analysis. While SPSS, SAS, and Stata are licensed with certain costs, R is publicly available for free. Each program has its advantages and disadvantages depending on researchers' preferences, topics, and data. Many websites and online videos guide and instruct how to use these software programs. The website by UCLA Statistical Methods and Data Analytics is one of the most structured and helpful resources for researchers in learning these software programs. Please visit the following website for more details and basic tutorials on software programs.

UCLA Statistical Methods and Data Analytics
https://stats.oarc.ucla.edu/

Appendix B
How to do a reliable empirical study

Data is not running itself.
Regression models without thoughtful considerations are pointless and useless.

What is the best way to start the empirical study, and how do we know that our empirical study is reliable? There are well-structured steps and guidance for sound empirical analysis. First, we need to clearly state what we would like to know, the research question or the study purpose. Second, we need to define the population of interest and the main information we need to collect or draw from the existing data. Third, it is important to consider the appropriate empirical methods that fit our study and the data we decide to use. Fourth, it is time to implement the methods and obtain the results. Fifth, we need to carefully interpret the results in terms of data perspectives and practical purposes. Sixth, we may draw interesting or meaningful implications from our interpretation.

Appendix C
z distribution table: standard normal curve tail probabilities

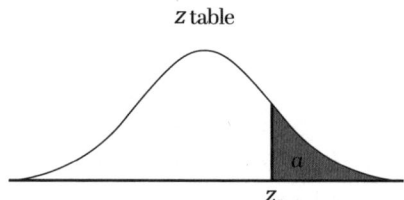

z table

z	0.00	0.01	0.02	0.03	0.04	0.05	0.06	0.07	0.08	0.09
0.0	0.5000	0.4960	0.4920	0.4880	0.4840	0.4801	0.4761	0.4721	0.4681	0.4641
0.1	0.4602	0.4562	0.4522	0.4483	0.4443	0.4404	0.4364	0.4325	0.4286	0.4247
0.2	0.4207	0.4168	0.4129	0.4090	0.4052	0.4013	0.3974	0.3936	0.3897	0.3859
0.3	0.3821	0.3783	0.3745	0.3707	0.3669	0.3632	0.3594	0.3557	0.3520	0.3483
0.4	0.3446	0.3409	0.3372	0.3336	0.3300	0.3264	0.3228	0.3192	0.3156	0.3121
0.5	0.3085	0.3050	0.3015	0.2981	0.2945	0.2912	0.2877	0.2843	0.2810	0.2776
0.6	0.2743	0.2709	0.2676	0.2643	0.2611	0.2578	0.2546	0.2514	0.2483	0.2451
0.7	0.2420	0.2389	0.2358	0.2327	0.2296	0.2266	0.2236	0.2206	0.2177	0.2148
0.8	0.2119	0.2090	0.2061	0.2033	0.2005	0.1977	0.1949	0.1922	0.1894	0.1867
0.9	0.1841	0.1814	0.1788	0.1762	0.1736	0.1711	0.1685	0.1660	0.1635	0.1611
1.0	0.1587	0.1562	0.1539	0.1515	0.1492	0.1469	0.1446	0.1423	0.1401	0.1379
1.1	0.1357	0.1335	0.1314	0.1292	0.1271	0.1251	0.1230	0.1210	0.1190	0.1170
1.2	0.1151	0.1131	0.1112	0.1093	0.1075	0.1056	0.1038	0.1020	0.1003	0.0985
1.3	0.0968	0.0951	0.0934	0.0918	0.0901	0.0885	0.0869	0.0853	0.0838	0.0823
1.4	0.0808	0.0793	0.0778	0.0764	0.0749	0.0735	0.0721	0.0708	0.0694	0.0681
1.5	0.0668	0.0655	0.0643	0.0630	0.0618	0.0606	0.0594	0.0582	0.0671	0.0559
1.6	0.0548	0.0537	0.0526	0.0516	0.0505	0.0495	0.0485	0.0475	0.0465	0.0455
1.7	0.0446	0.0436	0.0427	0.0418	0.0409	0.0401	0.0392	0.0384	0.0375	0.0367
1.8	0.0359	0.0351	0.0344	0.0336	0.0329	0.0322	0.0314	0.0307	0.0301	0.0294
1.9	0.0287	0.0281	0.0274	0.0268	0.0262	0.0256	0.0250	0.0244	0.0239	0.0233
2.0	0.0228	0.0222	0.0217	0.0212	0.0207	0.0202	0.0197	0.0192	0.0188	0.0183
2.1	0.0179	0.0174	0.0170	0.0166	0.0162	0.0158	0.0154	0.0150	0.0146	0.0143
2.2	0.0139	0.0136	0.0132	0.0129	0.0125	0.0122	0.0119	0.0116	0.0113	0.0110
2.3	0.0107	0.0104	0.0102	0.0099	0.0095	0.0094	0.0091	0.0089	0.0087	0.0084
2.4	0.0082	0.0080	0.0078	0.0075	0.0073	0.0071	0.0069	0.0068	0.0066	0.0064
2.5	0.0062	0.0060	0.0059	0.0057	0.0055	0.0054	0.0052	0.0051	0.0049	0.0048
2.6	0.0047	0.0045	0.0044	0.0043	0.0041	0.0040	0.0039	0.0038	0.0037	0.0036
2.7	0.0035	0.0034	0.0033	0.0032	0.0031	0.0030	0.0029	0.0028	0.0027	0.0026
2.8	0.0026	0.0025	0.0024	0.0023	0.0023	0.0022	0.0021	0.0021	0.0020	0.0019
2.9	0.0019	0.0018	0.0018	0.0017	0.0016	0.0015	0.0015	0.0015	0.0014	0.0014
3.0	0.0013	0.0013	0.0013	0.0012	0.0012	0.0011	0.0011	0.0011	0.0010	0.0010
3.1	0.0010	0.0009	0.0009	0.0009	0.0008	0.0008	0.0008	0.0008	0.0007	0.0007
3.2	0.0007	0.0007	0.0005	0.0005	0.0005	0.0006	0.0006	0.0005	0.0005	0.0005
3.3	0.0005	0.0005	0.0005	0.0004	0.0004	0.0004	0.0004	0.0004	0.0004	0.0003
3.4	0.0003	0.0003	0.0003	0.0003	0.0003	0.0003	0.0003	0.0003	0.0003	0.0002

Appendix D
t distribution table: critical values of the t distribution

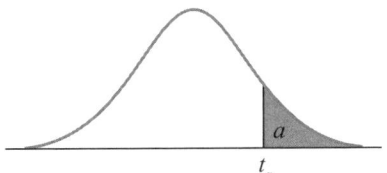

df	Right–Tail Probability					
	$t_{.100}$	$t_{.050}$	$t_{.025}$	$t_{.010}$	$t_{.005}$	$t_{.001}$
1	3.078	6.314	12.706	31.821	63.656	318.289
2	1.886	2.920	4.303	6.965	9.925	22.328
3	1.638	2.353	3.182	4.541	5.841	10.214
4	1.533	2.132	2.776	3.747	4.604	7.173
5	1.476	2.015	2.571	3.365	4.032	5.894
6	1.440	1.943	2.447	3.143	3.707	5.208
7	1.415	1.895	2.365	2.998	3.499	4.785
8	1.397	1.860	2.306	2.896	3.355	4.501
9	1.383	1.833	2.262	2.821	3.250	4.297
10	1.372	1.812	2.228	2.764	3.169	4.144
11	1.363	1.796	2.201	2.718	3.106	4.025
12	1.356	1.782	2.179	2.681	3.055	3.930
13	1.350	1.771	2.160	2.650	3.012	3.852
14	1.345	1.761	2.145	2.624	2.977	3.787
15	1.341	1.753	2.131	2.602	2.947	3.733
16	1.337	1.746	2.120	2.583	2.921	3.686
17	1.333	1.740	2.110	2.567	2.898	3.646
18	1.330	1.734	2.101	2.552	2.878	3.611
19	1.328	1.729	2.093	2.539	2.861	3.579
20	1.325	1.725	2.086	2.528	2.845	3.552
21	1.323	1.721	2.080	2.518	2.831	3.527
22	1.321	1.717	2.074	2.508	2.819	3.505
23	1.319	1.714	2.069	2.500	2.807	3.485
24	1.318	1.711	2.064	2.492	2.797	3.467
25	1.316	1.708	2.060	2.485	2.787	3.450
26	1.315	1.706	2.056	2.479	2.779	3.435
27	1.314	1.703	2.052	2.473	2.771	3.421
28	1.313	1.701	2.048	2.467	2.763	3.408
29	1.311	1.699	2.045	2.462	2.756	3.396
30	1.310	1.697	2.042	2.457	2.750	3.385
40	1.303	1.684	2.021	2.423	2.704	3.307
50	1.299	1.676	2.009	2.403	2.678	3.261
60	1.296	1.671	2.000	2.390	2.660	3.232
80	1.292	1.664	1.990	2.374	2.639	3.195
100	1.290	1.660	1.984	2.364	2.626	3.174
∞	1.282	1.645	1.960	2.326	2.576	3.091

Appendix E
Chi-square distribution table: critical values of the Chi-square distribution

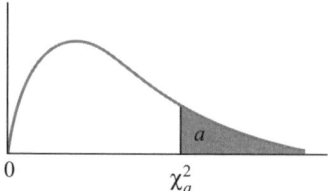

df	$\chi^2_{.995}$	$\chi^2_{.990}$	$\chi^2_{.975}$	$\chi^2_{.950}$	$\chi^2_{.900}$
1	.0000393	.0001571	.0009821	.0039321	.0157908
2	.0100251	.0201007	.0506356	.102587	.210720
3	.0717212	.114832	.215795	.351846	.584375
4	.206990	.297110	.484419	.710721	1.063623
5	.411740	.554300	.831211	1.145476	1.61031
6	.675727	.872085	1.237347	1.63539	2.20413
7	.989265	1.239043	1.68987	2.16735	2.83311
8	1.344419	1.646482	2.17973	2.73264	3.48954
9	1.734926	2.087912	2.70039	3.32511	4.16816
10	2.15585	2.55821	3.24697	3.94030	4.86518
11	2.60321	3.05347	3.81575	4.57481	5.57779
12	3.07382	3.57056	4.40379	5.22603	6.30380
13	3.56503	4.10691	5.00874	5.89186	7.04150
14	4.07468	4.66043	5.62872	6.57063	7.78953
15	4.60094	5.22935	6.26214	7.26094	8.54675
16	5.14224	5.81221	6.90766	7.96164	9.31223
17	5.69724	6.40776	7.56418	8.67176	10.0852
18	6.26481	7.01491	8.23075	9.39046	10.8649
19	6.84398	7.63273	8.90655	10.1170	11.6509
20	7.43386	8.26040	9.59083	10.8508	12.4426
21	8.03366	8.89720	10.28293	11.5913	13.2396
22	8.64272	9.54249	10.9823	12.3380	14.0415
23	9.26042	10.19567	11.6885	13.0905	14.8479
24	9.88623	10.8564	12.4011	13.8484	15.6587
25	10.5197	11.5240	13.1197	14.6114	16.4734
26	11.1603	12.1981	13.8439	15.3791	17.2919
27	11.8076	12.8786	14.5733	16.1513	18.1138
28	12.4613	13.5648	15.3079	16.9279	18.9392
29	13.1211	14.2565	16.0471	17.7083	19.7677
30	13.7867	14.9535	16.7908	18.4926	20.5992
40	20.7065	22.1643	24.4331	26.5093	29.0505
50	27.9907	29.7067	32.3574	34.7642	37.6886
60	35.5346	37.4848	40.4817	43.1879	46.4589
70	43.2752	45.4418	48.7576	51.7393	55.3290
80	51.1720	53.5400	57.1532	60.3915	64.2778
90	59.1963	61.7541	65.6466	69.1260	73.2912
100	67.3276	70.0648	74.2219	77.9295	82.3581

$X^2_{.100}$	$X^2_{.050}$	$X^2_{.025}$	$X^2_{.010}$	$X^2_{.005}$	df
2.70554	3.84146	5.02389	6.63490	7.87944	1
4.60517	5.99147	7.37776	9.21034	10.5966	2
6.25139	7.81473	9.34840	11.3449	12.8381	3
7.77944	9.48773	11.1433	13.2767	14.8602	4
9.23635	11.0705	12.8325	15.0863	16.7496	5
10.6446	12.5916	14.4494	16.8119	18.5476	6
12.0170	14.0671	16.0128	18.4753	20.2777	7
13.3616	15.5073	17.5346	20.0902	21.9550	8
14.6837	16.9190	19.0228	21.6660	23.5893	9
15.9871	18.3070	20.4831	23.2093	25.1882	10
17.2750	19.6751	21.9200	24.7250	26.7569	11
18.5494	21.0261	23.3367	26.2170	28.2995	12
19.8119	22.3621	24.7356	27.6883	29.8194	13
21.0642	23.6848	26.1190	29.1413	31.3193	14
22.3072	24.9958	27.4884	30.5779	32.8013	15
23.5418	26.2962	28.8485	31.9999	34.2672	16
24.7690	27.8571	30.1910	33.4087	35.7185	17
25.9894	28.8693	31.5264	34.8053	37.1564	18
27.2036	30.1435	32.8523	36.1908	38.5822	19
28.4120	31.4104	34.1696	37.5662	39.9968	20
29.6151	32.6705	35.4789	38.9321	41.4010	21
30.8133	33.9244	36.7807	40.2894	42.7956	22
32.0069	35.1725	38.0757	41.6384	44.1813	23
33.1963	36.4151	39.3641	42.9798	45.5585	24
34.3816	37.6525	40.6465	44.3141	46.9278	25
35.5631	38.8852	41.9232	45.6417	48.2899	26
36.7412	40.1133	43.1944	46.9630	49.6449	27
37.9159	41.3372	44.4607	48.2782	50.9933	28
39.0875	42.5569	45.7222	49.5879	52.3356	29
40.2560	43.7729	46.9792	50.8922	53.6720	30
51.8050	55.7585	59.3417	63.6907	66.7659	40
63.1671	67.5048	71.4202	76.1539	79.4900	50
74.3970	79.0819	83.2976	88.3794	91.9517	60
85.5271	90.5312	95.0231	100.425	104.215	70
96.5782	101.879	106.629	112.329	116.321	80
107.565	113.145	118.136	124.116	128.299	90
118.498	124.342	129.561	135.807	140.169	100

Appendix F

F distribution table: critical values of the F distribution

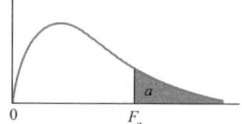

df_2	a	df_1								
		1	2	3	4	5	6	7	8	9
1	.100	39.86	49.50	53.59	55.83	57.24	58.20	58.91	59.44	59.86
	.050	161.4	199.5	215.7	224.6	230.2	234.0	236.8	238.9	240.5
	.025	647.8	799.5	864.2	899.6	921.8	937.1	948.2	956.7	963.3
	.010	4052	4999.5	5403	5625	5764	5859	5928	5982	6022
	.005	16211	20000	21615	22500	23056	23437	23715	23925	24091
2	.100	8.53	9.00	9.16	9.24	9.29	9.33	9.35	9.37	9.38
	.050	18.51	19.00	19.16	19.25	19.30	19.33	19.35	19.37	19.38
	.025	38.51	39.00	39.17	39.25	39.30	39.33	39.36	39.37	39.39
	.010	98.50	99.00	99.17	99.25	99.30	99.33	99.36	99.37	99.39
	.005	198.5	199.0	199.2	199.2	199.3	199.3	199.4	199.4	199.4
3	.100	5.54	5.46	5.39	5.34	5.31	5.28	5.27	5.25	5.24
	.050	10.13	9.55	9.28	9.12	9.01	8.94	8.89	8.85	8.81
	.025	17.44	16.04	15.44	15.10	14.88	14.73	14.62	14.54	14.47
	.010	34.12	30.82	29.46	28.71	28.24	27.91	27.64	27.49	27.35
	.005	55.55	49.80	47.47	46.19	45.39	44.84	44.43	44.13	43.88
4	.100	4.54	4.32	4.19	4.11	4.05	4.01	3.98	3.95	3.94
	.050	7.71	6.94	6.59	6.39	6.26	6.16	6.09	6.04	6.00
	.025	12.22	10.65	9.98	9.60	9.36	9.20	9.07	8.98	8.90
	.010	21.20	18.00	16.69	15.98	15.52	15.21	14.98	14.80	14.66
	.005	31.33	26.28	24.26	23.15	22.46	21.97	21.62	21.35	21.14
5	.100	4.06	3.78	3.62	3.52	3.45	3.40	3.37	3.34	3.32
	.050	6.61	5.79	5.41	5.19	5.05	4.95	4.88	4.82	4.77
	.025	10.01	8.43	7.76	7.39	7.15	6.98	6.85	6.76	6.68
	.010	16.26	13.27	12.06	11.39	10.97	10.67	10.46	10.29	10.16
	.005	22.78	18.31	16.53	15.56	14.94	14.51	14.20	13.96	13.77
6	.100	3.78	3.46	3.29	3.18	3.11	3.05	3.01	2.98	2.96
	.050	5.99	5.14	4.76	4.53	4.39	4.28	4.21	4.15	4.10
	.025	8.81	7.26	6.60	6.23	5.99	5.82	5.70	5.60	5.52
	.010	13.75	10.92	9.78	9.15	8.75	8.47	8.26	8.10	7.98
	.005	18.63	14.54	12.92	12.03	11.46	11.07	10.79	10.57	10.39
7	.100	3.59	3.26	3.07	2.96	2.88	2.83	2.78	2.75	2.72
	.050	5.59	4.74	4.35	4.12	3.97	3.87	3.79	3.73	3.68
	.025	8.07	6.54	5.89	5.52	5.29	5.12	4.99	4.90	4.82
	.010	12.25	9.55	8.45	7.85	7.46	7.19	6.99	6.84	6.72
	.005	16.24	12.40	10.88	10.05	9.52	9.16	8.89	8.68	8.51
8	.100	3.46	3.11	2.92	2.81	2.73	2.67	2.62	2.59	2.56
	.050	5.32	4.46	4.07	3.84	3.69	3.58	3.50	3.44	3.39
	.025	7.57	6.06	5.42	5.05	4.82	4.65	4.53	4.43	4.36
	.010	11.26	8.65	7.59	7.01	6.63	6.37	6.18	6.03	5.91
	.005	14.69	11.04	9.60	8.81	8.30	7.95	7.69	7.50	7.34
9	.100	3.36	3.01	2.81	2.69	2.61	2.55	2.51	2.47	2.44
	.050	5.12	4.26	3.86	3.63	3.48	3.37	3.29	3.23	3.18
	.025	7.21	5.71	5.08	4.72	4.48	4.32	4.20	4.10	4.03
	.010	10.56	8.02	6.99	6.42	6.06	5.80	5.61	5.47	5.35
	.005	13.61	10.11	8.72	7.96	7.47	7.13	6.88	6.69	6.54

				df_1								
10	12	15	20	24	30	40	60	120	∞	a	df_2
60.19	60.71	61.22	61.74	62.00	62.26	62.53	62.79	63.06	3.33	.100	1
241.9	243.9	245.9	248.0	249.1	250.1	251.2	252.2	253.3	254.3	.050	
968.6	976.7	984.9	993.1	997.2	1001	1006	1010	1014	1018	.025	
6056	6106	6157	6209	6235	6261	6287	6313	6339	6366	.010	
24224	24426	24630	24836	24940	25044	25148	25253	25359	25465	.005	
9.39	9.41	9.42	9.44	9.45	9.46	9.47	9.47	9.48	9.49	.100	2
19.40	19.41	19.43	19.45	19.45	19.46	19.47	19.48	19.49	19.50	.050	
39.40	39.41	39.43	39.45	39.46	39.46	39.47	39.48	39.49	39.50	.025	
99.40	99.42	99.43	99.45	99.46	99.47	99.47	99.48	99.49	99.50	.010	
199.4	199.4	199.4	199.4	199.5	199.5	199.5	199.5	199.5	199.5	.005	
5.23	5.22	5.20	5.18	5.18	5.17	5.16	5.15	5.14	5.13	.100	3
8.79	8.74	8.70	8.66	8.64	8.62	8.59	8.57	8.55	8.53	.050	
14.42	14.34	14.25	14.17	14.12	14.08	14.04	13.99	13.95	13.90	.025	
27.23	27.05	26.87	26.69	26.60	26.50	26.41	26.32	26.22	26.13	.010	
43.69	43.39	43.08	42.78	42.62	42.47	42.31	42.15	41.99	41.83	.005	
3.92	3.90	3.87	3.84	3.83	3.82	3.80	3.79	3.78	3.76	.100	4
5.96	5.91	5.86	5.80	5.77	5.75	5.72	5.69	5.66	5.63	.050	
8.84	8.75	8.66	8.56	8.51	8.46	8.41	8.36	8.31	8.26	.025	
14.55	14.37	14.20	14.02	13.93	13.84	13.75	13.65	13.56	13.46	.010	
20.97	20.70	20.44	20.17	20.03	19.89	19.75	19.61	19.47	19.32	.005	
3.30	3.27	3.24	3.21	3.19	3.17	3.16	3.14	3.12	3.10	.100	5
4.74	4.68	4.62	4.56	4.53	4.50	4.46	4.43	4.40	4.36	.050	
6.62	6.52	6.43	6.33	6.28	6.23	6.18	6.12	6.07	6.02	.025	
10.05	9.89	9.72	9.55	9.47	9.38	9.29	9.20	9.11	9.02	.010	
13.62	13.38	13.15	12.90	12.78	12.66	12.53	12.40	12.27	12.14	.005	
2.94	2.90	2.87	2.84	2.82	2.80	2.78	2.76	2.74	2.72	.100	6
4.06	4.00	3.94	3.87	3.84	3.81	3.77	3.74	3.70	3.67	.050	
5.46	5.37	5.27	5.17	5.12	5.07	5.01	4.96	4.90	4.85	.025	
7.87	7.72	7.56	7.40	7.31	7.23	7.14	7.06	6.97	6.88	.010	
10.25	10.03	9.81	9.59	9.47	9.36	9.24	9.12	9.00	8.88	.005	
2.70	2.67	2.63	2.59	2.58	2.56	2.54	2.51	2.49	2.47	.100	7
3.64	3.57	3.51	3.44	3.41	3.38	3.34	3.30	3.27	3.23	.050	
4.76	4.67	4.57	4.47	4.42	4.36	4.31	4.25	4.20	4.14	.025	
6.62	6.47	6.31	6.16	6.07	5.99	5.91	5.82	5.74	5.65	.010	
8.38	8.18	7.97	7.75	7.65	7.53	7.42	7.31	7.19	7.08	.005	
2.54	2.50	2.46	2.42	2.40	2.38	2.36	2.34	2.32	2.29	.100	8
3.35	3.28	3.22	3.15	3.12	3.08	3.04	3.01	2.97	2.93	.050	
4.30	4.20	4.10	4.00	3.95	3.89	3.84	3.78	3.73	3.67	.025	
5.81	5.67	5.52	5.36	5.28	5.20	5.12	5.03	4.95	4.86	.010	
7.21	7.01	6.81	6.61	6.50	6.40	6.29	6.18	6.06	5.95	.005	
2.42	2.38	2.34	2.30	2.28	2.25	2.23	2.21	2.18	2.16	.100	9
3.14	3.07	3.01	2.94	2.90	2.86	2.83	2.79	2.75	2.71	.050	
3.96	3.87	3.77	3.67	3.61	3.56	3.51	3.45	3.39	3.33	.025	
5.26	5.11	4.96	4.81	4.73	4.65	4.57	4.48	4.40	4.31	.010	
6.42	6.23	6.03	5.83	5.73	5.62	5.52	5.41	5.30	5.19	.005	

df_2	a	df_1 1	2	3	4	5	6	7	8	9
10	.100	3.29	2.92	2.73	2.61	2.52	2.46	2.41	2.38	2.35
	.050	4.96	4.10	3.71	3.48	3.33	3.22	3.14	3.07	3.02
	.025	6.94	5.46	4.83	4.47	4.24	4.07	3.95	3.85	3.78
	.010	10.04	7.56	6.55	5.99	5.64	5.39	5.20	5.06	4.94
	.005	12.83	9.43	8.08	7.34	6.87	6.54	6.30	6.12	5.97
11	.100	3.23	2.86	2.66	2.54	2.45	2.39	2.34	2.30	2.27
	.050	4.84	3.98	3.59	3.36	3.20	3.09	3.01	2.95	2.90
	.025	6.72	5.26	4.63	4.28	4.04	3.88	3.76	3.66	3.59
	.010	9.65	7.21	6.22	5.67	5.32	5.07	4.89	4.74	4.63
	.005	12.23	8.91	7.60	6.88	6.42	6.10	5.86	5.68	5.54
12	.100	3.18	2.81	2.61	2.48	2.39	2.33	2.28	2.24	2.21
	.050	4.75	3.89	3.49	3.26	3.11	3.00	2.91	2.85	2.80
	.025	6.55	5.10	4.47	4.12	3.89	3.73	3.61	3.51	3.44
	.010	9.33	6.93	5.95	5.41	5.06	4.82	4.64	4.50	4.39
	.005	11.75	8.51	7.23	6.52	6.07	5.76	5.52	5.35	5.20
13	.100	3.14	2.76	2.56	2.43	2.35	2.28	2.23	2.20	2.16
	.050	4.67	3.81	3.41	3.18	3.03	2.92	2.83	2.77	2.71
	.025	6.41	4.97	4.35	4.00	3.77	3.60	3.48	3.39	3.31
	.010	9.07	6.70	5.74	5.21	4.86	4.62	4.44	4.30	4.19
	.005	11.37	8.19	6.93	6.23	5.79	5.48	5.25	5.08	4.94
14	.100	3.10	2.73	2.52	2.39	2.31	2.24	2.19	2.15	2.12
	.050	4.60	3.74	3.34	3.11	2.96	2.85	2.76	2.70	2.65
	.025	6.30	4.86	4.24	3.89	3.66	3.50	3.38	3.29	3.21
	.010	8.86	6.51	5.56	5.04	4.69	4.46	4.28	4.14	4.03
	.005	11.06	7.92	6.68	6.00	5.56	5.26	5.03	4.86	4.72
15	.100	3.07	2.70	2.49	2.36	2.27	2.21	2.16	2.12	2.09
	.050	4.54	3.68	3.29	3.06	2.90	2.79	2.71	2.64	2.59
	.025	6.20	4.77	4.15	3.80	3.58	3.41	3.29	3.20	3.12
	.010	8.68	6.36	5.42	4.89	4.56	4.32	4.14	4.00	3.89
	.005	10.80	7.70	6.48	5.80	5.37	5.07	4.85	4.67	4.54
16	.100	3.05	2.67	2.46	2.33	2.24	2.18	2.13	2.09	2.06
	.050	4.49	3.63	3.24	3.01	2.85	2.74	2.66	2.59	2.54
	.025	6.12	4.69	4.08	3.73	3.50	3.34	3.22	3.12	3.05
	.010	8.53	6.23	5.29	4.77	4.44	4.20	4.03	3.89	3.78
	.005	10.58	7.51	6.30	5.64	5.21	4.91	4.69	4.52	4.38
17	.100	3.03	2.64	2.44	2.31	2.22	2.15	2.10	2.06	2.03
	.050	4.45	3.59	3.20	2.96	2.81	2.70	2.61	2.55	2.49
	.025	6.04	4.62	4.01	3.66	3.44	3.28	3.16	3.06	2.98
	.010	8.40	6.11	5.18	4.67	4.34	4.10	3.93	3.79	3.68
	.005	10.38	7.35	6.16	5.50	5.07	4.78	4.56	4.39	4.25
18	.100	3.01	2.62	2.42	2.29	2.20	2.13	2.08	2.04	2.00
	.050	4.41	3.55	3.16	2.93	2.77	2.66	2.58	2.51	2.46
	.025	5.98	4.56	3.95	3.61	3.38	3.22	3.10	3.01	2.93
	.010	8.29	6.01	5.09	4.58	4.25	4.01	3.84	3.71	3.60
	.005	10.22	7.21	6.03	5.37	4.96	4.66	4.44	4.28	4.14
19	.100	2.99	2.61	2.40	2.27	2.18	2.11	2.06	2.02	1.98
	.050	4.38	3.52	3.13	2.90	2.74	2.63	2.54	2.48	2.42
	.025	5.92	4.51	3.90	3.56	3.33	3.17	3.05	2.96	2.88
	.010	8.18	5.93	5.01	4.50	4.17	3.94	3.77	3.63	3.52
	.005	10.07	7.09	5.92	5.27	4.85	4.56	4.34	4.18	4.04
20	.100	2.97	2.59	2.38	2.25	2.16	2.09	2.04	2.00	1.96
	.050	4.35	3.49	3.10	2.87	2.71	2.60	2.51	2.45	2.39
	.025	5.87	4.46	3.86	3.51	3.29	3.13	3.01	2.91	2.84
	.010	8.10	5.85	4.94	4.43	4.10	3.87	3.70	3.56	3.46
	.005	9.94	6.99	5.82	5.17	4.76	4.47	4.26	4.09	3.96

				df_1								
10	12	15	20	24	30	40	60	120	∞	a	df_2
2.32	2.28	2.24	2.20	2.18	2.16	2.13	2.11	2.08	2.06	.100	10
2.98	2.91	2.85	2.77	2.74	2.70	2.66	2.62	2.58	2.54	.050	
3.72	3.62	3.52	3.42	3.37	3.31	3.26	3.20	3.14	3.08	.025	
4.85	4.71	4.56	4.41	4.33	4.25	4.17	4.08	4.00	3.91	.010	
5.85	5.66	5.47	5.27	5.17	5.07	4.97	4.86	4.75	4.64	.005	
2.25	2.21	2.17	2.12	2.10	2.08	2.05	2.03	2.00	1.97	.100	11
2.85	2.79	2.72	2.65	2.61	2.57	2.53	2.49	2.45	2.40	.050	
3.53	3.43	3.33	3.23	3.17	3.12	3.06	3.00	2.94	2.88	.025	
4.54	4.40	4.25	4.10	4.02	3.94	3.86	3.78	3.69	3.60	.010	
5.42	5.24	5.05	4.86	4.76	4.65	4.55	4.44	4.34	4.23	.005	
2.19	2.15	2.10	2.06	2.04	2.01	1.99	1.96	1.93	1.90	.100	12
2.75	2.69	2.62	2.54	2.51	2.47	2.43	2.38	2.34	2.30	.050	
3.37	3.28	3.18	3.07	3.02	2.96	2.91	2.85	2.79	2.72	.025	
4.30	4.16	4.01	3.86	3.78	3.70	3.62	3.54	3.45	3.36	.010	
5.09	4.91	4.72	4.53	4.43	4.33	4.23	4.12	4.01	3.90	.005	
2.14	2.10	2.05	2.01	1.98	1.96	1.93	1.90	1.88	1.85	.100	13
2.67	2.60	2.53	2.46	2.42	2.38	2.34	2.30	2.25	2.21	.050	
3.25	3.15	3.05	2.95	2.89	2.84	2.78	2.72	2.66	2.60	.025	
4.10	3.96	3.82	3.66	3.59	3.51	3.43	3.34	3.25	3.17	.010	
4.82	4.64	4.46	4.27	4.17	4.07	3.97	3.87	3.76	3.65	.005	
2.10	2.05	2.01	1.96	1.94	1.91	1.89	1.86	1.83	1.80	.100	14
2.60	2.53	2.46	2.39	2.35	2.31	2.27	2.22	2.18	2.13	.050	
3.15	3.05	2.95	2.84	2.79	2.73	2.67	2.61	2.55	2.49	.025	
3.94	3.80	3.66	3.51	3.43	3.35	3.27	3.18	3.09	3.00	.010	
4.60	4.43	4.25	4.06	3.96	3.86	3.76	3.66	3.55	3.44	.005	
2.06	2.02	1.97	1.92	1.90	1.87	1.85	1.82	1.79	1.76	.100	15
2.54	2.48	2.40	2.33	2.29	2.25	2.20	2.16	2.11	2.07	.050	
3.06	2.96	2.86	2.76	2.70	2.64	2.59	2.52	2.46	2.40	.025	
3.80	3.67	3.52	3.37	3.29	3.21	3.13	3.05	2.96	2.87	.010	
4.42	4.25	4.07	3.88	3.79	3.69	3.58	3.48	3.37	3.26	.005	
2.03	1.99	1.94	1.89	1.87	1.84	1.81	1.78	1.75	1.72	.100	16
2.49	2.42	2.35	2.28	2.24	2.19	2.15	2.11	2.06	2.01	.050	
2.99	2.89	2.79	2.68	2.63	2.57	2.51	2.45	2.38	2.32	.025	
3.69	3.55	3.41	3.26	3.18	3.10	3.02	2.93	2.84	2.75	.010	
4.27	4.10	3.92	3.73	3.64	3.54	3.44	3.33	3.22	3.11	.005	
2.00	1.96	1.91	1.86	1.84	1.81	1.78	1.75	1.72	1.69	.100	17
2.45	2.38	2.31	2.23	2.19	2.15	2.10	2.06	2.01	1.96	.050	
2.92	2.82	2.72	2.62	2.56	2.50	2.44	2.38	2.32	2.25	.025	
3.59	3.46	3.31	3.16	3.08	3.00	2.92	2.83	2.75	2.65	.010	
4.14	3.97	3.79	3.61	3.51	3.41	3.31	3.21	3.10	2.98	.005	
1.98	1.93	1.89	1.84	1.81	1.78	1.75	1.72	1.69	1.66	.100	18
2.41	2.34	2.27	2.19	2.15	2.11	2.06	2.02	1.97	1.92	.050	
2.87	2.77	2.67	2.56	2.50	2.44	2.38	2.32	2.26	2.19	.025	
3.51	3.37	3.23	3.08	3.00	2.92	2.84	2.75	2.66	2.57	.010	
4.03	3.86	3.68	3.50	3.40	3.30	3.20	3.10	2.99	2.87	.005	
1.96	1.91	1.86	1.81	1.79	1.76	1.73	1.70	1.67	1.63	.100	19
2.38	2.31	2.23	2.16	2.11	2.07	2.03	1.98	1.93	1.88	.050	
2.82	2.72	2.62	2.51	2.45	2.39	2.33	2.27	2.20	2.13	.025	
3.43	3.30	3.15	3.00	2.92	2.84	2.76	2.67	2.58	2.49	.010	
3.93	3.76	3.59	3.40	3.31	3.21	3.11	3.00	2.89	2.78	.005	
1.94	1.89	1.84	1.79	1.77	1.74	1.71	1.68	1.64	1.61	.100	20
2.35	2.28	2.20	2.12	2.08	2.04	1.99	1.95	1.90	1.84	.050	
2.77	2.68	2.57	2.46	2.41	2.35	2.29	2.22	2.16	2.09	.025	
3.37	3.23	3.09	2.94	2.86	2.78	2.69	2.61	2.52	2.42	.010	
3.85	3.68	3.50	3.32	3.22	3.12	3.02	2.92	2.81	2.69	.005	

df_2	a	df_1 1	2	3	4	5	6	7	8	9
21	.100	2.96	2.57	2.36	2.23	2.14	2.08	2.02	1.98	1.95
	.050	4.32	3.47	3.07	2.84	2.68	2.57	2.49	2.42	2.37
	.025	5.83	4.42	3.82	3.48	3.25	3.09	2.97	2.87	2.80
	.010	8.02	5.78	4.87	4.37	4.04	3.81	3.64	3.51	3.40
	.005	9.83	6.89	5.73	5.09	4.68	4.39	4.18	4.01	3.88
22	.100	2.95	2.56	2.35	2.22	2.13	2.06	2.01	1.97	1.93
	.050	4.30	3.44	3.05	2.82	2.66	2.55	2.46	2.40	2.34
	.025	5.79	4.38	3.78	3.44	3.22	3.05	2.93	2.84	2.76
	.010	7.95	5.72	4.82	4.31	3.99	3.76	3.59	3.45	3.35
	.005	9.73	6.81	5.65	5.02	4.61	4.32	4.11	3.94	3.81
23	.100	2.94	2.55	2.34	2.21	2.11	2.05	1.99	1.95	1.92
	.050	4.28	3.42	3.03	2.80	2.64	2.53	2.44	2.37	2.32
	.025	5.75	4.35	3.75	3.41	3.18	3.02	2.90	2.81	2.73
	.010	7.88	5.66	4.76	4.26	3.94	3.71	3.54	3.41	3.30
	.005	9.63	6.73	5.58	4.95	4.54	4.26	4.05	3.88	3.75
24	.100	2.93	2.54	2.33	2.19	2.10	2.04	1.98	1.94	1.91
	.050	4.26	3.40	3.01	2.78	2.62	2.51	2.42	2.36	2.30
	.025	5.72	4.32	3.72	3.38	3.15	2.99	2.87	2.78	2.70
	.010	7.82	5.61	4.72	4.22	3.90	3.67	3.50	3.36	3.26
	.005	9.55	6.66	5.52	4.89	4.49	4.20	3.99	3.83	3.69
25	.100	2.92	2.53	2.32	2.18	2.09	2.02	1.97	1.93	1.89
	.050	4.24	3.39	2.99	2.76	2.60	2.49	2.40	2.34	2.28
	.025	5.69	4.29	3.69	3.35	3.13	2.97	2.85	2.75	2.68
	.010	7.77	5.57	4.68	4.18	3.85	3.63	3.46	3.32	3.22
	.005	9.48	6.60	5.46	4.84	4.43	4.15	3.94	3.78	3.64
26	.100	2.91	2.52	2.31	2.17	2.08	2.01	1.96	1.92	1.88
	.050	4.23	3.37	2.98	2.74	2.59	2.47	2.39	2.32	2.27
	.025	5.66	4.27	3.67	3.33	3.10	2.94	2.82	2.73	2.65
	.010	7.72	5.53	4.64	4.14	3.82	3.59	3.42	3.29	3.18
	.005	9.41	6.54	5.41	4.79	4.38	4.10	3.89	3.73	3.60
27	.100	2.90	2.51	2.30	2.17	2.07	2.00	1.95	1.91	1.87
	.050	4.21	3.35	2.96	2.73	2.57	2.46	2.37	2.31	2.25
	.025	5.63	4.24	3.65	3.31	3.08	2.92	2.80	2.71	2.63
	.010	7.68	5.49	4.60	4.11	3.78	3.56	3.39	3.26	3.15
	.005	9.34	6.49	5.36	4.74	4.34	4.06	3.85	3.69	3.56
28	.100	2.89	2.50	2.29	2.16	2.06	2.00	1.94	1.90	1.87
	.050	4.20	3.34	2.95	2.71	2.56	2.45	2.36	2.29	2.24
	.025	5.61	4.22	3.63	3.29	3.06	2.90	2.78	2.69	2.61
	.010	7.64	5.45	4.57	4.07	3.75	3.53	3.36	3.23	3.12
	.005	9.28	6.44	5.32	4.70	4.30	4.02	3.81	3.65	3.52
29	.100	2.89	2.50	2.28	2.15	2.06	1.99	1.93	1.89	1.86
	.050	4.18	3.33	2.93	2.70	2.55	2.43	2.35	2.28	2.22
	.025	5.59	4.20	3.61	3.27	3.04	2.88	2.76	2.67	2.59
	.010	7.60	5.42	4.54	4.04	3.73	3.50	3.33	3.20	3.09
	.005	9.23	6.40	5.28	4.66	4.26	3.98	3.77	3.61	3.48
30	.100	2.88	2.49	2.28	2.14	2.05	1.98	1.93	1.88	1.85
	.050	4.17	3.32	2.92	2.69	2.53	2.42	2.33	2.27	2.21
	.025	5.57	4.18	3.59	3.25	3.03	2.87	2.75	2.65	2.57
	.010	7.56	5.39	4.51	4.02	3.70	3.47	3.30	3.17	3.07
	.005	9.18	6.35	5.24	4.62	4.23	3.95	3.74	3.58	3.45

				df_1								
10	12	15	20	24	30	40	60	120	∞	a	df_2
1.92	1.87	1.83	1.78	1.75	1.72	1.69	1.66	1.62	1.59	.100	21
2.32	2.25	2.18	2.10	2.05	2.01	1.96	1.92	1.87	1.81	.050	
2.73	2.64	2.53	2.42	2.37	2.31	2.25	2.18	2.11	2.04	.025	
3.31	3.17	3.03	2.88	2.80	2.72	2.64	2.55	2.46	2.36	.010	
3.77	3.60	3.43	3.24	3.15	3.05	2.95	2.84	2.73	2.61	.005	
1.90	1.86	1.81	1.76	1.73	1.70	1.67	1.64	1.60	1.57	.100	22
2.30	2.23	2.15	2.07	2.03	1.98	1.94	1.89	1.84	1.78	.050	
2.70	2.60	2.50	2.39	2.33	2.27	2.21	2.14	2.08	2.00	.025	
3.26	3.12	2.98	2.83	2.75	2.67	2.58	2.50	2.40	2.31	.010	
3.70	3.54	3.3	3.18	3.08	2.98	2.88	2.77	2.66	2.55	.005	
1.89	1.84	1.80	1.74	1.72	1.69	1.66	1.62	1.59	1.55	.100	23
2.27	2.20	2.13	2.05	2.01	1.96	1.91	1.86	1.81	1.76	.050	
2.67	2.57	2.47	2.36	2.30	2.24	2.18	2.11	2.04	1.97	.025	
3.21	3.07	2.93	2.78	2.70	2.62	2.54	2.45	2.35	2.26	.010	
3.64	3.47	3.30	3.12	3.02	2.92	2.82	2.71	2.60	2.48	.005	
1.88	1.83	1.78	1.73	1.70	1.67	1.64	1.61	1.57	1.53	.100	24
2.25	2.18	2.11	2.03	1.98	1.94	1.89	1.84	1.79	1.73	.050	
2.64	2.54	2.44	2.33	2.27	2.21	2.15	2.08	2.01	1.94	.025	
3.17	3.03	2.89	2.74	2.66	2.58	2.49	2.40	2.31	2.21	.010	
3.59	3.42	3.25	3.06	2.97	2.87	2.77	2.66	2.55	2.43	.005	
1.87	1.82	1.77	1.72	1.69	1.66	1.63	1.59	1.56	1.52	.100	25
2.24	2.16	2.09	2.01	1.96	1.92	1.87	1.82	1.77	1.71	.050	
2.61	2.51	2.41	2.30	2.24	2.18	2.12	2.05	1.98	1.91	.025	
3.13	2.99	2.85	2.70	2.62	2.54	2.45	2.36	2.27	2.17	.010	
3.54	3.37	3.20	3.01	2.92	2.82	2.72	2.61	2.50	2.38	.005	
1.86	1.81	1.76	1.71	1.68	1.65	1.61	1.58	1.54	1.50	.100	26
2.22	2.15	2.07	1.99	1.95	1.90	1.85	1.80	1.75	1.69	.050	
2.59	2.49	2.39	2.28	2.22	2.16	2.09	2.03	1.95	1.88	.025	
3.09	2.96	2.81	2.66	2.58	2.50	2.42	2.33	2.23	2.13	.010	
3.49	3.33	3.15	2.97	2.87	2.77	2.67	2.56	2.45	2.33	.005	
1.85	1.80	1.75	1.70	1.67	1.64	1.60	1.57	1.53	1.49	.100	27
2.20	2.13	2.06	1.97	1.93	1.88	1.84	1.79	1.73	1.67	.050	
2.57	2.47	2.36	2.25	2.19	2.13	2.07	2.00	1.93	1.85	.025	
3.06	2.93	2.78	2.63	2.55	2.47	2.38	2.29	2.20	2.10	.010	
3.45	3.28	3.11	2.93	2.83	2.73	2.63	2.52	2.41	2.29	.005	
1.84	1.79	1.74	1.69	1.66	1.63	1.59	1.56	1.52	1.48	.100	28
2.19	2.12	2.04	1.96	1.91	1.87	1.82	1.77	1.71	1.65	.050	
2.55	2.45	2.34	2.23	2.17	2.11	2.05	1.98	1.91	1.83	.025	
3.03	2.90	2.75	2.60	2.52	2.44	2.35	2.26	2.17	2.06	.010	
3.41	3.25	3.07	2.89	2.79	2.69	2.59	2.48	2.37	2.25	.005	
1.83	1.78	1.73	1.68	1.65	1.62	1.58	1.55	1.51	1.47	.100	29
2.18	2.10	2.03	1.94	1.90	1.85	1.81	1.75	1.70	1.64	.050	
2.53	2.43	2.32	2.21	2.15	2.09	2.03	1.96	1.89	1.81	.025	
3.00	2.87	2.73	2.57	2.49	2.41	2.33	2.23	2.14	2.03	.010	
3.38	3.21	3.04	2.86	2.76	2.66	2.56	2.45	2.33	2.21	.005	
1.82	1.77	1.72	1.67	1.64	1.61	1.57	1.54	1.50	1.46	.100	30
2.16	2.09	2.01	1.93	1.89	1.84	1.79	1.74	1.68	1.62	.050	
2.51	2.41	2.31	2.20	2.14	2.07	2.01	1.94	1.87	1.79	.025	
2.98	2.84	2.70	2.55	2.47	2.39	2.30	2.21	2.11	2.01	.010	
3.34	3.18	3.01	2.82	2.73	2.63	2.52	2.42	2.30	2.18	.005	

df_2	a	df_1								
		1	2	3	4	5	6	7	8	9
40	.100	2.84	2.44	2.23	2.09	2.00	1.93	1.87	1.83	1.79
	.050	4.08	3.23	2.84	2.61	2.45	2.34	2.25	2.18	2.12
	.025	5.42	4.05	3.46	3.13	2.90	2.74	2.62	2.53	2.45
	.010	7.31	5.18	4.31	3.83	3.51	3.29	3.12	2.99	2.89
	.005	8.83	6.07	4.98	4.37	3.99	3.71	3.51	3.35	3.22
60	.100	2.79	2.39	2.18	2.04	1.95	1.87	1.82	1.77	1.74
	.050	4.00	3.15	2.76	2.53	2.37	2.25	2.17	2.10	2.04
	.025	5.29	3.93	3.34	3.01	2.79	2.63	2.51	2.41	2.33
	.010	7.08	4.98	4.13	3.65	3.34	3.12	2.95	2.82	2.72
	.005	8.49	5.79	4.73	4.14	3.76	3.49	3.29	3.13	3.01
120	.100	2.75	2.35	2.13	1.99	1.90	1.82	1.77	1.72	1.68
	.050	3.92	3.07	2.68	2.45	2.29	2.17	2.09	2.02	1.96
	.025	5.15	3.80	3.23	2.89	2.67	2.52	2.39	2.30	2.22
	.010	6.85	4.79	3.95	3.48	3.17	2.96	2.79	2.66	2.56
	.005	8.18	5.54	4.50	3.92	3.55	3.28	3.09	2.93	2.81
∞	.100	2.71	2.30	2.08	1.94	1.85	1.77	1.72	1.67	1.63
	.050	3.84	3.00	2.60	2.37	2.21	2.10	2.01	1.94	1.63
	.025	5.02	3.69	3.12	2.79	2.57	2.41	2.29	2.19	2.11
	.010	6.63	4.61	3.78	3.32	3.02	2.80	2.64	2.51	2.41
	.005	7.88	5.30	4.28	3.72	3.35	3.09	2.90	2.74	2.62

df_1										a	df_2
10	12	15	20	24	30	40	60	120	∞		
1.76	1.71	1.66	1.61	1.57	1.54	1.51	1.47	1.42	1.38	.100	40
2.08	2.00	1.92	1.84	1.79	1.74	1.69	1.64	1.58	1.51	.050	
2.39	2.29	2.18	2.07	2.01	1.94	1.88	1.80	1.72	1.64	.025	
2.80	2.66	2.52	2.37	2.29	2.20	2.11	2.02	1.92	1.80	.010	
3.12	2.95	2.78	2.60	2.50	2.40	2.30	2.18	2.06	1.93	.005	
1.71	1.66	1.60	1.54	1.51	1.48	1.44	1.40	1.35	1.29	.100	60
1.99	1.92	1.84	1.75	1.70	1.65	1.59	1.53	1.47	1.39	.050	
2.27	2.17	2.06	1.94	1.88	1.82	1.74	1.67	1.58	1.48	.025	
2.63	2.50	2.35	2.20	2.12	2.03	1.94	1.84	1.73	1.60	.010	
2.90	2.74	2.57	2.39	2.29	2.19	2.08	1.96	1.83	1.69	.005	
1.65	1.60	1.55	1.48	1.45	1.41	1.37	1.32	1.26	1.19	.100	120
1.91	1.83	1.75	1.66	1.61	1.55	1.50	1.43	1.35	1.25	.050	
2.16	2.05	1.94	1.82	1.76	1.69	1.61	1.53	1.43	1.31	.025	
2.47	2.34	2.19	2.03	1.95	1.86	1.76	1.66	1.53	1.38	.010	
2.71	2.54	2.37	2.19	2.09	1.98	1.87	1.75	1.61	1.43	.005	
1.60	1.55	1.49	1.42	1.38	1.34	1.30	1.24	1.17	1.00	.100	∞
1.83	1.75	1.67	1.57	1.52	1.46	1.39	1.32	1.22	1.00	.050	
2.05	1.94	1.83	1.71	1.64	1.57	1.48	1.39	1.27	1.00	.025	
2.32	2.18	2.04	1.88	1.79	1.70	1.59	1.47	1.32	1.00	.010	
2.52	2.36	2.19	2.00	1.90	1.79	1.67	1.53	1.36	1.00	.005	

Notes: The statistical tables in this textbook are drawn from Mendenhall, Beaver, and Beaver (2012).

References

Abraham, K. G. & Kearney, M. S. (2020). Explaining the decline in the US employment-to-population ratio: A review of the evidence. *Journal of Economic Literature*, 58(3), 585-643.

Burnham, G., Lafta, R., Doocy, S., & Roberts, L. (2006). Mortality after the 2003 invasion of Iraq: a cross-sectional cluster sample survey. *The Lancet*, 368(9545), 1421-1428.

Cameron, A. C. & Trivedi, P. K. (2005). *Microeconometrics: methods and applications*. Cambridge University Press.

Einav, L., Finkelstein, A., Oostrom, T., Ostriker, A., & Williams, H. (2020). Screening and selection: The case of mammograms. *American Economic Review*, 110(12), 3836-70.

Glaeser, E. L., Ponzetto, G. A., & Shleifer, A. (2007). Why does democracy need education?. *Journal of economic growth*, 12(2), 77-99.

Kearney, M. S., Levine, P. B., & Pardue, L. (2022). The Puzzle of Falling US Birth Rates since the Great Recession. *Journal of Economic Perspectives*, 36(1), 151-76.

Korean Longitudinal Survey of Women and Families (KLoWF)
https://gsis.kwdi.re.kr/klowf/portal/eng/introSummaryPage.do

Mendenhall, W., Beaver, R. J., & Beaver, B. M. (2012). *Introduction to probability and statistics*. Cengage Learning.

NLSY79 (National Longitudinal Survey of Youth - 1979 Cohort) data set
https://www.nlsinfo.org/content/cohorts/nlsy79

Ott, J. C. (2010). Good governance and happiness in nations: Technical quality precedes democracy and quality beats size. *Journal of Happiness Studies*, 11(3), 353-368.

US Census Bureau. (2016). American Community Survey and Puerto Rico Community Survey. 2016 Subject Definitions.
https://www.census.gov/programs-surveys/acs/methodology/design-and-methodology.html

Wooldridge, J. M. (2012). *Introductory econometrics: a modern approach*. 5th. Cengage Learning.

Index

A

adjusted R-squared / 192
alternative hypothesis / 68
appropriate sample / 79
assumptions for the BLUE and inference of the OLS estimator / 128, 160
average marginal effects (AME) / 290

B

Bayes' Rule / 22
Bayes' Theorem / 22, 24
beta coefficients / 232
binary random variable / 15
binary variable / 201
BLUE / 115, 129, 278

C

causal paths / 244
Central Limit Theorem / 49, 54
Chi-square distribution / 297
concave relationships / 242
convex relationships / 242
cluster random sample / 24
confidence Interval (CI) / 56, 133
confidence intervals / 134
confounder / 244
consistency / 129, 160
continuous variables / 17, 18
covariance / 93
correlation coefficient / 96
counting variables / 17, 18
cumulative distribution function (CDF) / 282

D

dummy variables / 201

E

efficiency / 168
efficient / 114, 170
endogenous / 164
error term / 101
estimated intercept coefficient / 104
estimated slope coefficient / 104
estimation equation / 102
exogenous / 164
explained sum of squares / 111
explanatory variable / 100

F

F distribution / 186
F-test statistic / 184
Feasible Generalized Least Squares(F-GLS) / 272

G

Gauss-Markov Theorem / 115, 125, 238
Generalized Least Squares (GLS) / 270
group differences / 202

H

heteroscedasticity / 265
histogram / 33
Homoscedasticity / 112, 263
hypothesis / 179
hypothesis test / 68, 78, 137, 148

I

indicator variables / 201
interval variable / 211

L

Large sample OLS analysis / 128
Likelihood Ratio Test (LRT) / 296
linear and nonlinear specifications / 238
Linear Probability Model (LPM) / 277
linear regression model / 128
linearity / 238

logit and probit models / 281

M

marginal effects (ME) / 291
marginal of error / 80
median / 40
mediator / 249
mode / 40
moderator / 247
multicollinearity / 156, 157
multinomial random variable / 16
multivariate / 156

N

nominal variables / 17, 18
normal distribution / 32
null hypothesis / 68

O

OLS properties / 105
OLS regression analysis / 100
omitted variable bias / 164
one-sided hypothesis / 72
ordinal variables / 17, 18
outcome variable / 100

P

partialling out / 156
population / 27
population distribution / 51
population equation / 101
population variance / 27
pseudo R-squared / 299
p-value / 71, 140

Q

qualitative variables / 17, 18
quantitative variables / 17, 18

R

random sample assumption / 24
rescaling / 231
residual / 102

residual sum of squares (SSR) / 111, 189, 192
robust standard errors / 265, 269

S

sample distribution / 51
sample mean / 26
sample variance / 26
sampling distribution / 49, 51
SAS / 141, 159, 182
small sample OLS analysis / 128
standard error / 113
standard normal distribution / 34
Stata / 141, 159, 182
stratified random sample / 25

T

t distribution / 63
t-test statistic / 75, 127
total sum of squares / 111
two-sided hypothesis test / 68
Type I error / 74
Type II error / 74

U

unbiased OLS estimator / 107
unbiasedness / 129, 160
unexplained sum of squares / 111

W

Wald test / 296, 300
Weighted Least Squares (WLS) / 265, 270
White test / 267

Z

z table / 34

Data Analysis for Social Science
Fundamental Methods

About Author

Haeil Jung is a professor in the Department of Public Administration at Korea University in Seoul, South Korea. He earned his PhD degree in Public Policy from the University of Chicago, Chicago, USA. Before assuming his current role, he was an assistant professor in the Paul H. O'Neill School of Public and Environmental Affairs at Indiana University, Bloomington, IN, USA, from 2009 to 2015. Additionally, from 2012 to 2020, he served as a consultant for the World Bank, where he played a key role in the evaluation of the early childhood education program in Indonesia. His research expertise lies in policy analysis and program evaluation, particularly focusing on poverty, inequality, and related social policy interventions. He has authored numerous peer-reviewed research articles on diverse topics such as early childhood education, college education, labor market participation, immigration, fertility, obesity, incarceration, COVID-19, and empirical methods, making significant contributions to these fields. Along with his research, he has a comprehensive teaching background. He has taught introductory, intermediate, and advanced data analysis courses, as well as social policy courses, at the University of Chicago, Indiana University, and Korea University.